T0211016

Lecture Notes of the Institute for Computer Sciences, Social Informatics and Telecommunications Engineering   409

More information about this series at https://link.springer.com/bookseries/8197

Phan Cong Vinh · Abdur Rakib (Eds.)

Context-Aware Systems and Applications

10th EAI International Conference, ICCASA 2021
Virtual Event, October 28–29, 2021
Proceedings

 Springer

Editors
Phan Cong Vinh ⓘ
Nguyen Tat Thanh University
Ho Chi Minh City, Vietnam

Abdur Rakib ⓘ
University of the West of England
Bristol, UK

ISSN 1867-8211   ISSN 1867-822X (electronic)
Lecture Notes of the Institute for Computer Sciences, Social Informatics
and Telecommunications Engineering
ISBN 978-3-030-93178-0   ISBN 978-3-030-93179-7 (eBook)
https://doi.org/10.1007/978-3-030-93179-7

This Springer imprint is published by the registered company Springer Nature Switzerland AG
The registered company address is: Gewerbestrasse 11, 6330 Cham, Switzerland

Preface

ICCASA 2021 (the 10th EAI International Conference on Context-Aware Systems and Applications), was held during October 28–29, 2021, in cyberspace, due to the travel restrictions caused by the worldwide COVID-19 pandemic. The aim of the conference is to provide an internationally respected forum for scientific research in the technologies and applications of smart computing and communication. ICCASA provides an excellent opportunity for researchers to discuss modern approaches and techniques for smart computing systems and their applications. The proceedings of ICCASA 2021 are published by Springer in the series Lecture Notes of the Institute for Computer Sciences, Social Informatics and Telecommunications Engineering (LNICST; indexed by DBLP, EI, Google Scholar, Scopus, and Thomson ISI).

For this tenth edition of ICCASA, and repeating the success of the previous year, the Program Committee received submissions from authors in 8 countries and each paper was reviewed by at least three expert reviewers. We chose 25 papers after intensive discussions held among the Program Committee members. We really appreciate the excellent reviews and lively discussions of the Program Committee members and external reviewers in the review process. This year we had three prominent invited speakers, Francois Siewe from De Montfort University in the UK, Kurt Geihs from the University of Kessel in Germany, and Hafiz Mahfooz Ul Haque from the University of Lahore in Pakistan.

ICCASA 2021 was jointly organized by the European Alliance for Innovation (EAI), Ho Chi Minh City Open University (OU), and Nguyen Tat Thanh University (NTTU). This conference could not have been organized without the strong support of the staff members of the three organizations. We would especially like to thank Imrich Chlamtac (University of Trento), Aleksandra Śledziejowska (EAI), and Martin Karbovanec (EAI) for their great help in organizing the conference. We also appreciate the gentle guidance and help of Nguyen Minh Ha, Rector of OU.

October 2021

Phan Cong Vinh
Abdur Rakib

Organization

Steering Committee

Imrich Chlamtac (Chair) University of Trento, Italy
Phan Cong Vinh Nguyen Tat Thanh University, Vietnam

Organizing Committee

Honorary General Chair

Nguyen Minh Ha Ho Chi Minh City Open University, Vietnam

General Chair

Phan Cong Vinh Nguyen Tat Thanh University, Vietnam

Program Chair

Abdur Rakib University of the West of England, UK

Workshop Chair

Pham Van Dang Nguyen Tat Thanh University, Vietnam

Publicity Chair

Ijaz Uddin City University of Science and Information
Technology, Peshawar, Pakistan

Publication Chair

Phan Cong Vinh Nguyen Tat Thanh University, Vietnam

Sponsorship and Exhibits Chair

Vu Tuan Anh Industrial University of Ho Chi Minh City, Vietnam

Local Arrangement Chair

Le Xuan Truong Ho Chi Minh City Open University, Vietnam

Web Chair

Do Nguyen Anh Thu Nguyen Tat Thanh University, Vietnam

Technical Program Committee

Amando P. Singun Jr.	University of Technology and Applied Sciences, Oman
Bui Cong Giao	Saigon University, Vietnam
Chernyi Sergei	Admiral Makarov State University of Maritime and Inland Shipping, Russia
Chien-Chih Yu	National Chengchi University, Taiwan
David Sundaram	University of Auckland, New Zealand
Do Tri Nhut	Thu Dau Mot University, Vietnam
Gabrielle Peko	University of Auckland, New Zealand
Giacomo Cabri	University of Modena and Reggio Emilia, Italy
Hafiz Mahfooz Ul Haque	University of Lahore, Pakistan
Huynh Xuan Hiep	Can Tho University, Vietnam
Issam Damaj	American University of Kuwait, Kuwait
Jinfeng Li	Imperial College London, UK
Krishna Asawa	Jaypee Institute of Information Technology, India
Kurt Geihs	University of Kassel, Germany
Le Hong Anh	University of Mining and Geology, Vietnam
Manisha Chawla	Google, India
Muhammad Athar Javed Sethi	University of Engineering and Technology, Peshawar, Pakistan
Nguyen Hoang Thuan	RMIT University Vietnam, Vietnam
Nguyen Manh Duc	University of Ulsan, South Korea
Nguyen Thanh Binh	Ho Chi Minh City University of Technology, Vietnam
Nguyen Thanh Hai	Can Tho University, Vietnam
Pham Quoc Cuong	Ho Chi Minh City University of Technology, Vietnam
Shahzad Aahraf	Hohai University, China
Tran Huu Tam	University of Kassel, Germany
Tran Vinh Phuoc	Ho Chi Minh City Open University, Vietnam
Waralak V. Siricharoen	Silpakorn University, Thailand
Zhu Huibiao	East China Normal University, China

Contents

Adapt and Flex or Die: A Systems Approach to an Unhealthy
Healthcare Supply... 1
   Joshua Brodie, Gabrielle Peko, and David Sundaram

Knowledge Management Practices: Innovation the Path to Organizational
Performance.. 20
   Mina Cu, Johnny Chan, Gabrielle Peko, and David Sundaram

Predicting Humans' Balance Disorder Based on Center of Gravity Using
Support Vector Machine 38
   Tran Anh Vu, Hoang Quang Huy, Nguyen Viet Dung,
   Nguyen Phan Kien, Nguyen Thu Phuong, and Pham Thi Viet Huong

Internet of Things Big Data Management and Analytic for Developing
Smart City: A Survey and Future Studies.......................... 48
   Tuan Anh Vu, Cong Vinh Phan, and Cuong Pham-Quoc

Ensemble Learning for Mining Opinions on Food Reviews 56
   Phuc Quang Tran, Hai Thanh Nguyen, Hanh My Thi Le,
   and Hiep Xuan Huynh

Hidden Pattern: Toward Decision Support Fuzzy Systems 71
   Nguyen Van Han, Phan Cong Vinh, Bui Minh Phung,
   and Tran Ngoc Dan

Applying Segmented Images by Louvain Method into Content-Based
Image Retrieval 77
   Tuyet-Ngan Vo, Mickael Coustaty, Jean-Loup Guillaume,
   Thanh-Khoa Nguyen, and De Cao Tran

An Effective Approach for Mining k-item High Utility Itemsets
from Incremental Databases 91
   Nong Thi Hoa and Nguyen Van Tao

Recover Realistic Faces from Sketches 105
   Khoa Tan Truong, Khai Dinh Lai, Sang Thanh Nguyen,
   and Thai Hoang Le

Region of Interest Selection on Plant Disease.................... 119
   Hiep Xuan Huynh, Cang Anh Phan, Loan Thanh Thi Truong,
   and Hai Thanh Nguyen

Memory-Constrained Context-Aware Reasoning   133
  Ijaz Uddin, Abdur Rakib, Mumtaz Ali, and Phan Cong Vinh

Segmentation-Based Methods for Top-*k* Discords Detection in Static
and Streaming Time Series Under Euclidean Distance   147
  Huynh Thi Thu Thuy, Duong Tuan Anh, and Vo Thi Ngoc Chau

Hardware/Software Co-design for Convolutional Neural Networks
Acceleration: A Survey and Open Issues   164
  Cuong Pham-Quoc, Xuan-Quang Nguyen, and Tran Ngoc Thinh

Image Segmentation and Transfer Learning Approach
for Skin Classification   179
  *Hiep Xuan Huynh, Cang Anh Phan, Loan Thanh Thi Truong,
  and Hai Thanh Nguyen*

Blockchain and Identity Management   192
  Xin Yang and Johnny Chan

Binary Classification for Lung Nodule Based on Channel
Attention Mechanism.   205
  Khai Dinh Lai, Thai Hoang Le, and Thuy Thanh Nguyen

Design Cloud-Fog Systems Using Heuristic Solutions on the Energy
of IoT Devices   219
  Nguyen Thanh Tung

An International Overview and Meta-analysis for Using the Mechanical
Ventilation in the Medical Treatment.   226
  Ha Quang Thinh Ngo

Blockchain-Based Governance in Fractional Ownership:
Mitigating Zero-Sum Games Through Decentralized Autonomous Agents . . .   236
  Mina Cu, Johnny Chan, Gabrielle Peko, and David Sundaram

A Dynamic Programming Approach for Time Series Discord Detection.   255
  Duong Tuan Anh and Nguyen Van Hien

Recent Researches on Human-Aware Navigation for Autonomous System
in the Dynamic Environment: An International Survey.   267
  Ha Quang Thinh Ngo

Recommendation with Subjective Tendency Based on Statistical
Implicative Analysis   283
  *Hiep Xuan Huynh, Cang Anh Phan, Tu Cam Thi Tran,
  and Hai Thanh Nguyen*

Applying Convolutional Neural Network for Detecting Highlight Football
Events   300
   Tuan Hoang Viet Le, Hoang Thien Van, Hai Son Tran,
   Phat Kieu Nguyen, Thuy Thanh Nguyen, and Thai Hoang Le

Can Gaming be the Bad Escapism?   314
   Waralak V. Siricharoen

Applying CoKriging Method for Air Pollution Prediction PM10 in Binh
Duong Province   323
   Nguyen Cong Nhut

Author Index   337

Adapt and Flex or Die: A Systems Approach to an Unhealthy Healthcare Supply

Joshua Brodie, Gabrielle Peko[(⊠)], and David Sundaram

The University of Auckland, Auckland 1010, New Zealand
jbro777@aucklanduni.ac.nz,
{g.peko, d.sundaram}@auckland.ac.nz

Abstract. Healthcare supply chains are becoming increasingly complex and characterized by rapid and unpredictable changes, particularly during the Covid-19 pandemic. This unpredictability means supply chains are challenged from all levels. Patients, employees and society are all sources of uncertainty resulting with the need for supply chains to be healthier. This research explores the need for healthcare supply chains to be more adaptable and flexible. A literature informed design science approach was adopted as the methodology. We propose a systems view of an adaptive and flexible healthcare supply chain. Furthermore, we build system dynamic models to illustrate an unhealthy healthcare supply chain and a healthy healthcare supply chain. Theoretical supply chain conceptual frameworks and information systems concepts were synthesized to propose models that look to solve some of the supply chain problems arising from the Covid-19 pandemic.

Keywords: Healthcare supply chains · Unhealthy healthcare supply chains · Healthy healthcare supply chains · Covid-19 pandemic

1 Introduction

The concept that a healthy future is contingent on the health and well-being of the population is not new [7]. Yet, the Covid-19 pandemic has significantly disrupted the dispensing of healthcare throughout the world. Much of this disruption can be attributed to Healthcare Supply Chains (HSC) and how they functions [19], Flexibility [21], adaptability [16], collaboration, coordination and knowledge [26], elements of a fully functional supply chain (SC) have become the key differentiators between a Healthy Healthcare Supply Chain (HHSC) and an Unhealthy Healthcare Supply Chain (UHSC). The following research's motivation comes from seeing key problems arise from the vaccine distribution across the global SC network.

This research aims to identify issues within the HSC and provide solutions using principles of e-health, SC and information systems (IS). It follows a design science research (DSR) approach. We *observed* supply chains during the Covid-19 pandemic both through academic as well as grey literature. Based on these observations and further literature review we *theorized* both the current as well as potential solutions to the current problems. This theorization included the development of high level conceptual frameworks as well as system dynamic causal loop models. Based on this theorization we have proposed a set of core *systems* as a foundation for Healthy

P. Cong Vinh and A. Rakib (Eds.): ICCASA 2021, LNICST 409, pp. 1–19, 2021.
https://doi.org/10.1007/978-3-030-93179-7_1

Healthcare Supply Chains. These systems are already available in the technological ecosystem and can be integrated together to provide the functionality and requirements that we have proposed. The proposed concepts, models, including the system dynamic views of UHSC and HHSC, go some way to solving some of the issues identified by using modern e-care solutions, IS and traditional successful SC concepts.

Generally, the purpose of this paper is to promote resilient, health systems that are more sustainable and focus on the health and well-being of people [7]. Through simply highlighting the issues arising from an UHSC and propose requirements for its evolution to an HHSC through the utilization of different types of IS. Drawing on research that delves into the significant disruption in the HSC arising from the current global Covid-19 pandemic, several causal loop diagrams and models are presented. The following section outlines an HSC followed by what constitutes an UHSC. Different types of IS that can be utilized to transform an UHSC into an HHSC are then discussed in turn. Finally, the systems that deliver foundational elements of adaptability and flexibility are discussed.

2 Healthcare Supply Chains

2.1 Background

Sinha and Kohnke [38] suggest that an HSC can be viewed as three delineated sections labelled upstream, middle, and downstream. The upstream section refers to the part within the SC that is used to produce the different vaccines, medication, masks and equipment. The upstream section is more similar to traditional manufacturing supply chains. "The middle of the supply chain deals with financing and claims processing, and it is occupied by banks, insurance companies, and third-party administrators. These actors ensure that the developers and deliverers of care bundles are reimbursed" [38]. This part of the HSC deals with government regulations and pressure. "The downstream of the supply chain represented the health care delivery industry comprised entities such as hospitals, clinics, home-health services, and hospices" [38].

The healthcare industry's SC is different from traditional SCs in terms of the extent to which a partner or consumer participates, degree of customization of services provided, and the inherent process uncertainty [33]. All these cause a HSC be more dynamic and complex than other SCs [14]. The HSC is defined by Mathur et al. [26] as the "backbone of healthcare delivery...due to the healthcare industry being dependent on the availability of medical supplies at the right time and in the right quantities to the patients, lack of which may create customer dissatisfaction". Mathur et al. [27] also state that the HSC involves the flow of a variety of product types through the participation of people to fulfil patient requirements.

2.2 Motivation

The following discussion will focus on the Covid-19 vaccine distribution during the pandemic to illustrate and highlight the issues that arose within the supply chain. However, most of the identified issues apply to other SCs as well. Literature was used to highlight the key parts of an HHSC and an UHSC. Adaptable sustainable SC management operations can be best described as considering an entity towards adaptability and sustainability [4]. Each country or state has had a different response to the pandemic. In each instance, decision-makers prioritized the economic, environment, societal and cultural aspects of a country or state differently. It is implied in Fig. 1 that the HSC will often be directly correlated with a country or state approach.

An example of this is New Zealand's response to the pandemic. New Zealand was able to lock-down the country to have outstanding success in decreasing the amount of community transmitted cases [12]. This response allowed New Zealand's HSC to focus on being preventative and concentrate on vaccine distribution. Other places in the world do not have the luxury of New Zealand's geographic remoteness, which allows the country's boarders to be closed and effectively isolated it from the rest of the world. A preventative/proactive SC healthcare approach will set the standards for its processes ultimately effecting patients and employee's health (people in the area). All these key elements should be aligned, corrected, optimized and monitored through a sustainable learning flow.

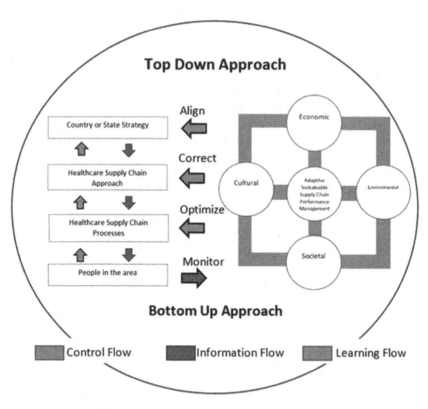

Fig. 1. Systems view of an adaptive and flexible healthcare supply chain

It is suggested by Maani and Cavana [23] that system thinking techniques are important to understanding complex systems. An HSC [24] falls under the category of a complex system considering its numerous elements. Modelling an HHSC and an UHSC needs to be done holistically rather than isolating each element of the system. This allows for relationships to be identified and variables to be highlighted. A SC model can be viewed as one system with several different elements and variables; allowing for problems to be highlighted and solutions to be provided. With all complex models, there are issues with illustrating all variables and relationships in one model. Figure 1 conceptualizes an adaptive and flexible HSC at a high level of abstraction while the Causal Loop Diagrams (CLD) in Fig. 2 and Fig. 4 are at a lower, more detailed, level of abstraction. For example, the problems that arose from the pandemic included a lack of coordination, fewer supplies available, a shortage of workers and limited capacity. The HHSC indicates that the adaptability and flexibility elements proposed (Fig. 3) are a way to solve some of these problems, highlighted in the CLDs, through IS.

3   Unhealthy Healthcare Supply Chains

Paché [30] argued that Europe's greatest HSC failure was its facemask supply. In the early stages of the pandemic, Europe could not accurately forecast how many face-masks were needed for both healthcare workers and the patients. "It is impossible to quantify the number of deaths due to the lack of face masks, but the reality of the dark side of healthcare SC management is indisputable" [30]. The lack of facemasks also allowed Covid-19 diagnosed patients to transmit the disease when moving from hospitals. If there were more IS and e-health measures in place within the SC network, Europe might have been able to better forecast how many masks would be needed. The lack of facemasks caused enormous pressure on the HSC, forcing hospitals to reach maximum capacity between March and April. The vaccine distribution in the HSC is facing similar problems throughout the world.

The model developed in Fig. 2 is used to illustrate a systems view of the current UHSC. The critical aspects in this model are the *Patients Health Deteriorating* module and the *Reactive e-health SC Measures*. As *a Lack of Coordination increases*, the *Patients' Health deteriorates* (decreases). When there are *Less Communication* and a *Lack of Coordination* between stakeholders in a supply chain, it can cost lives, particularly in the context of Covid-19 vaccine distribution. Suppose those who need the vaccine most do not receive the vaccine because of coordination failures between different elements outlined in Fig. 1. In that case, patients' overall good health might decrease, and the number of patients whose health deteriorates could increase.

The first loop is the 'employees health' loop. As the number of patients whose health deteriorates increases because of a lack of vaccine distribution, *Employee's Health* (i.e., those working in the healthcare field) worsens. Furthermore, the number of *Employees Working Overtime* increases as *Patients' Health Deteriorates*, further decreasing individual employee's health. Barnhill [3] also discusses that when *Employees Work Overtime*, it decreases the amount of *Personnel* available, increasing, a *Shortage of Workers*. Parris [32] suggests that an increase in strain on the HSC increases *Production Fluctuation* as the HSC cannot accurately forecast how many people still need the vaccine. Parris [32] claims that an increase in *Production Fluctuation* also increases *Service and Production Waste* [22]. O'Donnell [28] also suggests that this also decreases the HSC ability to *Scale Raw Materials* and distribute vaccines.

In line with Parris [32], Barnhill [3] claims that *Limited Capacity* for the vaccine increases the strain on the HSC. This further increases the amount of patients' health deteriorating due to not being unable to access the vaccine. The final loop is the relationship between *Reactive e-health SC Measures, Unsafe Practices* and *Production Fluctuation*. As long as the HSC continues to react to problems within the supply chain, fluctuation within the SC will increase. Decision-makers will always be on the backfoot and have less information than if they were able to engage with patients' proactively. These reactive measures will also ensure that the HSC will have to engage in *Unsafe Practices* to address these problems in the short term. Lack of Governance Risk Management and Compliance (GRC) might impact these unsafe practices, further extenuating these unhealthy SC loops. All these loops come together to increase *Work* which in turn may increase *Overall SC Waste*.

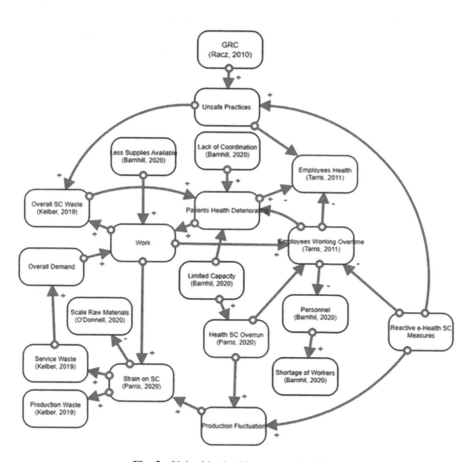

Fig. 2. Unhealthy healthcare supply chains

In summary, an UHSC Lacks Coordination which affects patient's health. An UHSC also has a Limited Capacity which increases the strain on the HSC. A Shortage of Workers, fewer Supplies Available, and Unsafe Practices are also core problems within an HSC. This paper's motivation comes from looking at these problems and finding potential solutions for them in literature. The solutions we propose will provide some basis for the HSC to transform the current way they operate. We then recommend different types of systems to help turn UHSC into an HHSC. Starting with Heinrich and Betts [16] visibility, we build our model's foundational steps.

4   Foundational Elements of Adaptability and Flexibility

A HHSC that can withstand the impacts of a global pandemic and respond effectively is one that is flexible and ultimately adaptive [40]. We propose that a certain level of education and automation can be achieved through achieving visibility, coordination, and collaboration [18]. Once education and automation are achieved, flexibility needs to be incorporated, which finally contributes to adaptability. When all these seven elements are obtained, the previous unhealthy SC will become healthier, and transformation will take place [16, 18]. These elements are illustrated in Fig. 3 and discussed in the following paragraphs.

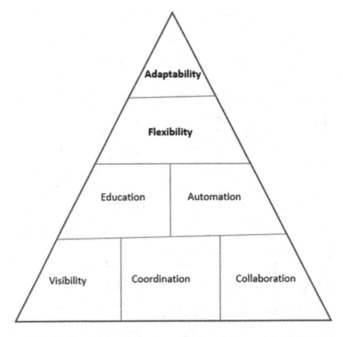

Fig. 3. Foundational elements of adaptability and flexibility

4.1   Visibility

Heinrich and Betts [16] argue that step one in achieving adaptability is visibility. The more fluctuation within the supply chain, the more significant the strain is on the overall supply chain. Heinrich and Betts [16] suggest that an increase in visibility between different partners reduces fluctuation. Heinrich and Betts [16] go on to say that "Processes are now readily visible, and achievements are measured and widely recognized when there is communication between all partners at all levels." In Heinrich and Betts [16], the recommended communication method is 'a phone call' with the frequency being a week. Briggs [6] suggests that different forms of technology should also be used within the context of increased visibility. Briggs [5] adds to Heinrich and Bett's [16] work by recommending that different forms of technology (like Zoom and Skype) could be used to increase visibility within the supply chain. This would allow partners to frequently discuss things like demand and supply, which are incredibly vital to a patient's health in the context of an HSC.

To solve the problems outlined in the descriptive model, Heinrich and Betts [16] recommend increased visibility in the SC and between all the different partners, mainly when working with partners to improve 'number accuracy'. Less unstable processes within a SC allow for more supplies to be available to all the partners. This is because SC members can more accurately collaborate and coordinate stock from one end to another. However, HSC must first have confidence in its own internal numbers before making decisions that will affect the whole HSC.

4.2   Coordination

Heinrich and Betts [16] suggest that after visibility, community coordination needs to take place to achieve adaptability. According to Heinrich and Betts [16], a core concept of community coordination is the ability to achieve "real time inventory count that is, having inventory counts that reflect what a company actually has on hand moment to moment, as close to instantaneously as possible". This can come from visibility of inventory levels and its located through coordination. Heinrich and Betts [16] recommend bar code scanner or radio frequency identification (RFID) technology, to record and track the movement of goods throughout the manufacturing process. These forms of technology contribute to a linked procedure or activity and increase coordination. In an HSC, the bar code system is perhaps the easiest and most cost-effective choice for inventory tracking, specifically when dealing with vaccines and other medication types. While barcode tracking is prevalent in the modern-day SC Near Field Communication and Bluetooth contact tracing is another type of e-health technology gaining popularity throughout the world.

4.3   Collaboration

Briggs et al. [6] argues that a SC design must have seven layers of collaboration (SLMC) to obtain collaboration. The HSC must have a Goal Layer in which all the partners within the HSC commit to collaborate even through challenging periods like a pandemic. Barnhill [3] argued that if the partners within the vaccine distribution were more committed to getting supplies to different countries, there would have been fewer capacity issues in the early stages of the vaccine distribution (see Fig. 2). The Products Layer within the SLMC also encourages the products made available to meet the standards and specifications set out in the first Goal Layer. This was a key issue in the vaccine distribution. For example, the Pfizer vaccine has to be kept in temperatures colder than Antarctica (−70 °C), causing infrastructure problems within the HSC [10]. Briggs et al. [6] argue that The Activities Layer points out that no activities have a purpose if there are no actual products. Mid 2020, there was no vaccine distribution plan. Fast forward to January 2021, there needs to be a robust SC vaccine distribution plan to administer the vaccine and get it to the places where people need it most. The final four layers include: The Patterns of Collaboration Layer, The Techniques Layer, The Techniques Layer, The Tools Layer, and The Scripts Layer [6]. The Patterns of Collaboration Layer refers to what patterns need to be identified to create a product. For example, there needs to be several different combinations or partnerships that need to take place to get the vaccine from one partner to another. When scientists created the first Pfizer/BioNTech Covid-19 vaccine, countries worldwide tried to build relationships with Europe to gain access to their HSC [15]. The Techniques Layer refers to what "techniques are used to invoke patterns of collaboration" [6] such as the brainstorming technique to invoke synergy and improve the number and quality of ideas produced by groups [29].

4.4   Education

Jansson [20] argues that with the introduction of technology, workers now need to have a baseline understanding of what different forms of technology (e.g. SAP) do to get by within a supply chain. Jansson [20] argues that workers education can be done in two different ways, either through a 'British way' or a 'Swedish way.' The British method involves splitting the SC into several various organizations and utilizing teacher-led hieratical classes. During different parts of the day, different workers spend time with a teacher to learn how to use different applications. These lessons will allow workers to understand how the entirety of the SC works. The classes will enable workers to be upskilled and better understand how the SC functions. An increase in education within the SC will allow workers to do their jobs better with the entire SC in mind. The Swedish way recommends that workers education is done through a more self-learning/democratic way. The method acknowledges that workers have different strengths and weaknesses. Jansson [20] recommends that workers teach each other how to do each other's roles at a low level. The method increases knowledge within the SC and increases flexibility. The form of education is traditionally organized through labour movement organizations.

4.5   Automation

Another element that will increase the number of skilled workers, increase education, and decrease work is automation. People throughout the SC should learn automation at a base level to understand how the different systems work within the supply chain. Automation involves routine tasks, structured data, and deterministic outcomes.

According to Aguirre and Rodriguez [1], recent studies report the benefits of the application of automation for productivity, costs, speed, and error reduction.

4.6   Flexibility

Once a certain level of education and automation have been completed, flexibility becomes the next target. SC flexibility can be achieved by adopting a three-stage approach, First, identify the flexibility required, second implement it and third monitor it through feedback and control [21]. The SC should formulate its competitive strategy in line with external environment, uncertainties, and relationships with suppliers and customers. If the SC can successfully target and eliminate unreliable suppliers and partners, fewer problems will occur due to members reliable nature [21]. Environmental uncertainties mean organizations have to create contingency plans which are included in an organization's business strategy. Hence, environmental uncertainties compel organization to develop different types of flexibilities [8]. Once developed, managers need to focus on implementing these flexibilities throughout the SC system along with the necessary people, processes and in particular, technology to achieve the flexibility requirements (e.g., information technology, relationship with key suppliers and customers, skilled workers, etc.). This implies that all of the HSC partners must consider sharing the responsibility for implementing and managing the required SC flexibility [20].We recommend that the IS requirements are pitched at a relatively low level as that is where the SC is least flexible [2].

The third and final stage highlights the importance of a control mechanism to monitoring and control the implemented flexibility [21]. Kumar [21] and Rosemann [36] recommend a feedback loop to assess the flexibility of the supply chain. If there was a feedback loop within the HSC that could provide meaningful feedback about its flexibility the HSC will come out of its vaccine distribution more resilient. Adaptability and flexibility ensure that a feedback loop exists. If not the control mechanism would signal that some adjustments are needed to realize the required flexibility necessary to improve the SC and subsequent business performance [21].

4.7   Adaptability

The top of the triangle and the final step of an HHSC is adaptability [16]. Haeckel [17] argues that there are four phases in adaptability. Sensing, interpreting, responding, and acting. According to Haeckel [17], environmental change is first sensed by adaptive individuals and adaptive organizations. These adaptive individual and organizations then interpret the changes based on their experience, aims, and capabilities, identifying threats and opportunities while discarding irrelevant information. They then decide on a response and implement it. This process of sense, interpret and respond becomes an iterative loop. The results are monitored by the adaptive system which enables the detection of environmental changes that have occurred since the previous cycle [17].

Adaptability is not a goal; it is a way for the SC to respond to environmental changes to survive [16]. When individual partners start the adaptability process, they establish a set of baseline key performance indicators for both the SC and themselves. This allows them to measure performance and set time frames for achieving critical objectives. The primary purpose of adaptability in an HHSC is to have information about patient demand communicated instantaneously to all partners. To achieve this, to some extent, automated decisions based on a set of pre-determined business rules should operate within the SC network. Adaptability requires standardization of services and processes across the network. This will allow for automate decision making and shared information throughout the network in near-real-time [16].

5 Healthy Healthcare Supply Chains

The adaptability and flexibility elements illustrated in Fig. 3 were applied to the UHSC model (Fig. 2) to provide potential solutions for the identified problems. The model developed in Fig. 4 is used to illustrate a systems view of an HHSC.

The elements increase *Automation* outlined by the academics Aguirre and Rodriguez [1], Dash et al. [9], and Parker [31]. We recommended that the HSC use robotic processing automation to achieve automation within the supply chain. The elements also increase *SC Coordination* which in turn increases *Employee's Health*. We recommend that collaboration systems are used to encourage coordination.

An increase in *Employees' Health* also contributes to enhanced adaptability and flexibility and improves *Patients' Health* when they are able to take care of more patients by giving them better healthcare. This reduces the number of *Employees Working Overtime* which improves their health as staff are able to better cover for each other when the aforementioned elements are implemented (see Education Sect. 4.4).

The adaptability and flexibility elements also increase *Knowledge in the SC* [26]. When there is increased knowledge in the supply chain, members in the HSC can proactively cover for each other as they understand the supply chain, increasing the supplies available [16]. We recommend that this is done through transaction processing systems along with decision support and knowledge management systems.

Automation increases *Capacity* and the number of *Skilled Workers within the SC* [1, 9]. Employees also experience increased *Job Enrichment* [31], which in turn increases the sufficient *Capacity* [3, 31]. Dash et al. [9] also link an increase in *Skilled Workers* and capacity to increased *Service Levels*.

An increase in *Automation* increases *Education* within the supply chain, according to Maier [26], Heinrich and Betts [16], Schlechty [37], and Watson and Watson [39]. In line with these academics, we recommended that SCs should use learning management systems and knowledge management systems together to maintain a high level of *Education* across the supply chain. Finally, through all these seven IS and *Waste Management* techniques decrease the strain on the HSC and reduces *Overall Waste*.

Briggs [5] argues that implementing models into networks can often be done more easily with IS. To better integrate adaptability and flexibility into the current UHSC we recommend that IS are used at every level of the model. We propose that Workflow Management Systems (WMS), Collaboration Systems (CS), Learning Management Systems (LMS), Robotic Processing Automation (RPA), Transaction Processing Systems (TPS), Knowledge Management Systems (KMS), and Decision Support Systems (DSS) can all be used help integrate the adaptability and flexibility into an HSC.

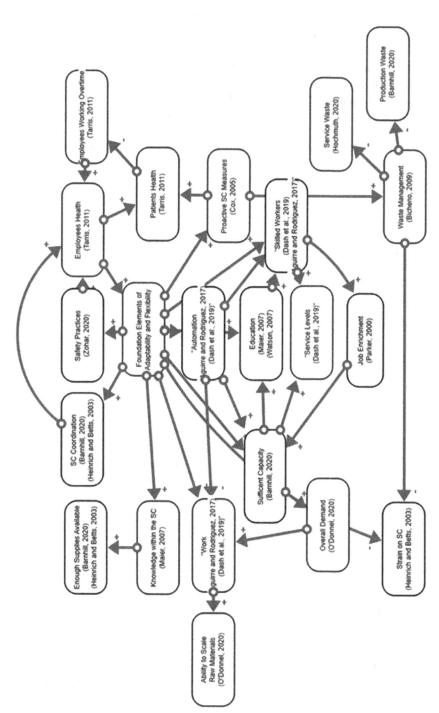

Fig. 4. Causal loop diagram of a healthy healthcare supply chain

6 Healthy Healthcare Supply Chains Systems

The problems identified by in the literature have made it extremely hard for the HSC to function effectively during the pandemic, for instance with the vaccine distribution. There is a significant amount of literature that reinforces the role of information systems to achieve adaptability and flexibility in HSC [35]. For example, Rakovska and Stratieva [35] identified from the literature HSC management practices, types of flows and IS that impact healthcare performance. The adaptability and flexibility elements illustrated in Fig. 3 are founded upon literature to optimize the current SC landscape through different types of IS.

Incorporating these elements through the implementation of appropriate information system can make the process easier [34]. These core IS are illustrated in Fig. 5 and discussed in detail in the following paragraphs.

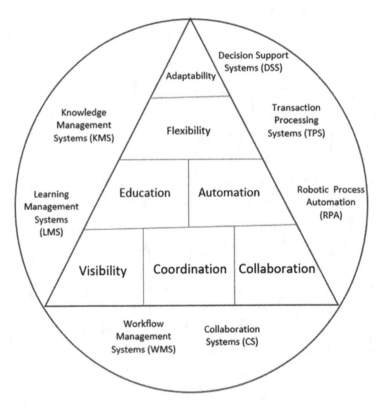

Fig. 5. Core systems to deliver adaptability and flexibility

6.1 Collaboration Systems

According to Heinrich and Betts [16] step four to build an adaptive SC network is collaboration. They recommend using enterprise systems, vendor managed inventory, and other forms of CS. "A collaborative Advanced Planning System is required for successful collaboration" [16]. Collaboration within a healthy SC refers to an increase in production speed between different partners within the supply chain. In Fig. 2 of an UHSC, the collaboration between various partners within the health care SC caused an increase in waste and an increase in the supply chain's overall strain (i.e., fewer resources within the SC causing significantly more pressure on all partners). CS should be used frequently to brainstorm solutions to problems within the SC in the context of an HSC. These meetings should be both internally and externally to ensure that the SC encourages visibility. Finally, the Tools Layer refers to "the capabilities required to instantiate a collaboration technique" [6]. These tools are the CS themselves and how the different partners communicate with each other within the supply chain. Examples of CS include various forms of technology that could increase visibility within the SC [5]. Scripts are "guidance about the things people in various roles should do and say with their tools to instantiate the techniques selected for the group" [6]. In the context of an HSC, partners might consider creating scripts of each other's roles so that in the event of large-scale SC disruption, the SC is not hugely affected. Scripts may require education and other types of IS to be successful.

Having stabilized processes and data, allows companies to better respond to unforeseen circumstances. Without stabilized processes and qualify information responding to these unplanned events will lead to further chaos [16]. Briggs [5] urges those within a complex SC to communicate using CS, mainly through group support systems, which will identify any inaccurate numbers that a supplier may be relying on, further reducing waste within the supply chain. Briggs [5] maintains that when CS is used to increase visibility in a supply chain, there is greater group cohesion and satisfaction and the SC will be able to flow with minimal waste. Further, it is generally agreed in the literature that in certain situations, people who engage with CS are significantly more productive than people who do not [13]. According to Heinrich and Betts [16], the benefits of CS are that there are significant cost savings within the SC and that it "reduces the need for costly emergency and less-than-full truckload shipments." Heinrich and Betts [16] claim that when companies increase visibility in the SC through CS it will reduce the frustration level between a supply chains' employee and its customers, making the company easier to do business with. Heinrich and Betts [16] also cite "better production schedule" as a benefit to increased visibility in the supply chain. Total personnel's cost will also decrease as enough staff will be hired and prepared to complete their roles.

6.2   Workflow Management Systems

Eder [11] suggests that WMS allows for coordination to occur more frequently between community members. WMS allows for traditional tasks like coordination to be done through an "automation of a business process, in whole or part, during which documents, information or tasks are passed from one participant to another for action, according to a set of procedural rules" [11]. Heinrich and Betts [16] builds on Eder [11] work when they suggest that a SC community needs to be able to coordinate and communicate with all the stakeholders to share up-to-date schedules, plans, and forecasts, and mechanize day-to-day orders and other transactions. They recommend inventory tracking systems which contribute to a more adaptable business network allowing for more automated streamlined data processing. Community coordination through WMS encourages activities like day to day ordering to be streamlined through coordination resulting in a more adaptable network [16]. WMS also allows for further cost saving measures, increased safety measures, increased coordination, and overall reduction in service and production waste as well as reduced strain on the supply chain.

For a SC to move towards automation and educating different community members, there are three key requirements: stable technology; accurate data and; procedures are standardized [16]. Referring to the key problems identified during the Covid-19 Pandemic (Fig. 2) the HSC has failed at almost all these steps. If the HSC were able to incorporate some of the WMS discussed above, there would be more stable technology within the SC allowing for medical supplies like the vaccine to be distributed to different countries without so many infrastructure problems [28]. Increased data accuracy would mean that the appropriate about of people would be able to distribute the vaccine, and there would be fewer problems with personnel [3].

6.3   Knowledge Management Systems and Learning Management Systems

One of the critical problems within the SC was 'personal,' according to Barnhill [3]. There was a large shortage of trained healthcare workers within the SC causing further issues with capacity and SC waste [3]. In line with [20] we propose a solution in which all HSC members are educated to do each other's work at a base level. The education process will be done through KMS and LMS. When the education process is done, skilled workers will increase, and further job enrichment will take place. Education will further contribute to flexibility as the SC will suffer less when workers get sick or have to quarantine for an extended period because other members within the SC will be able to fill in for each other.

Maier [26] argues that most KMS have an intranet and a groupware platform in place that offer basic knowledge management functionality and a solid foundation for KMS. Maier [26] goes on to say that these platforms come together with add-ons and extensions, further increasing the functionality of these KMS. Each organization can tailor its own KMS to fit its own organizations' needs. KMS is extremely important for internal visibility, especially with its inbuilt "advanced processes along with advanced information and communication needs" [26]. However, Maier [26] also notes that many KMS' functions are implemented, but not used intensively [26]. This is important as using a KMS as a forum for educational learning would come at a minimal cost to most organizations with an a robust KMS setup. "Therefore, there still seem to be considerable potentials when applying ICT to KM initiatives" [26]. We recommend that different key stakeholders within the SC create and upload videos, scripts, and other forms of notes to their organizations' KMS. The solution will ensure that when there is a reduced amount of personal or a shortage of workers [3] as different employees can step in and help each other out, encouraging flexibility with roles and responsibility and increasing adaptability [16]. It is important to note that currently organizations do not assign people for knowledge management tasks. "About a third of the organizations just assigned responsibility for basic tasks related to the publication and distribution of knowledge, but do not pay equally high attention to what happens to the knowledge once it is documented and inserted into the organizations' knowledge bases" [26]. This means that ideally for the model to flourish organization will need to assign some of these educational tasks to individual departments or specific people to ensure that employees are interacting with the KMS and are working with each other to complete their knowledge management tasks.

In line with the adaptability and flexibility elements, we also recommend that partners integrate an LMS with their KMS to enhance capability to achieve the education element. Schlechty [37] argues that technology will be needed to track each person's progress towards mastering a role. A LMS will assess each employee's learning and how quickly they are able to grasp different roles and responsibilities. An LMS is not common in traditional organizations, however, it is common in the healthcare industry [39]. An LMS could test an employee's understanding of another person's role, assess learners' knowledge and skill level. It will also allow management to work with workers to identify appropriate learning goals, identify and sequence instruction appropriate for the individual learner, store evidence of certification, support collaboration and generate reports [39] to provide information to maximize the effectiveness of learning within the entire HSC. The LMS could recognize if the employee has enough knowledge to assist another person with completing or doing their job.

6.4   Robotic Process Automation

"RPA is an automation technology based on software tools that could imitate human behavior for repetitive and non-value added tasks such as tipping, copying, pasting, extracting, merging and moving data from one system to another" [1]. Dash et al. [9] argue that Artificial Intelligence (AI) can be used as a type of automation to improve SC management at a decision-making level. "AI consists of a set of computational technologies developed to sense, learn, reason, and act appropriately" [9]. Supply-chain leaders use AI-powered technologies to make efficient designs, eliminate waste, increase service level, and increase the number of skilled workers within the SC when they learn how to automate tasks. Automation is essential in the critical role of work redesign and job enrichment [31]. They argue that when automation occurs within a supply chain, workers can be upskilled and learn how to automate. Automation will increase the number of skilled workers in the SC and encouraging job enrichment.

As RPA usually sits on top of an already existing system [1], we recommend that this RPA sits on top of the KMS discussed previously. This will allow employees within the SC to increasing their skills through job enrichment. Job enrichment aims to create more challenging activities for the involved employees. It combines activities on different levels of qualification. A main assumption of job enrichment is that people become motivated by more challenging tasks [1]. One example of job enrichment is the task of getting different employees to learn how to automate easier tasks to make their jobs much easier. The main benefit of RPA is cost reduction, based on productivity improvements, as the case study reveals [1]. In the context of an HSC, RPA could take over repetitive tasks like low-level reporting, purchasing stock, sending out emails, and making and creating meetings. According to Aguirre and Rodriguez [1], other benefits such as process agility are relative to the RPA configuration, hardware capacity, and response time of the applications that the robot needs to access. Error reduction is also a measure that was not measured in the case study [1], however, it could too be improved by using an RPA.

6.5   Transaction Processing Systems

The problems that have arisen from the pandemic have presented an opportunity for the HSC to redesign its systems to create more flexibility within the end-to-end supply chain. For a more flexible process, organization may consider process engineering is one of its main objectives [36]. We recommend that the process re-engineering takes place at the TP IS level. The lowest level TP supports the processing of a firm's business transactions. The HSC can reduce some of its problems by keeping an organization running smoothly by automating the processing of the voluminous amounts of paperwork that must be handled daily [25]. If TP is done by all business partners there may be a reduced strain on the supply chain, and increased information (through visibility) within the SC [21].

6.6   Decision Support Systems

We recommend that the HSC uses Decision Support Systems (DSS) to contribute towards adaptability. Often DSS are considered to be designed for collecting, manipulating and distributing information. Rather, DSS are primarily used by managers to support their decision making process [2]. In the context of adaptive business networks, such as adaptive HSC, Heinrich and Betts [16] posit that organizations have access to an abundance of accurate, real time information which enables operational agility and rapid response to market changes. For example, organizations will be able to gather information about actual patient healthcare and changes in patients' demands in real time. In addition, costly delays that may eventuate when engaging with patients and suppliers are reduced or eliminated when DSS are used to automate a wider range of decisions. Another important aspect of an adaptable SC is having each partner within the SC network exchange a wealth of information related to their business's success. This allows access to more timely and accurate information, which is shared among all appropriate parties in order to react immediately and solve problem when they occur [16]. A useful DSS in an HSC will combine all the relevant information from the entire network and predict what the decision-maker will do by allowing them to select the best response to a potential disruption in the SC or in the environment. A DSS can only have capability when a certain level of standardization takes place however it will only have functional capability when adaptability takes place [16].

7   Conclusion

The research conducted in the area of HSC has experienced growth over the years, particularly with the increased focus on technology and IS. To build upon and contribute to this research, we looked at HSC literature from a post Covid-19 pandemic perspective. This research aims to first look at the problems that arose from the pandemic and provide solutions using principles of e-health, SC and IS. Adaptability, flexibility, education, automation, visibility, coordination, and collaboration were all looked at in the context of a post-pandemic world. These elements were interwoven with seven types of relevant IS to enhance the model, and better allow a UHHSC to transform into an HHSC. The literature was viewed from two main views, an UHSC view and an HHSC view. Two system dynamic models were illustrated to showcase relationships between the different aspects and to elaborate on the views. Each aspect and its relevant relationship were taken from literature. This research is by no means definitive, and the solutions provided will not be applicable to every supply chain; however, at the least, the elements of adaptability and flexibility and the system dynamic views of UHSC and HHSC provide the basis for further research.

References

1. Aguirre, S., Rodriguez, A.: Automation of a business process using robotic process automation (RPA): a case study. In: Figueroa-García, J.C., López-Santana, E.R., Villa-Ramírez, J.L., Ferro-Escobar, R. (eds.) WEA 2017. CCIS, vol. 742, pp. 65–71. Springer, Cham (2017). https://doi.org/10.1007/978-3-319-66963-2_7
2. Alavi, M., Henderson, J.: An evolutionary strategy for implementing a decision support system. Manage. Sci. **27**(11), 1309–1323 (1981)
3. Barnhill, C.: The COVID-19 Vaccine Supply Chain: Potential Bottlenecks. https://poole. ncsu.edu/thought-leadership/the-covid-19-vaccine-supply-chain-potential-problems-and-bottlenecks/. Accessed 5 Jan 2021
4. Bi, Z., Pomalaza-Raez, C., Singh, Z.: Reconfiguring machines to achieve system adaptability and sustainability: a practical case study. Sage J. **1**, 5–100 (2014)
5. Briggs, R.: On theory-driven design and deployment of collaboration systems. Int. J. Hum. Comput. Stud. **3**(1), 573–582 (2006)
6. Briggs, R., Kolfschoten, G., Vreede, G., Albrecht, C.: A seven-layer model of collaboration: separation of concerns for designers of collaboration systems. In: Proceedings of the International Conference on Information Systems, pp. 1–14 (2009)
7. Colombo, F., Clark, H.E.: Overdue yet within reach: sustainable health systems that put people first. https://www.weforum.org/agenda/2020/09/overdue-yet-within-reach-sustainable-health-systems/. Accessed 1 Sept 2021
8. Correa, H.L.: Linking Flexibility, Uncertainty and Variability in Manufacturing Systems: Managing Unplanned Change in the Automotive Industry, Brookfield, USA (1994)
9. Dash, R., McMurtrey, M., Rebman, C., Kar, U.: Application of artificial intelligence in automation of supply chain management. J. Strateg. Innov. Sustain. **14**(3), 43–53 (2019)
10. Duffin, S.: Why does Pfizer's COVID-19 vaccine need to be kept colder than Antarctica? https://www.npr.org/sections/health-shots/2020/11/17/935563377/why-does-pfizers-covid-19-vaccine-need-to-be-kept-colder-than-antarctica. Accessed 20 Dec 2020
11. Eder, J.: Workflow management and workflow management system. In: Liu, L., Özsu, M.T. (eds.) Encyclopedia of Database Systems. Springer, Boston (2009). https://doi.org/10.1007/978-0-387-39940-9_471
12. Farrer, M.: New Zealand's Covid-19 response the best in the world, say global business leaders. https://www.theguardian.com/world/2020/oct/08/new-zealands-covid-19-response-the-best-in-the-world-say-global-business-leaders. Accessed 20 Dec 2020
13. Fjermestad, J., Hiltz, S.R.: An assessment of group support systems experimental research: methodology and results. J. Manag. Inf. Syst. **15**(3), 7–149 (1999)

14. Ford, E., Scanlon, D.: Promise and problems with supply chain management approaches to healthcare purchasing. Healthc. Manag. Rev. **32**, 192–202 (2007)
15. Fox, K., Pleitgen, F.: The scientists who developed the Pfizer/BioNTech Covid-19 vaccine are a Turkish-German power couple. https://edition.cnn.com/2020/11/10/europe/biontech-pfizer-vaccine-team-couple-intl/index.html. Accessed 20 Dec 2020
16. Heinrich, C., Betts, B.: Adapt or Die. Wiley, Hoboken (2003)
17. Haeckel, S.: Adaptive Enterprise: Creating and Leading Sense and Respond Organizations. Harvard Business School Press, Boston (1999)
18. Hossain, K., Thakur, V.: Modelling the emergency health-care supply chains: responding to the COVID-19 pandemic. J. Bus. Ind. Mark. (2021)
19. Iyengar, K.P., Vaishya, R., Bahl, S., Vaish, A.: Impact of the coronavirus pandemic on the supply chain in healthcare. Br. J. Healthc. Manag. **26**(6), 1–4 (2020)
20. Jansson, J.: Class formation in Sweden and Britain: educating workers. Int. Labor Work. Class Hist. **90**, 52–69 (2016)
21. Kumar, V., Fantazy, K., Kumar, U., Boyle, T.: Implementation and management framework for supply chain flexibility. Emerald Group Publ. Ltd. **19**(3), 303–316 (2006)
22. Kelber, J.: The 5 biggest areas of waste in logistics. https://blog.flexis.com/the-5-biggest-areas-of-waste-in-supply-chain-logistics. Accessed 20 Dec 2020
23. Maani, K., Cavana, R.: Systems Thinking and Modelling, 2nd edn. Pearson Education, Auckland (2007)
24. McKone-Sweet, K., Hamilton, P., Willis, S.: The ailing healthcare supply chain: a prescription for change. J. Supply Chain Manag. **1**(1), 4–14 (2004)
25. Mahar, F.: Role of information technology in transaction processing system. Dep. Electr. Eng. **2**(2), 128–134 (2003)
26. Maier, R.: Summary and critical reflection. In: Knowledge Management Systems. Springer, Heidelberg (2007). https://doi.org/10.1007/978-3-540-71408-8_16
27. Mathur, B., Gupta, S., Meena, M.L., Dangayach, G.S.: Healthcare supply chain management: literature review and some issues. J. Adv. Manag. Res. **15**(3), 265–287 (2018)
28. O'Donnell, C.: Pfizer says supply chain challenges contributed to slashed target for COVID-19 vaccine doses in 2020. https://www.reuters.com/article/uk-health-coronavirus-pfizer-vaccine/pfizer-says-supply-chain-challenges-contributed-to-slashed-target-for-covid-19-vaccine-doses-in-2020-idUKKBN28D3BH?edition-redirect=uk. Accessed 23 Jan 2021
29. Osborn, A.F.: Applied Imagination: Principles and Procedures of Creative Problem-Solving, 3rd edn. Charles Scribner's Sons, New York (1963)
30. Paché, G.: COVID-19: the two sides of healthcare supply chain management. Eur. J. Manag. **20**(1), 79–84 (2020)
31. Parker, L.E.: Current state of the art in distributed autonomous mobile robotics. In: Parker, L. E., Bekey, G., Barhen, J. (eds.) Distributed Autonomous Robotic Systems 4, pp. 3–12. Springer, Tokyo (2000). https://doi.org/10.1007/978-4-431-67919-6_1
32. Parris, C.: Supply-chain obstacles led to last month's cut to Pfizer's Covid-19 vaccine-rollout target. https://www.wsj.com/articles/pfizer-slashed-its-covid-19-vaccine-rollout-target-after-facing-supply-chain-obstacles-11607027787. Accessed 20 Dec 2020
33. Pitta, D.A., Laric, M.V.: Value chains in healthcare. J. Cust. Mark. **21**(7), 451–464 (2004)
34. Queiroz, M.M., Ivanov, D., Dolgui, A., Wamba, S.F.: Impacts of epidemic outbreaks on supply chains: mapping a research agenda amid the COVID-19 pandemic through a structured literature review. Ann. Oper. Res. 1–38 (2021)
35. Rakovska, M.A., Stratieva, S.V.: A taxonomy of healthcare supply chain management practices. Supply Chain Forum Int. J. **19**(1), 2–24 (2021)
36. Rosemann, M.: Business Process Lifecycle Management. Queensland University of Technology, pp. 2–29 (2001)

37. Schlechty, P.C.: Schools for the 21st Century: Leadership Imperatives for Educational Reform. Jossey-Bass Inc., San Francisco (1991)
38. Sinha, K., Kohnke, E.: Health care supply chain design: toward linking the development and delivery of care globally. Decis. Sci. **40**, 197–212 (2009)
39. Watson, W., Watson, S.: What are learning management systems, what are they not, and what should they become? TechTrends **51**(2), 28–34 (2007)
40. Winkler, H.: How to improve supply chain flexibility using strategic supply chain networks. Logist. Res. **1**(1), 19–25 (2009)

Knowledge Management Practices: Innovation the Path to Organizational Performance

Mina Cu[✉][ID], Johnny Chan[ID], Gabrielle Peko[ID],
and David Sundaram[ID]

The University of Auckland, Auckland 1010, New Zealand
{mina.cu, jh.chan, g.peko, d.sundaram}@auckland.ac.nz

Abstract. This paper investigates the current state of organizational knowledge management practices (KMP) to shed light on how the implementation of a knowledge management system impacts corporate performance. To this end, we include 52 research articles published in the high-ranked Information Systems (IS) journals from 2010 to 2021 to capture the continuously updating of research in the IS domain. Based on several bibliometric analyses using computer-aided qualitative data analysis software, we first survey relevant studies on KMP and diverse aspects of organizational performance (OP) such as finance, human resources, leadership, production, business relationship, and innovation. We use survey results to present the evolution of concepts, key themes, and research trends. We then demonstrate the research problems, particularly the limitations of existing studies on KMP and OP, and how these issues constitute knowledge gaps in the field. Building on these findings, we develop an object-oriented framework for representing the path of influence between KMP and OP. This paper presents an exploratory direction for academia, firms, and practitioners to further their of knowledge management practices and the criticality of innovation as a pathway to organizational performance.

Keywords: Knowledge management · Knowledge management practices · Organizational performance · Innovation

1 Introduction

In the last twenty years, interests in knowledge management practices (KMP) have been establishing among organizational performance (OP) studies [13, 52]. Alavi and Leidner [1] believe that KMP, which frequently depends on information technology (IT), would lead to a robust shift in firm performance such as improving internal communication, staff engagement, problem-solving, financial performance, team performance, innovation, and business strategy [5, 84]. As knowledge becomes inherently more consistent, safer, and faster in transferring, firms invested in KM systems show a remarkable transformation of internal communication and a decline in operational costs [12, 20]. Even though the implementation of KM systems has been proven to be crucial for organizations, the design of KMP is generally a challenge for managers. The success of such practices depends heavily on the optimal choice for other

© ICST Institute for Computer Sciences, Social Informatics and Telecommunications Engineering 2021
Published by Springer Nature Switzerland AG 2021. All Rights Reserved
P. Cong Vinh and A. Rakib (Eds.): ICCASA 2021, LNICST 409, pp. 20–37, 2021.
https://doi.org/10.1007/978-3-030-93179-7_2

organizational factors as a whole [17]. Therefore, there is a growing interest in KMP research from both academia and firms.

In addition to several symbolic qualitative research that laid the crucial conceptual framework and theoretical foundation for KM discipline [14, 58], a growing number of quantitative studies aim to test and measure the impact of KMP on OP using precise modeling methods. These works have been carried on large-scale datasets to efficiently deliver reliable empirical evidence that shows the significant effects of KMP on firm performance. Nevertheless, the descriptive analysis might not efficiently cover all the aspects of KMP and OP [88]. These studies generally focus on knowledge processes and/or practices on the financial performance of firms. Although there are several reviews regarding KMP and firm performance, we argue that KMP's path of influence to OP has received insufficient attention. For instance, in the exploratory study on KM and firm performance by Zack et al. [88], they did not provide a framework to address the relationships between KMP and firm performance adequately. Existing studies mainly focus on using data from literature review to assess the impact of KMP on OP [8, 32, 42], critical success factors of KMP impact on OP [79], KMP in the association of different configurations of intellectual capital and firm performance [30, 64, 83], and KMP and innovation [4, 22, 27, 73].

Existing literature displays a lack of concrete and systematic review of the current state of the art on the influence that KMP has on OP. This paper aims to deliver further insights into the relationship between KMP and firm performance by answering three research questions: (1) How do constructs of KMP and OP develop over time; (2) What aspects of OP absorb the impact of KMP, and what is the path of influence; and (3) What are the limitations/knowledge gaps of this research area? In seeking answers to these questions, we propose an object-oriented framework to address the path of influence between objects. While performance is a metric per se, we will include firm performance and KMP into the object-oriented framework to provide further insights on how these objects related to each other. Our work contributes to common knowledge and practices in several ways: (i) a thematic evolution of KMP and OP; (ii) a framework for assessing the relationship between KMP and OP; and (iii) an exploratory theme to support future research. We organize the paper as the following. Section 2 describes our research methodology. The material collection process is denoted in Sect. 3, followed by descriptive analysis in Sect. 4. Next, the findings are presented in Sect. 5. Section 6 details the material evaluation, and relevant discussions are presented in Sect. 7 before we conclude our paper in Sect. 8.

2   Research Methodology

This paper follows the literature review method outlined by Mayring [53] and bibliometric analysis using R programming language proposed by Nobre and Tavares [57] to provide a comprehensive systematic literature review. Mayring [53] denotes four steps in the content analysis method: material collection, descriptive analysis, category selection, and material evaluation. Nobre and Tavares [57] suggest that the bibliometric analysis method consists of citation analysis, network analysis, bibliographic coupling, cluster analysis, and findings. Both review and analysis methods have been recognized for their quality by publications in high-ranked IS journals. We thus follow the above framework to carry on this research. The four steps of our systematic literature review method are literature search, descriptive analysis, bibliography analysis, and findings.

Following the above methodology, we employ computer-aided qualitative data analysis software, an effective tool for conducting bibliometric analysis. We use the bibliometrics library in R programming to operate descriptive analysis, factorial analysis, and multifactor correspondence analysis. While descriptive analysis assists this paper in defining research trends, factorial and multifactor correspondence analyses are helpful to define concept revolution, literature clusters, author impact, conceptual structure, intellectual networks, current gaps, and tendency.

3 Literature Collection

Due to KMP and firm performance involve emergent concepts, information and communication technology, and information systems (IS), the review sets out to cover literature published in the last decade (from 2010 to 2021). This setting is to observe the evolution of critical concepts adequately. The search strings were developed to search by topic using exactly the search string of "knowledge management" practice* AND (organizational performance* OR firm performance*).

There are three layers in the literature search procedure, i.e., search on Google Scholar, search on leading journals, and search on the academic databases. The search strings remain the same in three layers. In the Google Scholar search layer, the search result gave us an initial picture of the existing studies in the review period. We then filtered out qualified and relevant articles published in the leading IS journals using the Advanced search function. We obtained 45 articles from the first and second search layers. Next, we use the same search strings to search on Web of Science (WoS) and Scopus databases. In this layer, the articles were sorted by descending order of citations. We then cross-checked the search results from the academic databases and Google Scholar to eliminate duplication and add essential studies. Finally, we selected 52 scientific articles to conduct bibliometric analysis.

4 Descriptive Analysis

Dodge and Commenges [16] argue that descriptive analysis is not to learn about the population but to summarize the data. Thus, descriptive analysis is typically to calculate the mean and standard variable, representing the central tendency and variability or dispersion of a dataset. In this paper, a total of 52 scientific articles published between 2010 to 2021 were taken into the descriptive analysis (Fig. 1). Our purpose in carrying on the descriptive analysis is to: (i) present an overview of research trends in KMP and OP, (ii) deliver interesting insights into the scientific domain, and (iii) establish supportive ground for further classification structure. Our descriptive analysis embedded two main criteria, including distribution of publications in the thematic area and source impact measurements based on total citations. Figure 1 indicates annual production and respective total citations of the selected articles.

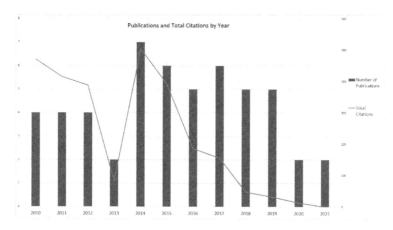

Fig. 1. The numbers of publications and total citations per year

It is notable that the numbers of publications and total citations had significantly increased in the period from 2014 to 2019, reaching the peak in 2014 with total citations of 504 for seven publications. This upward trend in research on KMP and OP could also be seen in the database search layer. It reflects the growing interest in the research area from academia. Although the number of publications from 2010 to 2012 remained the same, the citations rocketed for these scientific articles. This result indicates that the selected articles have received a high volume of citations, reflecting the recognition from academia. The total amount of citations would be one of the indicators to justify the quality of the selected articles in this literature review.

Regarding publication sources, studies on KMP and firm performance have been widely acknowledged in high-ranked IS journals. It is evident that all the articles selected in this review were from qualified sources. Significantly, the substantial number of citations over publication sources reveals that although the research domain of KM and OP is mature, the source impact tends to keep expanding. The high volume of citations highlights the potential of research on KMP and OP. This result also proves that the articles chosen for this literature review are outstanding and thus could represent a typical research stream in IS domain.

5 Findings

5.1 Concepts

The survey results of selected articles on KMP and OP show a solid bond to the concepts of organizational knowledge creation, tacit and explicit knowledge [58, 59], KMP [71], KM strategy [88], organizational KM [28] (Fig. 2). From these prior perspectives, Lee and Choi [42] define knowledge processes as the representation of fundamental operations of knowledge and enabler is essential infrastructure for firms to improve knowledge processes efficiency. On the other hand, firm performance could be addressed as the level to which firms meet their targeted propositions. Lee et al. [43]

develop a novel metric, namely, knowledge management performance index (KMPI), to measure OP under the implementation of a KM system. This metric could assign value and measure firms' intangible assets, for instance, financial index, stock price, and R&D expenses. Lee et al. [43] argue that KMP could impact the performance of workflow, processes, and management activities. Researchers thus can assess the relevant management performance by measuring the quality of organizational knowledge.

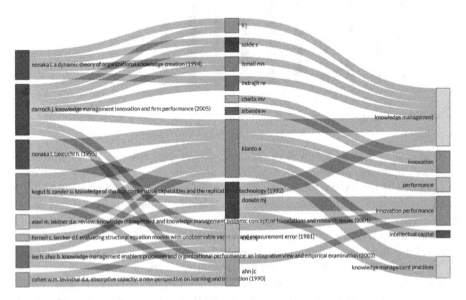

Fig. 2. Three fields plot of key concepts (reference sources-authors-concepts)

Andreevat and Klanto [2] suggest that KMP could be referred to as a set of management activities that allow organizations to produce value from knowledge assets. KM processes include phases such as knowledge creation, sharing, acquisition, and application. From a knowledge-based perspective, firm performance might be varied due to the discrepancy between their stocks of knowledge and capabilities of implementing knowledge applications. KMP thus could typically be seen as an integration of knowledge processes and firms' capabilities in supporting and advancing knowledge processes [28]. Donate [18] classifies KMP into two modes, namely, KM exploration practice (i.e., creation) and KM exploitation practice (i.e., storage, transfer, and application). Donate and Snchez de Pablo [19] believe that leadership is a critical factor that influences organizational KM. They measure the impact of knowledge-oriented leadership on several aspects of KM processes: knowledge creation, knowledge transfer and sharing, and knowledge application. They prove that KMP significantly impacts product innovation performance. Additionally, organizational KMP displays a vital role in the knowledge-oriented leadership of firms. Figure 2 illustrates the analysis of the three fields, i.e., key concepts, relative authors, and the reference sources.

The three fields analysis was conducted using R programming algorithm to define the unique terminology and associated references sources of the articles in review. We first calculated the broad area of indexed keywords and compared how the key concepts were connecting. We then selected the most outstanding concepts to represent in the form of a three fields plot. From Fig. 2, it is evident that the concepts of KM, KMP, and intellectual capital have intertwined in the studies of innovation, OP, and innovation performance. This means the research area of KMP relates to a broader domain, i.e., KM and intellectual capital. Similarly, the concept of performance bonds with innovation performance. Figure 2 represented a strong connection between KM, KMP, and symbolic studies in IS (reference sources), supporting our research focus and findings.

5.2 Conceptual Structure

The thematic map of concepts generally refers to the concept maps obtained from the thematic synthesis. Using bibliometric analysis with the assistance of R programming algorithm, the clusters of key concepts were obtained (Fig. 3). The inclusion index was weighted by word occurrences in the selected studies. We then developed a thematic map that describes synthesis results from 52 papers. Figure 3 displays key concepts and their relational networks. It visualizes the relatedness between KM and firm performance that was distributed into two main clusters. Each color represents one cluster connecting its network actors by the same color lines.

Analysis results show that "knowledge management" is the core concept interlinked to two main clusters. Notably, based on analysis results, we found that the concept of "innovation" establishes a broad network throughout two main clusters. This finding supports descriptive analysis results that were presented in the three fields plot of key concepts. Figure 3 shows multiple concepts of KMP link to diverse aspects of OP. In contrast, "OP" and "performance" create a cluster with relevant aspects of organizational KM systems, "firm performance" and "financial performance" bond to relevant aspects of KM and operational management. Based on the above analysis results, we summarized characteristics of OP and their respective clusters with KMP, and we then mapped the concepts back to the articles. We present the results in Table 1.

We provide further insights into the conceptual structure by carrying on a multiple correspondence analysis (MCA) [60], on the indexed keywords of the selected articles. The obtained results show the categories and hierarchical dimensions of the key concepts. It appears that while innovation and KM are at a lower level in information management, industrial research and OP are also interconnected. Knowledge-based systems and knowledge sharing are at the same levels of clusters under knowledge acquisition. This analysis results justified the significant relationships between industry, OP, KM, and information management. In the MCA analysis, dimensions are addressed in structured groups constituted by several sets of variables. We considered all the indexed keywords as individual variables and calculated the contribution of active variable groups to measure distances between variables. We used the Bibliometrix library (for MCA analysis) and multiple visualization packages (for data

Fig. 3. Clusters of concepts

Table 1. OP's clusters

Concepts	Associated word clusters	References
Firm performance, financial performance, industrial performance	New product performance, information and communication technology, industry, knowledge management tool, collaborative environment, business development, inter-organizational relationships, inter-firm collaboration, positive effects, significant impacts, collaborative innovation, knowledge-based	[5, 6, 10, 24, 32, 38, 39, 41, 46, 48, 49, 56, 61, 63, 66, 67, 69, 70, 78, 86]

(*continued*)

Table 1. (*continued*)

Concepts	Associated word clusters	References
	system, business value, research and development, business value, business units, speed-to-market, mutual trust, innovation. (1)	
OP, performance	Knowledge based systems, knowledge sharing, knowledge, knowledge application, external knowledge, knowledge acquisition, knowledge transfer, absorptive capacity, information management, best management practice, industrial research, management science, commerce, supply chains, manufacture, industry, computer networks, research models, product development, products and services, managerial implication. (2)	[3, 15, 26, 33–37, 51, 54, 56, 62, 66, 76, 80–83, 85, 89, 90]
Innovation	Involved in all nodes of cluster (1) and multiple nodes of cluster (2) such as performance, industrial research, best management practice, industry, knowledge sharing, knowledge, absorptive capacity, supply chains, commerce, and information management	[5, 6, 8, 10, 17–19, 24, 27, 32, 35, 37, 49, 61, 63, 66, 67, 69, 70, 72, 76, 78, 85, 86, 89]

visualization) from R. We put efforts to address the most critical variables that represent dimensions. We organized variable groups as below: (i) a group of variables that specifies the discipline of KM and KMP, including the variables that are relevant to theoretical approaches and research models; and (ii) a group of variables representing the factors of firms that would receive influences of the first group. Due to multiple sets of variables being considered simultaneously, we tried to balance the impact of the individual set by weighting the variables during the analysis, i.e., assigning the same weighting value to variables in the same group. In other words, the same variables in one group might be different in another group. Nevertheless, the nature of variables remains the same in the given groups [31]. Following the MCA analysis, we delivered an observation that contains (i) a set of variables that describes the KMP dimension and (ii) another set that describes OP dimension (Fig. 4).

28 M. Cu et al.

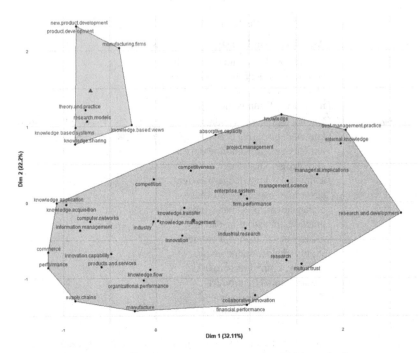

Fig. 4. Conceptual structure map using MCA method

Figure 4 shows the distinguished level of correlations between KMP and OP. The MCA results indicate that KMP relevant concepts are closely associated with firm performance, as suggested by prior qualitative studies [10, 24, 25, 58, 59, 88] and quantitative studies [2, 9, 13, 18]. In addition, the analysis results reveal a tighter correlation of OP in dimension 1 at 32.11%. The second dimension, which represents KMP, shows a lower correlation rate at 22.2%. In the first dimension, significantly, the variable "financial performance" reaches the highest value of the dimension, representing the value of the "performance" dimension. In the second dimension, "knowledge sharing," "knowledge base system," and "knowledge-based view" are the three key variables to observe. And these three variables are positively correlated with variables in OP clusters in both dimensions. These analysis results are similar to findings claimed by multiple earlier review studies [20, 50, 77].

5.3   Intellectual Structure

The intellectual structure analysis is to give insights into the outstanding contributors of the field. The bibliometric analysis results indicate that existing studies on KMP and OP were developed on the ground of high impact authors such as Fornell [23], Nonaka [58, 59], Cohen [11], Kogut [40], Szulanski [71], Grant [29], Zack [88], Gold [28], Alavi and Leidner [1], Zahra [90], Lee [44], and others. Analysis results on collaboration networks display a dominant collaboration between North America, Europe, Oceania, and North-East Asia. This result figures out the missing collaboration between other regions such as other European countries, Russia, and Oceania.

5.4   Object-Oriented Analysis

According to El Sawy and Majchrzak [21], KMP requires the integration of multiple perspectives. The classifications of KMP and OP thus are extra complex due to the multidimensional aspect. In seeking a solution that could help effectively addressing the relationships between KMP and OP, this study develops an object-oriented framework that acts as a categorization method. In this framework, each dimension of KMP and OP would be viewed as an object. Subsequently, we carry on a comparative analysis regarding the occurrences of objects and the association of arguments under these objects. The asterisk (*) represents the occurrence. In this object-oriented framework, we defined the reference-type arguments under KMP and OP objects. This means in our analysis, KMP might have a cluster with one argument (which represents one typical aspect) of OP. However, this argument might have another independent object (which is OP) that references it. In other words, one argument is related to two objects in the form of variable references. Following this framework, the details of objects in each study and their referenced factors will be properly illustrated. The analysis results of two fields (KMP and OP) would also reveal the gaps of the research domain: which areas are the mature research domain and which areas lack attention (Fig. 5).

Following the proposed framework, we conduct a further investigation on selected articles to deliver a comprehensive classification from multiple perspectives. The results show three main classes categorized based on research methods, i.e., design science research (main class 1), qualitative research (main class 2), and quantitative research (main class 3) (Fig. 6). Figure 5 and Fig. 6 indicate a mature image of research on KMP on OP with studies that sufficiently covered a wide range of both two research domains. Remarkably, they show that studies on KMP often simultaneously focus on knowledge creation, knowledge sharing, knowledge acquisition, and knowledge application. Similarly, studies on OP are often clustered with financial or economic performance and innovation. It is noteworthy that innovation is likely involved in almost all reviewed studies.

The frequent occurrence of innovation object across studies of KMP and OP might be a result of the high involvement between KMP and IT. This finding matches with the prior analysis results of conceptual structure in Sect. 5.2. It reveals that the significant path of influence that KMP produces to OP is likely via innovation and IT. Nevertheless, analysis results also reveal several issues of the current research on KMP and OP. We summarize these issues as follows.

Figure 5 could also be seen as a pre-mature state of research on KMP and leadership performance. Although several studies have been carried on KMP's influence on organizational strategy [9, 72], leadership styles, and management culture [6, 41], the rapid development of new technology would lead to a lack of further investigation on how and to what extent KMP would produce an additional impact on leadership performance.

In addition, the classification in Fig. 6 shows a short in research using design science research and qualitative methods. Current studies on KMP and OP display a dominant tendency of main class 3, representing quantitative research. Notably, most studies throughout three main classes were carried on under a positivism perspective,

No.	Authors	Year	Creation	Sharing/ Transfer	Acquisition/ Storage	Application/ Practice	Style/ Strategy	Capability	Finance/ Economic	Innovation	Team/HR/ Culture	Leadership	Business relationship	Production
1	Yan M.-R.	2021				•		•					•	
2	Lee M.-C.	2021	•	•								•		•
3	Williams & Mullane	2020				•				•				
4	Chaita & Sibanda	2020							•	•	•			
5	Marabelli & Newell	2019	•	•	•	•			•	•				
6	Gloet & Samson	2019							•	•				
7	Kaminska & Borzillo	2019					•		•	•	•			•
8	Valmohammadi & Ahmadi	2019	•	•	•				•				•	
9	Radaelli et al.	2019		•			•		•			•		
10	García-Merino et al.	2018	•	•	•	•				•				
11	Segarra-Ciprés et al.	2018	•	•	•						•	•		
12	Li et al.	2018	•	•	•	•	•			•			•	
13	Choi et al.	2018			•				•	•			•	
14	Taghizadeh et al.	2018		•			•	•				•		
15	Joshi & Chawla	2017		•			•			•				
16	Sheng M.L.	2017	•	•	•					•	•			
17	Pérez-Luño et al.	2017		•			•			•				
18	Durmuş-Özdemir &	2017				•				•				
19	Le & Lei	2017				•				•				
20	Turulja & Bajgorić	2017		•						•			•	
21	Khachlouf & Quélin	2016				•		•	•		•			
22	Chang et al.	2016	•	•	•	•				•				
23	Sun & Hou	2016	•	•					•	•	•			
24	Qin et al.	2016	•	•					•	•	•			
25	Jyoti & Rani	2016		•									•	
26	Hussinki et al.	2015		•				•	•					
27	Chen et al.	2015		•	•	•						•		
28	Mao et al.	2015	•	•	•	•				•	•			
29	Yang et al.	2015		•	•	•							•	
30	Van Reijsen et al.	2015	•	•	•					•		•		
31	Vicente-Oliva et al.	2015	•	•	•	•	•		•	•	•		•	
32	Donate & Guadamillas	2014		•	•					•				
33	Zhang et al.	2014	•	•					•					
34	Donate & Sánchez de Pablo	2014		•					•					
35	Villar et al.	2014	•	•	•	•					•			
36	Singh P.J., Power D.	2014		•							•	•		
37	Popaitoon & Siengthai	2014		•		•								
38	Wang et al.	2014		•	•	•			•				•	
39	Lipparini et al.	2013				•	•		•					•
40	Najafi Tavani et al.	2013	•	•	•	•			•		•			
41	Delen et al.	2012	•	•	•	•			•	•	•		•	
42	Fugate et al.	2012	•	•	•	•			•	•	•			
43	Andreeva & Kianto	2012		•			•				•			
44	Cao Y., Xiang Y.	2012	•	•	•	•			•		•			
45	Li et al.	2011		•							•			
46	Miranda et al.	2011		•		•			•	•	•			•
47	Hong et al.	2011		•			•		•				•	•
48	López et al.	2011					•		•	•				
49	Young et al.	2010	•	•	•	•			•			•		
50	Vaccaro et al.	2010	•	•	•	•				•	•			
51	Joshi et al.	2010					•				•			
52	Ko D.-G.	2010			•				•		•			

Fig. 5. Two-fields object occurrences

i.e., providing evidence to prove theory [55]. This finding reflects a lack of attention towards theory-building perspective using qualitative research methods such as field study and grounded theory. Additionally, there was no appearance of research conducted under a critical perspective.

No.	Class	Author	Year	Philosophical Perspective	Methodoly	Model/ Data Analysis	Data Unit	Data Collect	Approach
1	Main Class 1	Yan M.-R.	2018	Post.	DSR	Strategic Decision Support System (SSDSS)	2 business cases	Simulated	System dynamic
2		Lee M.-C.	2016	Int.	DSR	Conceptual model	N/A	Simulated	Resource-based view
3	Main Class 2	Williams & Mullane	2019	Int.	Qual	Hermeneutic	concepts	LR	Resource-based view
4		Chaita & Sibanda	2021	Int.	Qual. Case	Hermeneutic	4 firms	Survey	Innovation behavior
5		Marabelli & Newell	2019	Int.	Qual. Case	Synthesis	1 firm	Survey	Practice-based
6		Gloet & Samson	2016	Int.	Qual. Case	Crosscase analysis	16 firms	Survey	Innovation capability
7		Kaminska & Borzillo	2016	Int.	Qual. Case	Hermeneutics	1 firm	Survey	Longtitudinal
8		Valmohammadi & Ahmadi	2015	Int.	Qual. Case	Factor analysis	3 firms	Survey	Balanced scorecard
9		Radaelli et al.	2011	Int.	Qual. Case	Interpretive analysis	3 firms	Survey	Mediating effect
10		García-Merino et al.	2010	Int.	Qual. Field	Hermeneutics	1 firm	Survey	Intagible asset
11		Segarra-Ciprés et al.	2014	Int.	Qual. LR	Interpretive analysis	Literature	Archival	Accessing knowledge
12	Main Class 3	Li et al.	2021	Post.	Quan. Emp.	Structural equation modeling (SEM)	173 firms	Survey	Ethics theory
13		Choi et al.	2020	Post.	Quan. Emp.	SEM	285 firms	Survey	Community practice
14		Taghizadeh et al.	2020	Post.	Quan. Emp.	SEM	202 owners	Survey	Environmental dynamism
15		Joshi &Chawla	2019	Post.	Quan. Emp.	Conceptual model	313 respondents	Survey	Literature review
16		Sheng M.L.	2019	Post.	Quan. Emp.	SEM	205 firms	Survey	Dynamic capabilities
17		Pérez-Luño et al.	2019	Post.	Quan. Emp.	Multi-item scales and indexes	105 firms	Survey	Cross functional Integration
18		Durmuş-Özdemir & Abdukhoshimov	2018	Post.	Quan. Emp.	Factor analysis	59 respondents	Survey	Competitiveness-based view
19		Le & Lei	2018	Post.	Quan. Emp.	SEM	56 firms	Survey	Trust-based view
20		Turulja & Bajgorić	2018	Post.	Quan. Emp.	SEM	N/A	Survey	Mediating effect
21		Khachlouf & Quélin	2018	Post.	Quan. Emp.	SEM	43 firms	Survey	Managerial ties
22		Chang et al.	2017	Post.	Quan. Emp.	SEM	499 responses	Survey	Knowledge intensive
23		Sun & Hou	2017	Post.	Quan. Emp.	SEM	800 firms	Survey	Stock and flow
24		Qin et al.	2017	Post.	Quan. Emp.	SEM	225 firms	Survey	Cultural distance
25		Jyoti & Rani	2017	Post.	Quan. Emp.	SEM	304 responses	Survey	Work system
26		Hussinki et al.	2017	Post.	Quan. Emp.	Difference in difference	259 firms	Survey	Mean differences
27		Chen et al.	2017	Post.	Quan. Emp.	SEM	1012 data	Archival	SECI Model
28		Mao et al.	2016	Post.	Quan. Emp.	Regression analysis	168 firms	Archival	IT resources
29		Yang et al.	2016	Post.	Quan. Emp.	SEM	137 respondents	Survey	Social exchange
30		Van Reijsen et al.	2015	Post.	Quan. Emp.	SEM	55 firms	Survey	Dynamic capability
31		Vicente-Olivae t al.	2015	Post.	Quan. Emp.	Descriptive statistics	69 responses	Survey	Absorptive capacity
32		Donate & Guadamillas	2015	Post.	Quan. Emp.	SEM	111 firms	Survey	Knowledge-based
33		Zhang et al.	2015	Post.	Quan. Emp.	SEM	276 firms	Survey	Absorptive capacity
34		Donate & Sánchez de Pablo	2015	Post.	Quan. Emp.	SEM	Four industries	Survey	Knowledge-based
35		Villar et al.	2014	Post.	Quan. Emp.	SEM	157 firms	Survey	Dynamic capability
36		Singh P.J., Power D.	2014	Post.	Quan. Emp.	SEM	418 firms	Survey	Knowledge-based
37		Popaitoon & Siengthai	2014	Post.	Quan. Emp.	SEM	198 projects	Survey	Project team
38		Wang et al.	2014	Post.	Quan. Emp.	Multiple phase model	288 responses	Archival	Mediating effect
39		Lipparini et al.	2014	Post.	Quan. Emp.	Multiple phase model	982 projects	Survey	Knowledge dynamics
40		Najafi Tavani et al.	2013	Post.	Quan. Emp.	SEM	161 firms	Survey	Firm capacity
41		Delen et al.	2013	Post.	Quan. Emp.	Machine learning	277 firms	Survey	KM implementation
42		Fugate et al.	2012	Post.	Quan. Emp.	SEM	336 responses	Survey	Global manufacturing
43		Andreeva & Kianto	2012	Post.	Quan. Emp.	SEM	234 firms	Survey	ICT and HRM for KM
44		Cao Y., Xiang Y.	2012	Post.	Quan. Emp.	SEM	399 employees	Survey	"Guanxi" effect
45		Li et al.	2012	Post.	Quan. Emp.	SEM	411 firms	Survey	Collaborative KM
46		Miranda et al.	2011	Post.	Quan. Emp.	Regression analysis	218 firms	Survey	KM capability
47		Hong et al.	2011	Post.	Quan. Emp.	SEM	285 projects	Survey	Strategic fit
48		López et al.	2011	Post.	Quan. Emp.	SEM	310 firms	Survey	Strategic KM
49		Young et al.	2010	Post.	Quan. Emp.	SEM	743 individuals	Survey	Resource-based view
50		Vaccaro et al.	2010	Post.	Quan. Emp.	Factor analysis	113 respondents	Survey	KM tools
51		Joshi et al.	2010	Post.	Quan. Emp.	Multiple phase model	110 firms	Archival	IT-enabled
52		Ko D.-G.	2014	Int.	Quanl. LR	Interpretive analysis	Literature	Archival	Mutual trust effect

*Abbreviations: LR: literature review, Post.: Positivistic, Int.: Interpretive, Quan.: Quantitative, Qual.: Qualitative, N/A: Not applicable, Field: Field study, Emp.: Empirical, DSR: Design Science Research.

Fig. 6. Literature classification

6 Research Methodology Evaluation

This paper follows the qualitative research framework outlined by Myers [55] and the systematic review method [53, 57]. The rigor of this paper thus could be seen in multiple aspects. Firstly, this review followed a rigorous search procedure with evidence of search strings provided. Secondly, the selected articles were published in high-ranked IS journals with a substantial number of total citations that indicate the recognition from academia is sufficient to represent the research mainstreams. Finally, the use of computer-aided qualitative data analysis software, particularly the bibliometrix library of the R programming [60], in conducting multiple types of bibliometric analysis such as descriptive, MCA, and comparative analysis produce precise and consistent results. The relevance and rigor could eliminate the restraint of the number of articles in review (n = 52).

7 Discussion

Literature reviews on KMP usually have problems with the complex and multidimensional definition of knowledge [1]. Although the concept of KMP has gradually become a common term in the OP research area, existing studies often use one aspect of KMP to assess one to few indicators of firm performance. This one aspect assessment produces difficulties in delivering a precise measurement model of the impact that organizational KM has on OP [46, 77, 81]. This review treats the aspects of both KMP and firm performance as "objects" in assessing the occurrences of concepts to overcome this challenge. By which, it would mitigate the problems in categorizations. The limitation of this review would lay in the restraint in the number of the selected article (n = 52). This paper might miss some exploratory concepts and aspects of studies on organizational KM and firm performance. Nevertheless, the selected articles were published in high-ranked IS journals with a substantial number of total citations. Thus, it could deliver reliable analysis results. Overall, KMP is found directly associated with several types of measurement on OP such as finance, economic, operation, innovation, human resource, team, and leadership. The measure of OP shows a strong bond with financial performance or financial indicators. From this perspective, several studies argue that although KMP improves one typical type of OP, it will result in overall a positive financial performance [65, 87, 88]. The connection between OP and financial performance thus could extend to the areas of intermediate OP under the indirect impact of KM. We expect this could provide a direction for future research.

It is necessary to mention the argument regarding the path of influence that KMP produces on OP. The analysis results show a significant cluster between innovation and KMP. As KM systems and KMP are basically constructed on IT [68, 75], it would show that IT is the core factor that drives to firm's innovation [45, 50] and would be a primary element that constitutes the path of influence for KMP to impact organizational innovation [47, 74]. Therefore, the innovation factor would be concerned as an aspect of OP and should be an independent object that might impact both KMP and OP. This finding is interesting as most existing studies lack focus on the KMP's path of influence on OP and thus only consider innovation as one aspect of OP. This might be a consequence of the dominant research trend using structural equation modeling analysis that leads to a failure in addressing latent variables such as the path of influence. Future qualitative research could focus more on this area to deliver further insights.

8 Conclusion

This paper is a systematic literature review on KMP and OP. By carrying on multiple analyses such as descriptive, MCA, and object-oriented analysis of 52 articles published in the period from 2010–2021 in high-ranked IS journals, we answered three research questions regarding thematic evolution of concepts, KMP's path of influence on OP, and knowledge gaps of the field. Notably, this paper proposes an object-oriented framework to address the relationships between KMP and OP. The proposed framework integrates almost all the relevant aspects of existing studies in assessing KMP and OP. Analysis results show that research on KMP and firm performance should look at the objects in three key fields – KM, OP, and innovation. The assessment results indicate that KMP is directly associated with several types of OP, namely, finance, economics, operation, innovation, human resources, team, and leadership. Nevertheless, the measurement of firm performance usually refers to financial performance or financial indicators. Current literature shows a lack of studies regarding the impact of management style and KM process on new product development strategy and leadership performance. There is a lack of studies using qualitative research methods such as field study and grounded theory. In addition, there is an absence of research conducted under a critical perspective. This literature review delivers to academia, firms, and practitioners a better understanding of knowledge management practices and the vital role of innovation in improving organizational performance.

References

1. Alavi, M., Leidner, D.E.: Review: knowledge management and knowledge management systems: conceptual foundations and research issues. MIS Q. **25**(1), 107–136 (2001)
2. Andreeva, T., Kianto, A.: Does knowledge management really matter? Linking knowledge management practices, competitiveness and economic performance. J. Knowl. Manag. **16**(4), 617–636 (2012)
3. Cao, Y., Xiang, Y.: The impact of knowledge governance on knowledge sharing. Manag. Decis. **50**(4), 591–610 (2012)
4. Cavusgil, S.T., Calantone, R.J., Zhao, Y.: Tacit knowledge transfer and firm innovation capability. J. Bus. Ind. Mark. **18**(1), 6–21 (2003)
5. Chaita, M.V., Sibanda, W.: The role of knowledge in enhancing SME innovation: the case of knowsley-northwest region of England. Int. J. Knowl. Manag. **17**(1), 93–112 (2021)
6. Chang, W., Liao, S., Wu, T.: Relationships among organizational culture, knowledge sharing, and innovation capability: a case of the automobile industry in Taiwan. Knowl. Manag. Res. Pract. **15**(3), 471–490 (2017)
7. Chen, C., Huang, J.: Strategic human resource practices and innovation performance - the mediating role of knowledge management capacity. J. Bus. Res. **62**(1), 104–114 (2009)

8. Chen, H., Yuan, Y., Wu, C., Dai, C.: Moderator effects of proactive knowledge transfer among knowledge transfer usefulness, management, and innovation: a study of knowledge innovation effective model construction. Int. J. Knowl. Manag. **13**(1), 16–33 (2017)

9. Choi, B., Lee, H.: An empirical investigation of KM styles and their effect on corporate performance. Inf. Manag. **40**(5), 403–417 (2003)

10. Choi, H., Ahn, J., Jung, S., Kim, J.: Communities of practice and knowledge management systems: effects on knowledge management activities and innovation performance. Knowl. Manag. Res. Pract. **18**(1), 53–68 (2020)

11. Cohen, W.M., Levinthal, D.A.: Absorptive capacity: a new perspective on learning and innovation. Adm. Sci. Q. **35**, 128–152 (1990)

12. Cummings, J.N.: Work groups, structural diversity, and knowledge sharing in a global organization. Manage. Sci. **50**(3), 352–364 (2004)

13. Darroch, J.: Knowledge management, innovation and firm performance. J. Knowl. Manag. **9** (3), 101–115 (2005)

14. Davenport, T.H., Prusak, L.: Working Knowledge: How Organizations Manage What They Know. Harvard Business Press, Cambridge (1998)

15. Delen, D., Zaim, H., Kuzey, C., Zaim, S.: A comparative analysis of machine learning systems for measuring the impact of knowledge management practices. Decis. Support Syst. **54**(2), 1150–1160 (2013)

16. Dodge, Y., Commenges, D.: The Oxford Dictionary of Statistical Terms. Oxford University Press, Oxford (2006)

17. Donate, M.J., Guadamillas, F.: An empirical study on the relationships between knowledge management, knowledge-oriented human resource practices and innovation. Knowl. Manag. Res. Pract. **13**(2), 134–148 (2015)

18. Donate, M.J., Sánchez de Pablo, J.D.: The role of knowledge-oriented leadership in knowledge management practices and innovation. J. Bus. Res. **68**(2), 360–370 (2015)

19. Durmuş-Özdemir, E., Abdukhoshimov, K.: Exploring the mediating role of innovation in the effect of the knowledge management process on performance. Technol. Anal. Strateg. Manage. **30**(5), 596–608 (2018)

20. Dyer, J.H., Hatch, N.W.: Relation-specific capabilities and barriers to knowledge transfers: creating advantage through network relationships. Strateg. Manag. J. **27**(8), 701–719 (2006)

21. El Sawy, O.A., Majchrzak, A.: Critical issues in research on real-time knowledge management in enterprises. J. Knowl. Manag. **8**(4), 21–37 (2004)

22. Fosfuri, A., Tribó, J.A.: Exploring the antecedents of potential absorptive capacity and its impact on innovation performance. Omega **36**(2), 173–187 (2008)

23. Fornell, C., Larcker, D.F.: Structural equation models with unobservable variables and measurement error: Algebra Stat. **18**, 382 (1981)

24. Fugate, B.S., Autry, C.W., Davis-Sramek, B., Germain, R.N.: Does knowledge management facilitate logistics-based differentiation? The effect of global manufacturing reach. Int. J. Prod. Econ. **139**(2), 496–509 (2012)

25. Fugate, B.S., Stank, T.P., Mentzer, J.T.: Linking improved knowledge management to operational and organizational performance. J. Oper. Manag. **27**(3), 247–264 (2009)

26. García-Merino, J.D., Arregui-Ayastuy, G., Rodríguez-Castellanos, A., García-Zambrano, L.: The intangibles mindset of CFOs and corporate performance. Knowl. Manag. Res. Pract. **8** (4), 340–350 (2010)

27. Gloet, M., Samson, D.: Knowledge management and systematic innovation capability. Int. J. Knowl. Manage. **12**(2), 54–72 (2016)

28. Gold, A.H., Malhotra, A., Segars, A.H.: Knowledge management: an organizational capabilities perspective. J. Manag. Inf. Syst. **18**(1), 185–214 (2001)

29. Grant, R.M.: Toward a knowledge-based theory of the firm. Strateg. Manag. J. **17**(S2), 109–122 (1996)
30. Grant, R.M.: The knowledge-based view of the firm. Strateg. Manage. Intellect. Cap. Organ. Knowl. **17**(2), 133–148 (2002)
31. Greenacre, M.: Correspondence Analysis in Practice. Chapman and Hall, CRC, Boca Raton (2017)
32. Hong, P., Doll, W.J., Revilla, E., Nahm, A.Y.: Knowledge sharing and strategic fit in integrated product development projects: an empirical study. Int. J. Prod. Econ. **132**(2), 186–196 (2011)
33. Hussinki, H., Ritala, P., Vanhala, M., Kianto, A.: Intellectual capital, knowledge management practices and firm performance. J. Intellect. Cap. **18**(4), 904–922 (2017)
34. Joshi, H., Chawla, D.: How knowledge management influences performance? Evidences from Indian manufacturing and services firms. Int. J. Knowl. Manag. **15**(4), 56–77 (2019)
35. Joshi, K.D., Chi, L., Datta, A., Han, S.: Changing the competitive landscape: continuous innovation through IT-enabled knowledge capabilities. Inf. Syst. Res. **21**(3), 472–495 (2010)
36. Jyoti, J., Rani, A.: High performance work system and organisational performance: role of knowledge management. Pers. Rev. **46**(8), 1770–1795 (2017)
37. Kaminska, R., Borzillo, S.: Organizing for sustained innovation: the role of knowledge flows within and between organizational communities. Knowl. Manag. Res. Pract. **14**(1), 46–54 (2016)
38. Khachlouf, N., Quélin, B.V.: Interfirm ties and knowledge transfer: the moderating role of absorptive capacity of managers. Knowl. Process. Manag. **25**(2), 97–107 (2018)
39. Ko, D.: The mediating role of knowledge transfer and the effects of client-consultant mutual trust on the performance of enterprise implementation projects. Inf. Manag. **51**(5), 541–550 (2014)
40. Kogut, B., Zander, U.: Knowledge of the firm, combinative capabilities, and the replication of technology. Organ. Sci. **3**(3), 383–397 (1992)
41. Le, P.B., Lei, H.: Fostering knowledge sharing behaviours through ethical leadership practice: the mediating roles of disclosure-based trust and reliance-based trust in leadership. Knowl. Manag. Res. Pract. **16**(2), 183–195 (2018)
42. Lee, H., Choi, B.: Knowledge management enablers, processes, and organizational performance: an integrative view and empirical examination. J. Manag. Inf. Syst. **20**(1), 179–228 (2003)
43. Lee, K.C., Lee, S., Kang, I.W.: KMPI: measuring knowledge management performance. Inf. Manag. **42**(3), 469–482 (2005)
44. Lee, M.: Knowledge management and innovation management: best practices in knowledge sharing and knowledge value chain. Int. J. Innov. Learn. **19**(2), 206–226 (2016)
45. Li, J., Saide, S., Ismail, M.N., Indrajit, R.E.: Exploring IT/IS proactive and knowledge transfer on enterprise digital business transformation (EDBT): a technology-knowledge perspective. J. Enterp. Inf. Manag. (2021)
46. Li, Y., Tarafdar, M., Rao, S.S.: Collaborative knowledge management practices: theoretical development and empirical analysis. Int. J. Oper. Prod. Manag. **32**(4), 398–422 (2012)
47. Lichtenthaler, U., Lichtenthaler, E.: A capability-based framework for open innovation: complementing absorptive capacity. J. Manage. Stud. **46**(8), 1315–1338 (2009)
48. Lipparini, A., Lorenzoni, G., Ferriani, S.: From core to periphery and back: a study on the deliberate shaping of knowledge flows in interfirm dyads and networks. Strateg. Manag. J. **35**(4), 578–595 (2014)
49. López-Nicolás, C., Meroño-Cerdán, A.L.: Strategic knowledge management, innovation and performance. Int. J. Inf. Manage. **31**(6), 502–509 (2011)

50. Mao, H., Liu, S., Zhang, J., Deng, Z.: Information technology resource, knowledge management capability, and competitive advantage: the moderating role of resource commitment. Int. J. Inf. Manage. **36**(6), 1062–1074 (2016)

51. Marabelli, M., Newell, S.: Absorptive capacity and enterprise systems implementation: the role of prior-related knowledge. Data Base Adv. Inf. Syst. **50**(2), 111–131 (2019)

52. Massey, A.P., Montoya-Weiss, M.M., O'Driscoll, T.M.: Knowledge management in pursuit of performance: insights from Nortel Networks. MIS Q. **26**, 269–289 (2002)

53. Mayring, P.: Qualitative content analysis: theoretical background and procedures. In: Bikner-Ahsbahs, A., Knipping, C., Presmeg, N. (eds.) Approaches to Qualitative Research in Mathematics Education. Advances in Mathematics Education, pp. 365–380. Springer, Dordrecht (2015). https://doi.org/10.1007/978-94-017-9181-6_13

54. Miranda, S.M., Lee, J., Lee, J.: Stocks and flows underlying organizations' knowledge management capability: synergistic versus contingent complementarities over time. Inf. Manag. **48**(8), 382–392 (2011)

55. Myers, M.D.: Qualitative Research in Business and Management. SAGE, New York (2020)

56. Najafi Tavani, S., Sharifi, H., Soleimanof, S., Najmi, M.: An empirical study of firms absorptive capacity dimensions, supplier involvement and new product development performance. Int. J. Prod. Res. **51**(11), 3385–3403 (2013)

57. Nobre, G.C., Tavares, E.: Scientific literature analysis on big data and internet of things applications on circular economy: a bibliometric study. Scientometrics **111**(1), 463–492 (2017)

58. Nonaka, I.: A dynamic theory of organizational knowledge creation. Organ. Sci. **5**(1), 14–37 (1994)

59. Nonaka, I., Takeuchi, H.: The Knowledge-Creating Company. Oxford University Press, Oxford (1995)

60. Husson, F., Lê, S., Pagès, J.: Exploratory Multivariate Analysis by Example Using R, vol. 15. CRC Press, Boca Raton (2011)

61. Pérez-Luño, A., Bojica, A.M., Golapakrishnan, S.: When more is less: the role of cross-functional integration, knowledge complexity and product innovation in firm performance. Int. J. Oper. Prod. Manag. **39**(1), 94–115 (2019)

62. Popaitoon, S., Siengthai, S.: The moderating effect of human resource management practices on the relationship between knowledge absorptive capacity and project performance in project-oriented companies. Int. J. Project Manage. **32**(6), 908–920 (2014)

63. Qin, C., Wang, Y., Ramburuth, P.: The impact of knowledge transfer on MNC subsidiary performance: does cultural distance matter? Knowl. Manag. Res. Pract. **15**(1), 78–89 (2017)

64. Radaelli, G., Mura, M., Spiller, N., Lettieri, E.: Intellectual capital and knowledge sharing: the mediating role of organisational knowledge-sharing climate. Knowl. Manag. Res. Pract. **9**(4), 342–352 (2011)

65. Saraf, N., Langdon, C.S., Gosain, S.: IS application capabilities and relational value in interfirm partnerships. Inf. Syst. Res. **18**(3), 320–339 (2007)

66. Segarra-Ciprés, M., Roca-Puig, V., Bou-Llusar, J.C.: External knowledge acquisition and innovation output: an analysis of the moderating effect of internal knowledge transfer. Knowl. Manag. Res. Pract. **12**(2), 203–214 (2014)

67. Sheng, M.L.: Foreign tacit knowledge and a capabilities perspective on MNEs' product innovativeness: examining source-recipient knowledge absorption platforms. Int. J. Inf. Manage. **44**, 154–163 (2019)

68. Sher, P.J., Lee, V.C.: Information technology as a facilitator for enhancing dynamic capabilities through knowledge management. Inf. Manag. **41**(8), 933–945 (2004)

69. Singh, P.J., Power, D.: Innovative knowledge sharing, supply chain integration and firm performance of Australian manufacturing firms. Int. J. Prod. Res. **52**(21), 6416–6433 (2014)

70. Sun, Q., Hou, R.: Knowledge forms and enterprise innovation performance: an evidence from the dimensions of stock and flow. Int. J. Knowl. Manag. **13**(3), 55–70 (2017)
71. Szulanski, G.: The process of knowledge transfer: a diachronic analysis of stickiness. Organ. Behav. Hum. Decis. Process. **82**(1), 9–27 (2000)
72. Taghizadeh, S.K., Karini, A., Nadarajah, G., Nikbin, D.: Knowledge management capability, environmental dynamism and innovation strategy in Malaysian firms. Manag. Decis. **59**(6), 1386–1405 (2020)
73. Tamer Cavusgil, S., Calantone, R.J., Zhao, Y.: Tacit knowledge transfer and firm innovation capability. J. Bus. Ind. Mark. **18**(1), 6–21 (2003)
74. Tanriverdi, H.: Information technology relatedness, knowledge management capability, and performance of multibusiness firms. MIS Q. Manag. Inf. Syst. **29**(2), 311–334 (2005)
75. Tippins, M.J., Sohi, R.S.: IT competency and firm performance: is organizational learning a missing link? Strateg. Manag. J. **24**(8), 745–761 (2003)
76. Turulja, L., Bajgorić, N.: Knowledge acquisition, knowledge application, and innovation towards the ability to adapt to change. Int. J. Knowl. Manag. **14**(2), 1–15 (2018)
77. Uotila, J., Maula, M., Keil, T., Zahra, S.A.: Exploration, exploitation, and financial performance: analysis of S&P 500 corporations. Strateg. Manag. J. **30**(2), 221–231 (2009)
78. Vaccaro, A., Parente, R., Veloso, F.M.: Knowledge management tools, inter-organizational relationships, innovation and firm performance. Technol. Forecast. Soc. Chang. **77**(7), 1076–1089 (2010)
79. Valmohammadi, C., Ahmadi, M.: The impact of knowledge management practices on organizational performance: a balanced scorecard approach. J. Enterp. Inf. Manag. **28**(1), 131–159 (2015)
80. Van Reijsen, J., Helms, R., Batenburg, R., Foorthuis, R.: The impact of knowledge management and social capital on dynamic capability in organizations. Knowl. Manag. Res. Pract. **13**(4), 401–417 (2015)
81. Vicente-Oliva, S., Martínez-Sánchez, Á., Berges-Muro, L.: Research and development project management best practices and absorptive capacity: empirical evidence from Spanish firms. Int. J. Project Manage. **33**(8), 1704–1716 (2015)
82. Villar, C., Alegre, J., Pla-Barber, J.: Exploring the role of knowledge management practices on exports: a dynamic capabilities view. Int. Bus. Rev. **23**(1), 38–44 (2014)
83. Wang, Z., Wang, N., Liang, H.: Knowledge sharing, intellectual capital and firm performance. Manag. Decis. **52**(2), 230–258 (2014)
84. Williams, R.I., Mullane, J.: Family leadership succession and firm performance: the moderating effect of tacit idiosyncratic firm knowledge. Knowl. Process. Manag. **26**(1), 32–40 (2019)
85. Yan, M.: Improving entrepreneurial knowledge and business innovations by simulation-based strategic decision support system. Knowl. Manag. Res. Pract. **16**(2), 173–182 (2018)
86. Yang, J., Yu, G., Liu, M., Rui, M.: Improving learning alliance performance for manufacturers: does knowledge sharing matter? Int. J. Prod. Econ. **171**, 301–308 (2016)
87. Young Choi, S., Lee, H., Yoo, Y.: The impact of information technology and transactive memory systems on knowledge sharing, application, and team performance: a field study. MIS Q. Manag. Inf. Syst. **34**(4), 833–854 (2010)
88. Zack, M., McKeen, J., Singh, S.: Knowledge management and organizational performance: an exploratory analysis. J. Knowl. Manag. **13**(6), 392–409 (2009)
89. Zhang, M., Zhao, X., Lyles, M.A., Guo, H.: Absorptive capacity and mass customization capability. Int. J. Oper. Prod. Manag. **35**(9), 1275–1294 (2015)
90. Zahra, S.A., George, G.: The net-enabled business innovation cycle and the evolution of dynamic capabilities. Inf. Syst. Res. **13**(2), 147–150 (2002)

Predicting Humans' Balance Disorder Based on Center of Gravity Using Support Vector Machine

Tran Anh Vu[1], Hoang Quang Huy[1], Nguyen Viet Dung[1],
Nguyen Phan Kien[1], Nguyen Thu Phuong[1,2],
and Pham Thi Viet Huong[3(✉)]

[1] School of Electronics and Telecommunications, Hanoi University of Science
and Technology, Hanoi, Vietnam
[2] National Geriatric Hospital, Hanoi, Vietnam
[3] International School, Vietnam National University, Hanoi, Vietnam
huongptv@isvnu.vn

Abstract. Currently, vestibular disorders are quite common in Vietnam. However, as far as we know, methods for vestibular diagnosis are only qualitative, which are mostly based on experiences and doctors' observations. Therefore, a demand for a quantitative method is needed to help doctors accurately diagnose the vestibular disease. Moreover, the method is expected to allow monitoring the patient's situation during the treatment. To response to this demand, this paper applied machine learning technique to build a model to predict a person who has balance disorder. The data is obtained by a self-made device to measure the Center of Gravity (CoG) from people with and without vestibular. Results show that our proposed quantitative method had high accuracy in predicting whether a certain person has balance disorder or not.

Keywords: Vestibular disorder · Center of Gravity (CoG) · Data analysis · SVM

1 Introduction

When a person has balance disorder, they may have the feeling of dizziness, unsteadiness, or a lightheaded status. They feel hard to keep balance or fall down when changing position. There are 4 main systems in the body that work together to ensure a good postural balance: inner ear (vestibular system), vision, muscle and joints, and sensory input [1]. When one of these systems does not work well, it interferes your life by making you uncomfortable and uncontrollably. Balance disorder can be the symptom of following diseases: benign paroxysmal positional vertigo (BPPV), Meniere's disease, Migraine, acoustic neuroma, vestibular neuritis, Ramsay Hunt syndrome, cardiovascular disease, vestibular problems [2]. To diagnose these diseases, doctors need to perform a complex process, including physical examination such as Romberg's sign, the rotary chair test, etc., and using medical equipment for Electronystagmography test and Videonystagmography test [3]. Hence, more advanced

P. Cong Vinh and A. Rakib (Eds.): ICCASA 2021, LNICST 409, pp. 38–47, 2021.
https://doi.org/10.1007/978-3-030-93179-7_3

medical techniques for better diagnosis are in high demand. A promising technique for determining balance disorder is to apply the Center of Gravity (CoG). The Center of Gravity (CoG) is an imaginary point around which the body's weight is evenly distributed. For patients with balance disorder, their CoG points oscillate around normal ones due to bad ability to keep balance, so their CoG patterns may be different.

In this paper, we use the CoG data, which is the measurement of people's CoG location, to determine whether a person has balance disorder or not. The CoG data are collected in some hospitals, universities, … etc. and stored in a system made by our group. The raw data can be transformed to a new dataset which is more meaningful to doctors. We process the data by using support vector machine (SVM) technique, which is a supervised data mining technique for classification. In recent years, SVM has been applied widely in medical diagnosis. In 2013, patients with diabetes are classified by SVM with the accuracy of 78% [4]. In 2010, SVM is used for prediction of medication adherence in Heart Failure patients with 11 attributes. They tried Kernel method with 4 kernel functions and found that Radial Basis Function had the best accuracy - up to 77.6% for 2 groups of patients [5]. This paper proposed a method for processing CoG data with 2 stages. Stage 1 is to convert CoG raw data into useful parameters and to access the influence of each parameter in patient's postural balance. Stage 2 is to apply SVM for binary classification using corresponding parameters obtained in stage 1.

The paper is organized as follow. Section 2 is the methodology and the setup of the experiment. Section 3 is the results and discussion. Section 4 concludes the paper.

2 Methodology

2.1 Data Preparation and Processing

Sets of CoG data from patients with and without balance disorder are collected with CoG device. This device is made by our group to record real time CoG signals, which is shown in Fig. 1 [6].

It is a simple design with Arduino microprocessor and 4 loadcells, which is designed based on postural sway analysis. A postural sway analysis is a method based on the distribution of force in the four directions of the human body when standing on a rectangular or square board as illustrated in Fig. 2.

The device collects data on the mass that the human body produces over 4 sensors and sends signals to user interface via COM port or Bluetooth. Then, the CoG of each person is calculated as below:

$$x = \frac{[(F4 + F2) - (F1 + F3)] \times L}{W} \tag{1}$$

$$y = \frac{[(F3 + F4) - (F1 + F2)] \times L}{W} \tag{2}$$

where $W = F1 + F2 + F3 + F4$.

The platform demonstrates the projection of CoG onto 2-dimentional space, represented as a set of (x, y) coordinates. There are totally 78 participants at the age

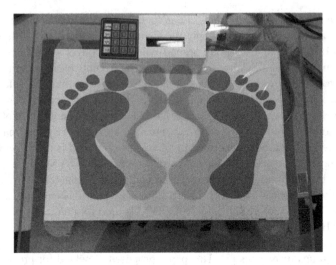

Fig. 1. Self-made CoG device

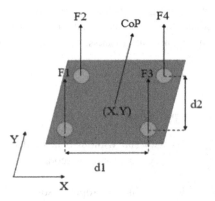

Fig. 2. CoG Platform design

between 22 and 60. All patients are required to stand on the CoG device twice, for the duration of 45 s each, with leg-open and leg-closed status. Base on each patient's medical record and treatment, patients are divided into two groups: with and without balance disorder. The patients in group "with balance disorder" are diagnosed with a disease that has balance disorder symptom, such as vestibular disorder, high blood pressure, BPPV, cerebral circulation insufficiency, etc. People in this group currently complain about high frequency of unstability and dizziness. They stayed in the hospital for less than one week (this ensures they do not undergo so many treatment procedures). The "without balance disorder" group includes healthy patients who are not diagnosed with any diseases relating to balance disorder and rarely feel dizzy and unstable. All patients do not have any leg injury that interferes them from standing on the device and do not use stimulants before measurement.

Each dataset for each patient contains 300 samples, or 300 pairs of (x, y) measured in time series, which represents the CoG of each person in 45 s. When changing from leg-open to leg-closed position, the patient's coordinate might have insignificant numerical errors, so the first 100 samples collected in the first 15 s are eliminated and the rest are kept for processing. The mean of x and y, denoted by $\bar{x}$ and $\bar{y}$, are used as the new origin coordinate around which patients sway to keep balance. According to [7], this dataset can be transformed to a new dataset which is more meaningful to doctors: mean distance, root mean squared (RMS) distance, range, mean velocity, 95% confident circle area, 95% confident ellipse area, sway area, mean frequency, fractal dimension, total power, etc. In this paper, only some of these parameters are chosen for calculation for each dataset.

The first purpose is to figure out the influence of such parameters on human balance by examining two independent groups, which is done by Independent Sample T-test. Group 1 includes 28 patients with balance disorder, group 2 includes 50 patients without balance disorder, and each patient in each group corresponds to a set of values, including mean distance, mean distance x, mean distance y, RMS distance, RMS distance x, RMS distance y, mean velocity, mean velocity x, mean velocity y, mean frequency, mean frequency x, mean frequency y, 95% confidence circle area, 95% confidence ellipse area and sway area, drawn out from the raw set of (x, y) data. When considering each parameter, the Independent Sample T-test is used to check whether the mean values of two group for each parameter are statistically different from each other. If yes, then that parameter could have impact on human's balance disorder.

The second purpose is to use SVM to classify patients with and without balance disorder, which requires above parameters as the input of SVM. The inputs of SVM should include attributes that have significant impact on human balance. According to independent sample T-test value, if there is any parameter that makes the mean values of two group not different from each other, it will be ignored temporarily, and the rest will be considered as the input of SVM. A user interface by C# programming language and Microsoft Visual Studio is created to support parameter calculations for the purpose of binary classification.

All calculations will be done in reference to the mean CoG, which means each pair (x, y) is transformed to a new pair (X, Y) in the new coordinate so that the new origin is the mean CoG ($\bar{x}$, $\bar{y}$). It is also necessary to do additional calculations for only x or y direction. The resultant distance (RD) is the distance from each data point to the mean CoG in the new coordinate.

$$X = x - \bar{x}, Y = y - \bar{y} \tag{3}$$

$$RD[n] = \left(X[n]^2 + Y[n]^2\right)^{1/2}, n = 1, \ldots, N \tag{4}$$

where N is the number of samples for each dataset. The mean distance is the average distance from the mean CoG and the RMS distance from the mean CoG is the RMS value of the RD, which is calculated as:

$$\text{Mean distance} = 1/N \sum RD[n] \tag{5}$$

$$\text{RMS distance} = \left[1/N \sum RD[n]^2\right] 1/2 \tag{6}$$

When considering only x direction, the mean and rms distance for each direction is:

$$\text{Mean distance x} = 1/N \sum |X[n]| \tag{7}$$

$$\text{RMS distance x} = \left[1/N \sum X[n]^2\right]^{1/2} \tag{8}$$

The total excursion is the total length of the CoG path, and is approximated by the sum of the distances between consecutive points on the CoG path

$$\text{Total path} = \sum_{n=1}^{N-1} \left[(X[n+1] - X[n])^2 + (Y[n+1] - Y[n])^2\right]^{1/2} \tag{9}$$

The total path when considering only x direction is:

$$\text{Total path x} = \sum_{n=1}^{N-1} |X[n+1] - X[n]| \tag{10}$$

The mean velocity (v) is the distance that the coordinates move in a time unit:

$$v = \text{Total path}/T \tag{11}$$

The increase in total path or mean velocity may suggest a poorer ability to keep balance. The 95% confidence circle is defined as the circle that contains 95% of the distance from the mean CoG, and the 95% confidence ellipse is defined similarly.

$$\text{Area CC} = \pi(\text{MD} + z_{0.5}s_{RD})^2 \tag{12}$$

$$\text{Area CE} = 2\pi\, F_{.05[2,n-2]}\left[s_{x^2}s_{y^2} - s_{xy^2}\right]^{1/2} \tag{13}$$

Where s_{RD}, s_x, s_y are the standard deviation of RD, X and Y, s_{xy} is the covariance; $z_{0.5} = 1.645$ is the z statistic at the 95% confidence interval. $F_{.05[2, n-2]}$ is the F statistic at 95% confidence level for a bivariate distribution with n data points. It has the value of 3.00 for a large number of samples (n > 120).

Sway area (AREA-SW) estimates the area enclosed by the CoG path per unit of time.

$$\text{Sway area} = \frac{1}{2T} \sum_{n=1}^{N-1} |X[n+1]Y[n] + +X[n]Y[n+1]| \tag{14}$$

The mean frequency is the rotational frequency, in revolutions per second or Hz, of the CoG if it had travelled the total excursions around a circle with a radius of the mean distance

$$\text{Mean } f = \frac{Total\ path}{2\pi MDT} = \frac{v}{2\pi MD} \tag{15}$$

2.2 Support Vector Machine Technique

Support Vector Machine Methodology. Support Vector Machine is a supervised data mining technique mainly used for classification. It aims at both minimizing misclassification and maximizing the geometric margin. The most basic form of SVM is linear SVM in which all data are linearly separable, but in fact, the dataset is too complex to simply solve by linear SVM. Fortunately, SVM can work efficiently for non-linear classification by applying kernel trick, which implicitly maps the inputs into a new space with higher dimensions to minimize nonlinear complexity. In this paper, we use a mapping function $x \rightarrow \varphi(x)$ to cast the original input data into a higher dimension space to deal with nonlinearity. However, calculating $\varphi(x)$ for each sample is very complex, especially when the dimension of the data set increases, and the number of samples is large. We need to simplify the process by using kernel trick in which only inner products (dot product) of the mapped inputs in the feature space need to be determined without explicitly calculate φ. Four kernel functions are summarized in Table 1 [8]:

Table 1. Four kernel functions

Name of kernel function	Definition
Polynomial	$k(x, z) = (r + \gamma x^T z)^d$
Laplacian	$k(x, z) = \exp(-\|x - y\|/(2\delta^2)), \gamma > 0$
Radial basis function	$k(x, z) = \exp(-\gamma \|x - y\|^2), \gamma > 0$
Sigmoid	$k(x, z) = \tanh(\gamma x^T z + r)$

The kernel trick converts the objective function into a new form:

$$\lambda = \arg \max_{\lambda} \sum_{n=1}^{N} \lambda_n - \frac{1}{2} \sum_{n=1}^{N} \sum_{m=1}^{N} \lambda_n \lambda_m y_n y_m k(x_n, x_m) \tag{16}$$

$$\text{subject to} \quad \sum_{n=1}^{N} \lambda_n y_n = 0; 0 \leq \lambda_n \leq C, \forall n = 1, 2, \ldots, N$$

where N is the number of data point in the training set; xn is the nth vector in the training set; yn is the label of nth data point (yn can be 1 or −1); λn is the Lagrange factor of nth data point; C is a constant described above. After this function is solved, support vectors will be found, and labelling can be performed next.

Experiment Setup. We divided the data into training and testing dataset. Training dataset includes 50 samples, in which 18 samples are labelled as 1 (which means they are in group "with balance disorder"), and others are labelled as −1 (which means they are in group "without balance disorder"). Testing dataset includes 28 samples, in which 10 samples are labeled as 1 and 18 samples are labeled as −1. The division of training and testing data is based on hold-out technique (training set/testing set = 64/36) [9].

We selected parameters using SVM library in C#. It allows parameter optimization by grid search tool, in which cross-validation accuracy is obtained for each parameter and the one with highest cross-validation accuracy will be considered the optimal value [10].

In order to evaluate our methodology, we calculate the accuracy, sensitivity and specificity for each classification. Each classification gives us values of TP (true positive), TN (true negative), FP (False positive), FN (False negative) which help to measure accuracy, sensitivity and specificity [11]. These values are critical in assessment of a specific test's reliability. Sensitivity shows the probability a test can correctly give a positive result for people who have disease. For a test with high sensitivity, it will generate positive result for almost everyone who has the disease and return just few false-negative results. Specificity of a test is the ability to correctly generate a *negative* result for people who *do not* have that disease. A test with high specificity will correctly identify almost people who *do not* have the disease and the rate for false-positive results is very low. The calculation of accuracy, sensitivity and specificity is given as below.

$$\text{Accuracy} = \frac{TN + TP}{TN + TP + FN + FP} \tag{17}$$

$$\text{Sensitivity (TP rate)} = \frac{TP}{TP + FN} \tag{18}$$

$$\text{Specificity (FP rate)} = \frac{FP}{FP + TN} \tag{19}$$

3 Results and Discussion

According to Independent Sample t-test, the mean values of two group for each parameter are statistically different from each other, so all above parameters have impact on human's balance and could be useful for clinical assessment. Especially, parameters calculated for solely x or y direction also reflect a significant difference between 2 groups, which is identical to the results obtained in [12]. Theoretically, patients with balance disorder will agitate more than normal people, so their coordinate also swing more around the origin. Hence, there is an increase in all above parameters, which is identical to the results of Independent Sample t-test. The p-value for each parameter is summarized in Table 2. In this t-test, the null hypothesis H0 and H1 is expressed as "the two means of the two groups are equal" and "the two means of the two groups are not equal", respectively. When p-value is less than α ($\alpha = 0.05$), it indicates a significant difference between 2 groups and vice versa.

Table 2. p-values of all parameters when comparing means between 2 groups (group 1: n = 28; group 2: n = 50)

Parameter	Mean distance	Mean distance x	Mean distance y	RMS distance	RMS distance x	RMS distance y
P-value	0.003	0.024	0.001	0.002	0.009	0.001
Parameter	Mean velocity	Mean velocity x	Mean velocity y	Mean frequency	Mean frequency x	Mean frequency y
P-value	0.000	0.000	0.000	0.000	0.000	0.005
Parameter	95% confidence circle area		95% confidence ellipse area		Sway area	
P-value	0.002		0.001		0.000	

All parameters are eligible for the input of SVM. The first trial for SVM involves the use of 7 attributes: mean distance, RMS distance, mean velocity, mean frequency, 95% confidence circle area, 95% confidence ellipse area and sway area, in which movement of the coordinate in solely x or y direction is not taken into account, and the second one has 15 attributes, which means 8 attributes is added: mean distance x, mean distance y, RMS distance x, RMS distance y, mean velocity x, mean velocity y, mean frequency x, mean frequency y.

These two trials help to figure out whether a better result can be obtained when adding more parameters relating to the movement of patients' CoG data in one direction. When using SVM with 7 attributes, the accuracy for the training and testing data sets is obtained and described in Table 3:

Table 3. Performance of 7-attribute SVM

Kernel functions	Data set	Accuracy	Sensitivity	Specificity
Gaussian (RBF)	Training set	88%	77.2%	96.9%
	Testing test	78.6%	70%	83.3%
Polynomial	Training set	62%	100%	40.6%
	Testing set	57.1%	100%	33.3%
Laplacian	Training set	76%	33.3%	100%
	Testing set	67.9%	20%	94.4%
Sigmoid	Training set	64%	0%	100%
	Testing set	64.3%	0%	100%

When using SVM with 15 attributes, the accuracy for training and testing data sets is obtained and described in Table 4:

Table 4. Performance of 15-attribute SVM

Kernel functions	Data set	Accuracy	Sensitivity	Specificity
Gaussian (RBF)	Training set	90%	72.2%	100%
	Testing test	82.1%	80%	83.3%
Polynomial	Training set	84%	100%	75%
	Testing set	82.1%	100%	72.2%
Laplacian	Training set	90%	83.3%	93.8%
	Testing set	75%	80%	72.2%
Sigmoid	Training set	64%	0%	100%
	Testing set	64.3%	0%	100%

Referring to Table 3 and Table 4, the RBF is the most effective function among 4 kernel functions with the highest accuracy. The accuracy of RBF when performing classification on training dataset is 88% for 7 attributes and 90% for 15 attributes. The accuracy of RBF when performing classification on testing dataset is 78.6% for 7 attributes and 82.1% for 15 attributes. Sigmoid function brings up the lowest accuracy ($\sim 64\%$) and sensitivity (0%) so it is not a promising function. In 15-attribute SVM with 3 kernel functions, the accuracy, sensitivity, and specificity for classification of training and testing set are greater than or equal to those in 7-attribute SVM. Therefore, SVM with more attributes has better outcomes, and the movement of CoG data in solely one direction, indicated by 8 additional parameters, can influence on classification accuracy. Laplacian function and Polynomial function do not seem to work well with 7-attribute SVM but they have better results in 15-attribute SVM. We can see that through experiment, RBF is the most effective function. Moreover, SVM with 15 attributes has better results than SVM with 7 attributes since it almost increases the accuracy, sensitivity, and specificity of classification for both training and testing set.

4   Conclusion

In this paper, SVM on the CoG data is used to diagnose diseases with balance disorder. Parameters that can be used to assess human's postural balance include: mean distance, mean distance x, mean distance y, rms distance, rms distance x, rms distance y, mean velocity, mean velocity x, mean velocity y, mean frequency, mean frequency x, mean frequency y, 95% confidence circle area, 95% confidence ellipse area and sway area. When classifying patients with and without balance disorder by SVM algorithm, RBF is the function that is the most effective. Moreover, SVM with 15 attributes has better results than SVM with 7 attributes since it almost increases the accuracy, sensitivity and specificity of classification for both training and testing set. One limitation of this research is that the impact of age on human's postural balance is ignored. The CoG pattern for young and old people may differ, because the older usually has poorer ability to keep balance due to the degradation of skeleton system. This fact opens a future direction for the topic. In conclusion, 15 parameters listed above can demonstrate patient's balance status, and SVM algorithm is a potential technique to classify patients with and without balance disorder with high accuracy.

References

1. Watson, M.A., Owen Black, F., Crowson, M.: The human balance system: a complex coordination of central and peripheral systems by vestibular disorders association. https://vestibular.org/sites/default/files/page_files/Documents/Human%20Balance%20System_36.pdf
2. Lava, N.: A visual guide to balance disorder, 10 April 2008. http://www.webmd.com
3. Robinson, B.S.: Common vestibular function tests. http://www.neuropt.org
4. Chitra, R., Anuja Kumari, V.: Classification of diabetes diseases using support vector machine. Int. J. Eng. Res. Appl. **3**(2), 1797–1801 (2013)
5. Lee, S.-K., et al.: Application of support vector machine for prediction of medication adherence in heart failure patients. Healthc. Inform. Res. **16**, 253–259 (2010)
6. Huy, H.Q., et al.: A design of a vestibular disorder evaluation system. In: Solanki, V.K., Hoang, M.K., Lu, Z., Pattnaik, P.K. (eds.) Intelligent Computing in Engineering. AISC, vol. 1125, pp. 1105–1117. Springer, Singapore (2020). https://doi.org/10.1007/978-981-15-2780-7_114
7. Prieto, T.E.: Measures of postural steadiness: differences between healthy young and elderly adults. IEEE Trans. Biomed. Eng. **43**(9), 956–966 (1996)
8. Souza, C.R.: Kernel functions for machine learning applications, 17 March 2010. http://crsouza.blogspot.com/2010/03/kernel-functions-for-machine-learning.html
9. Allibhai, E.: Hold-out vs. cross-validation in machine learning, 03 October 2018. https://medium.com
10. Hsu, C.-W., Chang, C.-C., Lin, C.-J.: A practical guide to support vector classification (2016)
11. Parikh, R., Mathai, A., Parikh, S., Chandra Sekhar, G., Thomas, R.: Understanding and using sensitivity, specificity and predictive values. Indian J. Ophthalmol. **56**, 45 (2008)
12. Hossein, T., et al.: Static balance in patients with vestibular impairments: a preliminary study. Scientifica **56**(1), 1–5 (2016)

Internet of Things Big Data Management and Analytic for Developing Smart City: A Survey and Future Studies

Tuan Anh Vu[1,2,3]($\boxtimes$)(iD), Cong Vinh Phan[4](iD), and Cuong Pham-Quoc[1,2](iD)

[1] Ho Chi Minh University of Technology (HCMUT), Ho Chi Minh City, Vietnam
{vtanh.sdh19,cuongpham}@hcmut.edu.vn
[2] Vietnam National University, Ho Chi Minh City, Vietnam
[3] Faculty of Electronics Technology, Industrial University of Ho Chi Minh City,
Ho Chi Minh City, Vietnam
[4] Faculty of Information Technology, Nguyen Tat Thanh University,
Ho Chi Minh City, Vietnam
pcvinh@ntt.edu.vn

Abstract. The progress of computing helps us to analyze a large set of data, called big data. Nowadays, there are many Data Analytic Tools for Big Data Analysis, such as Xplenty, Analytics, Microsoft HDInsight, etc.. Big data is a new research field of many research fields as cameras, mobile devices, RFIDs, remote sensing, software log, and wireless sensor network, and IoT (Internet of Things) that is not an exception. Many types of sensors are used to build smart houses, smart cities, and many intelligent things. Smart cities are the future of many countries. A massive data is collected throughout sensors and stored in data centers. It needs to be analyzed in detail to get meaningful information for particular purposes or reduce the database system's size. This paper surveys IoT big data management and analysis. Besides, the study of IoT big data will helps us to find a way to build an intelligent traffic light system in a smart city.

Keywords: Internet of Things · Big Data · Smart traffic light systems · Smart city

1 Introduction

The more progressive social is, the more requirements are. The first need is how to connect some network devices such as modems, switches, and routers for communication in the early days of a computer networking. In human society development, people want more information about cars, devices inside the house (fan, light, door, air controller), and healthcare devices, etc. People use sensors to help things become more intelligent. The sensors get some information about temperature, humidity, speed, action, place, status, situation, etc. Then the data is sent to the data center for analysis or other purposes. Therefore, a smart city

P. Cong Vinh and A. Rakib (Eds.): ICCASA 2021, LNICST 409, pp. 48–55, 2021.
https://doi.org/10.1007/978-3-030-93179-7_4

is researched very much especially in my countries. Our city wants to become better and smarter in 2030. Traffic jam is a real big problem of big cities. The congestion is at a high level and appears usually in corners in rush hours. Traffic police are hard to control traffic jams because of massive corners in the big city (maybe a few thousand corners). The big cities don't have enough traffic police to do this work. It is a waste of time and money. The big cities need an intelligent light system that can solve congestion situations by changing green or red light duration to reduce congestion levels in the corners.

In addition, if the next corner is also in congestion status, cars can't pass through the observed corner. Therefore, the congestion level is higher in the observed corner. Obviously, there is a relationship between the observed corner and next corner. To solve this problem, we need four cameras and controller devices. Besides, we can attach RFID (Radio Frequency Identification) card to emergency vehicles to define when they come to the observed corner. At that time, the observed corner need to turn on the green light first, and then turn back to the red light status after the emergency vehicles already pass through the observed corner. Therefore, the emergency vehicles can save a time of running on the road. Because of massive corners, data of sensors and RFID card are too large and called IoT big data. The traffic controllers analyze it to get much important information. It helps to define the priority of the ways, and the duration of red light and green light. For example, the higher priority the road has, the longer duration the green light has. This is a reason why we need to analyze big data. Next section, we survey IoT big data management and analytic.

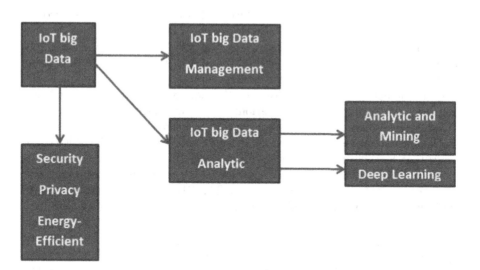

Fig. 1. Overview of IoT Big Data

2   A Survey of IoT Big Data Management and Analytic

In the big data problem of intelligent traffic light systems, the vital thing is classifying the data's position. For example, data belongs to which corner, district, and place. Therefore, we can create a data distribution on Google map. In addition, the time field of data shows congestion's duration. That will also help define place and time of congestion. The congestion status is repeated or not at the same time. The congestion maybe appears every day with higher congestion and more extended time.

The overview of the survey is shown in Fig. 1. The first branch is survey of IoT Big Data Management, the second branch is survey of Analytic, and the remaining one is survey of Security, Privacy, Energy-Efficient. IoT Big Data Analytic is divided into two branches, including Analytic & Mining and Deep Learning.

2.1   A Survey of IoT Big Data Management

Data source of IoT environment has many types and levels. Therefore, we can't compare two types of data due to features such as size, types, and structure. Data includes structured data, semi-structured data, and unstructured data. When data center receives a data flow, it should to classify data due to above features and types. Then we can storage it in database. However, unstructured data is a special type that should be focused on. Because of massive data, we need to scale it down on size.

The paper [13] proposes a Cognitive Oriented Framework (COIB-framework). The framework help to manage data effectively. The framework includes five layers. The first layer, named IoT big-data aggregators, collects all data of IoT sensors network. Then, it divides data into small pieces. This is raw data without encoding or scaling. The raw data is unstructured type and still in same name, scale, and structure level. Anomalies of the data steam can be checked and eliminated due to data fusion operation. The second layer help to categorize cleaned data and save it in clusters according to behaviors and characteristics. The framework can get access to domain and cloud easily. Next layer is HBase storage that have scaling and storing function. In this layer, data is reduced in its size and saved to nodes. The HBase table has two features as key names and data relationship for setting storage nodes. The HBase table can scale big data effectively. The last layer is Iot big-data analysis. It have a tool, named Cognitive CI-Toll, to do a process of knowing data. Then it can decide, plant, and act something with data in next step. The authors believe in success of the framework in the automation environment because of many computing tools. The paper also instructs deploying the framework and cloud computing in the life. However, the paper just give out an ideal without any stimulation or deployment. Therefore, we need to add some features of data like place, number of congestion, priority level of the way. This helps to build intelligent traffic light system so much.

Paper [1] proposes a HEP Framework (Unified Heterogeneous Event Processing Framework) for event data. The event data, collected from sensors and intelligent objects, is transferred to the framework via Common Event Adapter. Next, the framework has a space to save it according to relationship and XML type. In here, a cache helps data formatting and data processing to be run faster. The data categorizing in before layers also helps data processing effectively in next layer, named Event Processing space. All works should make sure real time constraint because of data streaming. Finally, the data is transferred to end-points. The framework is very suitable for analyzing data of streaming, but the intelligent traffic light system has no data streaming.

The following paper [7] proposes Smart Flood Management Framework. The framework has three layers:

- The first layer is the Internet of Things. The sensor measures water level and speed of water flow, and satellite take some pictures of the water flow. In addition, buoys measure deep factor.
- The second layer is Food Data Storage. This layer has some tasks such us processing, analyzing and reducing. We maybe integrate some tools inside this layer.
- The last layer is the Presentation Layer with Flood Map, where each color presents a level of Flood correspondingly. The authors' setup Food Attributes included Velocity of Catchment, Density of Forests per Acre, and Food Preventing Attributes had Current season, Drainage system, and soil type.

Food Causing Attributes are divided into five levels: the significantly less, the less, the moderate, the high, and the extreme to classify and store big data. In addition, Flood Preventing has the same five levels as >1000, 800–1000, 500–800, 100–500, and <100. Therefore, we can refer to the paper to build three levels of way and congestion, as usual, medium, and high. The considered factors of the system are the car's velocity, congestion level, distance between emergency vehicles and corners, etc. We will explain all things in more detail in future studies section.

2.2   A Survey of IoT Big Data Analytic

In some exceptional cases, we need to make some critical decisions to control the traffic light system. To decide, we should analyze data to help actuators to do some actions. However, big data of the sensors and cameras are a big problem because of the massive traffic lights in the big cities. In the before part, the survey of IoT extensive data management is done already. The management process classifies big data in some attributes for storing and later analyzing. We start discussing the Analytic and Mining section first. The following subsection discusses Deep Learning.

2.2.1 Analytic and Mining

Paper [4] proposes an IoT Big Data Analytic Framework (IBDA framework). The framework is developed on the basics of Python Language and Big Data

Cloudera Platform. They simulate sensors and analyze the data with python code and PySpart tool. Sensors create data and transfer it to HDFS storage. To get it, HDFS need Flume Agent as an agent for get the data Flume Agents is a top-level project of Apache Software Foundation, requiring Java Runtime Environment 1.6, Memory and Disk space, channels or sinks, Directory permissions for reading and writing by the agent. Flume Agents is a data flow unit where events flow is transferred from an external source (like a web server) to the next destination (called hop). The hop is HDFS storage in the next layer. Then the authors use Spark as major software for analyzing data as soon as it arrives into HDFS storage. The last layer is the actuators (turn oxygen pumps, fire alarms, and lights ON and OFF) and Cloudera visualization data. Spark is a unified Analytics Engine for Big Data developed by Apache. Spark also is necessary soft for future researches on building an intelligent traffic light system. Maybe, we also can use Python Code to simulate virtual sensors before applying them in life. Flume Agents is a data flow unit, set by the framework. The external source is a web server where data get out and go to the next-hop named HDFS storage. In the storage, they use Spark to analyze big data. We can apply it to our research on the intelligent light system. We can refer to the paper about sensor stimulation with python code in the lab.

Paper [5] introduces IoTSim as stimulation and analytic software. The IoT-Sime has total five layers. The first layer is the core layer for stimulating Clouds. This layer has network topologies, added sources, added services or already services. It also has a UI structure for users. The network also have delay factors that can be calculated. We can build sensors in the cloud source with some functions as Events Handling. Besides, Datacenter help to manage and analyze data to get results. The second layer is stimulating CloudSim for storing online. The next layer is used for storing data in the system. Data processing is the fourth layer. And the last layer is a layer for coding. The user use this layer to program or code application. We can refer to the paper for simulating the intelligent traffic light system in the lab.

Next, paper [3] explains IoT Fundamentals and IoT Stream Mining Algorithms. The paper also focuses on open-source tools to mine big data such as Spark, Flink, Storm, and Samza. This paper is a good reference for the beginner who needs to be used to data mining tools. Data mining can help to get a map of congestion distribution in the city. Data mining will be discussed in more detail in the future researches part later. The paper introduces some tools to mine big data. Tools, like Spark, Flink, Storm, and Samza, are very popular with users. The beginners should be used to them easily, and we can be the same. We will discuss data mining in a later section.

2.2.2 Deep Learning

The paper [15] proposed a model for deep computing. This is a first step and important thing. The mode integrates tensor (3D data) that have ability to be coded automatically. The paper also instructs calculating errors when the sample is reconstructed. However, the paper doesn't explain data mining in more detail, and just concern with the results and problem of data.

The paper [5] also proposes a model to do deep learning on data. The paper has the same authors as the paper [15]. The model uses an adaptive distribution that has a rate with a probability named p. There are some attributes been set for the model. The probabilistic model is used for calculating the activating rate, and Maximum Likelihood Estimation is used for estimating parameters of probabilistic distribution to statistic data. The authors used CUAVE and SNAE2 datasets with Matlab R2014 and a high-performance laptop (core i7 and 8G RAM). The DCM results are about 13.3 to 21.3% and are the same with DDCM and ADDCM (about 10.5 to 18.5%). We can refer to the model and apply it to the intelligent light system.

3 Security Privacy and Energy Efficient

Security and Privacy requirements and Innovative Demand of uses conflict in collecting, using, and managing Big Data. Paper [6] is also a survey made by Karen R. Sollins. The author wants to clarify challenges in future researches. Therefore, we will not survey Security Privacy in more detail. The following paper [8] is a request-based, secured, and energy-efficient architecture for handling IoT big data. The nodes have a small battery for actions. The spending energy is due to far distance or near distance between nodes. Therefor, the authors want to save the energy by reducing the distance. Some relay nodes are put in the middle, or use multi-hop system. They have ability to relay data when it is transferred from source to destination. This helps to reduce the distance and save more energy. Besides, the system can turn off passive sensors and turn on them again when they are necessary for actions. Multi-hop system can be used in transferring data to the sink. All of works will increase the lifetime of the system.

4 Future Studies

The survey of IoT Big Data helps to find a way to build an intelligent traffic light system. Basing on all before researches, we need some factors as follows:

- To define some attributes of an intelligent light system, we should have three levels of congestion, speed, and distance, as usual, medium, and high. Suppose the congestion is medium or high level in the next corner. The observed corner should increase more duration of the red light to decrease the congestion of the next corner. The more duration can be from 30 to 60 s according to medium and high levels. However, it still depends on target countries. In addition, the green light needs to be turned on for emergency vehicles and turned back to before status. But, the normal cars can't stop immediately at crossroads, so we need to turn on the yellow light before the red light for about 3 s. That is a reason why we need to know the distance from emergency cars to the corner. This helps the system know the time to turn on the yellow light.

- Using some software such as PySpart, Spark, etc. and some platforms such as COIB, IBDA. It helps build framework and analyze data to create a congestion map. Based on the congestion level in areas, the computer can automatically calculate and define priority levels of ways in the regions.
- The survey helps to decrease spending power so that relay nodes and multi-hop systems can be applied. In addition, the passive nodes is turned off to decrease spending energy. This increase efficiency and lifetime of the system because of limited energy.

5 Conclusion

The development of IoT is speedy today. In the early days of IoT, the intelligent house is approached very much. The inside devices have become more thoughtful and give more convenience. The other directions research on agriculture, manufacturer, industry, and so on. However, the traffic is also the same field. To build a smart city, we need to develop intelligent traffic light systems. It is a system that can change the duration of red and green lights automatically. The changes depend on the congestion level of the observed corner, congestion of the next corner, and priority level of the way. All attributes are divided into three classes, including usual, medium, and high. The receiving data is categorized and saved to in HDFS. We can refer to the survey papers to use the framework like COIB and IBDA. But, we need to replace 5 attribute level with to 3 attribute level as usual, medium, and high. Next step, some analytic tool are applied to the system. Finally, we can use medium nodes and hops to decrease the distance to help to increase a lifetime of the system. We also refer IoTSim or Python to simulate the intelligent traffic light system in the lab before applying it in life.

Acknowledgments. This research is funded by Ho Chi Minh City University of Technology (HCMUT), VNU-HCM, under grant number BK-SDH-2021-1980918.

References

1. Wang, W., Guo, D.: Towards unified heterogeneous event processing for the Internet of Things. In: 2012 3rd IEEE International Conference on the Internet of Things, pp. 84–91 (2012). https://doi.org/10.1109/IOT.2012.6402308
2. Marjani, M., et al.: Big IoT data analytics: architecture, opportunities, and open research challenges. IEEE Access **5**, 5247–5261 (2017). https://doi.org/10.1109/ACCESS.2017.2689040
3. De Francisci Morales, G., Bifet, A., Khan, L., Gama, J., Fan, W.: IoT big data stream mining. In: Proceedings of the 22nd ACM SIGKDD International Conference on Knowledge Discovery and Data Mining, KDD 2016, pp. 2119–2120 (2016). https://doi.org/10.1145/2939672.2945385
4. Bashir, M.R., Gill, A.Q.: Towards an IoT big data analytics framework: smart buildings systems. In: 2016 IEEE 18th International Conference on High-Performance Computing and Communications, IEEE 14th International Conference on Smart City, and IEEE 2nd International Conference on Data Science and

Systems (HPCC/SmartCity/DSS), vol. 1, pp. 1325–1332 (2016). https://doi.org/10.1109/HPCC-SmartCity-DSS.2016.0188

5. Zhang, Q., Yang, L.T., Chen, Z., Li, P., Bu, F.: An adaptive dropout deep computation model for industrial IoT big data learning with crowdsourcing to cloud computing. IEEE Trans. Ind. Inform. **15**(4), 2330–2337 (2019). https://doi.org/10.1109/TII.2018.2791424

6. Sollins, K.R.: IoT big data security and privacy vs. innovation. IEEE Internet Things J., Special Issue on Security and Privacy Protection for Big Data and IoT. ISSN 2327-4662 CD 2372-2541

7. Sooda, S.K., Sandhuab, R., Singla, K., Chang, V.: IoT, big data and HPC based smart flood management framework. Sustain. Comput. Inform. Syst. **20**, 102–117 (2018). https://doi.org/10.1016/j.suscom.2017.12.001

8. Ahad, M.A., Biswas, R.: Request-based, secured and energy-efficient (RBSEE) architecture for handling IoT big data. J. Inf. Sci. 1–12 (2018). https://doi.org/10.1177/0165551518787699

9. Hajiheydari, N., Talafidaryani, M., Khabiri, S.: IoT big data value map: how to generate value from IoT data. In: 5th International Conference on e-Society, e-Learning and e-Technologies, pp. 98–103 (2019). https://doi.org/10.1145/3312714.3312728

10. Saheb, T., Izadi, L.: Paradigm of IoT big data analytics in the healthcare industry: a review of scientific literature and mapping of research trends. Telemat. Inform. 70–85 (2019). https://doi.org/10.1016/j.tele.2019.03.005

11. Misra, N.N., Dixit, Y., Al-Mallahi, A., Bhullar, M.S., Upadhyay, R., Martynenko, A.: IoT, big data and artificial intelligence in agriculture and food industry. IEEE Internet Things J. (Early Access) 1–18 (2020). https://doi.org/10.1109/JIOT.2020.2998584

12. Atitallah, S.B., Driss, M., Boulila, W., Ghézala, H.B.: Leveraging deep learning and IoT big data analytics to support the smart cities development: review and future directions. Comput. Sci. Rev. **38** (2020). https://doi.org/10.1016/j.cosrev.2020.100303

13. Mishra, N., Lin, C.-C., Chang, H.-T.: A cognitive adopted framework for IoT big-data management and knowledge discovery prospective. Int. J. Distrib. Sens. Netw. (2015). https://doi.org/10.1155/2015/718390

14. Zeng, X., Garg, S.K., Strazdins, P., Jayaraman, P.P., Georgakopoulos, D., Ranjan, R.: IOTSim: a simulator for analysing IoT applications. J. Syst. Archit. **72**, 93–107 (2017). https://doi.org/10.1016/j.sysarc.2016.06.008

15. Zhang, Q., Yang, L.T., Chen, Z.: Deep computation model for unsupervised feature learning on big data. IEEE Trans. Serv. Comput. **9**(1), 161–171 (2016). https://doi.org/10.1109/TSC.2015.2497705

16. Tuan Anh, V., Cuong, P.Q., Cong Vinh, P.: Context-aware mobility based on π-calculus in internet of thing: a survey. In: Vinh, P.C., Rakib, A. (eds.) ICCASA/ICTCC -2019. LNICST, vol. 298, pp. 38–46. Springer, Cham (2019). https://doi.org/10.1007/978-3-030-34365-1_4

17. Anh, V.T., Cuong, P.Q., Vinh, P.C.: Context-aware mobility in internet of thing: a survey. EAI Endorsed Trans. Context-Aware Syst. Appl. **6**(16), e3 (2019). https://doi.org/10.4108/eai.13-7-2018.158875

Ensemble Learning for Mining Opinions on Food Reviews

Phuc Quang Tran[1] , Hai Thanh Nguyen[2] , Hanh My Thi Le[3] ,
and Hiep Xuan Huynh[2](✉)

[1] Faculty of Foreign Language and Informatics,
People's Police College II, Ho Chi Minh City, Vietnam
[2] College of Information and Communication Technology,
Can Tho University, Can Tho City, Vietnam
{nthai.cit,hxhiep}@ctu.edu.vn
[3] Faculty of Information Technology, University of Science and Technology
Da Nang University, Da Nang City, Vietnam
ltmhanh@dut.udn.vn

Abstract. This paper proposes an ensemble learning model for opinion mining on food reviews. The proposed model is built on an ensemble of decision trees called Random classification forest. This model performs the task of classifying sentiment about food as positive, negative, or neutral. The ensemble learning model was evaluated on two scenarios, which we built based on important features of the reviews. The experimental results on the food reviews data set have shown the effectiveness of the proposed model.

Keywords: Opinion mining · Opinion ensemble learning · Food reviews

1 Introduction

Opinion mining or sentiment analysis is widely applied in social life [1]. The aims of opinion mining to extract opinions and sentiments from natural language text using computational methods. The computational methods of opinion mining are based on the ones used in data mining, machine learning, and others [2]. Currently, there are many studies on opinion mining with supervised machine learning approaches to classify sentiment such as Naive bayes classification, Maximum entropy classification, Support vector machines, and classification based on Decision tree are used [3–5]. Ensemble methods [6,7] for sentiment classification also used with the classifiers of individual same(Decision trees) e.g. Random forest algorithm [8] for sentiment classification with data from Twitter. The accuracy of measurements in this study is around 75%. Different supervise machine learning algorithms such as Random forest, Gradient boosting,

P. Cong Vinh and A. Rakib (Eds.): ICCASA 2021, LNICST 409, pp. 56–70, 2021.
https://doi.org/10.1007/978-3-030-93179-7_5

and Voting classifier are used in sentiment classification of Music Lyrics reviews [9]. Sentiment classification results of Random forest algorithm is better than other algorithm with accuracy of 89.1%. In the sentiment analysis of reviews on social networking like WhatsApp, Facebook, and Twitter [10]. A technique used that is machine learning algorithm-Random forest to sentiment classification of comments are positive or negative. A study on sentiment analysis of Online Food Reviews using Big Data Analytics [11]. The techniques of sentiment analysis using apache spark data processing system for big datasets of Amazon Fine Food reviews. The accuracy named as Linear SVC, Logistic Regression, and Naïve Bayes have more than 80%. Moreover, sentiment analysis on food reviews was performed using machine learning algorithms such as Random forest, Naïve Bayes, SVM, and Logistic regression to classify sentiments based on review text features for multiclass classification. The resulting accuracy of the corresponding classifiers are Random forest 48.80%, Naïve bayes 42.45%, SVM 51.80%, and Logistic regression 55.40% [12].

At present, opinion mining techniques on food reviews have not yet focused on the majority sentiment classification and the important features of the reviews such as product aspects e.g. "quality", "flavor", "size" of the product, and sentiment orientation of opinion to opinion target of more detail, more clearly. The studies on food reviews also did not take into the holder and the time offers an opinion of the product reviews. Although this is a very important factor to sentiment orientation for opinion.

In this paper, we propose a new approach to ensemble learning for mining opinions on food reviews. We performed opinion discovery tasks on food reviews to convert the reviews into important features which are then used for classification using an ensemble learning algorithm such as Random classification forest into sentiment orientation is positive, negative, or neutral.

The rest of this paper is organized as follows. Section 2 some concepts related to opinion. Section 3 performs opinion discovery tasks. Section 4 how to build an opinion ensemble learning from features. Section 5 is an opinion summary from the previous tasks. Section 6 presents the result of the experiment, and the section finally is the conclusion of the paper.

2   Opinion Modeling

2.1   Opinion

An opinion [2] is a quadruple.

$$(g, s, h, t)$$

where g is the sentiment target, s is the sentiment of the opinion about the target g, h is the opinion holder, and t is the time when the opinion is expressed.

2.2   Simplify Definition

An opinion is a quintuple [2]

$$(e, a, s, h, t)$$

where e is the target entity, a is the target aspect of entity e on which the opinion has been given, s is the sentiment of the opinion on aspect a of entity e, h is the opinion holder, and t is the opinion posting time; s can be positive, negative, or neutral, or a rating (e.g., 1–5 stars).

In the case opinion directed at a whole entity, the special aspect GENERAL is used to express that opinion.

2.3   Reason and Qualifier

Reason. [2] A reason is the cause or explanation of the opinion.
Qualifier. [2] A qualifier of an opinion limits or modifies the meaning of the opinion.

2.4   Entity

An entity [1] e is represented by itself as a whole and a finite set of aspects.

$$A = \{ a_1, a_2, ..., a_n \}$$

e can be expressed in text with any one of a finite set of its entity expressions $\{ ee_1, ee_2, ..., ee_s \}$. Each aspect $a \in A$ of entity e can be expressed with any one of a finite set of its aspect expressions $\{ ae_1, ae_{i2}, ..., ae_m \}$.

Aspect. The aspects $a \in A$ of an entity e are the components and attributes of e.

2.5   Document

An opinion document [1] D contains opinions on a set of entities $\{ e_1, e_2, ..., e_r \}$ and a subset of their aspects from a set of opinion holders h contains opinions on a set of entites $\{ h_1, h_2, ..., h_p \}$ at some particular time point t.

3   Opinion Discovery

Given an opinion documents D, mining opinions consists of the following eight main tasks [2]:

Task 1 (Entity Extraction and Resolution). Perform the task of extracting entities expressions in documents D and group entities synonyms into clusters (or categories). Each entity represents a clustering expression of the entity.

Task 2 (Aspect Extraction and Resolution). Perform the task of extracting aspects expressions in document D and group aspects synonyms into clusters (or categories). Each aspect represents a clustering expression of the aspect.

Task 3 (Opinion Holder Extraction and Resolution). Extract the expression of the holder of each opinion from the review or structured data and group them.

Task 4 (Time Extraction and Standardization). Extract the posting time of each opinion and time format.

Task 5 (Aspect Sentiment Classification or Regression). In the case of sentiment classification, determine the aspect (or entity) whose opinion is positive, negative, or neutral. In the case of regression, determine the numeric sentiment rating score of the aspect(or entity).

Task 6 (Opinion Quintuple Generation). This task is generate all opinion quintuples (e, a, s, h, t) expressed in D from previous tasks.

Task 7 (Opinion Reason Extraction and Resolution). Perform the task of extracting reason expressions for each opinion and group reason synonyms into clusters. Each reason represents a clustering expression of the reason for the opinion.

Task 8 (Opinion Qualifier Extraction and Resolution). Perform the task of extracting qualifier expressions for each opinion and group qualifier synonyms into clusters. Each qualifier represents a clustering expression of the qualifier for the opinion.

For example about a review such as:

(1) These Chips are quite tasty and the price is right. (2) Packaged very well, would buy again. (Posted by: Swannie, time: Oct-4-2011).

The task should six generate the following opinion quintuples:

(Chips, GENERAL, Positive, Swannie, Oct-4-2011).
(Chips, Price, Positive, Swannie, Oct-4-2011).
(Chips, Packaged, Positive, Swannie, Oct-4-2011).
The task seven and eight are find the reasons and qualifier for opinion:
(Chips, Price, Positive, Swannie, Oct-4-2011).
The reason for opinion: none.
The qualifier of opinion: none.

4   Opinion Ensemble Learning

Given a set of n individual classifiers $O = \{o_1, o_2, ..., o_n\}$, each o_i is an opinion quintuples (e, a, s, h, t) and K classes, each one labelled as c_k with $k \in [1, ...K]$. Given a classifier o_i, $i \in [1, ...n]$. The vector K-dimensional $v = (o_i^1, o_i^2, ..., o_i^k)$ is represented for the output.

In the case of class label where $o_i^k \in \{0, 1\}$ that obtain value 1 if the class is k and 0 otherwise.

In the case of class probability where $o_i^k \in [0, 1]$. An estimate of the posterior probability for classifier o_i is $P(c_k|v)$.

The model aggregates the classification by obtaining the value that occurs most often for each classification

$$H(v) = c_{\arg\max_j \sum_{i=1}^{n} h_i^j(v)}$$

where $H(v)$ is output of opinion ensemble learning Fig. 1.

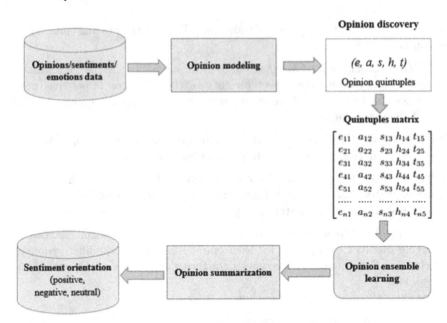

Fig. 1. Illustrate an opinion ensemble learning graph.

4.1 Quintuples Matrix

Given an opinion quintuple (e, a, s, h, t). A matrix $n \times 5$ of opinion quintuple is shown as follows:

$$\begin{bmatrix} e_{11} & a_{12} & s_{13} & h_{14} & t_{15} \\ e_{21} & a_{22} & s_{23} & h_{24} & t_{25} \\ e_{31} & a_{32} & s_{33} & h_{34} & t_{35} \\ e_{41} & a_{42} & s_{43} & h_{44} & t_{45} \\ e_{51} & a_{52} & s_{53} & h_{54} & t_{55} \\ \cdots & \cdots & \cdots & \cdots & \cdots \\ e_{n1} & a_{n2} & s_{n3} & h_{n4} & t_{n5} \end{bmatrix}$$

The quintuples matrix is called a feature matrix as an input to the process of building an opinion forest as the basis for mining and summarizing opinion.

4.2 Decision Tree

Given X_i is the sentiment orientation classification predictor variable [13] that takes values from a finite set of categories $O_i = \{e_{i,1}, a_{i,2}, s_{i,3}, h_{i,4}, t_{i,5}\}$. A split sends a subset of these categories $O \in O_i$ to the left and the remaining categories to the right in Figure.2.

The tree is split one node into two nodes by looking at the split on every predictor variable and choosing the best split to be the splitting criterion.

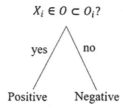

Fig. 2. The split on a opinion quintuples predictor variable X_i.

In the case of classification [14] where there are K classes denoted $1, ..., K$ a typical splitting criterion is the Shannon entropy, given by

$$H(S) = -\sum_{k \in K} p(k) \log(p(k)) \qquad (1)$$

where S is a collection of training opinion quintuples and denotes k is the class label. The collection of all classes is denoted K and $p(k)$ designates the empirical distribution extracted from the training opinion quintuples within collection S. A measure of node purity by measuring the information gain by the following formula:

$$I = H(S) - \sum_{i \in \{L, R\}} \frac{|S^i|}{|S|} H(S^i) \qquad (2)$$

The decision tree includes decision rules. The path from the root node to the leaf node is represented as root → leaf. As a rule, to the right of the denote "→" has a value and to the left of the denote "→" has at least one value. The denote "∩" is the intersection mark. For example in Fig. 3 has a decision rules:

$$(Entity = Lemon) \cap (Aspect = Price) \rightarrow Opinion = Negative$$

4.3 Random Forests

Given a random vector have p-dimensional, denoted by $X = (X_1, X_2, ...X_p)^T$ where $X_i \in \{e_{i,1}, a_{i,2}, s_{i,3}, h_{i,4}, t_{i,5}\}$ representing the predictor variables and a random variable Y representing the response variables. Assume an unknown joint distribution $P_{XY}(X, Y)$. The object is to find a prediction function $f(X)$ for predicting Y. The prediction function [15] is determined by a loss function $L(Y, f(X))$. This function is determined by minimizing the expected value of the loss:

$$E_{X,Y}(L(Y, f(X))) \qquad (3)$$

where the subscripts denote expectation with respect to the joint distribution of X and Y; $L(Y, f(X))$ is a measure of how close $f(X)$ is to Y. The loss function for a typically chosen classifier is as follows:

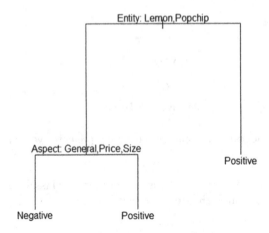

Fig. 3. An example of a decision tree for leaf node represents the sentiment.

$$L(Y, f(X)) = I(Y \neq f(X)) = \begin{cases} 0 & \text{if } L(Y, f(X)) \\ 1 & \text{otherwise.} \end{cases} \quad (4)$$

In the case of classification, if the collection of possible values of Y is denoted by Υ, $E_{X,Y}(L(Y, f(X)))$ is minimized for loss gives:

$$f(x) = \arg\max_{y \in \Upsilon} P(Y = y | X = x)) \quad (5)$$

Ensembles of base learners $h_1(x), h_2(x), ... h_j(x)$ and these base learners are combined to give the ensemble predictor $f(x)$. In classification, $f(x)$ is the most frequently predicted class:

$$f(x) = \arg\max_{y \in \Upsilon} \sum_{j=1}^{J} I(y = h_j(x)) \quad (6)$$

In Random forests [15,16] the jth base learner is a tree denoted $h_j(X, \Theta_j)$, where Θ_j is a collection of random variables and the Θ_j's are independent for $j = 1, ..., J$.

4.4   Evaluation

Performance is measured using the confusion matrix as follows in Table 1.

Table 1. Confusion matrix.

	Predicted positive	Predicted negative
Positive actual	TP	FP
Negative actual	FN	TN

Based on the confusion matrix, evaluate the sentiment classifier through the measures are Accuracy, Precision, Recall, and F-Measure [17].

Accuracy is the proportion of correct predictions for both true positives and true negatives among the total number opinion quintuples of cases examined.

$$Accuracy = \frac{TP + TN}{TP + TN + FP + FN} \quad (7)$$

Precision is calculated between the number of true positives and the total number of true positives and false positives. If the result of this calculation has a value of 1, it represents the fact that all positively classified samples were true.

$$Precision = \frac{TP}{TP + FP} \quad (8)$$

Recall is the percentage of correct items selected. If the recall result is 1 it means all positive examples were found.

$$Recall = \frac{TP}{TP + FN} \quad (9)$$

where TP is count of opinion quintuples correctly classified "Positive" sentiments, TN is count of opinion quintuples correctly classified "Negative" sentiments, FP is count of opinion quintuples incorrectly classified "Positive" sentiments, FN is count of opinion quintuples incorrectly classified "Negative" sentiments.

F-measure is used to evaluate the system's overall performance by harmoniously combining the two metrics of recall and precision. The following formula defines F1 score.

$$F1 = \frac{2 * (Recall * Precision)}{Recall + Precision} \quad (10)$$

5   Opinion Summarization

Opinion summarization [2] based on the product aspect is made as follows:
GENERAL.
Positive. Total number of opinion holders who gave a positive opinion about the entity e.
Negative. Total number of opinion holders who gave a negative opinion about the entity e.
Aspect a_1.
Positive. Total number of opinion holders who gave a positive opinion about the aspect a_1 of the entity e.
Negative. Total number of opinion holders who gave a negative opinion about the aspect a_1 of the entity e.
Aspect a_2.
Positive. Total number of opinion holders who gave a positive opinion about the aspect a_2 of the entity e.

Negative. Total number of opinion holders who gave a negative opinion about the aspect a_2 of the entity e.

Aspect a_n.

Positive. Total number of opinion holders who gave a positive opinion about the aspect a_n of the entity e.

Negative. Total number of opinion holders who gave a negative opinion about the aspect a_n of the entity e.

where $GENERAL$ deputizes the entity e itself and n is the total number of aspects of the entity e.

Given an opinion document D. The opinion summarization is modeled as follows in Fig. 4, where D is opinion document; e_i is entity; a_i is aspect of entity e_i ; o_i is opinion of aspect a_i of entity e_i.

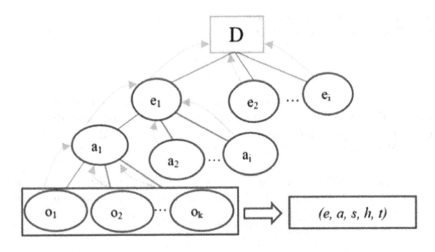

Fig. 4. Opinion hierarchy.

In the example of opinion summarization below. A structured opinion summary of aspects of a "Popchips" product such as "Flavor quality", "Weight", "Size" is described. There are 208 customer reviews expressing the positive opinion of "Flavor quality", and only 4 negative. Meanwhile, the "Weight" aspect of the Popchips product has 128 positive reviews and only two negative reviews. Similar in terms of "Size" there are 228 positive reviews and 2 negative reviews. There are more positive reviews than negative reviews. This is common on food reviews. The $<$ *individual review sentence* $>$ link points to specific sentences or the entire review that gives a positive or negative comment about the aspect.

For an example of opinion summarization the "Popchips" product:

Popchips.

Aspect: **Flavor quality.**

Positive: 208

$<$ *individual review sentence* $>$.

Negative: 4.
> < *individual review sentence* >.

Aspect:**Weight**.
> Positive: 128.
>> < *individual review sentence* >.
> Negative: 2.
>> < *individual review sentence* >.

Aspect: **Size**.
> Positive: 228.
>> < *individual review sentence* >.
> Negative: 6.
>> < *individual review sentence* >.

6 Experiment

6.1 Data Used

The Amazon Food Reviews dataset [18] containing 568454 reviews is used to experimented. Each review contains the product identity, user identity, user name, user ratio (who found the reviews is helpful), product rating, review time, review summary, review text. Dataset details are described in Table 2.

Table 2. Amazon food reviews dataset.

Data set statistics	Number of records
Reviews	568,454
Users	256,059
Products	74,258
Users with >50 reviews	260
Median no. of words per review	56

6.2 Preprocessing

The first one we prepossessing and remove Null values in the data set. The remaining data is 568411 reviews. The percentage according to the rating of the reviews in Table 3.

The second, processing balanced distribution of dataset, we split the dataset into positive and negative ratings with scores of 1 and 2 are negative, and scores of 3 and 4 are positive, and the score remove is 5. Figure 6. Illustration of the distribution of the number of positive and negative reviews. There are 59167 reviews that are negative, and 62856 reviews are positive out of a total of 568411 reviews.

Table 3. Detail of percentage according to the rating of the reviews.

Score	Total reviews	Percent
5	363111	63.88
4	80655	14.19
3	42638	7.5
2	29743	5.23
1	52264	9.19
Total	568411	100

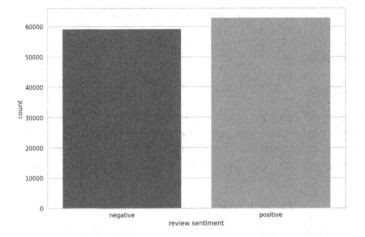

Fig. 5. The distribution of the number of positive and negative reviews.

The next is randomly take 5411 reviews from the dataset 568411 reviews to perform the opinion discovery tasks in Sect. 3. The results obtained from the set of opinion quintuples, and then randomly divide the set of opinion quintuplets into training opinion quintuplets and test opinion quintuplets in the ratio 8:2 respectively such in Table 4. It is used as input for opinion ensemble learning.

Table 4. Data train and test.

Opinion quintuples	Train	Test
8020	6416	1604

6.3   Tool Used

We proposed a technique implemented using R language [19]. Package "tree"[1], and "randomForest"[2] were implemented for this experiment. In addition, we also proposed to implement package "NLP"[3] to perform text preprocessing data.

6.4   Scenario 1. Food Product Aspects

From the data set of food reviews, we have constructed a Random classification forest (or random forest) for opinion mining on food product aspects that have been commented on by customers. We first split the data into n bootstrap samples, then classify the weak learners as decision trees. We aggregate the classification by acquiring the value that occurs most often for each classification. The results of Random classification forest based on aspects of food products in Fig. 6.

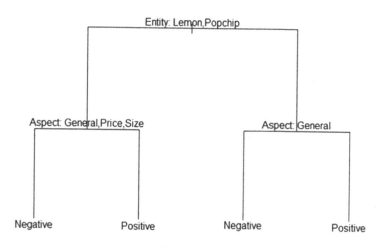

Fig. 6. Random classification forest summary for product aspect.

Table 5. Detail of the measure of Random forest algorithm for product aspect.

Algorithm	Accuracy	Precision	Recall	F1
Random classification forest	0.805	0.8	0.76	0.78

The results on the measure of Random classification forest on the food reviews dataset with the participation of food product aspect have an accuracy of 0.805%, Precision is 0.8%, Recall is 0.76%, F1 is 0.78% in Table 5.

---

[1] https://cran.r-project.org/web/packages/tree/.

[2] https://cran.r-project.org/web/packages/randomForest/.

[3] https://cran.r-project.org/web/packages/NLP/index.html.

6.5   Scenario 2. Food Product Holders or Time Reviewers

In this scenario, we are interested in the important attributes of holder or time reviewer to consider whether sentiment orientation is positive or negative. The person evaluates his or her opinion and time to determine the direction of the point of view more accurately. Frequent reviewers with reviews are often more accurate than those who do not. The time reviewer is also important.

A review today will have a different opinion than previous reviews. Therefore, the scenario we propose is to have more important attributes of opinion evaluator and opinion evaluation time. The results of Random classification forest for food product holders or time reviewers are summarized in Fig. 7 and Fig. 8.

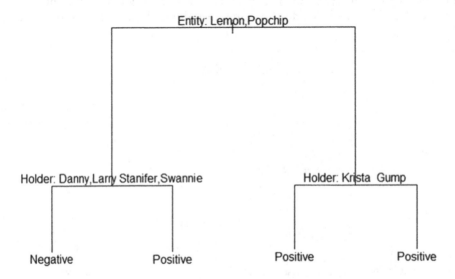

Fig. 7. Random classification forest summary for food product holders.

The results on the measure of Random classification forest on the food reviews dataset with the participation of food product holders or time reviewers have an accuracy of 0.82%, Precision is 0.85%, Recall is 0.67%, F1 is 0.75% in Table 6.

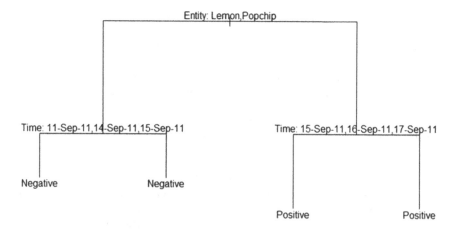

Fig. 8. Random classification forest summary for food product time reviewers.

Table 6. The measure of Random classification forest algorithm for food product holders or time reviewers.

Algorithm	Accuracy	Precision	Recall	F1
Random classification forest	0.82	0.85	0.67	0.75

7 Conclusion

We have approached ensemble learning modeling for opinion mining on food reviews. This model is based on a set of decision trees to classify affective orientation as positive, negative, or neutral. Each tree is built on a subset of random variables that are the attributes of the product name, product aspect, product reviewer, reviewer time, and the decision attribute which are sentiment attributes. Our experimental results on food reviews dataset based on two scenarios to explore important attributes in the construction of random forest classification have shown effectiveness.

References

1. Liu, B.: Sentiment analysis and opinion mining. Synth. Lect. Hum. Lang. Technol. **5**(1), 1–167 (2012). https://doi.org/10.2200/s00416ed1v01y201204hlt016
2. Liu, B.: Sentiment Analysis: Mining Sentiments, Opinions, and Emotions, 2nd edn. Cambridge University Press, Cambridge (2020)
3. Pang, B., Lee, L., Vaithyanathan, S.: Thumbs up? Sentiment classification using machine learning techniques. In: Proceedings of the 2002 Conference on Empirical Methods in Natural Language Processing, pp. 79–86 (2002)
4. Abinash Tripathy, A., KumarRath, S.: Classification of sentimental reviews using machine learning techniques. Procedia Comput. Sci. **57**, 821–829 (2015). 3rd International Conference on Recent Trends in Computing 2015 (ICRTC-2015)

5. Moret, B.M.E.: Decision trees and diagrams. ACM Comput. Surv. **14**(4), 593–623 (1982)
6. Zhou, Z.H.: Ensemble Methods: Foundations and Algorithms. Chapman & Hall/CRC, Boca Raton (2012)
7. Srivastava, R., Bhatia, M.: Ensemble methods for sentiment analysis of on-line micro-texts. In: 2016 International Conference on Recent Advances and Innovations in Engineering (ICRAIE), pp. 1–6 (2016)
8. Karthika, P., Murugeswari, R., Manoranjithem, R.: Sentiment analysis of social media network using random forest algorithm. In: 2019 IEEE International Conference on Intelligent Techniques in Control, Optimization and Signal Processing (INCOS), pp. 1–5 (2019)
9. Ahuja, M., Sangal, A.L.: Opinion mining and classification of music lyrics using supervised learning algorithms. In: 2018 First International Conference on Secure Cyber Computing and Communication (ICSCCC), pp. 223–227 (2018)
10. Arnav Munshi, M.A., Thirunavukkarasu, K.: Random Forest Application of Twitter Data Sentiment Analysis in Online Social Network Prediction. Wiley Online Library (2021)
11. Ahmed, H., Awan, M., Khan, N., Yasin, A., Shehzad, F.: Sentiment analysis of online food reviews using big data analytics. İlköğretim Online **20**, 827–836 (2021)
12. Islam, N., Akter, N., Sattar, A.: Sentiment analysis on food review using machine learning approach. In: 2021 International Conference on Artificial Intelligence and Smart Systems (ICAIS), pp. 157–164 (2021)
13. Amit, Y., Geman, D.: Shape quantization and recognition with randomized trees. Neural Comput. **9**, 1545–1588 (1997)
14. LI, B., Friedman, J., Olshen, R., Stone, C.: Classification and Regression Trees (CART), vol. 40 (1984)
15. Breiman, L.: Random forests. Mach. Learn. **45**, 5–32 (2001)
16. Cutler, A., Cutler, D., Stevens, J.: Random forests. Mach. Learn. **45**, 157–176 (2011)
17. Sammut, C., Webb, G.I.: Encyclopedia of Machine Learning, 1st edn. Springer, Heidelberg (2011). https://doi.org/10.1007/978-0-387-30164-8
18. McAuley, J.J., Leskovec, J.: From amateurs to connoisseurs: modeling the evolution of user expertise through online reviews. Association for Computing Machinery (2013). https://doi.org/10.1145/2488388.2488466
19. Team, R.C.: R: A language and environment for statistical computing. R Foundation for Statistical Computing, Vienna, Austria (2019)

Hidden Pattern: Toward Decision Support Fuzzy Systems

Nguyen Van Han[1]📙, Phan Cong Vinh[1(✉)]📙, Bui Minh Phung[2],
and Tran Ngoc Dan[3]

[1] Faculty of Information Technology, Nguyen Tat Thanh University,
300A Nguyen Tat Thanh Street, Ward 13, District 4, Ho Chi Minh City, Vietnam
{nvhan,pcvinh}@ntt.edu.vn
[2] Faculty of Information Technology, Van Lang University,
45 Nguyen Khac Nhu Street, Ward Co Giang District 1, Ho Chi Minh City, Vietnam
phung.bm@vlu.edu.vn
[3] University of Labor - Society (CSII), 1018 To Ky, Tan Chanh Hiep Ward,
District 12, Ho Chi Minh City, Vietnam
dantn@ldxh.edu.vn

Abstract. In this paper, we introduce a method for computing with words to find linguistic hidden pattern ($\mathbb{LHP}$) as well as decision support system ($\mathbb{DSS}$) based on hedge algebra ($\mathbb{HA}$) using linguistic cognitive map ($\mathbb{LCM}$). Our model consists of a set of vertices and edges whose values are linguistic variables that are constrained by a linguistic lattice. The algorithm for the system studied will convert to hidden pattern.

Keywords: Fuzzy logic · Hedge algebra · Hidden pattern · Decision support system

1 Introduction

Fuzzy set and fuzzy logic have been applied in neural network as well as machine learning. Fuzzy set or "computing with words" (CWW) was made in the 1990s by Zadeh's idea [1] which was just a tool to realize an intelligent system [2]. As Zadeh points out, human cognition is nothing more than CWW. In everyday life, we see the real world through words. Many intelligent systems that based on CWW such as fuzzy neural network, fuzzy machine learning, fuzzy classifying and so on have been studied [3–6].

The remainder of this paper is organized as follows: Sect. 2 reviews some of the main concepts of modeling with words based on $\mathbb{HA}$ [9,10,14]. Section 3 proposes a computational method for computing hidden pattern and decision support system. Section 4 outlines the conclusion and future work.

P. Cong Vinh and A. Rakib (Eds.): ICCASA 2021, LNICST 409, pp. 71–76, 2021.
https://doi.org/10.1007/978-3-030-93179-7_6

2 Preliminary: Linguistic Fuzzy Cognitive Map

Linguistic Fuzzy Cognitive Maps
Fuzzy cognitive map (FCM) [7] is a combination of fuzzy logic and neural network, in which learning process depends on numerical domain in unit interval $[0, 1]$. Paper stands on LCM which is extended from fuzzy cognitive map FCM [7]. The LCM model, based on linguistic variables, is constructed from linguistic hedge of HA in [11–13,15].

Definition 1. *A linguistic cognitive map (LCM) is a 4- Tuple:*

$$LCM = \{C, E, \mathbb{C}, f\} \tag{1}$$

In which:

1. $C = \{C_1, C_2, \ldots, C_n\}$ *is the set of N concepts forming the nodes of a graph.*
2. $E : (C_i, C_j) \longrightarrow e_{ij} \in \mathbb{L}$; $e_{ij} =$ *weight of edge directed from C_i to C_j. The connection matrix $E(N \times N) = \{e_{ij}\}_{N \times N} \in \mathbb{L}^{N \times N}$*
3. *The map: $\mathbb{C} : C_i \longrightarrow C_i^t \in \mathbb{L}, t \in N$*
4. $\mathbb{C}^0 = [C_1^0, C_2^0, \ldots, C_n^0] \in \mathbb{L}^N$ *is the initial vector, recurring transformation function f is defined as:*

$$C_j^{t+1} = f(\sum_{i=1}^{N} e_{ij}C_i^t) \in \mathbb{L} \tag{2}$$

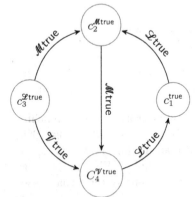

Example 1. Figure 1 shows a simple LCM. Let

$$HA = <\mathcal{X} = \text{truth}; c^+ = \text{true}; \mathcal{H} = \{\mathcal{L}, \mathcal{M}, \mathcal{V}\}> \tag{3}$$

be an HA with order as $\mathcal{L} < \mathcal{M} < \mathcal{V}$ ($\mathcal{L}$ for less, $\mathcal{M}$ for more and $\mathcal{V}$ for very are hedges). $C = \{c_1, c_2, c_3, c_4\}$ is the set of 4 concepts with corresponding values $\mathcal{C} = \{\text{true}, \mathcal{M}\text{true}, \mathcal{L}\text{true}, \mathcal{V}\text{true}\}$

Fig. 1. A simple LCM

3 Computational Fuzzy DSS

Hidden Patterns (HP) in combined and adaptive knowledge networks, that was introduced by B. Kosko in [8] have been applied in both fuzzy logic and neural network as a foundation for development in artificial intelligence. Applications from HP in pattern classification as well as pattern recognition were presented in [3,4] in which patterns were studied numerical values.

This paper researches on a special HP that called $\mathbb{LHP}$ which uses linguistic variable for three computational phases: modeling, reasoning and verifying. $\mathbb{DSS}$ is the fuzzy $\mathbb{KB}$ which inferred from $\mathbb{LHP}$, the special state in state space $\mathfrak{C} = \{\mathbb{C}^0, \mathbb{C}^1, \ldots \mathbb{C}^N\}$ when system reaches stable state.

3.1   Computational Algorithm to Compute $\mathbb{DSS}$

Pseudo Algorithm for Computing Processes

With notation $\mathfrak{s}_{ij} \in \mathbb{Adj} \subset \mathbb{L}^N$ being strength of directed edge (C_i, C_j) or $\mathfrak{s}_{ij} \leftarrow \|(C_i, C_j)\|$ and $\mathbb{Adj}$ is the $\mathbb{LCM}$'s connection matrix. Algorithm 1 points out that the processes of computation to find $\mathbb{DSS}$ and $\mathbb{LHP}$ are implemented in some simple steps:

- Initial system to first state $\mathbb{C}^0$ in state space $\mathfrak{C}$ that uses linguistic variables.
- Recursive computation until system reaches final state.
- The final stable state $C_j^{\mathcal{T}ime+1} = C_j^{\mathcal{T}ime}$ and $\mathbb{LHP} \leftarrow C_j^{\mathcal{T}ime}$
- Finally, linguistic $\mathbb{DSS}$ is derived from $\mathbb{LHP}$: $\mathbb{DSS} \leftarrow \mathbb{LHP}$

Algorithm 1. Computational $\mathbb{DSS}$ algorithm

           ▷ firstly, initialize first state vector $\mathbb{C}^0 \subset \mathfrak{C}$

1: **for** $\mathcal{T}ime \leftarrow 1$ to N **do**
2:      $\|C_i^0\| \leftarrow \mathscr{Linguistic\ value} \in \mathbb{L}$

           ▷ Iterate on $\mathfrak{C}$ space by discrete-time $\mathcal{T}ime$

3: **while** $\|C_j^{\mathcal{T}ime+1}\| \neq \|C_i^{\mathcal{T}ime}\|$ **do**
4:      $\|C_j^{\mathcal{T}ime+1}\| \leftarrow \bigvee_{i=0}^{N} \|C_i^{\mathcal{T}ime}\| \wedge \mathfrak{s}_{ij}$
5: $\mathbb{DSS} \leftarrow \mathbb{LHP} \leftarrow C_j^{\mathcal{T}ime}$

An Example for Implementing Processes

Figure 2 is an example to illustrate the processes of the Algorithm 1, in which:

- System $\mathfrak{C}$ consists five states: $\mathbb{LCM}^0, \mathbb{LCM}^1, \mathbb{LCM}^2, \mathbb{LCM}^3, \mathbb{LCM}^4$
- The initial state is $\mathbb{LCM}^0$ and final stable state is $\mathbb{LCM}^4$
- Edges's linguistic values present *What-If* relation between $\mathbb{LCM}$'s
- System reaches stable state $\mathbb{LCM}^4$ after looping four times.
- And, finally: $\mathbb{DSS} \leftarrow \mathbb{LHP} \leftarrow \mathbb{LCM}^4$

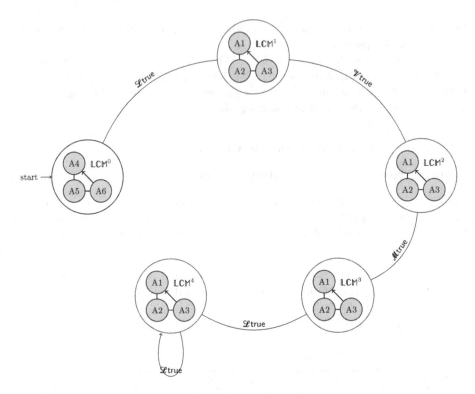

Fig. 2. State space $\mathfrak{C}$: $\mathbb{LCM}^0, \mathbb{LCM}^1, \mathbb{LCM}^2, \mathbb{LCM}^3, \mathbb{LCM}^4$ for finding $\mathbb{DSS}$

3.2 Applying Algorithm in Medical Decision Problem

Chondromalacia patellae problem (CPP) is modelled by $\mathbb{FCM}$ in [6]. By using domain transformation method as in [15], see Table 1. Concepts space is denoted in Table 2.

With converting as in Table 1, negative linguistic values are converted to linguistic variable in $\mathbb{L}$ of $\mathbb{HA}$ and CPP is remodeled in $\mathbb{LCM}$ form. This allows to use $\mathbb{HA}$ as tool for computing with word. From Table 2, CPP now is modeled by linguistic values in $\mathbb{LCM}$ form as Fig. 3.

Table 1. Domains conversion

Range [−1, 1]	Positive range [0, 1]	Domain of $\mathbb{L}$	Meaning
[−1, −0.7)	[0, 0.15)	$\mathcal{VV}$low	Very very low
[−0.7, −0.4)	[0.15, 0.3)	$\mathcal{LM}$low	Less more low
[−0.4, −0.1)	[0.3, 0.45)	$\mathcal{LL}$low	Less less low
[−0.1, 0.1)	[0.45, 0.55)	$\mathcal{W}$	Trung hòa
[0.1, 0.4)	[0.55, 0.7)	$\mathcal{VL}$high	Very less high
[0.4, 0.7)	[0.7, 0.85)	$\mathcal{LM}$high	Less more high
[0.7, 1]	[0.85, 1]	$\mathcal{VV}$high	More more high

Table 2. Table concept space.

Concepts $C \in \mathbb{C}$	Meaning	Linguistic domain
C_1	Extracellular matrix	Linguistic value in $\mathbb{L}$
C_2	Chondromalacia	Linguistic value in $\mathbb{L}$
C_3	Cells	Linguistic value in $\mathbb{L}$
C_4	Physical exercises	Linguistic value in $\mathbb{L}$
C_5	Weight	Linguistic value in $\mathbb{L}$

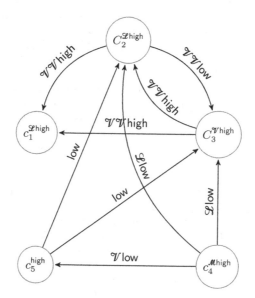

Fig. 3. $\mathbb{LCM}$ models Chondromalacia

Property 1. Following the Algorithm 1, CPP always converges to hidden pattern $\mathbb{LHP}$

Proof. This property is immediately inferred from convergence in Theorem 2 [15].

4   Conclusion and Future Work

We have introduced a method to computational linguistic fuzzy $\mathbb{DSS}$ as well as making $\mathbb{DSS}$ In the future, two studies will be:

- Considering a complete algorithm to construct $\mathbb{DSS}$.
- Verifying soundness and completeness for the algorithms.

References

1. Zadeh, L.A., Kacprzyk, J.: Computing with Word in Information Intelligent System 1. Springer, Heidelberg (1999). https://doi.org/10.1007/978-3-7908-1873-4
2. Zadeh, L.A.: Computing with Words - Principal Concepts and Ideas. Studies in Fuzziness and Soft Computing, Springer, Heidelberg (2012). https://doi.org/10.1007/978-3-642-27473-2
3. Glykas, M.: Fuzzy Cognitive Maps, Advances in Theory, Tools and Applications. Springer, Heidelberg (2010). https://doi.org/10.1007/978-3-642-03220-2
4. Papageorgiou, E.I.: Fuzzy Cognitive Maps for Applied Science and Engineering From Fundamentals to Extensions and Learning Algorithms. Springer, Heidelberg (2014). https://doi.org/10.1007/978-3-642-39739-4
5. Caarvalho, J.: On the semantics and the use of fuzzy cognitive maps and dynamic cognitive maps in social sciences. Fuzzy Sets Syst. **214**, 6–19 (2013)
6. Frias, M., Yaima, F., Nápoles, G., Vahoof, K., Bello, R.: Fuzzy cognitive maps reasoning with words based on triangular fuzzy numbers. In: ISFUROS (2017)
7. Kosko, B.: Fuzzy cognitive maps. Int. J. Man-Mach. Stud. **24**, 65–75 (1986)
8. Kosko, B.: Hidden patterns in combined and adaptive knowledge networks. Int. J. Approx. Reason. **2**(4), 377–393 (1988)
9. Ho, N.C., Wechler, W.: Hedge algebras: an algebraic approach to structure of sets of linguistic truth values. Fuzzy Sets Syst. **35**(3), 281–293 (1990)
10. Ho, N.C., Son, T.T., Khang, T.D., Viet, L.X.: Fuzziness measure, quantified semantic mapping and interpolative method of approximate reasoning in medical expert systems. J. Comput. Sci. Cybern. **18**(3), 237–252 (2002)
11. Han, N.V., Vinh, P.C.: Toward modeling and reasoning with words based on hedge algebra. EAI Endor. Trans. Context-aware Syst. Appl. **5**(15), e5 (2018)
12. Van Han, N., Vinh, P.C.: Modeling with words based on hedge algebra. In: Cong Vinh, P., Alagar, V. (eds.) ICCASA/ICTCC -2018. LNICST, vol. 266, pp. 211–217. Springer, Cham (2019). https://doi.org/10.1007/978-3-030-06152-4_18
13. Van Han, N., Hao, N.C., Vinh, P.C.: Toward aggregating fuzzy graphs a model theory approach. In: Vinh, P.C., Rakib, A. (eds.) ICCASA/ICTCC -2019. LNICST, vol. 298, pp. 215–222. Springer, Cham (2019). https://doi.org/10.1007/978-3-030-34365-1_17
14. Ho, N.C., Long, N.V.: Fuzziness measure on complete hedge algebras and quantifying semantics of terms in linear hedge algebras. Fuzzy Sets Syst. **158**(4), 452–471 (2007)
15. Han, N.V., Vinh, P.C.: Reasoning with words: a hedge algebra linguistic cognitive map approach. Concurr. Comput. Pract. Exp. **33**(2), e5711 (2020)

Applying Segmented Images by Louvain Method into Content-Based Image Retrieval

Tuyet-Ngan Vo[1], Mickael Coustaty[2], Jean-Loup Guillaume[2],
Thanh-Khoa Nguyen[1(✉)], and De Cao Tran[3]

[1] Ca Mau Community College, Ca Mau, Vietnam
{vtngan,khoant}@cmcc.edu.vn
[2] L3i Laboratory, University of La Rochelle, La Rochelle, France
{mickael.coustaty,jean-loup.guillaume}@univ-lr.fr
[3] Can Tho University, Can Tho, Vietnam
tcde@cit.ctu.edu.vn

Abstract. The amount of multimedia data has increased on personal computers and the Internet requires the essential to finding a particular image or a collection of images have enhanced of demands. It urges researchers to propose new sophisticated methods to retrieve the information one desires. In the case of, the legacy approach cannot grow up with the rapid rate of available data anymore. Therefore, content-based image retrieval (CBIR) has attracted many researchers to various fields. Content-based image retrieval models attempt to effort to automate data analysis and indexing. In this paper, we propose a content-based image retrieval system for real images. This method is using segmented images by the Louvain method [26] to create features in order to apply to the CBIR system based on the Bag-of-Visual-Words (BoVW) model. In order to evaluate the proposed method, we selected the Corel dataset which is composed of 10 classes [14] total of 1000 images in the dataset for the experiment. The experimental results are shown using qualitative and quantitative evaluations.

Keywords: Louvain method · Image content-based retrieval · Bag of Visual Words · Shape representation · Image content-based searching · Image retrieval

1 Introduction

Recently, image retrieval (IR) has become a fascinated topic in the computer vision field. Especially, with the dramatic increase in multimedia data, the classical information retrieval techniques do not meet the demand for users. Content-based image retrieval (CBIR) has become an alternate technique for information retrieval.

Image retrieval is the discipline of research that focused on finding, searching, and retrieving digital images that are stored. For traditional image retrieval systems, embedded metadata such as captioning, keywords, or descriptions of the

© ICST Institute for Computer Sciences, Social Informatics and Telecommunications Engineering 2021
Published by Springer Nature Switzerland AG 2021. All Rights Reserved
P. Cong Vinh and A. Rakib (Eds.): ICCASA 2021, LNICST 409, pp. 77–90, 2021.
https://doi.org/10.1007/978-3-030-93179-7_7

images is used in order to perform image retrieval through the annotation words. Recently, the amount of digital multimedia data has increased rapidly. Therefore, information retrieval techniques have shifted from text-based to become semantic-based or content-based.

Text-based image retrieval (TBIR) is a traditional image retrieval method that uses artificial notes to retrieve image results. This image retrieval method not only requires huge labors to manually annotate the images but also takes time-consuming and complicated work.

The content-based image retrieval (CBIR) means that the search analyzes the content of the image based on features related to color, texture, shape, or any other informative that can be derived from image properties themselves. This image retrieval method is desirable since most image search engines reply purely on metadata, and this process produces a lot of unrelated images.

The semantic-based image retrieval (SBIR) is an automatic method of extracting semantically meaningful representations from low-level features of images to support queries by high-level semantic concepts in the user's mind. Reducing the semantic gap between the low-level features and high-level semantic concept is a main concern of semantic image retrieval efforts.

In fact, the way of image features can distinguish and what people perceive from the image are not common. Semantic-based image retrieval is often built by using extracted low-level features methods to determine meaningful while interesting objects related to the similarity properties of the visual features. In a sense, the semantic process extracts object features to produce a semantic description of images in order to be stored in database. To grab Image, we can make a query based on high-level concepts. The query could work thanks to a set of textual words which translate into semantic features in the query. The local features is used for the semantic mapping process that will be performed through supervised or unsupervised learning tools to cooperate the low-level features. [35,36]. The Semantic content can be retrieved by textual annotation or by high sophisticated inference procedures based on visual content. Recently, deep learning has enabled detection objects belong to many classes exceed traditional computer vision techniques [28,29,34].

2   Bag of Visual Words Model

The Bag-of-Visual-Words (BoVW) model is used popularly in CBIR models. The image is represented as a collected local feature. The local features are used to represent groups of local descriptors. The local descriptors obtained by the extraction process for each image could be extremely huge. Moreover, it takes a lot of time to search in the image query to find the nearest neighbors for the local descriptors. For this reason, bag-of-visual-words were proposed as an approach to solving this problem by quantizing descriptors into "visual words" to reduce the number of descriptors significantly. Bag-of-Visual-Words can create the descriptor that becomes more robust to change. The BoVW model is more likely to the traditional description of texts in information retrieval, however, we consider for images retrieval in this case [6, 16]. Commonly, Bag-of-Visual-Words reply on the Keypoint detectors and Keypoint descriptors. Besides, there are many researches using methodology with graphs [5, 30, 31], Strokes [17, 27], Bag-of-ARSRG (attributed relational SIFT (scale-invariant feature transform) regions graph) words (BoAW) [18], and *etc.*

In our work, we attempt to use our image segmentation method in the BoVW model by extracting features in that one segmented image to build a CBIR. The CBIR based on the BoVW method comprises three main stages: (1) finding the region of interests (interesting part) of an image using Keypoint detectors in general; (2) computing a summary of the Region through the use of a feature vector (like the Keypoint descriptors); and (3) building the vocabulary to define a common subspace (the vocabulary) for all images. This subspace will then make images comparable. We present a detailed description in the following sequential subsections.

2.1 Keypoint Detection

Keypoint detection is a process that uses a feature detector to determine the unique content regions in an image, for instance, corners. Feature detection is used to search points of interest (keypoints) in the image. Keypoints are guaranteed to be no change. Therefore, the feature detector can detect them in case of the presence of scaling or rotation.

Detecting Keypoints is used for the first step in the bag-of-visual-words method. In order to extract features from interest points, these features are counted at predefined locations and scales [15]. The extraction of features is an individually separated process from represented features in the bag-of-visual-words method [20]. In the literature, there are several keypoint detectors that have been used in researches, such as Harris-Laplace, Difference of Gaussian (DoG), Hessian Laplace, and Maximally Stable Extremal Regions (MSER) [8, 21, 33].

2.2 Keypoint Descriptors

Based on the detected interest points, it is computed a local descriptor. Local descriptors are implemented by image processing of the transformation of a local pixel neighborhood into a compacity of the represented vector.

According to the content of Keypoints, local descriptors are described as multi-dimensional vectors. In fact, features descriptors could use to construct the representation of the neighbor pixels around a localized keypoint [20]. The literature witnesses many kinds of feature descriptors, such as the scale-invariant feature transform (SIFT) [16], speeded up robust features (SURF) [1], gradient location and orientation histogram (GLOH) [19] and histogram of oriented gradients (HOG) [7].

2.3 Building Vocabulary

The amount of extracted feature descriptors are enormous. In order to solve this issue, we need to build a visual vocabulary by using a clustering algorithm to cluster the feature descriptors, for instance, K-Means technique [10]. In the vocabulary, each cluster is represented by its respective cluster center and treated as a distinct visual word. The clustering algorithm determines the size of the vocabulary and is affected by the size and the types of the dataset [1].

The Bag-of-Visual-Words model could be formulated as below. First of all, the Bag-of-Visual-Words defines the training dataset as S including images represented by $S = s_1, s_2, \ldots, s_n$, where s is the extracted visual features. Secondly, Apply the clustering algorithm like K-Means, which is based on a fixed number to visual words W represented by $W = w_1, w_2, \ldots, w_v$, where v is the cluster number. After that, the data is summarized in a $V \times N$ occurrence table of counts $N_{ij} = n(w_i, s_j)$, where $n(w_i, s_j)$ denotes how often the word w_i is presented in an image s_j [16].

3 Our CBIR Architecture

3.1 Converting Images to Complex Networks

We can represent an image as an undirected graph $G = (V, E)$, where V is a set of vertices ($V = \{v_1, v_2, \ldots, v_n\}$) and E is a set of edges ($E = \{e_1, e_2, \ldots, e_k\}$). Every vertex $v_i \in V$ corresponds to a pixel and an edge $e_{ij} \in E$ links vertices v_i and v_j. In this research, we define paths towards other pixels that are considered when the distance of two pixels is lower or equal L neighbors pixels. We have also tested for many cases of distances of L for rows and columns directions (see Fig. 2). Empirically, the $L = 15$ value reaches a relatively good performance. The obtained networks by this pattern have few edges (2.L per pixel) which offer a good condition for the Louvain algorithm to compute communities faster. It is also useful to create edges for distant pixels which can offer good criteria for the Louvain method operates [26]. Moreover, edges are weighted. Its weight w_{ij} is a value of the similarities between v_i and v_j. They are defined as:

$$w_{ij} = \begin{cases} 1 & if \quad d_{ij}^c \leq t \text{ for all color channels } c \\ nil & otherwise \end{cases} \tag{1}$$

where t is a threshold, d_{ij}^c is a measure of the similarity of pixels i and j intensity for color channel c (among R, G and B). It is defined by $d_{ij}^c = \left| I_i^c - I_j^c \right|$ where I_i^c and I_j^c are the intensity value of pixel i and j.

3.2 Detection Communities in Complex Networks

Community detection is finding the best partition of a network. The community is dense of the internal link of nodes while sparse external connected with others. In the literature, it is witnessed the existence of several algorithms have been

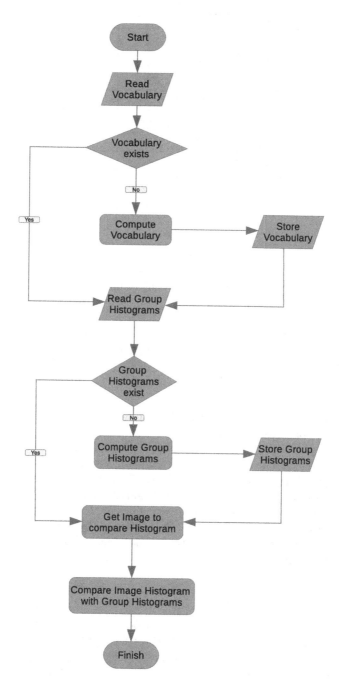

Fig. 1. A general Bag-of-Visual-Word model

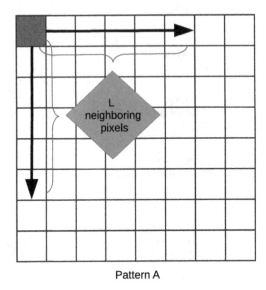

Pattern A

Fig. 2. A pattern for generating complex networks

proposed to find good partitions in a fast way [9]. It is known that the Newman-Girvan modularity [22] is used to measure the qualities of partition results. It is formulated as below:

$$Q = \sum_i (e_{ii} - a_i^2) \tag{2}$$

where e_{ii} denotes the fraction of edges in community i and $a_i (= \sum_j e_{ij})$ if the fraction of ends of edges in community i.

The stronger community structure of the network is indicated by the value of the modularity Q. The community detection algorithms are usually heuristics algorithms. In our research, the Louvain method [2] is used, a hierarchical greedy algorithm, to detect the communities on weighted graphs. The performance of the Louvain method is very quick and very efficient. Its properties are vital to working on graphs built from images. It is inferred that images involve many pixels so graphs are huge and to obtain well-segmented images, communities must be well-identified.

3.3   Extraction of Feature

To extract image features, we consider two aspects of image properties are color and texture. Building a 15-dimensional vector feature for each sub-segmented, namely HOGMeanSD feature [24–26], including 6 elements from Mean and Standard deviation and 9 elements come from HOG feature, detailed in [25].

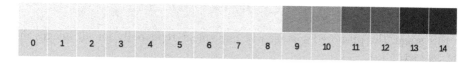

Fig. 3. A 15-dimensional vector for each segment

Based on the results we got in the image segmentation task, we build a content-based image retrieval using the bag-of-visual-words of local features on the segmented regions. The system computes the feature descriptor for those segmented regions. For the validation of our system, we decided to use the K-Means algorithm to cluster the visual vocabulary. As shown in Fig. 4, the proposed system includes two stages: a training stage and a testing stage.

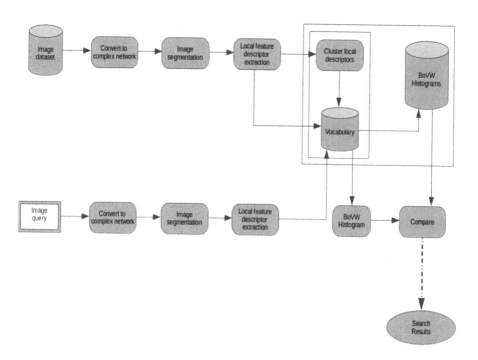

Fig. 4. An illustration of our proposed CBIR model

3.4 Training Stage

In this stage, the proposed system will implement repeatedly for all images in the dataset.

   1) For every image
   - Read each image individually
   - Convert image to a complex network (Graph)
   - Segment the image based on community detection: Louvain method and ARA algorithm [23]
   - Extract features based on the sub-segments and associates these characteristics to feature descriptors
   - Using a K-Means algorithm to cluster the set of local descriptors into K clusters.
   2) For every feature descriptor in the image:
   - Find the nearest visual word from the vocabulary for each feature vector using distance matching, for instance, BFMatcher, knnMatch, radiusMatch or FlannBasedMatcher
   - Compute the Bag-of-Words image descriptor as a normalized histogram of vocabulary words encountered in the image
   - Save the Bag-of-Words descriptors for all images in the dataset.

3.5 Testing Stage

In this step, the proposed system will perform for each input image query.

- The query image is converted to a graph
- Segment the image based on community detection: Louvain method and ARA algorithm [23]
- Extract features based on the sub-segments and associates these characteristics to feature descriptors
- Compute the Bag-of-Words vector with the method defined above
- Compare the histogram of query image with groups histograms and retrieve the best results.

4 Experimental Results

We have implemented our CBIR systems to search in the database for images of similarities to a query image. The database is the collected images from the Corel dataset.

4.1 Dataset

In order to evaluate the proposed method, we selected the Corel dataset which is included 10 classes [14]. Each class contains 100 images on the same topic namely, Africans, Beaches, Buildings, Buses, Dinosaurs, Elephants, Flowers, Horses, Mountains, and Food. There is a total of 1000 images in the dataset for the experiment. We tested 1 image to all images in the dataset, so total test cases are 1000 × 1000 images. The experimental results are shown using qualitative and quantitative evaluations.

4.2 Results

For qualitative evaluations, we present some retrieved images from image queries implemented by proposed CBIR system. Detail of this qualitative evaluations are displayed in Figs. 5, 6, 7 and 8.

For quantitative evaluations, we present a comparison of our method to others of which used the same Corel dataset. We implement of each image is taken as a query image if an obtained image is within the exactly right class of the query image, it is a recorded success; otherwise, it recorded fail. The precision is given as Eq. 3. In Table 1, we present Top 1 retrieved image including the query image itself on every test case. We also display the statistics of Top 5 and Top 10 first candidates images on retrieved images results. The results infer that our method will reduce the ability to retrieve the similarities images in a large dataset. Table 2 presents the top 5 results of our study compared with those of other studies in the literature. Our experimental results are pretty fine however we need to do more experiments and enhance this method in many ways but this is left for future investigations.

$$Precision = \frac{Number\ of\ Relevant\ Images}{Number\ of\ Relevant\ Images + Number\ of\ Irrelevant\ Images} \tag{3}$$

Table 1. Precision proportion of Top 1, Top 5 and Top 10 implemented on dataset including all classes.

Class name	Top 1	Top 5	Top 10
10 classes	92.25%	60.15 %	52.81%

Fig. 5. Qualitative evaluation of results using image query. *First line*: image query, *Second line*: images retrieved (Top 5), *Third line*: images retrieved (5 last images from Top 10)

Fig. 6. Qualitative evaluation of results using image query. *First line*: image query, *Second line*: images retrieved (Top 5), *Third line*: images retrieved (5 last images from Top 10)

Fig. 7. Qualitative evaluation of results using image query. *First line*: image query, *Second line*: images retrieved (Top 5), *Third line*: images retrieved (5 last images from Top 10)

Table 2. Comparison of the top 5 results of proposed method with others.

Methods	10 classes	9 classes	6 classes	5 classes
Huang's method [11]	74.41%	78.71%	86.51%	94.23%
Khosla's method [13]	55.00%	–	–	–
Srivastava's method [32]	67.16%	–	–	–
Choudhary's method [4]	–	75.00%	–	–
Choudhari's method [3]	–	–	–	72.00%
Janani's method [12]	–	–	79.00%	–
Our method	60.15%	63.84%	77.20%	80.49%

Fig. 8. Qualitative evaluation of results using image query. *First line*: image query, *Second line*: images retrieved (Top 5), *Third line*: images retrieved (5 last images from Top 10)

5 Conclusion

The proposed content-based image retrieval system has been implemented to look for the most similar images to a given image. Our CBIR system of which the Bag-of-Visual-Words model using the local feature that we have proposed and extracted offers an efficient image retrieval method. Although our CBIR system has not been implemented on a large dataset or in deep and extensive experimental results, it has demonstrated its usefulness. We strongly believe that our research will be more advanced and deeper in several future studies [24].

References

1. Bay, H., Tuytelaars, T., Van Gool, L.: SURF: speeded up robust features. In: Leonardis, A., Bischof, H., Pinz, A. (eds.) ECCV 2006. LNCS, vol. 3951, pp. 404–417. Springer, Heidelberg (2006). https://doi.org/10.1007/11744023_32
2. Blondel, V.D., Guillaume, J.L., Lambiotte, R., Lefebvre, E.: Fast unfolding of communities in large networks. J. Stat. Mech: Theor. Exp. **10**, 10008 (2008). https://doi.org/10.1088/1742-5468/2008/10/P10008
3. Chaudhari, R., Patil, A.M.: Content based image retrieval using color and shape features. Int. J. Adv. Res. Electr. Electron. Instrum. Eng. **1**, 386–392 (2012)
4. Choudhary, R., Raina, N., Chaudhary, N., Chauhan, R., Goudar, R.H.: An integrated approach to content based image retrieval. In: 2014 International Conference on Advances in Computing, Communications and Informatics (ICACCI), pp. 2404–2410 (2014). https://doi.org/10.1109/ICACCI.2014.6968394

5. Cortés, X., Conte, D., Cardot, H.: Bags of graphs for human action recognition. In: Bai, X., Hancock, E.R., Ho, T.K., Wilson, R.C., Biggio, B., Robles-Kelly, A. (eds.) S+SSPR 2018. LNCS, vol. 11004, pp. 429–438. Springer, Cham (2018). https://doi.org/10.1007/978-3-319-97785-0_41

6. Csurka, G., Dance, C.R., Fan, L., Willamowski, J., Bray, C.: Visual categorization with bags of keypoints. In: In Workshop on Statistical Learning in Computer Vision, ECCV, pp. 1–22 (2004)

7. Dalal, N., Triggs, B.: Histograms of oriented gradients for human detection. In: 2005 IEEE Computer Society Conference on Computer Vision and Pattern Recognition (CVPR 2005), vol. 1, pp. 886–893, June 2005. https://doi.org/10.1109/CVPR.2005.177

8. Dang, Q.B., Coustaty, M., Luqman, M.M., Ogier, J.M.: A comparison of local features for camera-based document image retrieval and spotting. IJDAR **22**(3), 247–263 (2019)

9. Fortunato, S.: Community detection in graphs. Phys. Rep. **486**(3–5), 75–174 (2010)

10. Hartigan, J.A., Wong, M.A.: Algorithm AS 136: A K-Means clustering algorithm. Appl. Stat. **28**(1), 100–108 (1979)

11. Huang, Y.F., Chen, B.R.: Content-based image retrieval system for real images. In: Benzmüller, C., Sutcliffe, G., Rojas, R. (eds.) GCAI 2016. 2nd Global Conference on Artificial Intelligence. EPiC Series in Computing, vol. 41, pp. 95–108. EasyChair (2016). https://doi.org/10.29007/w4sr, https://easychair.org/publications/paper/Z3T

12. Janani, R.G.: An improved CBIR method using color and texture properties with relevance feedback. Int. J. Innovative Res. Comput. Commun. Eng. **2**, 47–54 (2014)

13. Khosla, G., Rajpal, N., Singh, J.: Evaluation of Euclidean and Manhanttan metrics in content based image retrieval system. In: 2015 2nd International Conference on Computing for Sustainable Global Development (INDIACom), pp. 12–18, March 2015

14. Liu, G.H., Yang, J.Y., Li, Z.: Content-based image retrieval using computational visual attention model. Pattern Recogn. **48**(8), 2554–2566 (2015)

15. Liu, J.: Image retrieval based on bag-of-words model. CoRR abs/1304.5168 (2013). http://arxiv.org/abs/1304.5168

16. Lowe, D.G.: Distinctive image features from scale-invariant keypoints. Int. J. Comput. Vis. **60**(2), 91–110 (2004). https://doi.org/10.1023/B:VISI.0000029664.99615.94

17. Mandal, R., Roy, P.P., Pal, U., Blumenstein, M.: Bag-of-visual-words for signature-based multi-script document retrieval. Neural Comput. Appl. **31**(10), 6223–6247 (2018). https://doi.org/10.1007/s00521-018-3444-y

18. Manzo, M., Pellino, S.: Bag of ARSRG words (BoAw). Mach. Learn. Knowl. Extr. **1**, 871–882 (2019). https://doi.org/10.3390/make1030050

19. Mikolajczyk, K., Schmid, C.: A performance evaluation of local descriptors. IEEE Trans. Pattern Anal. Mach. Intell. **27**(10), 1615–1630 (2005). https://doi.org/10.1109/TPAMI.2005.188

20. Mikolajczyk, K., et al.: A comparison of affine region detectors. Int. J. Comput. Vis. **65**(1), 43–72 (2005). https://doi.org/10.1007/s11263-005-3848-x

21. Mukherjee, J., Mukhopadhyay, J., Mitra, P.: A survey on image retrieval performance of different bag of visual words indexing techniques. In: Proceedings of the 2014 IEEE Students' Technology Symposium, pp. 99–104 (2014). https://doi.org/10.1109/TechSym.2014.6807922

22. Newman, M.E., Girvan, M.: Finding and evaluating community structure in networks. Phys. Rev. E **69**(2), 026113 (2004)

23. Nguyen, T., Coustaty, M., Guillaume, J.: A new image segmentation approach based on the Louvain algorithm. In: 2018 International Conference on Content-Based Multimedia Indexing (CBMI), pp. 1–6 (2018). https://doi.org/10.1109/CBMI.2018.8516531
24. Nguyen, T.: Image segmentation and extraction based on pixel communities. Segmentation et extraction d'images basées sur des communautés de pixels. Ph.D. Thesis, University of La Rochelle, France (2019). https://tel.archives-ouvertes.fr/tel-03223157
25. Nguyen, T., Coustaty, M., Guillaume, J.: A combination of histogram of oriented gradients and color features to cooperate with Louvain method based image segmentation. In: Proceedings of the 14th International Joint Conference on Computer Vision, Imaging and Computer Graphics Theory and Applications - Volume 4: VISAPP, pp. 280–291. INSTICC, SciTePress (2019). https://doi.org/10.5220/0007389302800291
26. Nguyen, T.K., Guillaume, J.L., Coustaty, M.: An enhanced Louvain based image segmentation approach using color properties and histogram of oriented gradients. In: Cláudio, A.P., et al. (eds.) Computer Vision, Imaging and Computer Graphics Theory and Applications, pp. 543–565. Springer International Publishing, Cham (2020)
27. Okawa, M.: Offline signature verification based on bag-of-visualwords model using KAZE features and weighting schemes. In: 2016 IEEE Conference on Computer Vision and Pattern Recognition Workshops (CVPRW), pp. 252–258 (2016). https://doi.org/10.1109/CVPRW.2016.38
28. Potapov, A., Zhdanov, I., Scherbakov, O., Skorobogatko, N., Latapie, H., Fenoglio, E.: Semantic image retrieval by uniting deep neural networks and cognitive architectures. CoRR abs/1806.06946 (2018). http://arxiv.org/abs/1806.06946
29. Sadeghi-Tehran, P., Angelov, P., Virlet, N., Hawkesford, M.J.: Scalable database indexing and fast image retrieval based on deep learning and hierarchically nested structure applied to remote sensing and plant biology. J. Imaging **5**(3), 33 (2019). https://doi.org/10.3390/jimaging5030033
30. Silva, F., Goldenstein, S., Tabbone, S., Torres, R.: Image classification based on bag of visual graphs, pp. 4312–4316 (2013). https://doi.org/10.1109/ICIP.2013.6738888
31. Silva, F.B., de O. Werneck, R., Goldenstein, S., Tabbone, S., da S. Torres, R.: Graph-based bag-of-words for classification. Pattern Recogn. **74**, 266–285 (2018). https://doi.org/10.1016/j.patcog.2017.09.018
32. Srivastava, P., Prakash, O., Khare, A.: Content-based image retrieval using moments of wavelet transform. In: The 2014 International Conference on Control, Automation and Information Sciences (ICCAIS 2014), pp. 159–164 (2014). https://doi.org/10.1109/ICCAIS.2014.7020550
33. Tsai, C.F.: Bag-of-words representation in image annotation: a review. ISRN Artif. Intell. **2012** (2012). https://doi.org/10.5402/2012/376804
34. Wan, J., et al.: Deep learning for content-based image retrieval: a comprehensive study. In: Proceedings of the 22Nd ACM International Conference on Multimedia, pp. 157–166. MM 2014, ACM (2014). https://doi.org/10.1145/2647868.2654948
35. Wang, H., Mohamad, D., Ismail, N.A.: Image retrieval: techniques, challenge, and trend. World Acad. Sci. Eng. Technol. **60**, 716–718 (2009)
36. Wang, H.H., Mohamad, D., Ismail, N.A.: Approaches, challenges and future direction of image retrieval. CoRR abs/1006.4568 (2010). http://arxiv.org/abs/1006.4568

An Effective Approach for Mining k-item High Utility Itemsets from Incremental Databases

Nong Thi Hoa[1][✉] and Nguyen Van Tao[2]

[1] School of Computer Science, Duy Tan University, Da Nang, Vietnam
nongthihoa@duytan.edu.vn
[2] Thai Nguyen University of Information and Communication Technology,
Thai Nguyen, Vietnam
nvtao@ictu.edu.vn

Abstract. Mining High Utility Itemset (HUI) from incremental database discovers itemsets making much profit from newest transactions. Therefore, mining HUIs from incremental database are important for planing business. Previous studies on mining exact HUIs consume both time and memory for computing. Therefore, fast algorithms for mining compact HUIs have proposed. However, studies on mining compact HUIs still take a long time and consume much memory because of considering all itemsets of items in a transaction. Moreover, decision making in business is more effective based on HUIs containing several items. In this paper, we propose a novel effective algorithm for mining k-item HUIs that meets the need of decision makers and overcomes the limits of mining compact HUIs. We present a simple list to store k-itemsets appearing during scanning database. This list stores items and utility of each itemset. Our approach perform two ways of database segmentation to mine all k-itemsets. For each way of database segmentation, we run the following algorithm. It consists of two main steps including segmenting the current database to form sub-partitions and mining k-itemsets from each sub-partition. k-item HUIs are extracted from the list based on the utility. The proposed algorithm obtain advantages including without candidate generation and without re-scanning when changing the threshold of utility. Experiments are conducted on dense benchmark databases. Results of experiments show that our algorithm is better than state-of-the-art methods.

Keywords: High utility itemset · HUI · Mining high utility itemset · Mining HUI · k-item HUI · Data mining

1 Introduction

Mining HUIs discovers itemsets whose utility overcome a given threshold. Mining HUIs from incremental databases updates HUIs from newest transactions. Therefore, mining HUIs from incremental databases is essential for activities of

P. Cong Vinh and A. Rakib (Eds.): ICCASA 2021, LNICST 409, pp. 91–104, 2021.
https://doi.org/10.1007/978-3-030-93179-7_8

business. Algorithms of mining HUIs usually consume both time and memory for computing because of generating many itemsets and computing the utility of itemsets. Many studies on mining HUIs from incremental databases have developed to update newest HUIs. These studies can be divided into two categories including using a tree structure and pruning strategies [4–6], and using a list structure and properties of itemset utility [1–3]. In the first category, a tree structure is used to compress transactions in branchs of the tree. As a result, memory for computing decreases. Then, pruning strategies based on properties of HUIs helps remove parts of the tree that contain unpromising itemsets. Therefore, dropping time for tree traversal. In the second one, list structures store information of itemsets containing in transactions. Next, larger itemsets is generated from smaller itemsets based on the same of Transaction Identification. Utilities of larger itemsets is estimated from information of small itemsets generating them. Then, using properties of utility of itemsets to avoid generating larger unpromising itemsets. However, these studies still consume time and memory because there are too many itemsets in large databases.

Recently, several fast algorithms for discovering compact HUIs are proposed to decrease representation of HUIs. These studies use list structures to mined closed HUIs [7–10] and maximal HUIs [7,11]. Properties of compact HUIs is discovered to find compact HUIs more quickly. However, studies on compact HUIs still consume both time of CPU and memory because of processing all items in each transaction. Moreover, planing business is more effectively based on HUIs containing several items. HUIs with a few items is not enough information for making a good decision. HUIs including many items require decision makers to consider the importance of each item. Additionally, a transaction database contains a few of HUIs with many items. In this paper, we propose a novel effective algorithm for mining k-item HUIs that meets the need of business managers and decreases both time and memory by mining on each sub-partition of databases. We present a simple list structure to store the most important information of k-itemsets. This list is updated when scanning both the original database and incremental databases. Our algorithm consists of following steps. First, a vertical segmentation is performed for the current database to form sub-partitions. As a result, rows of each sub-partition contain k items. Next, k-itemsets in each sub-partition are mined and stored in a global list. Then, k-item HUIs is extracted from the global list based on utility of itemsets. Experiments are conducted on benchmark dense databases which have various different characteristics. We compare the performance of our algorithm to state-of-the-art algorithms. Experiment results show that the proposed algorithm significantly decreases both time and memory for computing, and it outperforms compared algorithms.

This paper is organized as follows. Next section is Related work. In Sect. 3, we present our approach for mining k-item HUIs. Section 4 shows experiment results and compares to other studies. Finally, conclusions are written in Sect. 5.

2   Related Works

Studies on mining HUIs focus on decreasing both time and memory for computing. We summarise studies on mining HUIs from incremental databases and mining compact HUIs to present our motivation. Mining HUIs from incremental databases finds HUIs from newest transactions. Therefore, knowledge from databases is frequently updated to support better for decision makers. Y. Unil and et al. [1] presented an algorithm for mining HUPs with one database scan. They used set of utility lists to store information of candidate patterns. After the global data structure was constructed from the original database or updated from increased data, it was restructured according to a *twu* ascending order. Then, a algorithm mined from a utility list for a promising candidate pattern composed of an item with the smallest *twu* value. The mining process was performed based on HUI-Miner [14]. L. Judae and et al. [4] proposed an approach of pre-large concept to mine high utility patterns (HUPs). This method required only one scan as well as mined in dynamic environments. They used a tree structure (PIHUPL-tree) includes a header and a tail list. After the construction, the header was reordered by a *twu* descending. Mining HUIS was performed by tree traversal. R. Heungmo and Y Unil [5] proposed an algorithm for mining HUPs from data streams. A tree structure (SHU-Tree) was used to maintain information of transactions and HUPs in the current window. The proposed tree was restructured by updating information with overestimation utilities. Y. Unil and H. Ryang [6] proposed algorithm HUPID-Growth (HUPs in Incremental Databases Growth) for mining HUPs. Authors used a HUPID-Tree, and a restructuring method with a TIList (Tail-node Information List). This algorithm composed of three steps. In the first step, a global HUPID-Tree, TIList were constructed with a single database scan. Then, the tree was restructured by arranging nodes in a *twu* descending order. If new transactions were added to the original database, this tree and the TIList were updated. In the second step, candidate patterns were generated from the tree by the HUPID-Growth. All HUPs were identified from the extracted candidates in the last step. L. Chun-Wei and et al. [12, 13] presented an algorithm based on pre-large concepts to update discovered HUIs. Itemsets were partitioned into three parts: large, pre-large, or small transaction-weighted utilization in the original database and in inserted transactions. Then, computing procedures were executed for each part. The downward closure property was applied to reduce the number of candidate itemsets. Only a small number of itemsets which were less than a threshold must be rescanned. L. Jerry Chun-Wei and et al. [3] proposed a memory-based incremental approach to build utility list structures for mining HUIs. An Estimated Utility Co-Occurrence Structure (EUCS) was applied to keep the relationship of 2-itemsets and eliminated the extension itemsets with lower utility. P. Fournier-Viger and et al. [2] proposed an algorithm EIHI (Efficient Incremental HUI miner) to maintain HUIs in dynamic databases. This algorithm scanned the database to calculate the *twu* of each item. A second database scan was performed to collect data for the EUCS structure. All itemsets were stored on a trie-like structure (HUI-trie). Each node represented an item and each itemset was represented by a path starting from the tree root and ending by an inner node or a leaf. Then, the depth-first search exploration of itemsets was performed to find HUIs.

Studies on mining compact HUIs have developed to find general HUIs such as closed HUIs, maximal HUIs. Therefore, both time of CPU and memory decrease

by avoiding to consider many itemsets. C. W. Wu and et al. [10] proposed the
EU-List (Extended Utility-List) to maintain and calculate the utility of itemsets
without scanning the original database. Next, a novel algorithm, CHUI-Miner
(Closed HUI Miner), adopted the divide-and-conquer methodology to mine the
complete set of close HUIs without producing candidates. For each closed itemset X, it used EU-List to calculate its utility to determine whether it was a
closed HUI. Property of remaining utility was used to prune the search space.
P. Fournier-Viger and et al. [9] presented EFIM-Closed (EFficient HUI Mining
- Closed) based on the strict constraint of each itemset in the search space.
EFIM-Closed proposed three strategies to discover close HUIs: closure jumping,
forward closure checking, and backward closure checking. EFIM-Closed reduced
the cost of database scans based on techniques: High-utility Database Projection
and High utility Transaction Merging. Moreover, it used two new upper-bounds
on the utility of itemsets named sub-tree utility and local utility to effectively
prune the search space, and applied an efficient Fast Utility Counting technique
to compute utility of itemsets. P. Fournier-Viger and et al. [7] proposed a novel
algorithm named CHUI-Mine (Compact HUI Miner) to discover closed HUIs
and maximal HUIs. It was a one-phase algorithm and discovered representations
without generating candidates. Authors used the proposed PUDC (Pivot Utility
Downward Closure) property to prune the search space. Moreover, an efficient
algorithm, RHUI (Recover all HUIs from maximal patterns), was presented to
recover all HUIs and their exact utilities from the set of maximal HUIs. This algorithm reused EU list in [10] during mining closed HUIs or maximal HUIs. N.T.T.
Loan and et al. [11] presented optimized versions of CHUI-Mine [7] to mine maximal HUIs using P-Set, Estimated Utility Co-occurrence Pruning (EUCP), and
First Utility Co-occurrence Structure (FUCS). P-set of itemset X listed identification of transactions containing X. EUCP pruned candidate itemsets based
on the EUCS structure. FUCS was a structure to store sum of twu of itemsets containing two items. D. Thu-Lan and et al. [8] presented IncCHUI that
mined close HUIs efficiently from incremental databases. They used an utility
list structure that built and updated from one database scan. Next, pruning
strategies was applied to increase the speed of construction of utility lists and
eliminate candidates. Then, they suggested an hash based method to update
or insert new closed sets. Previous studies show an idea approach for mining
HUIs need obtain advantages including without generating candidates, without
re-scanning database to compute the utility of itemsets. However, these studies
still consume both time of CPU and memory because of processing all items in
each transaction. Therefore, we propose a novel effective algorithm that obtains
these advantages and overcome this limit.

3   Our Approach

Problem Statement: Given a DB, number of items of each itemset k, and an
utility threshold $minutil$, mining k-item HUIs from DB discovers all k-itemsets
whose utilities are greater than or equal to $minutil$.

Our idea is discovered from knowledge of process of making business decision, observation of recommendation systems, and properties of transaction databases. We see that decision makers plan business more effectively based on HUIs containing several items. HUIs with a few items are not enough information for decisions. HUIs including many items require decision makers to consider the importance of each items. Moreover, big recommendation systems usually show from 3 to 6 related items of the current item. Additionally, most HUIs in transaction databases contain several items and a few HUIs have many items. Therefore, we propose a fast effective algorithm for mining k-item HUIs with small number of items. The proposed algorithm is called inc-k-HUI-Miner (mining k-item HUIs from Incremental databases). We introduce a simple list to store k-itemsets containing in databases. This list is called Items-Utility list (IU list). Our algorithm perform on two ways of database segmentation. For each way of database segmentation, we run the following process. This process includes two main steps. In the first step, a vertical segmentation of the current database is performed to form sub-partitions (SPs) based on the value of k. Each row in a SP contains k items. In the second one, k-itemsets is listed from each SP and stores them in a global IU list. k-item HUIs are extracted from the global IU list based on the utility of itemsets. We explain our approach more detail in next subsections.

3.1 Structure of the IU List

We propose the IU list to store k-itemsets containing in the current database. Structure of this list includes *items, utility* of itemsets. Table 1 shows an example of the IU list.

Table 1. An example of the IU list with $k = 5$

Items	Utility
1, 2, 3, 5, 6	10309
4, 5, 6, 7, 8	16778

The IU list is added or updated during browsing transactions. When a new itemset appears, a new row is added. If an itemset exists then updating its utility. Structure of the IU list is simple and only contains two important information for mining HUIs. Therefore, the IU list uses a small capacity of memory and helps to decrease time for searching existing itemsets.

3.2 The Proposed Algorithm for Mining k-item HUIs

Firstly, we perform a vertical segmentation for the current database. This database is divided into SPs whose rows contain k items. As a result, items in a transaction belong to many SPs. If number of items of the last SP is not enough k items then adding default items. For example, adding item 0 to last SP. Database segmentation is done two times to find all k-item HUIs. In the first way for segmenting database, items in $1..k$ belong to SP 1 and items in $k+1..2*k$ belong to SP 2, ... Do until the last item is assigned for the last SP. Similarly, the second way for segmenting database is done from $k/2$-th item if k is a even number. Meaning, $k/2..k/2 + k$ belong to SP 1 and $k/2 + k+1..k/2 + 2 * k$ belong to SP 2. Do until the last item is assigned for the last SP. If k is a odd number then SP 1 start $(k+1)/2$-th. As a result, k-itemsets appearing between two adjacent SPs of the first way are mined by running the process listing k-itemsets with the second way. Assuming that we choose $k = 5$ for an example database. The first way for segmenting database is done in Fig. 1 and Fig. 2 shows the second one of segmenting database.

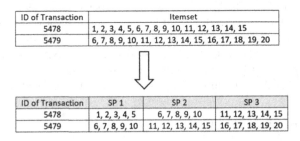

Fig. 1. The first way for segmenting database with $k = 5$.

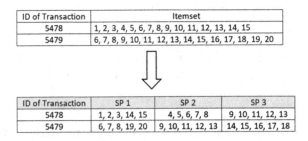

Fig. 2. The second way for segmenting database with $k = 5$.

Users assign a value of k to meet the need of making decisions. Choosing a proper value of k helps improve the performance of mining k-item HUIs. We observe big recommendation systems in retail. We see that an item usually links to from 3 to 6 related items. Therefore, we recommend values of k that is from 4 to 7.

The top-down strategy is applied for exploring transactions in each SP. Our algorithm finds an k-itemset that appears in adjacent transactions. Assuming, a

k-itemset X appears in transactions from m to n. We formulate the utility of X in transactions from m to n and store in an available. Then, searching X from the IU list. If X exists then updating the utility of X. Otherwise, adding a new row to the IU list to store X. Repeat this process until browsing the last row of each SP. We only use a single IU list. As a result, an IU list stores itemsets appearing in all SPs of two ways of database segmentation.

When adding new transactions from an incremental database, the IU list is continuously added or updated. Meaning, we combine data of both the original database and incremental databases in an IU list. Therefore, inc-k-HUI-Miner still finds new HUIs without re-scanning the original database. Moreover, the proposed algorithm still outputs HUIs without re-scanning databases when changing *minutil*. Similarly, mining HUIs from a incremental database is done.

Process of mining k-item HUIs by inc-k-HUI-Miner is presented by Algorithm 1 and Algorithm 2. Algorithm 1 shows the method that are applied for a way of database segmentation. Algorithm 2 shows the performance of the proposed algorithm for mining k-item HUIs. Steps of Algorithm 1 is described as follow

Algorithm 1: Mining k-itemsets

Input: Given a way of database segmentation
   DB - transaction database
   P - a sub-partition, **L** - the IU list, **T** - a transaction
   X - an itemset appearing in adjacent transactions
   Y - an itemset appearing in the current row
Output: k-itemsets in the global IU list **L**.
   1:   Divide DB into SPs .
   2:   for each **P** in DB do
   3:        Set X to the itemset in the first transaction of **P**
   4:        for each $T \in \mathbf{P}$ do
   5:            if $\mathbf{X} = \mathbf{Y}$ then
   6:               Update the utility of **X**
   7:            end if
   8:            if $\mathbf{X} \neq \mathbf{Y}$ then
   9:               if $X \notin \mathbf{L}$ then
   10:                  Add **X** to **L**
   11:               else
   12:                  Update the utility of X in **L**.
   13:               end if
   14:            end if
   15:            **X=Y**

Our approach for mining k-item HUIs is shown in Algorithm 2. Two ways for database segmentation is done to overlap SPs of the first way and SPs of the second one. A single IU list is used to store k-itemsets during mining k-item HUIs.

Algorithm 2: inc-k-HUI-Miner
Input: Given a database DB
    $minutil$ - the threshold of utility
    k - the number of items of an itemset
    M_1, M_2: Two ways of database segmentation
    L - the IU list that obtain from the Algorithm 1
    Z - an itemset appearing in **L**
Output: k-item HUIs.
    1:   Mining k-itemsets with parameter k according to M_1.
    2:   Mining k-itemsets with parameter k according to M_2.
    3:   for each **Z** $\in L$ do
    4:     if **Z**.Utility $\geq minutil$ then
    5:       **Z** is a k-item HUI.
    6:     end if

3.3   Discussion

Our approach obtains following advantages

- Mine on a small part of databases to drop memory
- Avoid generation of candidate itemsets.
- Mine new HUIs without re-scanning databases when changing $minutil$.
- Propose a simple list to decrease memory and time for searching elements.
- Apply for both a original database and incremental databases.
- Be simple to understand and perform.

As a result, inc-k-HUI-Miner significantly decreases both time and memory for computing. We conduct experiments to prove the effectiveness of our algorithm.

4   Experiments

Experiments are conducted to measure influence of the utility threshold, influence of the insertion ratio, and scalability. Our approach is compared to state-of-the-art algorithms including EFIM-Closed [9], and CHUI-Miner, CHUI-MinerMax [10].

4.1   Experiment Setup

We performed experiments on dense benchmark databases having various characteristics. Three databases were used in experiments including *mushroom* (8124 transactions, 119 items), *chess* (3196 transactions, 75 items), *connect* (67557 transactions, 129 items). They were downloaded from FIMI Repository [15]. Most databases do not provide item utility and item count for each transaction. Like some previous studies [8], external utilities for items are generated between 0.01 and 10 by using a log-normal distribution and internal utilities for items are randomly generated from 1 to 10.

All algorithms were implemented in Java, where EFIM-Closed, CHUI-Miner, CHUI-MinerMax were obtained from SPMF [16]. We conducted experiments on a computer equipped with a 64 bit, Core i3 (2 GHz x 2 GHz) Intel Processor, 4 GB of main memory, and running Windows 10. Each data is an average of 5 experiment results. Time of CPU consists of time for inputting transactions and mining HUIs.

4.2   Performance of inc-k-HUI-Miner

Experiments measure influence of the utility threshold, influence of the insertion ratio, and scalability on *chess* and *connect* to evaluate the effectiveness of the proposed algorithm.

Results on *chess*
Influence of the Utility Threshold: We select values of *minutil* including 50, 100, 150, 200, 250 because *chess* is a small database. Value of k is greater, time and memory for computing is smaller. We choose $k = 5$ to obtain higher values of time and memory for computing. Number of 5-itemsets of *chess* is 260. Table 2 presents the influence of the utility threshold on *chess*. Data from Table 2 show the maximal time is 1409 (ms) and memory consumption is stable at 1.66 (MB).

Table 2. Influence of changing *minutil* on *chess*

minutil	#5-item HUI	Time of CPU (ms)	Memory (MB)
250	216	1388.8	1.65912
200	225	1409.6	1.65915
150	235	1360.4	1.65912
100	244	1359.0	1.65915
50	258	1386.6	1.65912

Influence of the Insertion Ratio: We setup *minutil* = 100 and $k = 5$ to run experiments. Selected insertion ratios are 10%, 15 %, 20%, and 25%. Data of each insertion ratio are different because we select 10% first transactions, 15% next ones, 20% next ones, and 25% next ones. Meaning, 70% first transactions are used. For *chess*, 300 transactions are 10% of transactions. Table 3 presents the influence of the insertion ratio on *chess*. Data in Table 3 show time of CPU increases from 83.3 (ms) to 286.7 (ms) and memory for computing is stable at 1.66 (MB).

Scalability Tests: We setup *minutil* = 100 and $k = 5$ to run experiments. Number of transactions are 20%, 40%, 60%, and 80%. For *chess*, selected transactions are from 1 to 600, 1200, 1800, 2400. Table 4 presents the scalability tests on *chess*. Data in Table 4 show values of time are from 140.7 (ms) to 879.7 (ms) and memory is about 1.66 (MB).

We see that the ratio of k-item HUIs and k-itemsets is high in all sub-tests. Memory of our algorithm is stable because it store k-itemsets of the current

Table 3. Influence of the insertion ratio on *chess* with *minutil* = 100

Insertion ratio	#5-item HUI	#5-itemset	Time of CPU (ms)	Memory (MB)
10%	86	93	83.3	1.65912
15%	102	113	125.0	1.65912
20%	137	149	171.7	1.65912
25%	185	201	286.7	1.65912

Table 4. Scalability tests on *chess* with *minutil* = 100

Scalability	#5-item HUI	#5-itemset	Time of CPU (ms)	Memory (MB)
20%	109	118	140.7	1.65912
40%	147	158	328.0	1.65912
60%	181	194	536.7	1.65912
80%	217	227	879.7	1.65912

database. Moreover, time and memory for computing are smaller many times than performance of modern computers.

Results on *connect*

Influence of the Utility Threshold: We select values of *minutil* including 100, 150, 200, 250, 300 on *connect*. We choose $k = 5$ and small values of *minutil* to obtain higher values of time and memory for computing. The newest transactions of *connect* are used to run experiments which is in from 50000 to 67557. With $k = 5$, number of 5-itemsets of *connect* is 691. Table 5 presents the influence of the utility threshold on *connect*. Data from Table 5 show the maximal time is 25187 (ms) and memory is stable at 26.85 (MB).

Table 5. Influence of changing *minutil* on *connect*

minutil	#5-item HUI	Time of CPU (ms)	Memory (MB)
300	564	25067.8	26.84734
250	579	25187.2	26.84730
200	590	25217.6	26.84741
150	620	24900.4	26.84730
100	645	25136.4	26.84742

Influence of the Insertion Ratio: We setup *minutil* = 100 and $k = 5$ to run experiments. Selected insertion ratios are 10%, 15 %, 20%, and 25%. 2000 transactions are 10% of *connect* (running from the 50000-th transaction). Table 6 presents the influence of the insertion ratio on *connect*. Data in Table 6 show time of CPU increases from 1453 (ms) to 5566.3 (ms) and memory is about 26.85 (MB).

Table 6. Influence of the insertion ratio on *connect* with $minutil = 100$

Insertion ratio	#5-item HUI	#5-itemset	Time of CPU (ms)	Memory (MB)
10%	274	302	1453.0	26.84735
15%	294	336	2374.7	26.84735
20%	397	444	3967.7	26.84735
25%	481	536	5566.3	26.84742

Scalability Tests: We setup $minutil = 100$ and $k = 5$ to run experiments. Number of transactions are 20%, 40%, 60%, and 80%. For *connect*, they are 50001..54000, 50001..58000, 50001..62000, 50001..66000. Table 7 presents the scalability on *connect*. Data in Table 7 show values of time are from 3447.3 (ms) to 19604.3 (ms) and memory is about 26.85 (MB).

Table 7. Scalability tests on *connect* with $minutil = 100$

Scalability	#5-item HUI	#5-itemset	Time of CPU (ms)	Memory (MB)
20%	337	376	3447.3	26.84735
40%	415	462	7586.7	26.84742
60%	546	611	13814.0	26.84742
80%	609	663	19604.3	26.84742

We also see that the ratio of k-item HUIs and k-itemsets is high and memory of the proposed algorithm is stable. Running on a computer equipped with a 64 bit, Core i3 Intel Processor, 4 GB of main memory, the maximal time on *connect* is 19.6 (s) and 26.85 (MB) is the highest memory. Time and memory of our approach are much smaller than performance of modern computers. Therefore, our approach is suitable for online analytical processing.

4.3   Comparing to the State-of-the-Art Methods

Values of $minutil$ for inc-k-HUI-Miner are selected as follow. Values of $minutil$ are selected to reach a high ratio of number of k-item HUIs and number of k-itemsets. As a result, time and memory of the proposed algorithm reach to the largest values. Experiments are conducted on *mushroom* to limit the running time.

Influence of Changing the *minutil*
We setup $k = 5$. *minutil* for inc-k-HUI-Miner is lower 10 times than compared algorithms to obtain a large number of k-item HUIs. We select values of *minutil* for EFIM-Closed, CHUI-Miner, and CHUI-MinerMax including 1000, 2000, 3000, 4000, 5000. Values of *minutil* in our algorithm are 100, 200, 300, 400,

500 respectively. Figure 3 presents the time of CPU and memory consumption of *mushroom* when changing *minutil*. Figure 3(a) shows time of the proposed algorithm is lowest. EFIM-Closed and CHUI-Miner are the second and third one. The last one is CHUI-MinerMax. inc-*k*-HUI-Miner's time is lower 2.5 times than the second algorithm. Data from Fig. 3(b) show memory of our approach is smallest. It is lower 5 times than CHUI-Miner (the second one).

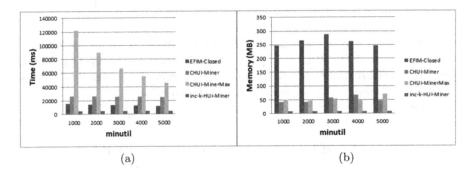

(a)   (b)

Fig. 3. Results of *mushroom* when changing *minutil*

Influence of the Insertion Ratio

We setup *minutil* = 100 and *k* = 5 to run experiments. Selected insertion ratios are 10%, 15 %, 20%, and 25%. Data of each insertion ratio are different. For *mushroom*, 800 transactions are 10% of transactions. Figure 4 presents CPU's time and memory consumption of algorithms to measure the influence of the insertion ratio. Data from Fig. 4(a) show that inc-*k*-HUI-Miner is the best algorithm. The last one is CHUI-MinerMax. Similarly, our approach is better than compared methods in Fig. 4(b). Memory of the proposed algorithm is sharply lower than CHUI-Miner (the second one).

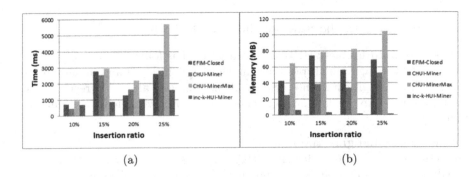

(a)   (b)

Fig. 4. Results of *mushroom* when changing the insertion ratio

Scalability Tests

We setup $minutil = 100$ and $k = 5$ to run experiments. Number of transactions are 20%, 40%, 60%, and 80%. For *mushroom*, data are selected from the first transaction to 1600, 3200, 4800, 6400 respectively. Figure 5 presents CPU's time and memory consumption of algorithms on scalability tests. Data from Fig. 5 show that both time and memory of the proposed algorithm is better than compared methods. Especially, both time and memory of our algorithm sharply drop.

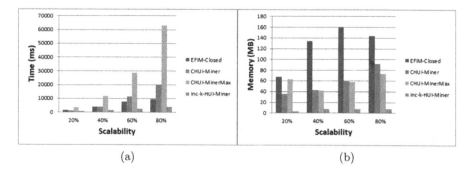

(a)   (b)

Fig. 5. Results of *mushroom* for scalability tests

Results of experiments show that our approach is better than state-of-the-art methods. Both time and memory of the proposed are smaller many times than both hardware and performance of modern computers. Therefore, our algorithm is effective for applications running online analytic processing.

5   Conclusions

In this paper, we propose a novel effective algorithm for mining k-item HUIs that meets the need of business activities and improves the performance of mining HUIs. We use a simple list structure to store important information of k-itemsets during browsing transactions. The proposed algorithm perform two times of a process which finds k-itemsets from databases. This process includes two main steps. First, the current database is vertically segmented into sub-partitions. Then, k-itemsets are mined from each sub-partition. All k-itemsets are stored in a global list. k-item HUIs is extracted from the global list based utility of each itemset. Our approach obtains advantages including without candidate generation, without re-scanning database when changing the utility threshold. Experiments are conducted on dense benchmark databases including *mushroom*, *chess*, and *connect*. Experiment results show that our algorithm is better than state-of-the-art methods. Both time and memory of the proposed sharply decrease.

We will investigate to optimize the time for computing and conduct experiments on larger databases in the future.

References

1. Unil, Y., Ryang, H., Gangin, L., Fujita, H.: An efficient algorithm for mining high utility patterns from incremental databases with one database scan. Knowl.-Based Syst. **124**, 188–206 (2017)
2. Fournier-Viger, P., Jerry, L.C., Gueniche, T., Barhate, P.: Efficient incremental high utility itemset mining. In: Proceedings of 5th ASE International Conference on Big Data (2015)
3. Lin, J.C.-W., Gan, W., Hong, T.-P., Pan, J.-S.: Incrementally updating high-utility itemsets with transaction insertion. In: Luo, X., Yu, J.X., Li, Z. (eds.) ADMA 2014. LNCS (LNAI), vol. 8933, pp. 44–56. Springer, Cham (2014). https://doi.org/10.1007/978-3-319-14717-8_4
4. Judae, L., Unil Yun, Y., Gangin, L., Eunchul, Y.: Efficient incremental high utility pattern mining based on pre-large concept. Eng. Appl. Artif. Intell. **72**, 111–123 (2018)
5. Heungmo, R., Unil, Y.: High utility pattern mining over data streams with sliding window technique. Expert Syst. Appl. **57**, 214–231 (2016)
6. Yun, U., Ryang, H.: Incremental high utility pattern mining with static and dynamic databases. Appl. Intell. **42**(2), 323–352 (2014). https://doi.org/10.1007/s10489-014-0601-6
7. Wu, C.-W., Fournier-Viger, P., Gu, J.-Y., Tseng, V.S.: Mining compact high utility itemsets without candidate generation. In: Fournier-Viger, P., Lin, J.C.-W., Nkambou, R., Vo, B., Tseng, V.S. (eds.) High-Utility Pattern Mining. SBD, vol. 51, pp. 279–302. Springer, Cham (2019). https://doi.org/10.1007/978-3-030-04921-8_11
8. Thu-Lan, D., Heri, R., Kjetil, N., Quang-Huy, D.: Towards efficiently mining closed high utility itemsets from incremental databases. Knowl.-Based Syst. **165**, 13–29 (2019)
9. Fournier-Viger, P., Zida, S., Lin, J.C.-W., Wu, C.-W., Tseng, V.S.: EFIM-closed: fast and memory efficient discovery of closed high-utility itemsets. In: MLDM 2016. LNCS (LNAI), vol. 9729, pp. 199–213. Springer, Cham (2016). https://doi.org/10.1007/978-3-319-41920-6_15
10. Wu, C.W., Fournier-Viger, P., Gu, J.Y., Tseng, V.S.: Mining closed+ high utility itemsets without candidate generation. In: Proceedings of Conference on Technologies and Applications of Artificial Intelligence (TAAI), pp. 187–194 (2015)
11. Loan, N.T.T., Bao, V.D., Trinh, N.D.D., Bay, V.: Mining maximal high utility itemsets on dynamic profit databases. Cybern. Syst. **51**(2), 140–160 (2020)
12. Chun-Wei, L., Wensheng, G., Tzung-Pei, H., Binbin, Z.: An incremental high-utility mining algorithm with transaction insertion. Sci. World J. (2015)
13. Lin, C.-W., Hong, T.-P., Lan, G.-C., Wong, J.-W., Lin, W.-Y.: Incrementally mining high utility patterns based on pre-large concept. Appl. Intell. **40**(2), 343–357 (2013). https://doi.org/10.1007/s10489-013-0467-z
14. Liu, J., Wang, K., Fung, B.: Direct discovery of high utility itemsets without candidate generation. In: International Conference on Data Mining, pp. 984–989 (2012)
15. Frequent Itemset Mining Dataset Repository (2012). http://fimi.ua.ac.be/
16. Fournier-Viger, P., Gomariz, A., Soltani, A., Lam, H., Gueniche, T.: Spmf: Open-source data mining platform (2014). http://www.philippe-fournier-viger.com/spmf

Recover Realistic Faces from Sketches

Khoa Tan Truong[1,2,3], Khai Dinh Lai[1,2,3], Sang Thanh Nguyen[3],
and Thai Hoang Le[1,2(✉)]

[1] Faculty of Information Technology, University of Science,
Ho Chi Minh City, Vietnam
lhthai@fit.hcmus.edu.vn
[2] Vietnam National University, Ho Chi Minh City, Vietnam
[3] Faculty of Information Technology, Saigon University,
Ho Chi Minh City, Vietnam
{truongtankhoa,laidinhkhai,thanhsang}@sgu.edu.vn

Abstract. Currently, Generative Adversarial Networks (GANs) is considered as the best method to solve the challenge of synthesizing realistic images from sketch images. However, the effectiveness of this method depends mainly on setting up a loss function to learn the mapping between sketches and realistic images. This leads to how to choose an optimal loss function to map them. In this paper, we investigate and propose a loss function that combines pixel-based error and context-based error on a proper ratio to obtain the best training result. The proposed loss function will be utilized to train the generator's U-Net architecture in greater detail. To convert a drawing to an actual image, the trained architecture will be applied. Based on two metrics that are the Structural Similarity Index (SSIM) and visual observations, the assessment results on the CUHK Face Sketch Database (CUFS), AR database (AR), and the CUHK ColorFERET Sketch Database (CUFSF) prove that the suggested method is feasible.

Keywords: Face sketch to image translation · Generative adversarial networks (GANs) · Sketch-based synthesis · Face image generation · Spatial attention · Dual generator · Conditional generative adversarial networks

1 Introduction

The application of image processing in criminal tracking is a much concerning issue today. By applying computer vision, we can 'translate' an input image to a corresponding output one. This is quite useful when we have an input sketch of a criminal through the description of the witness, then we can reproduce a photo-realistic face of that criminal [1]. Traditionally, current methods suggest different techniques to solve the problem, but the general idea is mostly the same: predict pixels from pixels [2–5]. Our goal in this paper is to improve a loss function in GANs [6] to enhance the realistic image prediction from the sketch.

© ICST Institute for Computer Sciences, Social Informatics and Telecommunications Engineering 2021
Published by Springer Nature Switzerland AG 2021. All Rights Reserved
P. Cong Vinh and A. Rakib (Eds.): ICCASA 2021, LNICST 409, pp. 105–118, 2021.
https://doi.org/10.1007/978-3-030-93179-7_9

GANs have been greatly evolved over the past decade and many of the techniques we explore in this article have been suggested previously [7–9]. Within a deep-learning network, like GANs, the most prevalent method is to minimize a loss function which is the main target for scoring the quality of results. Though the learning process is automatic, we must still spend much manual effort on designing effective loss functions. Besides, previous articles have focused on specific applications and it has remained limitations that we can optimize more for translating images. Our contribution is to customize the loss function based on pixels error and contextual error and suggest a new evaluation for synthesized images based on the Structural Similarity Index Measure (SSIM) [10] and visual inspection.

In this paper, the authors suggest a solution to enhance the quality of synthesizing photo/sketch in GANs based on improving the loss function by combining pixel and context loss evaluations. Concurrently, the paper also suggests a method to evaluate experimental results via SSIM and visual inspection.

2   Background and Related Work

2.1   Background

Currently, there are many research groups in the world that perform facial image synthesis from sketch images in many different ways. In general, these methods can be classified into two categories: data-oriented methods and model-oriented methods. Previously, to synthesize a photo/sketch, researchers used to rely on linear matching of similar training photo/sketch patches [11–16]. These approaches include two major sections: search similar photo/sketch and calculate linear association weight. Such processes consume a lot of computational time. For model-oriented method, it is essential to learn an offline mathematical function to map the image to sketch or inverse [17–20]. Usually, researchers must figure out handmade features, neighbor searching strategies, and learning techniques. However, these methods often cause image blur and large distortion in results.

Recently, the appearance of deep convolutional neural networks [13, 21, 22] has come up with great solutions for photo synthesis. Among them, Generative Adversarial Networks (GANs) [6] is the most effective method. The GAN training model behaves like a zero-sum game between the generator and the discriminator. The aim of discriminator is to decide whether a specific image is fake or real, while the generator tries to create realistic images much sophisticated that the discriminator cannot distinguish they are real or fake. Sketch-based image synthesis can be constructed as a conditional image translation problem based on an input sketch (see Fig. 1). There are several methods of using GAN to translate images from one domain to another [20, 23]. However, they are not specifically designed for photo synthesis from facial sketches.

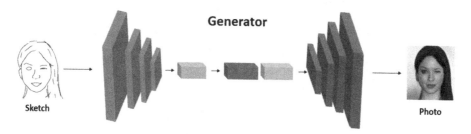

Fig. 1. General model for image translation in GANs

2.2 Related Work

Sketch to Photo Conversion in GANs. Through many studies, GANs have proven effective in creating realistic and natural images [24, 25]. Instead of directly optimizing and correcting per-pixel errors, which often affect the quality of the synthesized image, the GAN uses a discriminator to distinguish the unrealistic image among real images, then it forces the generator to produce sharper images. In the paper "pix2pix" of Isola et al. [26], he illustrated a direct approach to translate an image into another using conditional GANs. This motivates many researches on image-to-image translation methods afterward like CoupledGAN [27], CycleGAN [28], etc. These methods all yield good and promising results.

Sketch-Based Datasets. There are a few datasets on hand-drawing sketches, and they are usually small due to the effort needed to make hand-drawing images. One of the most common sketch datasets is CUHK Face Sketch dataset (CUFS) [29] which contains 188 faces from the Chinese University of Hong Kong's students. Besides, we have experienced on AR sketch dataset (AR) [30] and the CUHK ColorFERET Sketch Database (CUFSF) [31, 32].

3 Proposal Methods for Sketch-Image Translation

3.1 GANs Model Architecture

In this section, we present a Generative Adversarial Network framework that convert input sketches to images in Fig. 2. Our GANs model uses a U-Net [33] based generator with seven convolutional layers and a discriminator with four convolution layers. Here, the special improved point is the loss function which combines two evaluation methods: pixel loss (Sect. 3.2) and context loss (Sect. 3.3).

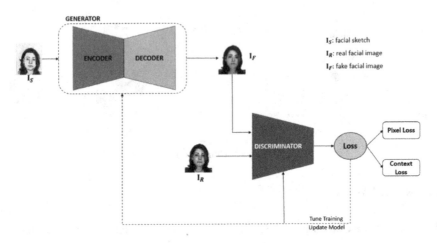

Fig. 2. Training model using GANs in proposed method

Figure 3 shows the model of the generator network based on the U-Net symmetric architecture, with n encoding units and n decoding units. The model uses a 4 × 4 convolutional filter with stride 2 and a Leaky-ReLU [34] activation function with a slope of 0.2 for downsampling. The number of channels will be doubled with each successive layer during this process. For upsampling, the preceding step's output will be doubled in size. Next, the model also uses a 4 × 4 filter with stride 1 and the ReLU [34] activation function to produce the convolution. Following batch normalization and the ReLU activation function, the output will be normalized and concatenated with the activation map of the mirrored layer in the contracting path. The network's last layer is a 1 × 1 convolution, which is the same as a cross-channel parametric pooling layer. For the last layer, we use the "*tanh*" function [35].

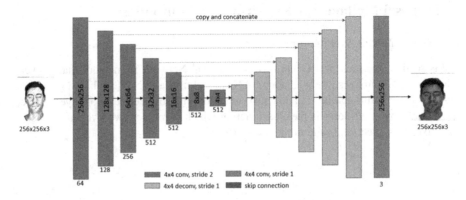

Fig. 3. The "U-Net" Generator network's architecture

Furthermore, we utilize the PatchGAN architecture [36] for the discriminator: 4×4 convolutional layers with stride 2 and the number of channels doubled after each downsampling. As illustrated in Fig. 4, all convolutional layers are followed by batch normalization and a Leaky-ReLU activation function with a slope of 0.2. For the last layer, we do a convolution operator with a filter size $4 \times 4 \times 1$ and stride 1.

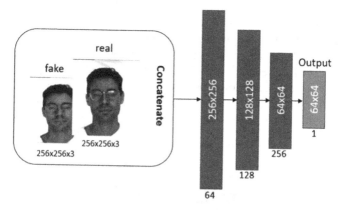

Fig. 4. Architecture of the Discriminator network

3.2 Pixel Loss

To evaluate the pixel difference between a true image and a predicted image in our model, we suggest to use the Mean Absolute Error (MAE) [37] to perform. The formula of this regression loss function is as (1).

$$\text{Pixel loss} = \frac{\sum_{i=1}^{n} |y_i - x_i|}{n} \tag{1}$$

Where:

y_i is ground truth image which is used for training.

x_i is faked image generated by the generator.

3.3 Context Loss

The main idea behind this function is that it assumes the image as a collection of features, and then determines the similarity between the images by measuring the similarity between the features. This loss function allows the local deformation of the image to a certain extent, therefore the requirement for the data to be aligned at the pixel level is moderate. In addition, this function also aims to constrains the local features, which enables it to operate on the region with similar semantics. Specifically, it first finds similar features in these regions with similar semantic meanings and forms a match between these features.

The loss function is operated based on following coding steps: 1) convert two images (real and fake image) to grayscale; 2) normalize them to range [0, 1]; 3) divide non-zero pixel each other in two pixel-matrix; 4) reduce the same pixels (e.g., pixels in boundary) because their ratios are similar (Fig. 5). Mathematically, the context similarity between the uncorrupted portions, e.g., portions in ground truth and translated image, are measured by a contextual loss [38], which is defined in formula (2).

$$\mathcal{L}_{\text{contextual}}(z) = D_{\text{KL}}(M \odot y, M \odot G(z)) \tag{2}$$

where M is the binary mask of corrupted ground truth image, z is the input sketch, and $\odot$ denotes the Hadamard production [39]. We use KL-divergence [40] to compare two images: a generator-generated image G(z) and a ground truth image y. All of these photos have been binary-normalized previously. If two images y and G(z) are exactly the same ideally, then $\mathcal{L}_{\text{contextual}}(z) = 0$, but if they aren't, we punish G(z) for not producing the same image as the ground truth y.

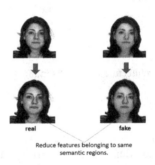

real   fake

Reduce features belonging to same
semantic regions.

Fig. 5. Illustration for context loss evaluation

3.4   Total Loss

To increase sharpness and ensure similar semantic structure of images synthesized by the generator, we suggest to unify both previous loss function based on formula (3).

$$\text{Total loss} = \lambda * \text{Pixel loss} + \beta * \text{Context loss} \tag{3}$$

where λ is the important coefficient of pixel loss, β is the important coefficient of context loss, and $\lambda + \beta = 1$.

4   Experiment

4.1   Experiment Settings

Dataset Splitting. We experiment the proposed approach on three sketch-photo databases: the CUHK Face Sketch Database (CUFS), the AR database (AR) and the

CUHK ColorFERET Sketch Database (CUFSF). In detail, CUHK includes 188 faces, AR includes 123 face in various ages and CUFSF includes 1194 persons from the FERET database [41]. For each person, there are a face photo with lighting variation and a sketch with shape exaggeration drawn by an artist when viewing this photo. To experiment, we divide to two rounds. For the first round, in Sect. 4.2 and 4.3, we train on a small dataset mixed from CUFS and AR based on the following rule: choose randomly 90 sketch-photo pairs which compose about 50% pairs from CUFS and 50% remains from AR. In order to testing, we apply the same strategy to form 5 subsets with size: 20, 40, 60, 80, 100. The aim of the first round that combine SSIM and visual observation to find the most proper total loss from which the generator in Fig. 2 is trained. To prepare for the second round suggested in Sect. 4.4, we build a larger dataset mixed from CUFSF and CUFS based on database splitting strategy in [42]. All these images are resized in dimension 256×256. The aim of second round is to compare the generator trained from the total loss in the first round to state-of-art methods.

Implementation Details. In all experiments, we use a batch size of 16 and epoch is 100. Besides, we use the Adam optimizer [43], and set the initial learning rate 0.0001 to both generator and discriminator.

Experiment Environment. All experiments are implemented on a server PC with the configuration: Intel(R) Xeon(R) CPU E5-2609 v4 @1.70 GHz, 16 cores, 32 GB RAM, GPU NVIDIA TITAN Xp 12 GB.

Evaluation Metrics. To evaluate our task of image synthesis, we propose to use the Structural Similarity Index Measure metric to build a simple recognition framework in Fig. 6. The principle of this framework is quite simple. It is used to check if our synthesized image from the sketch is realistic enough for the facial recognition system to successfully identify the subject. The synthesis process is judged successful if the translated image is acknowledged as being comparable to the true image of the subject itself. Extensively, for each sketch-photo pair in testing subset, we pass the sketch to the generator obtained in Fig. 2 to translate it to a 2D realistic photo. Then, we compare this realistic one to the photo in the same pair with the sketch translated and to other photos in other pairs using the SSIM metric. Since all images are labeled, so we can easily calculate the accuracy of the method. In addition, we also carry out a perceptual study to consider how realistic the generated images are and how faithful they are to the input sketches. Because the suggested method is tested mostly based on the structure, so we concern much on color and visual quality on synthesized images. To resolve the problem, we manually take randomly some output samples and observe them by eyes. Fortunately, all results are as expected though some cases are abnormal.

4.2 Experimental Results

In the first testing round, we test the effect of training model based on evaluating total loss function mentioned in Sect. 3.4. This function includes one parameter tuple (λ, β) that describes combination between pixel loss and context loss. First, we initialize (λ, β) to $(0, 1)$ and combine them 11 times with shift step 0.1 as following Table 1.

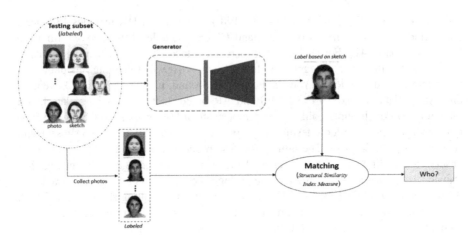

Fig. 6. Proposed recognition framework for testing

Table 1. Splitting training configurations

Total loss configuration	λ	β
0_10	0	1
1_9	0.1	0.9
2_8	0.2	0.8
3_7	0.3	0.7
4_6	0.4	0.6
5_5	0.5	0.5
6_4	0.6	0.4
7_3	0.7	0.3
8_2	0.8	0.2
9_1	0.9	0.1

For each setting, we retrain the generator model and use the testing framework in Fig. 6 to calculate accuracy scores through 5 data subsets (20, 40, 60, 80, 100).

According to Table 2, some configurations such as 0_10, 2_8, 3_7, 5_5, 7_3, 10_0 get high accuracy. Therefore, we use them to compare each other (see Fig. 7). The results in Table 2 demonstrate the effectiveness of this approach when we alter the combined ratio of pixel loss and context loss. Thereby, we learn that when the context loss is scaled down, the matching based on Structural Similarity Index Measure metric is affected negatively because the metric is mainly calculated based on context and semantics in images.

Table 2. Accuracy statistics of generator model in testing round 1

Configuration	Subset				
	20	40	60	80	100
0_10	95.00	87.50	88.33	78.75	82.00
1_9	95.00	85.00	86.67	78.75	78.00
2_8	95.00	85.00	86.67	78.75	80.00
3_7	95.00	85.00	85.00	78.75	81.00
4_6	95.00	85.00	85.00	78.75	80.00
5_5	95.00	85.00	85.00	77.50	80.00
6_4	95.00	87.50	86.67	78.75	80.00
7_3	95.00	85.00	86.67	78.75	80.00
8_2	95.00	82.50	85.00	77.50	79.00
9_1	90.00	87.50	88.33	78.75	78.00
10_0	90.00	85.00	86.67	78.75	83.00

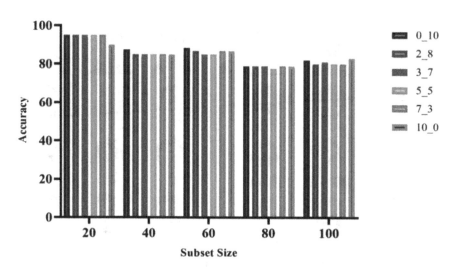

Fig. 7. Accuracy comparison for training configurations

4.3 Perceptual Validation

In addition, as shown in Fig. 7, we use the SSIM metric to evaluate the generator model, and we also use human visual perception to validate the results. Evaluation in Sect. 4.2 mainly depends on similar contextual structures, not rely on the color. We took effort to look over generated results when applying each different training configuration. After observing whole outputs over 11 settings of training configurations, we recognize that: when optimizing the generator based on high ratio of the pixel loss function, the color quality of outputs is realistic and more similar to the ground truth though they are a little blurry and unsharp; in contrast, if we decrease the ratio of the pixel loss and increase the ratio of the context loss, the output is sharp, but their color is distorted unrealistically (Fig. 8).

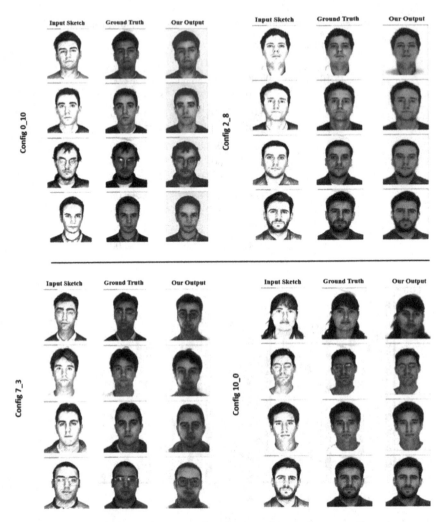

Fig. 8. Visual observation on results of proposed method over configurations

4.4   Comparison with Other Methods

Figure 7 shows an analysis of the experimental results in Sect. 4.2, which shows that the results are nearly identical. However, configurations 0_10, 2_8, 3_7 favor contextual factors that are not close to human vision (evaluating images through color); the configuration 5_5 balanced between pixel color and contextual elements also does not properly reflect human visual judgment of the image (in favor of pixel color values rather than contextual factors); configuration 10_0 does not care about the context factor, only cares about the color of the pixel, will result in a not sharp (blurred). More over, based on our visual observations in Sect. 4.3, we discover that configuration 7_3 is the best choice. Therefore, the generator trained from configuration 7_3 will be used for image synthesis. Table 3 compares the proposed method's accuracy to that of some other modern approaches mentioned in [42]. In summary, the proposed strategy is feasible and produces positive outcomes on both huge data sets, according to statistics.

Table 3. A comparison of our method to others in testing round 2

Methods	SSIM
Baseline	0.487
cGAN-Final generator 1	0.579
cGAN-Final generator 2	0.524
cGAN-Initial generator 1	0.581
cGAN-Initial generator 2	0.608
cGAN-Both generator 1	0.564
cGAN-Both generator 2	0.529
cGAN-Final gray	0.526
cGAN-Final w/ spectral norm & self-attn, gen. 1	0.571
cGAN-Final w/ spectral norm & self-attn, gen. 2	0.530
Ours	**0.690**

5 Conclusions

With the aim of building a model with the ability to translate sketch to realistic image, our paper suggests some modifications to traditional GANs and gain some results promising. Based on analysis in Sect. 4.4, we suggest training configure 7_3 where the total loss defined as the following: 0.7 * Pixel loss + 0.3 * Context loss is the best one used for training model. Summarily, in the paper, we have three main contributions that are: 1) Improve the GAN training model to select an effective generator by the combination of pixel loss and context loss according to the set of scale factors (λ, β), of which the prominent is the proposal to use the context loss function to help ensure the basic structure of the face; 2) Suggest a new recognition framework using SSIM metric to test accuracy of realistic images translated by generator; 3) Finally, evaluate results by visual perception.

Moreover, the quality of synthesized images are still a challenge, we will be going to research and innovate the structure of the GANs to win better. The paper contributes a new approach to customize the existing GANs model to solve an interesting problem: translate sketch to image. It's a meaningful way to help police to detect criminals quickly and effectively.

References

1. Wang, N., Tao, D., Gao, X., Li, X., Li, J.: A comprehensive survey to face hallucination. Int. J. Comput. Vis. **106**(1), 9–30 (2014)
2. Efros, A.A., Freeman, W.T.: Image quilting for texture synthesis and transfer. In: SIGGRAPH (2001)
3. Hertzmann, A., Jacobs, C.E., Oliver, N., Curless, B., Salesin, D.H.: Image analogies. In: SIGGRAPH (2001)
4. Chen, T., Cheng, M.-M., Tan, P., Shamir, A., Hu, S.-M.: Sketch2Photo: internet image montage. ACM Trans. Graph. (TOG) **28**(5), 124 (2009)
5. Long, J., Shelhamer, E., Darrell, T.: Fully convolutional networks for semantic segmentation. In: CVPR (2015)
6. Goodfellow, I.J., et al.: Generative adversarial nets. In: International Conference on Neural Information Processing Systems, pp. 2672–2680 (2014)
7. Wang, N., Zha, W., Li, J., Gao, X.: Back projection: an effective postprocessing method for GAN-based face sketch synthesis. Pattern Recogn. Lett. **107**, 59–65 (2018)
8. Di, X., Patel, V.M.: Face synthesis from visual attributes via sketch using conditional VAEs and GANs. arXiv:1801.00077 (2017)
9. Zhang, S., Ji, R., Hu, J., Gao, Y., Chia-Wen, L.: Robust face sketch synthesis via generative adversarial fusion of priors and parametric sigmoid. In: Proceedings of the Twenty-Seventh International Joint Conference on Artificial Intelligence (IJCAI-18), pp. 1163–1169 (2018)
10. Wang, Z., Bovik, A.C., Sheikh, H.R., Simoncelli, E.P.: Image quality assessment: from error visibility to structural similarity. IEEE Trans. Image Process. **13**(4), 600–612 (2004)
11. Song, Y., Zhang, J., Bao, L., Yang, Q.: Fast preprocessing for robust face sketch synthesis. In: Proceedings of International Joint Conference on Artificial Intelligence, pp. 4530–4536 (2017)
12. Song, Y., Bao, L., He, S., Yang, Q., Yang, M.-H.: Stylizing face images via multiple exemplars. Comput. Vis. Image Underst. **162**, 135–145 (2017)
13. Gao, X., Wang, N., Tao, D., Li, X.: Face sketchphoto synthesis and retrieval using sparse representation. IEEE Trans. Circuits Syst. Video Technol. **22**(8), 1213–1226 (2012)
14. Song, Y., Bao, L., Yang, Q., Yang, M.-H.: Real-time exemplar-based face sketch synthesis. In: Fleet, D., Pajdla, T., Schiele, B., Tuytelaars, T. (eds.) ECCV 2014. LNCS, vol. 8694, pp. 800–813. Springer, Cham (2014). https://doi.org/10.1007/978-3-319-10599-4_51
15. Pan, Q., Liang, Y., Zhang, L., Wang, S.: Semi-coupled dictionary learning with applications to image super-resolution and photo-sketch synthesis. In: Computer Vision and Pattern Recognition, pp. 2216–2223 (2012)
16. Wang, X., Tang, X.: Face photo-sketch synthesis and recognition. IEEE Trans. Pattern Anal. Mach. Intell. **31**(11), 1955–1967 (2009)
17. Peng, C., Gao, X., Wang, N., Tao, D., Li, X., Li, J.: Multiple representations-based face sketch-photo synthesis. IEEE Trans. Neural Netw. Learn. Syst. **27**(11), 2201–2215 (2016)
18. Zhang, S., Gao, X., Wang, N., Li, J., Zhang, M.: Face sketch synthesis via sparse representation-based greedy search. IEEE Trans. Image Process. **24**(8), 2466–2477 (2015)
19. Zhang, S., Gao, X., Wang, N., Li, J.: Robust face sketch style synthesis. IEEE Trans. Image Process. **25**(1), 220 (2016)
20. Wang, N., Tao, D., Gao, X., Li, X., Li, J.: Transductive face sketchphoto synthesis. IEEE Trans. Neural Netw. Learn. Syst. **24**(9), 1364–1376 (2013)
21. Peng, C., Wang, N., Li, J., Gao, X.: Face sketch synthesis in the wild via deep patch representation-based probabilistic graphical model. IEEE Trans. Inf. Forensics Secur. **15**, 172–183 (2020)

22. Wang, L., Sindagi, V., Patel, V.: High-quality facial photo-sketch synthesis using multi-adversarial networks. In: 2018 13th IEEE International Conference on Automatic Face & Gesture Recognition (FG 2018), pp. 83–90. IEEE (2018)
23. Zhang, L., Zhang, L., Mou, X., Zhang, D.: FSIM: a feature similarity index for image quality assessment. IEEE Trans. Image Process. **20**(8), 2378 (2011)
24. Gulrajani, I., Ahmed, F., Arjovsky, M., Dumoulin, V., Courville, A.C.: Improved training of Wasserstein GANs. In: Advances in Neural Information Processing Systems, pp. 5769–5779 (2017)
25. Nguyen, A., Clune, J., Bengio, Y., Dosovitskiy, A., Yosinski, J.: Plug & play generative networks: conditional iterative generation of images in latent space. In: The IEEE Conference on Computer Vision and Pattern Recognition (CVPR), July 2017
26. Isola, P., Zhu, J.-Y., Zhou, T., Efros, A.A.: Image-to-image translation with conditional adversarial networks. In: The IEEE Conference on Computer Vision and Pattern Recognition (CVPR), July 2017
27. Liu, M.-Y., Tuzel, O.: Coupled generative adversarial networks. In: Advances in Neural Information Processing Systems, pp. 469–477 (2016)
28. Zhu, J.-Y., Park, T., Isola, P., Efros, A.A.: Unpaired image-to-image translation using cycle-consistent adversarial networks. In: The IEEE International Conference on Computer Vision (ICCV), October 2017
29. Zhang, W., Wang, X., Tang, X.: Coupled information-theoretic encoding for face photo-sketch recognition. In: CVPR 2011, pp. 513–520 (2011). https://doi.org/10.1109/CVPR.2011.5995324
30. Martinez, A.M., Benavente, R.: The AR Face Database. CVC Technical Report #24, June 1998
31. Wang, X., Tang, X.: Face photo-sketch synthesis and recognition. IEEE Trans. Pattern Anal. Mach. Intell. (PAMI) **31**(11), 1955–1967 (2009)
32. Zhang, W., Wang, X., Tang, X.: Coupled information-theoretic encoding for face photo-sketch recognition. In: Proceedings of IEEE Conference on Computer Vision and Pattern Recognition (CVPR) (2011)
33. Long, J., Shelhamer, E., Darrell, T.: Fully convolutional networks for semantic segmentation. IEEE Trans. Pattern Anal. Mach. Intell. **39**(4), 640–651 (2014)
34. Maas, A.L., Hannun, A.Y., Ng, A.Y.: Rectifier nonlinearities improve neural network acoustic models. In: Proceedings of the ICML, vol. 30 (2013)
35. Abramowitz, M., Stegun, C.A. (eds.): Hyperbolic Functions. §4.5 in Handbook of Mathematical Functions with Formulas, Graphs, and Mathematical Tables, 9th printing, pp. 83–86. Dover, New York (1972)
36. Isola, P., Zhu, J.Y., Zhou, T., Efros, A.A.: Image-to-image translation with conditional adversarial networks. In: 2017 IEEE Conference on Computer Vision and Pattern Recognition (CVPR), pp. 5967–5976 (2016)
37. Willmott, C.J., Matsuura, K.: Advantages of the mean absolute error (MAE) over the root mean square error (RMSE) in assessing average model performance. Climate Res. **30**, 79–82 (2005)
38. Radford, A., Metz, L., Chintala, S.: Unsupervised representation learning with deep convolutional generative adversarial networks. CoRRabs/1511.06434 (2015)
39. Davis, C.: The norm of the Schur product operation. Numer. Math. **4**(1), 343–344 (1962). https://doi.org/10.1007/bf01386329
40. Joyce, J.M.: Kullback-Leibler divergence. In: Lovric, M. (ed.) International Encyclopedia of Statistical Science, pp. 720–722. Springer, Heidelberg (2011). https://doi.org/10.1007/978-3-642-04898-2_327

41. Phillips, P.J., Moon, H., Rizvi, S.A., Rauss, P.J.: The FERET evaluation methodology for face-recognition algorithms. In: NISTIR 6264, 7 January 1999 and IEEE Trans. Pattern Anal. Mach. Intell. **22**(10) (2000)
42. Gong, J., Mistele, M.: sketch2face: Conditional Generative Adversarial Networks for Transforming Face Sketches into Photorealistic Images (2018). https://web.stanford.edu/~jxgong/docs/sketch2face.pdf
43. Kingma, D., Ba, J.: Adam: a method for stochastic optimization. arXiv preprint arXiv:1412.6980 (2014)

Region of Interest Selection on Plant Disease

Hiep Xuan Huynh[1]([✉]), Cang Anh Phan[2], Loan Thanh Thi Truong[3], and Hai Thanh Nguyen[1]

[1] College of Information and Communication Technology,
Can Tho University, Can Tho 900000, Vietnam
{hxhiep,nthai.cit}@ctu.edu.vn
[2] Faculty of Information Technology, Vinh Long University
of Technology Education, Vinh Long, Vietnam
cangpa@vlute.edu.vn
[3] Cai Nhum Town High School, Vinh Long, Vietnam

Abstract. Plant diseases is one of the most influential factors in agricultural production. It can affect product quality, quantity, or yield of crops. Diagnosis of plant diseases is made mainly based on the experience of farmers. This work is done based on the naked eye. It is often misleading, time-consuming, and laborious. Machine learning methods based on leaf images have been proposed to improve disease identification. Transfer learning is accepted and proven to be effective. In this paper, we used the transfer learning method to classify apple tree diseases. The research data were used from the Fine-Grained Visual Categorization (FGVC7) Kaggle PLANT PATHOLOGY 2020, expert-annotated to create a pilot dataset for apple scab, cedar apple rust, multiple diseases, and healthy leaves. The InceptionV3 architecture trained with the Adam optimizer attained the highest validation accuracy.

Keywords: Plant disease · Classification · Transfer learning

1 Introduction

Plant diseases [1] is one of the most influential factors in agricultural production. It can affect product quality, quantity, or yield of crops. Diagnosis is the first step in the study of any disease. A rapid and accurate diagnosis of the disease is required before appropriate control measures can be instituted. Unfortunately, diagnosis of plant diseases is made mainly based on the experience of farmers. This is very time-consuming and error-prone. Moreover, due to significant crop numbers, complex disease symptoms, the farmer's experience should lead to undesirable treatment results [1]. Methods have been developed to assist

© ICST Institute for Computer Sciences, Social Informatics and Telecommunications Engineering 2021
Published by Springer Nature Switzerland AG 2021. All Rights Reserved
P. Cong Vinh and A. Rakib (Eds.): ICCASA 2021, LNICST 409, pp. 119–132, 2021.
https://doi.org/10.1007/978-3-030-93179-7_10

in plant disease identification. Laboratory-based techniques have been developed and established over the past decades. The techniques commonly used to detect plant diseases are ELISA and PCR [2]. The segmentation and classification of leaf images with a complicated background using deep learning are studied [3]. The results show that the average Misclassification Error (ME) of 80 test images using Mask R-CNN is 1.15%. The average accuracy value for the leaf classification of 150 test images using VGG16 is up to 91.5%. The authors [4] introduces Few-Shot Learning (FSL) algorithms for plant leaf classification using deep learning with small datasets. FSL using Siamese networks and Triplet loss was used and compared to classical fine-tuning transfer learning. The authors [5] propose an automatic detection framework based on deep learning is investigated for apple leaves disease classification. A combination of parameters like learning rate, batch size, and optimizer is analyzed, and the best combination of ResNetV2 with Adam optimizer provided the best classification accuracy of 94%.

In plants, some common diseases are brown and yellow spots, early and late scorch. Identifying the disease correctly when it first appeared is an essential step in effective disease management. Inaccurate diagnosis and treatment can lead to excessive or insufficient chemical use, increased production costs, or potentially significant disease outbreaks [6]. In recent years, digital imaging and machine learning have shown tremendous potential to speed up diagnosing plant diseases [7]. Therefore, the automatic classification of plant diseases is an important research topic in agriculture. It helps to detect diseases at a very early stage.

Transfer learning [8] is an advantageous approach to building strong taxonomy networks using little data. Using transfer learning to adapt existing neural models for visual categorization tasks in image classification and many other domains has been successful [9]. In this paper, we propose a new approach to classify plant disease based on transfer learning. To help enhance the classification results, we have looked at two segmentation approaches: Region Of Interest (ROI) selection uses Canny edge detection [10] and watershed transformation [11]. Then, we performed transfer learning with six pre-trained models VGG16 [12], VGG19 [12], DenseNet [13], InceptionV3 [14], Resnet50 [15] and InceptionResNetV2 [16] to develop a leaf classifier. With this method, plant diseases can be identified at an early stage, and pest and infection control tools can be used to solve pest problems while minimizing risks to plants, people, and the environment.

The remainder is organized as follows: Sect. 2 introduces the plant disease. Section 3 introduces the proposed method for plant disease classification with transfer learning. Section 4 we give a short description of the dataset, tools, and our experimental results. Finally, we conclude in Sect. 5 and point out future work directions.

2   Plant Disease

Plant disease [1] is the deterioration of a plant's normal state. Plant diseases develop due to a timely combination of the same factors that lead to plant diseases: susceptible host plants, toxic pathogens, and favorable environmental conditions over a relatively long time. Humans can inadvertently help initiate and develop disease through some of their activities by planting or pruning trees in wet weather.

Plant diseases are a normal part of nature and are one of many ecological factors that help keep hundreds of thousands of plant and animal species living in balance. Plant cells contain special signaling pathways that enhance their defenses against insects, animals and pathogens.

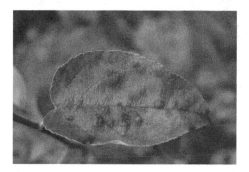

Fig. 1. Images from the Apple scab

Plant diseases affect the survival, adequate growth, and yield of all crops and thus affect one or more of the basic prerequisites for a healthy, safe human life. Plant diseases can be classified according to the nature of their main pathogens, infectious or non-infectious.

Fig. 2. Images from the Apple rust

Apple, Malus Domestica, is a species of deciduous tree in the family Rosaceae, grown for its fruit, called an apple. The apple is one of the most commonly grown fruits in the world, having around (pome) shape and a variety of colors from green to red. When grown from seed, apple trees can take six to ten years to mature and bear fruit. The leaves of the plant are oval, the length can be up to 13 cm, the width is 7 cm. Some diseases on Apple leaf: Apple Scab[1] Fig. 1, Apple Rust[2] Fig. 2, Powdery Mildew[3] (Fig. 3), Multiple diseases (Fig. 4) denotes the plant is suffering both scab and rust.

Fig. 3. Images from the Apple Powdery mildew.

Plant disease causes great economic loss to farmers worldwide. The Food and Agriculture Organization estimates that pests are responsible for about 25% of crop losses[4]. Diagnosis is the process of identifying the plant disease. A good diagnostician must go through many iterations of the scientific method,

Fig. 4. Images from the Apple multiple diseases.

---

[1] https://www.thespruce.com/apple-scab-disease-4845572.
[2] https://extension.psu.edu/apple-diseases-rust.
[3] https://extension.psu.edu/apple-disease-powdery-mildew.
[4] https://en.wikipedia.org/wiki/Plant_pathology/.

Table 1. Comparison of the characteristics of the Apple disease.

Disease	Symptoms	Pathogen	Survival and spread	Influence
Scab	- First appears as, small pale yellow dots on the upper surface - Finally, tiny, black, fruiting bodies become visible - Black, scabby lesions on leaves and fruit	fungus Venturia inaequalis	The pathogen survives through perithecia in the soil debris	- Severely affected leaves may turn yellow and drop - The apples are so blemished
Rust	- Appear on the upper surface of apple leaves shortly after bloom - Small, pale yellow spots appear on the upper surface of leaves - Lesions on apple leaves, telial gall on cedar	fungus Gymnosporangium juniperi-virginianae	If a spore lands on a susceptible apple leaf and environmental conditions are favorable infection can occur in as little as four hours	- Infected leaves may remain on the plant or may become yellow and fall - Rust in leaves and fruit will not cause other infections in the plant
Powdery Mildew	- 3–4 day delay in the opening of infected buds - Become covered with a white to light gray powder	fungus Podosphaera leucotricha	- The fungus overwinters in fallen, infected leaves. Spores blow up onto healthy leaves to infect them	- It's unlikely to kill your plant, but it will sap its strength - Reduce the size of the entire shoot

through observations of plants, the environment, and information from growers. Incorrectly identifying diseases and pathogens, disease control measures can be a waste of time and money and can lead to crop damage (Table 1).

3 Plant Disease Classification

Apple rust, apple scab, and multiple diseases may affect the plant. Manual inspection is sluggish, vulnerable to mistakes, and requires a lot of human resources and time. The method proposes for plant disease classification can achieve high classification accuracy, outperforming humans in many cases.

We have used the concept of transfer learning for classification. With transfer learning, instead of starting the learning process from scratch, you start from patterns that have been learned when solving a different problem. In image classification, transfer learning is often manifested through the use of pre-trained models. The model of plant disease classification using transfer learning consists of three phases: image pre-processing, image segmentation and classification. Figure 5 shows the proposed system that is used in this study.

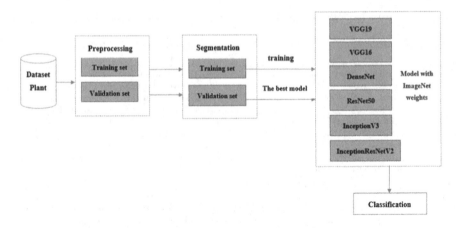

Fig. 5. The proposed method for plant classification with transfer learning technique.

3.1 Pre-processing

Image pre-processing [17] is an important step in image analysis. The aim of image preprocessing is to improve contrast. Pre-processing can include simple operations image cropping, contrast improvement, dimensionality reduction.

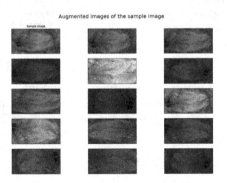

Fig. 6. Data augmentation.

The data contains many images of healthy and infected leaves. The input images in the dataset were downscaled to 512 × 512 pixels resolution from the original size. As a result, the Plant Pathology 2020 dataset has an unbalance distribution of samples among the four classes. Image data augmentation [18] is a technique used to extend the size of the training dataset. In our training set, we have applied many geometric transformations to the increased data. We use vertical flipping and horizontal flipping, random zoom, and images with different brightness levels. Image data augmentation techniques are shown in Fig. 6.

3.2   Segmentation

Segmentation [19] is a step in image analysis to subdivide an image into meaningful regions. Image segmentation can help enhance the classification results. We need to separate the diseased leaves from the unnecessary background. We have looked at two segmentation approaches.

We use the Region Of Interest (ROI) selection, to detect the edges of the leaf, ROI selection using watershed transformation. Method Canny edge detection will only work if the target leaf is in the middle area and the image is of good quality. Results are shown in Fig. 7.

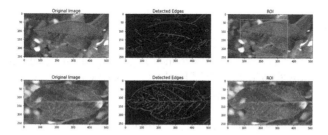

Fig. 7. ROI selection used Canny edge detection.

For many images, the ROI selection method does not give accurate results. Therefore, we try another method to determine the ROI according to the shape of the target leaf.

Watershed transformation is one of the most reliable methods for automatic and unsupervised segmentation is watershed transformation. This technique has been successfully applied to solve a variety of difficult image segmentation problems. The basic idea is to treat the image as a topographic surface, the gray level of the pixels in the image corresponds to the local minimum, elevation, and it influence areas defined as watersheds. The purpose of the watershed transformation is to define hydrolysis lines on the topographic surface. Results are shown in Fig. 8.

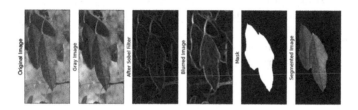

Fig. 8. ROI selection using watershed transformation.

3.3 Classification

Transfer learning is a type of machine learning technique, in which the pre-trained models [20] are reused to leverage their weights to introduce them as the initialization of a new CNN model for a different purpose. In this paper, we use pre-trained neural network models in the ImageNet dataset[5] such as VGG16, VGG19, DenseNet, InceptionV3, Resnet50 and InceptionResNetV2.

With transfer learning, we use pre-trained models and fine-tuning them to our problem. We use features learned from the ImageNet dataset by eliminating the final classifier and combining them with logistic regression as a general classifier predicting our class labels in the new domain.

4 Experiment

In this section, our method's performance is evaluated on a data of plant disease from the Kaggle PLANT PATHOLOGY 2020 competition. This work is presented as follows: Sect. 4.1 description the experimental data. Then, the tools used for the experiment are presented in Sect. 4.2. Finally, we formulate experimental scenarios and some remarks of results in Sects. 4.3 and 4.10, respectively.

4.1 Data Used

The data were used from the FGVC7 Kaggle PLANT PATHOLOGY 2020 competition [6]. The data included 1821 labeled training images of apple tree leaves. There are 516 images of healthy leaves, 91 images of multiple diseases, 622 images of apple rust, and 592 images apple scab.

The distribution of the four classes is shown in Fig. 9. The column chart shows that the "Multiple diseases" layer makes up only a tiny fraction of the entire dataset. On the other hand, the "Rust" layer took the most quantity, the "Scab" layer was the second most, and the "Healthy" layer took the third place.

4.2 Tools

Our method has been implemented with Python[6]. Keras and Tensorflow are used to deploy deep learning models. Numpy is used to perform basic math. For the prior training, we used ImageNet weights for each model. The input shape of the leaf image is $512 \times 512 \times 3$. We will use TPU for training for grading purposes. The escribed model was trained for 40 epochs, using Adam optimizer while minimizing categorical cross-entropy loss.

---

[5] https://papers.nips.cc/paper/2012/hash/c399862d3b9d6b76c8436e924a68c45b-Abstract.html.

[6] https://www.python.org/.

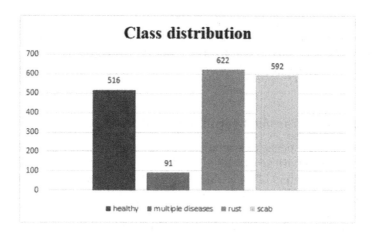

Fig. 9. Plant disease distribution.

4.3 Model Used

This study used 1,548 training images and 273 validation images of disease and healthy leaves (ratio into 85:15). Each of these experiments runs for 40 epochs. We performed transfer learning with six models InceptionV3, DenseNet, InceptionResNetV2, ResNet50, VGG16 and VGG19.

4.4 Scenario 1: Transfer Learning with InceptionV3

The pre-trained InceptionV3 model is used. InceptionV3 model used 21,776,548 trainable parameters and 34,432 non-trainable parameters of InceptionV3 layers. The initialized weights of ImageNet are used for each layer. The weight value was updated using Adam Optimizer for each epoch. The last layer is used for the classification with softmax as the activation function. The loss function used is categorical cross-entropy.

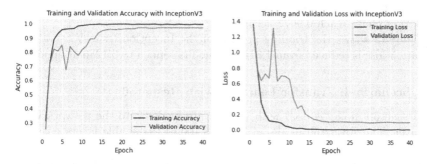

Fig. 10. Plant disease classification performance in training and validation phases of the InceptionV3 model.

Figure 10 shows the training process of the InceptionV3 model. The accuracy improves quickly from 0.2555 in epoch 1 to 0.9745 and stabilizes after 40 epochs. From the above plots, we can see that the losses decrease and accuracies increase. The training accuracy of 0.9976 was obtained, while a validation accuracy of 0.9745 was achieved.

4.5   Scenario 2: Transfer Learning with DenseNet

With the number of epochs as scenario 1, we experiment with DenseNet model. The DenseNet model utilized 18,100,612 trainable layers parameter and 229,056 non-trainable parameters of DenseNet layers. The training accuracy of 0.9965 was obtained, while a validation accuracy of 0.9635 was achieved.

The training process of the DenseNet model is shown in Fig. 11. The accuracy improves quickly from 0.0657 in epoch 1 to 0.9635 and stabilizes after 35 epochs.

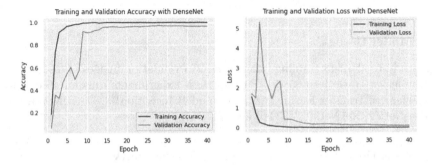

Fig. 11. Accuracy and Loss with DenseNet.

4.6   Scenario 3: Transfer Learning with InceptionResnetV2

The InceptionResnetV2 model is experimented. InceptionResnetV2 model used 54,282,340 trainable layers parameter and 60,544 non-trainable parameters of InceptionResnetV2 layers. With the number of epochs is 40, the results of the Validation phase reach 0.9672 accuracies.

Figure 12 shows the training process of the InceptionResnetV2 model. The validation loss is reduced from 1.3154 at the first epoch to 0.1286 at epoch is 40.

4.7   Scenario 4: Transfer Learning with Resnet50

The Resnet50 model is used with weights are loaded into the network with no top layer. The Resnet50 model utilized 18,100,612 trainable layers parameters and 229,056 non-trainable parameters of Resnet50 layers.

The Accuracy and Loss of the Resnet50 model is shown in Fig. 13. The training accuracy of 0.9967 was obtained, while a validation accuracy of 0.9635 was achieved. The validation loss is reduced from 1.6323 to 0.1922 at epoch 40.

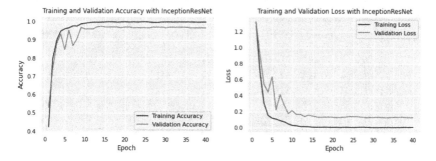

Fig. 12. Accuracy and Loss with InceptionResnet.

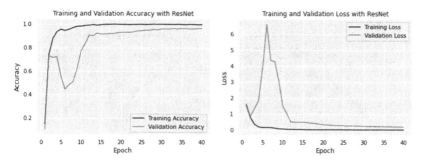

Fig. 13. Accuracy and Loss with Resnet50.

4.8   Scenario 5: Transfer Learning with VGG16

The VGG16 model operates with 14,716,740 trainable layers parameters. We used just 40 epochs, the VGG16 model achieving a probability validation accuracy of 0.9453. The training loss is 0.1466 and the validation loss is 0.2028. The Accuracy and Loss vs epoch with the VGG16 model is shown in Fig. 14.

4.9   Scenario 6: Transfer Learning with VGG19

The VGG19 model used 20,026,436 trainable layers parameters. Model is trained using the training dataset with a limit of 40 epochs. The results of the validation phase reach an accuracy of 0.9161.

The loss reduce quickly from 1.2072 in epoch 1 to 0.2028 after 40 epochs. The training process of the VGG19 model is shown in Fig. 15.

For input data disease, samples of apple rust, apple scab, multiple diseases and healthy leaves are considered. Segmented images can be classified into different plant diseases. Figure 16 shows the input and output image where the input image is an apple leaf with rust disease and output image shows the classification of disease "rust" using selection watershed transformation. The results of the experiment scenarios were provided in the following Table 2.

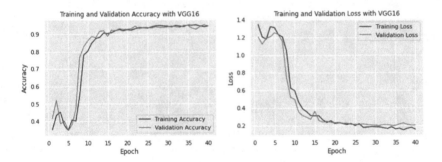

Fig. 14. Accuracy and Loss with VGG16.

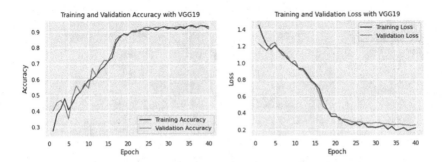

Fig. 15. Accuracy and Loss with VGG19.

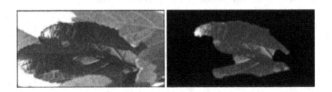

Fig. 16. Input image of "apple rust" and output disease is "apple rust".

Table 2. Experimental results.

Model	Trainable params	Accuracy train	Accuracy val
InceptionV3	21.776.548	0.9976	**0.9745**
DenseNet	18.100.612	0.9965	0.9635
InceptionResnetV2	54.282.340	0.9994	0.9672
Resnet50	23.527.556	0.9967	0.9635
VGG16	14.716.740	0.9485	0.9453
VGG19	20.026.436	0.9328	0.9161

4.10 Discussion

Six pre-trained models are performed with transfer learning technique and achieved an accuracy of over 90%, with InceptionV3 reaching the highest accuracy.

From Table 2, the accuracy of the InceptionV3 model is the highest at 0.9745. InceptionResnetV2 model obtained the second-highest validation accuracy probability of 0.9672. VGG19 ranks behind all five pre-trained models, achieving a probability validation accuracy of 0.9161.

Compare the performance of the proposed method with published results. The accuracy of our training model gives better results, as shown in Table 3.

Table 3. Comparison with published results.

Model	Accuracy
ResNetV2 [5]	0.947
Deep learning [3]	0.915
Proposed Model	**0.9745**

5 Conclusion

Plant disease causes significant damage to the agricultural industry. Plant disease identification and classification play an important role in disease detection, mitigation, and management. This study introduces an approach using transfer learning method for the classification of plant diseases. The proposed model is ensemble of six CNN architectures (VGG16 [12], VGG19 [12], DenseNet [13], InceptionV3 [14], Resnet50 [15] and InceptionResNetV2 [16]). The system was experimental on the Kaggle PLANT PATHOLOGY 2020 dataset and had an accuracy of 97.45%. Besides, The method can save compute time and resources and successfully learn a new task. In the future, more data at different stages of different diseases will be collected and classified.

References

1. Ferentinos, K.P.: Deep learning models for plant disease detection and diagnosis. Comput. Electron. Agric. **145**, 311–318 (2018). https://doi.org/10.1016/j.compag.2018.01.009
2. Sankaran, S., Mishra, A., Ehsani, R., Davis, C.: A review of advanced techniques for detecting plant diseases. Comput. Electron. Agric. **72**(1), 1–13 (2010). https://doi.org/10.1016/j.compag.2010.02.007
3. Yang, K., Zhong, W., Li, F.: Leaf segmentation and classification with a complicated background using deep learning. Agronomy **10**(11), 1721 (2020). https://doi.org/10.3390/agronomy10111721

4. Argueso, D., et al.: Few-Shot Learning approach for plant disease classification using images taken in the field. Comput. Electron. Agric. **175**, 105542 (2020). https://doi.org/10.1016/j.compag.2020.105542
5. Alsayed, A., Alsabei, A., Arif, M.: Classification of apple tree leaves diseases using deep learning methods. Int. J. Comput. Sci. Netw. Secur. (IJCSNS) **21**(7), 324–330 (2021). https://doi.org/10.22937/IJCSNS.2020.20.10.01
6. Thapa, R., Zhang, K., Snavely, N., Belongie, S., Khan, A.: The Plant Pathology Challenge 2020 data set to classify foliar disease of apples. Appl. Plant Sci. **8**(9) (2020). https://doi.org/10.1002/aps3.11390
7. Mahlein, A.-K.: Plant disease detection by imaging sensors - parallels and specific demands for precision agriculture and plant phenotyping. Plant Dis. **100**(2), 241–251 (2016). https://doi.org/10.1094/pdis-03-15-0340-fe
8. Pan, S.J., Yang, Q.: A survey on transfer learning. IEEE Trans. Knowl. Data Eng. **22**(10), 1345–1359 (2010). https://doi.org/10.1109/tkde.2009.191
9. Beikmohammadi, A., Faez, K.: Leaf classification for plant recognition with deep transfer learning. In: Iranian Conference on Signal Processing and Intelligent Systems (ICSPIS) (2018). https://doi.org/10.1109/icspis.2018.8700547
10. Cheng, J., Foo, S.W., Krishnan, S.M.: Automatic detection of region of interest and center point of left ventricle using watershed segmentation. In: IEEE International Symposium on Circuits and Systems (2005). https://doi.org/10.1109/iscas.2005.1464546
11. Roerdink, J.B.T.M., Meijster, A.: The watershed transform: definitions, algorithms and parallelization strategies. Fundamenta Informaticae **41**(1,2), 187–228 (2000). https://doi.org/10.3233/fi-2000-411207
12. Simonyan, K., Zisserman, A.: Very deep convolutional networks for large-scale image recognition. In: Computer Science - Computer Vision and Pattern Recognition (2015). http://arxiv.org/abs/1409.1556
13. Huang, G., Liu, Z., van der Maaten, L., Weinberger, K.Q.: Densely connected convolutional networks. In: Computer Vision and Pattern Recognition (2018). http://arxiv.org/abs/1608.06993
14. Szegedy, C., Vanhoucke, V., Ioffe, S., Shlens, J., Wojna, Z.: Rethinking the inception architecture for computer vision. In: Computer Science - Computer Vision and Pattern Recognition (2015). http://arxiv.org/abs/1512.00567
15. He, K., Zhang, X., Ren, S., Sun, J.: Deep residual learning for image recognition. In: IEEE Conference on Computer Vision and Pattern Recognition (CVPR), pp. 770–778 (2016). https://doi.org/10.1109/cvpr.2016.90
16. Szegedy, C., Ioffe, S., Vanhoucke, V.: Inception-v4, Inception-ResNet and the impact of residual connections on learning. In: Computer Science - Computer Vision and Pattern Recognition (2016). https://arxiv.org/abs/1602.07261
17. Hurtik, P., Molek, V., Hula, J.: Data preprocessing technique for neural networks based on image represented by a fuzzy function. IEEE Trans. Fuzzy Syst. **28**(7), 1195–1204 (2020). https://doi.org/10.1109/TFUZZ.2019.2911494
18. Fawzi, A., Samulowitz, H., Turaga, D., Frossard, P.: Adaptive data augmentation for image classification. In: IEEE International Conference on Image Processing (ICIP) (2016). https://doi.org/10.1109/icip.2016.7533048
19. Mizushima, A., Lu, R.: An image segmentation method for apple sorting and grading using support vector machine and Otsu's method. Comput. Electron. Agric. **94**, 29–37 (2013). https://doi.org/10.1016/j.compag.2013.02.009
20. Simon, M., Rodner, E., Denzler, J.: ImageNet pre-trained models with batch normalization. In: Computer Science - Computer Vision and Pattern Recognition (2016). http://arxiv.org/abs/1612.01452

Memory-Constrained Context-Aware Reasoning

Ijaz Uddin[1](✉), Abdur Rakib[2], Mumtaz Ali[1], and Phan Cong Vinh[3]

[1] Department of Computer Science, City University of Science and Information Technology, Peshawar, Pakistan
mumtazali@cusit.edu.pk
[2] Department of Computer Science and Creative Technologies, The University of the West of England, Bristol, UK
Rakib.Abdur@uwe.ac.uk
[3] Nguyen Tat Thanh University, Ho Chi Minh City, Vietnam
pcvinh@ntt.edu.vn

Abstract. The context-aware computing paradigm introduces environments, known as smart spaces, which can unobtrusively and proactively assist their users. These systems are currently mostly implemented on mobile platforms considering various techniques, including ontology-driven multi-agent rule-based reasoning. Rule-based reasoning is a relatively simple model that can be adapted to different real-world problems. It can be developed considering a set of assertions, which collectively constitute the working memory, and a set of rules that specify how to act on the assertion set. However, the size of the working memory is crucial when developing context-aware systems in resource constrained devices such as smartphones and wearables. In this paper, we discuss rule-based context-aware systems and techniques for determining the required working memory size for a fixed set of rules.

Keywords: Context-aware systems · Rule-based reasoning · Working memory

1 Introduction

Rule-based reasoning attempts to emulate the capabilities of human reasoning and problem solving. The technique models how a human expert analyses a particular scenario by applying rules to the facts so that a conclusion can be drawn [1]. The reasoning process in a forward chaining rule-based system starts with known facts and progresses by using inference rules to extract more data. The facts are represented in a working memory which is continually updated. In rule-based systems, the knowledge is represented as a set of rules. The rules serve

© ICST Institute for Computer Sciences, Social Informatics and Telecommunications Engineering 2021
Published by Springer Nature Switzerland AG 2021. All Rights Reserved
P. Cong Vinh and A. Rakib (Eds.): ICCASA 2021, LNICST 409, pp. 133–146, 2021.
https://doi.org/10.1007/978-3-030-93179-7_11

as long-term memory, whereas the facts serve as short-term memory [2,3]. While humans perceive their surroundings through their senses of sight, hearing, smell, taste, and touch, computers employ the context-awareness technique to become aware of their surroundings. In sensor-rich systems, sensor data is collected from a variety of sources by a device with various sensors attached to it. It is often difficult to interpret this sensed raw data. As a result, in the literature Semantic Web technologies have been used in the design and implementation of sensor-rich systems [4,5]. In Semantic Web technology, ontological representation allows context representation in terms of concepts and roles, context sharing and semantic interoperability of heterogeneous systems [6]. A framework for constructing context-aware systems in resource-bounded devices has been proposed in [6], where a context-aware system is modelled as a distributed rule-based agents. In the proposed model, the working memory containing facts (contexts) is conceptually divided into two parts, such as static and dynamic parts. The dynamic part of the working memory stores the newly derived contexts while the static part holds the initial contexts. The initial facts in the static memory are vital to start running any system, and therefore can not be removed or overwritten. More details of the setting can be found in [6]. In resource constrained systems, as a system moves, all the derived contexts cannot be stored in the working memory. That is old contexts could be overwritten by the newly derived contexts. In [5], it was shown how we can formally model and verify resource requirements of a system of rule-based context-aware reasoning agents. In this paper, we discuss techniques for determining the required working memory size of a rule-based context-aware reasoning system with a fixed set of rules.

The rest of the paper is structured as follow. Section 2 reviews related literature. Section 3 discusses an approach to smart space system modelling. Section 4 describes multi-agent rule-based reasoning and the basic components of rule-based systems. Section 5 discusses the management of working memory. Finally, Sect. 6 concludes the paper and discusses the scope for future work.

2   Related Work

Users can access context-aware services in the mobile environment due to the advent of small-scale microelectronic sensors and recent improvements in smartphones and other modern mobile devices such as smartwatches and wearable devices. Furthermore, the social network plays an important role in this regard, as users provide information primarily about their preferences, likes, and dislikes. In a different context, it can also provide contextual information about users, their surroundings, and their behavioural activities [7]. In other words, these smart devices are now a valuable source of data for determining context and understanding user behavioural activities in various situations [8]. The SociaCircuit Platform [9], for example, tracks various social interactions among users and, as a result, causes a change in the user's preferences. The developers of [10] came up with the idea of identifying a social interaction between users using data mining tools. The sociometric badge [11] tracks different activities of employees throughout office hours, forecasts job satisfaction, and coworker inter-action based on that data/patterns. Although recent work on monitoring user activities and relationships with other users has provided us with a wealth of data and relevant information to analyse and draw conclusions, the domain still lacks various features. The authors of [12], for example, developed an expert sys-tem that functions as an academic advisor. It's a monotonous system that takes six user inputs and provides recommendations based on those inputs. However, this system is unable to run an alternative set of rules since the rules are linked to the given interface. Other research [13–18] focused on developing a client-server architecture model, in which the smartphone acts as an interface for an applica-tion installed on it, with the server acting as a knowledge base. Another iPhone platform research article [19] employs the same client-server architecture for a safe emergency evacuation from a university campus (case scenario). However, the authors did not specify the set of rules that define expert knowledge.

There have already been attempts to bring advanced expert systems to the Android platform. Although Android is based on Java, it lacks some classes that are only available in desktop environments. A book for Android smart applica-tions has been published by [20]. Throughout the book, the rule engines that can be used with the Android platform are thoroughly described. These rule engines, however, lack context awareness and resource friendliness, as well as the ability to apply preferences for dynamic context awareness. Furthermore, according to the author, these engines have several significant limitations. For example, the Jrule engine and Zilonis do not support OR operators; in Termware, rules must be written in code and are difficult to update later; and in Roolie, each rule must be coded in its own file, which is also a time-consuming task that is nearly impossible in larger systems. Some technical challenges were encountered while porting various other rule engines. Since Drools is a memory-intensive engine, Eclipse quickly runs out of memory while converting files to Dalvik format. Take requires a Java compiler at runtime, and JLisa fails to function on Android due to a stake overflow issue. Jess, on the other hand, is extremely expensive and not recommended because its significant licencing costs, it is not compatible with Android, and it consumes a significant amount of memory.

The majority of rule engines are based on the RETE algorithm, according to our review and analysis of the literature. RETE is a memory-intensive algo-rithm that loads all of the rules into memory before checking them one by one in practise to see if they should be fired [21]. Similarly, checking all of the rules for each instance takes a long time. To save memory, the work by [21] introduced preferences. Instead of putting all of the rules into memory at once, their tech-nique just loads the rules that are in the preference set. Although the approach consumes less memory during loading due to preference sets, it does not remove the already loaded rules from memory over time. In [6], the size of the memory allocation is fixed. If the algorithm claims a random fixed size memory while accounting for the size of the preference sets, it may run into issues if the system has to invoke rules that are not currently in the preference set. In [6, 21], there is no systematic technique for removing rules if the memory limit is reached. The rules are remove from the memory at random, which is a problem because the rule(s) selected for removal could be a key one that will be needed again soon for the execution.

3   Smart Space System Modelling

Developing intelligent, autonomous, and adaptable systems that work in complex dynamic environments is a goal that has been around for decades. In recent years work on this area has been a more focus of discussion and research [22–26]. A smart space provides an interoperable heterogeneous environment within which users, devices and services communicate. Such an environment ultimately provides users with unobtrusive assistance based on contextual knowledge [27]. Interoperability is critical here, since smart spaces contain many different devices and software components. It is a system's ability to exchange information, so that information is correctly interpreted by the receiving device in the same way that the transmitting device intends. One way to achieve this is by using the Semantics Web technology [28]. While Semantic Web technologies can be used to achieve interoperability on mobile devices, it is important to take into account the resource limitations and unique characteristics of mobile and embedded devices.

Context awareness is a key aspect of smart spaces, and context modelling is a fundamental step in developing context-aware systems that operate in these environments. By context, we refer to any physical or conceptual information that can be used to identify the status of an entity. An entity can be a person, a place, a physical or a computing object. This context is relevant to a user and application, and reflects the relationship among themselves [29]. A smart space serves its users by sensing and interpreting the situation they are in, identifying their needs and delivering the necessary functionality according to the available resources. This process involves three major steps, namely context acquisition, context modelling and context-aware reasoning. Among other approaches, ontology-based context modelling and rule-based context reasoning are widely used techniques to enable semantic interoperability and interpreting user situations in smart spaces [6]. The context acquisition process involves acquiring context in raw format from a wide variety of sensors. It may also allow the user to manually provide the contextual information [30]. To model a context and adapt it to any domain, an ontology is requires which captures the generic concepts to a higher level. The context model needs to provide frameworks for expanding the specific context knowledge in a hierarchical way. The context ontology provides a shared vocabulary for representing knowledge about a domain and for describing specific situations in a domain. The goal of contextual reasoning is to deduce higher-level contexts from the sensed low-level contexts as well as to deduce new relevant knowledge for the use of applications and users from various context-data sources. This stage is therefore primarily responsible for interpreting the situation in a smart environment, and for deciding how its users can be assisted [31]. The OWL 2 Web Ontology Language is one possible knowledge representation language for ontologies. The W3C recommended OWL specification includes the definition of three variants of OWL, with different levels of expressiveness, namely OWL Lite, OWL DL and OWL Full. OWL DL and OWL Lite are based on Description Logics, for which sound and complete reasoners exits. The W3C also recommended three profiles OWL 2 EL, OWL 2 QL and OWL 2 RL, which are restricted sublanguages of OWL 2. For context modelling and reasoning, OWL 2 RL and SWRL [32] languages can be used. OWL 2 RL is suitable for the design and development of rule-based systems, which can be implemented using rule-based reasoning engines [5]. An OWL 2 RL ontology can be translated into a set of Horn clause rules based on [33]. Moreover, more complex rule-based concepts can be expressed using SWRL which allow us to write rules using OWL concepts. In our framework, a context-aware system composed of a set of rule-based agents, and firing of rules that infer new facts may determine context changes and representing overall behaviour of the system. A more detailed discussion of this approach can be found in [34].

4 Multi-agent Rule-Based Reasoning Systems

Multi-agent systems (MASs) are based on the concept of a decentralised working group being able to deal with problems that are difficult to solve using the conventional centralised computing approach. Intelligent agents are used to work more effectively and in a versatile and interactive way to solve problems. Multi-agent systems are considered to be a promising approach to dealing with ubiquitous systems development because of their ability to adapt themselves to dynamic environments. Such features together with collaborative behaviour, autonomy, reactivity and pro-activity facilitate the modelling and reasoning about complex context-aware system behaviour [5].

An agent is called a rule-based agent, if its behaviour and/or its knowledge is expressed by means of rules. A rule-based reasoning agent, as can be seen in Fig. 1, has few components such as a rule-base, an inference engine and a working memory. A rule-base contains a collection of rules, where rules are IF(antecedent)—THEN(consequent) statements. The antecedent is a sufficient condition for the consequent and the consequent is a necessary condition for the antecedent. The antecedent part is matched with the elements in the working memory. If the antecedent of a rule is fully matched with the elements of the working memory then the rule is said to be eligible for firing and the corresponding rule instance(s) can be added to the agenda. The working memory of an agent consists of facts. The facts are initial contexts, derived contexts and/or communicated contexts received as messages from other agents in the system. The inference engine loops through three sequential phases: Match, Select and Act. In the Match phase, rules are matched with facts, if more than one rule is eligible to fire then a conflict arises. The strategy to decide which is the next rule to be fired is called conflict resolution. The next step is to resolve this conflict in the Select phase. Once a conflict is resolved than its time to fire the rule in the Act phase. Firing a rule instance can add a context to the working memory by

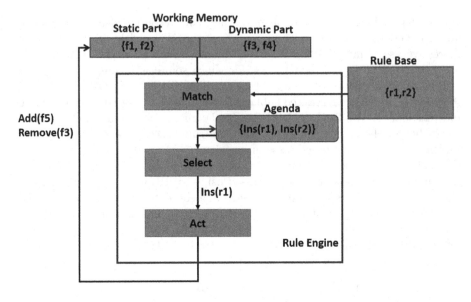

Fig. 1. Reasoning process of a rule-based agent

possibly overriding an element from its dynamic part. Mostly the literature discusses the rule-based reasoning from a point of view where the resources (e.g., working memory size) are not considered. In our work, however, we consider memory to be a limited resource. In the following, we will concentrate our discussion on the rule-based reasoning algorithm and working memory management and updating.

5   Management of Working Memory

As previously discussed, the working memory is divided into two parts. Each part plays its own role. Part of the emphasis in this discussion is dynamic working memory. A newly created context may be added to the dynamic working memory by firing a rule instance, or a context may be added as a message received from another device or agent. In order to accommodate this new context, we must first review our current working mechanism and then suggest new techniques to substitute the current framework for efficient use of the working memory.

5.1   Working Memory Updating

The working memory acts as a holder for the currently available contexts and helps to perform context-aware reasoning. Where the emphasis is on resource limitations, memory is one of the primary resources we aim to save during the entire system design and implementation stages. The restriction on the size of the working memory is to ensure that it does not exceed the maximum number of contexts it can hold at any given time. However, contexts can be generated at every iteration, and preserving those contexts that are more crucial for execution is a critical task. In our implementation, the working memory is basically a fixed size container, which is divided into static memory and dynamic parts. The dynamic memory is bounded in size, where one unit of memory corresponds to the ability to store an arbitrary context. Only facts stored in the dynamic memory may get overwritten, and this happens if an agent's memory is full or a contradictory context arrives in the working memory (even if the memory is not full) [5]. Whenever a newly derived context arrives in the memory, it is compared with the existing contexts to see if any conflict arises. If so then the corresponding contradictory context will be replaced with the newly derived context, otherwise, the new context will be added to the working memory by overwriting an arbitrary context if the working memory is full. Since the dynamic memory is bounded in size, the system possibly can go through an infinite execution if a goal is not achievable and there is no way to forcefully stop the inference engine. For example, let's assume an instance of a rule r_1 generates a new context that can activate another rule r_2 and vice versa. If we have a single memory unit then the system will be in the infinite running state, unless otherwise controlled. To overcome this issue, we set the number of iterations equal to the number of rules. This will ensure that each rule is tested and, if no matches are found, the system will stop itself instead of abrupt behaviour. This also saves the resources of the host system. The Algorithm 1 describes the steps involved in executing the instance of the selected rule and updating the working memory.

5.2 Estimating Size of the Working Memory

Estimating the working memory size can help to minimise context loss, in particular the critical contexts. It can be achieved using the following techniques.

Distinct Working Memory (DWM). In the database analogy, the distinct returns all the results so that the duplicated values are only seen once instead of being replicated. Similarly, the working memory size can be set equal to the number of distinct consequences of the rules. Let R be the total number of rules in the rule base, R_c be the total number of consequences of the rules and R_{dc} be the total number of distinct consequences such that $R_{dc} \leq R_c$ and $R_{dc} > 0$. Then the required size of the working memory will be R_{dc}.

Average of the Preference Sets (APS). In this technique, the sets of preferences are taken into account. The primary idea is to customize user preferences so that resource-bounded context-aware applications can be personalised [30]. When preferences need to be implemented, the procedure is more complex than the prior method, but it saves space. This method considers the rules of several different groups of preferences. To begin, it calculates an average working memory size based on the overall average of rule base sizes. It then determines

Input: **to_ fire:** A selected rule instance to be fired [$\mathbf{R}_c$: A communication rule instance, $\mathbf{R}_g$: A rule instance contains a goal context, $\mathbf{R}_d$: A deduction rule instance, $\mathbf{R}_f$: Rule Flag, $\mathbf{R}_{cons}$: Consequent, **MAX_SIZE**: memory size]

Output: Rule instance executed, consequent added to **WM** and corresponding action performed.

1 **START**
2 **to_ fire** from conflict resolution and $\mathbf{R}_{cons}$ is the consequent
3 **if** R_g **then**
4   **if** R_{cons} *is a conflicting context* **then**
5 | Overwrite the contradictory context with $\mathbf{R}_{cons}$
6   **end**
7   **else if** $|WM| < MAX\_SIZE$ **then**
8 | Add $\mathbf{R}_{cons}$ to **WM**
9   **end**
10   **else**
11 | Overwrire an existing context with $\mathbf{R}_{cons}$
12   **end**
13   Goal Reached
14   Execution Halts
15 **end**
16 **else**
17   **if** R_{cons} *is a conflicting context* **then**
18   Overwrite the contradictory context with $\mathbf{R}_{cons}$
19   **if** R_c **then**
20 | initiate communication module
21   **end**
22   **end**
23   **else if** $|WM| < MAX\_SIZE$ **then**
24   Add $\mathbf{R}_{cons}$ to **WM**
25   **if** R_c **then**
26 | initiate communication module
27   **end**
28   **end**
29   **else**
30   Overwrite an existing context with $\mathbf{R}_{cons}$
31   **if** R_c **then**
32 | initiate communication module
33   **end**
34   **end**
35 **end**
36 **END**

Algorithm 1: Execution of a rule

how many preference sets have WM requirements that are higher than the computed average. In the second stage, the technique will verify these preference sets (which have higher requirements than the average size) for distinct values in their consequent parts. If the number of distinct consequent parts in any of these preference sets checked for WM is less than the average, the system will request WM size equal to the calculated average. However, if the value is higher than the average, the system will request a WM size that is equal to this value. To avoid context loss, the system will use the largest calculated value as the WM size in both cases. Let R be a rule base with $n = |R|$ number of rules and there are m preference sets $P_1, P_2, \ldots P_m$ with varied preference methods. Then the size of the working memory will be $(|P_1| + |P_2| + \ldots + |P_m|)/m$, where $|P_i|$ is the size of the preference set P_i for $1 \leq i \leq m$. However, the memory size may be larger than the calculated average if any preference set requires more memory as discussed above.

Smart Average of the Preference Sets (SAPS). Preference sets are another focus of the SAPS technique. This technique is similar to APS, but it has the added benefit of reducing the computation factor if certain conditions are met. Otherwise, it will function in the same way as APS does. In this approach, the standard deviation (SD) of the available preference sets is first calculated. A low standard deviation implies that the values are close to the set's mean, whereas a high standard deviation shows that the values are spread out over a larger range. Therefore, if the SD is small (less than a threshold value 2) then the number of rules in the preference sets will be close to the mean. In this case, among the available preference sets, the system will request the preference set that requires the most memory units. There will be no need to do any further calculations because the size will be enough for any other preference sets. However, if the SD is large (greater than or equal to a threshold value 2), it will function similarly to APS.

5.3   An Example

Let us consider an example system developed using a set of rules presented in Table 1 [30]. There are 18 different rules in this rule base. Some rules have the same consequence, and some of the rules have the same preference set. We have shown below how the aforementioned techniques are applied to Table 1.

Distinct Working Memory. As previously explained, this technique returns all distinct results and does not display duplicated values; duplicated values are displayed just once. The following terms are used to apply the DWM approach to the table. Here, $|R| = 18$ (total number of rules), $|R_c| = 7$ (total number of consequences of the rules) and $|R_{dc}| = 4$ (total number of distinct consequences). In this case, $|R_c| \geq R_{dc}$ and the size of WM $= R_{dc}$. We get 12 distinct rules out

Table 1. Blood pressure and heart rate rules

Blood pressure category rules				
Category	m	Corresponding rule	F	CS
Low BP	1	Person(?p), hasSystolicBloodPressure(?p,?sbp), hasDiastolicBloodPressure(?p, ?dbp), lessThan(?sbp, '90), lessThan(?dbp,60) ⟶ hasBPCategory(?p,LowBP)	D	-
Normal	1	Person(?p),hasSystolicBloodPressure(?p,?sbp), hasDiastolicBloodPressure(?p, ?dbp), greaterThan(?sbp,90), greaterthan(?dbp,60), lessThan(?sbp,120), less-Than(?dbp,80) ⟶ hasBPCategory(?p,Normal)	D	-
Pre high	1	Person(?p), hasSystolicBloodPressure(?p,?sbp), hasDiastolicBloodPressure(?p, ?dbp),greaterThan(?sbp,120), greaterThan(?dbp,80),lessThan(?sbp,140), less-Than(?dbp,90)⟶ hasBPCategory(?p,PreHigh)	D	-
High	1	Person(?p), hasSystolicBloodPressure(?p,?sbp), hasDiastolicBloodPressure(?p, ?dbp), greaterThan(?sbp,140), greaterThan(?dbp,90)⟶ hasBPCategory(?p, HighBP)	D	-
Heart rate category rules				
Category	m	Corresponding rule	F	CS
Athlete	1	Person(?p), hasHeartRate(?p,?hrt), greaterThan(?hrt,48), lessThan(?hrt,55) ⟶ hasHRCategory(?p, Athlete)	D	-
Excellent	1	Person(?p), hasHeartRate(?p,?hrt), greaterThan(?hrt,54), lessThan(?hrt,62) ⟶ hasHRCategory(?p,Excellent)	D	-
Good	1	Person(?p), hasHeartRate(?p,?hrt), greaterThan(?hrt,61), lessThan(?hrt,66) ⟶ hasHRCategory(?p,Good)	D	-
Above Average	1	Person(?p), hasHeartRate(?p,?hrt), greaterThan(?hrt,65), lessThan(?hrt,71) ⟶ hasHRCategory(?p,AboveAverage)	D	-
Average	1	Person(?p), hasHeartRate(?p,?hrt), greaterThan(?hrt,70), lessThan(?hrt,75) ⟶ hasHRCategory(?p,Average)	D	-
Below Average	1	Person(?p), hasHeartRate(?p,?hrt), greaterThan(?hrt,74),lessThan(?hrt,82) ⟶ hasHRCategory(?p,BelowAverage)	D	-
Poor	1	Person(?p), hasHeartRate(?p,?hrt), greaterThan(?hrt,81) ⟶ hasHRCategory(?p,Poor)	D	-
Some example rules to derive different situations				
Category	m	Corresponding rule	F	CS
Emergency	2	Patient(?p), hasBPCategory(?p,HighBP), hasHRCategory(?p,Poor) → hasSituation (?p,Emergency)	D	H
Emergency	2	Patient(?p), hasBPCategory(?p,PreHigh), hasHRCategory(?p,Poor) → hasSituation (?p,Emergency)	D	H
Emergency	2	Patient(?p),hasBPCategory(?p,Normal), hasHRCategory(?p,Poor) → hasSituation (?p,Emergency)	D	N
Emergency	2	Patient(?p),hasBPCategory(?p,LowBp), hasHRCategory(?p,Poor) →hasSituation (?p,Emergency)	D	L
Non Emergency	1	Patient(?p),hasBPCategory(?p,Normal), hasHRCategory(?p,Average) → ~hasSituation (?p,Emergency)	D	N
Non Emergency	1	Patient(?p),hasBPCategory(?p,Normal), hasHRCategory(?p,AboveAverage) → ~hasSituation (?p,Emergency)	D	N
Non Emergency	1	Patient(?p),hasBPCategory(?p,Normal), hasHRCategory(?p,Good) → ~hasSituation (?p,Emergency)	D	N

of a total of 18 rules if we use the DWM technique to group the rules that have the same consequence and define the working memory on DWM bases. In this specific case, the DWM technique decreases the number of rules by almost 33.33%. This technique mainly depends on the number of rules having the same consequences. It will work more efficiently as the number of rules with the same consequence grows.

Average of the Preference Sets (APS). The APS approach is primarily concerned with preference sets. This technique takes into account the rules in various preference sets and calculates an average; the WM size is determined by the calculated average. The WM is the same size as the average. There can be four different preference sets based on the rule-base in Table 1, consisting of 11, 2, 1, and 4 rules, with an average $(11 + 2 + 1 + 4)/4 = 4.5$. However, the preference set $P1$ having $9(> 5)$ distinct consequences. Thus, the size of the working memory WM is 9. This method will reduce the amount of time it takes to calculate and check each rule for distinct consequences. In this example, instead of 18 rules, only 9 rules were checked, which is a 50 percent reduction. In other circumstances, depending on the number of rules in the preference sets with values higher than the average calculated, it can be reduced from 20 to 60%. In the general case, the required WM size for the DWM technique is 12, whereas it is for the APS technique is 9, which is roughly 25% less than the DWM technique. However, the results may vary from one example to another. It's also worth mentioning that this just applies to the size of the dynamic working memory.

Smart Average of the Preference Sets (SAPS). In the above example, $|P1| = 11, |P2| = 2, |P3| = 1$, and $|P4| = 4$. Therefore, the average is 4.5, while the standard deviation is 3.90. As a result, it will function similarly to APS, and the required WM size will be 9. However, for example, if we have a scenario where $|P1| = 5, |P2| = 6, |P3| = 7$, and $|P4| = 8$, the average and standard deviation would be 6.5 and 1.11, respectively. In this case, the WM size will be 8 since standard deviation is smaller than the threshold value and the memory requirement of the preference set with the most rules is 8.

6   Discussion and Future Work

In this paper we have addressed the issues with the working memory in resource constrained devices and proposed a possible solution as to how much dynamic memory size of an agent is required with a fixed set of rules. There can be more complex solutions but resources should be considered. In the future we intend to work on the reverse engineering of the preference sets. Although, in our proposed system, we have a well-explained mechanism for deriving a preference set from a set of rules. This set depends on a variety of choices by a user such as context-based, derived or live preferences. However, it is unavoidable to make a strategy that can reverse a set of rules when not required. The preference set may be able to remove rules which are not likely to fire in the future by its own. As a result, redundancy will be reduced, allowing the system's output to be maximised. Another area where further development could be made is with the rule generating strategy. Because the rules are created in software or with a tool and then processed in a typical manner, in our situation, we have several options for creating and changing rules, including a web-based interface, writing to a JSON file, and utilising the Onto-HCR tool [24]. We would also like to make changes to the generated rules for preferences and other factors. It would be more convenient to do devoted research in this regard in order to develop a standalone framework capable of automating all of the processes mentioned above.

References

1. Ligeza, A.: Logical Foundations for Rule-Based Systems, vol. 11, no. 2. Springer, Heidelberg (2006)
2. Giarratano, J.C., Riley, G.: Expert systems, principles and programming, Thomson course of technology. Boston, Australia (2005)
3. Luger, G.F.: Artificial Intelligence: Structures and Strategies for Complex Problem Solving, 6th edn. (2005)
4. Tai, W., Keeney, J., O'Sullivan, D.: Resource-constrained reasoning using a reasoner composition approach. Semant. Web **6**, 35–59 (2015)
5. Rakib, A., Haque, H.M.U.: A logic for context-aware non-monotonic reasoning agents. In: Gelbukh, A., Espinoza, F.C., Galicia-Haro, S.N. (eds.) MICAI 2014. LNCS (LNAI), vol. 8856, pp. 453–471. Springer, Cham (2014). https://doi.org/10.1007/978-3-319-13647-9_41
6. Rakib, A., Uddin, I.: An efficient rule-based distributed reasoning framework for resource-bounded systems. Mob. Netw. Appl. **24**(1), 82–99 (2019)
7. Sarker, I.H.: Mobile data science: towards understanding data-driven intelligent mobile applications. arXiv preprint arXiv:1811.02491 (2018)
8. Sarker, I.H.: BehavMiner: mining user behaviors from mobile phone data for personalized services. In: 2018 IEEE International Conference on Pervasive Computing and Communications Workshops (PerCom Workshops), pp. 452–453. IEEE Computer Society (2018)
9. Chronis, I., Madan, A., Pentland, A.: SocialCircuits: the art of using mobile phones for modeling personal interactions. In: Proceedings of the ICMI-MLMI 2009 Workshop on Multimodal Sensor-Based Systems and Mobile Phones for Social Computing, pp. 1–4 (2009)
10. Jung, J.J.: Contextualized mobile recommendation service based on interactive social network discovered from mobile users. Expert Syst. Appl. **36**(9), 11950–11956 (2009)
11. Olguín, D.O., Waber, B.N., Kim, T., Mohan, A., Ara, K., Pentland, A.: Sensible organizations: technology and methodology for automatically measuring organizational behavior. IEEE Trans. Syst. Man Cybern. Part B (Cybern.) **39**(1), 43–55 (2008)
12. Aly, W.M., Eskaf, K.A., Selim, A.S.: Fuzzy mobile expert system for academic advising. In: 2017 IEEE 30th Canadian Conference on Electrical and Computer Engineering (CCECE), pp. 1–5. IEEE (2017)
13. Ghasempour, A.: Optimized scalable decentralized hybrid advanced metering infrastructure for smart grid. In: 2015 IEEE International Conference on Smart Grid Communications (SmartGridComm), pp. 223–228. IEEE (2015)
14. Ghasempour, A.: Optimum packet service and arrival rates in advanced metering infrastructure architecture of smart grid. In: 2016 IEEE Green Technologies Conference (GreenTech), pp. 1–5. IEEE (2016)

15. Ghasempour, A.: Optimized advanced metering infrastructure architecture of smart grid based on total cost, energy, and delay. In: 2016 IEEE Power & Energy Society Innovative Smart Grid Technologies Conference (ISGT), pp. 1–6. IEEE (2016)
16. Ghasempour, A.: Optimizing the advanced metering infrastructure architecture in smart grid. Utah State University (2016)
17. Sharma, V., Song, F., You, I., Atiquzzaman, M.: Energy efficient device discovery for reliable communication in 5G-based IoT and BSNs using unmanned aerial vehicles. J. Netw. Comput. Appl. **97**, 79–95 (2017)
18. Sharma, V., You, I., Andersson, K., Palmieri, F., Rehmani, M.H., Lim, J.: Security, privacy and trust for smart mobile-internet of things (M-IoT): a survey. IEEE Access **8**, 167123–167163 (2020)
19. Abulkhair, M.F., Ibrahim, L.F.: Using rule base system in mobile platform to build alert system for evacuation and guidance. Int. J. Adv. Comput. Sci. Appl. **7**(4), 68–79 (2016)
20. Mukherjee, C.: Build Android-Based Smart Applications: Using Rules Engines, NLP and Automation Frameworks. Apress (2017)
21. Uddin, I.: A rule-based framework for developing context-aware systems for smart spaces. Ph.D. thesis, University of Nottingham (2019)
22. Alirezaie, M., et al.: An ontology-based context-aware system for smart homes: E-care@home. Sensors (Basel, Switzerland) **17** (2017)
23. Abdur, R.: Smart space system interoperability. In: Proceedings of the 3rd International Workshop on (Meta)Modelling for Healthcare Systems, Bergen, Norway, vol. 2336, pp. 16–23. CEUR Workshop Proceedings (2018)
24. Uddin, I., Rakib, A., Haque, H.M.U., Vinh, P.C.: Modeling and reasoning about preference-based context-aware agents over heterogeneous knowledge sources. Mob. Netw. Appl. **23**, 13–26 (2018)
25. Streitz, N.A., Charitos, D., Kaptein, M., Böhlen, M.: Grand challenges for ambient intelligence and implications for design contexts and smart societies. J. Ambient Intell. Smart Environ. **11**, 87–107 (2019)
26. Mahalle, P.N., Dhotre, P.S.: Context-Aware Pervasive Systems and Applications. ISRL, vol. 169. Springer, Singapore (2020). https://doi.org/10.1007/978-981-32-9952-8
27. Cook, D., Das, S.: Smart Environments: Technology, Protocols and Applications (Wiley Series on Parallel and Distributed Computing). Wiley, Hoboken (2004)
28. Noy, N., McGuinness, D., Hayes, P.J.: Semantic integration & interoperability using RDF and OWL. W3C Editor's Draft 3, November 2005
29. Dey, A.K.: Understanding and using context. Pers. Ubiquit. Comput. **5**, 4–7 (2001)
30. Uddin, I., Rakib, A.: A preference-based application framework for resource-bounded context-aware agents. In: Kim, K.J., Joukov, N. (eds.) ICMWT 2017. LNEE, vol. 425, pp. 187–196. Springer, Singapore (2018). https://doi.org/10.1007/978-981-10-5281-1_20
31. Wang, X.H., Zhang, D.Q., Gu, T., Pung, H.K.: Ontology based context modeling and reasoning using OWL. In: IEEE Annual Conference on Pervasive Computing and Communications Workshops, pp. 18–22 (2004)
32. Horrocks, I., Patel-Schneider, P.F., Boley, H., Tabet, S., Grosof, B., Dean, M.: SWRL: a Semantic Web rule language combining OWL and RuleML. Acknowledged W3C submission, standards proposal research report: Version 0.6, April 2004

33. Grosof, B., Horrocks, I., Volz, R., Decker, S.: Description logic programs: combining logic programs with description logics. In: The Twelfth International World Wide Web Conference, Budapest, pp. 48–57. ACM (2003)

34. Rakib, A., Ul Haque, H.M., Faruqui, R.U.: A temporal description logic for resource-bounded rule-based context-aware agents. In: Vinh, P.C., Alagar, V., Vassev, E., Khare, A. (eds.) ICCASA 2013. LNICST, vol. 128, pp. 3–14. Springer, Cham (2014). https://doi.org/10.1007/978-3-319-05939-6_1

Segmentation-Based Methods for Top-*k* Discords Detection in Static and Streaming Time Series Under Euclidean Distance

Huynh Thi Thu Thuy[1,2(✉)], Duong Tuan Anh[1,3], and Vo Thi Ngoc Chau[1]

[1] Faculty of Computer Science and Engineering, Ho Chi Minh City University of Technology - VNU-HCM, Ho Chi Minh City, Vietnam
{8141217, chauvtn}@hcmut.edu.vn, anh.dt@huflit.edu.vn
[2] Center for Applied Information Technology, Ton Duc Thang University, Ho Chi Minh City, Vietnam
[3] Department of IT, HCM City University of Foreign Languages and Information Technology, Ho Chi Minh City, Vietnam

Abstract. Detecting top-*k* discords in time series is more useful than detecting the most unusual subsequence since the result is a more informative and complete set, rather than a single subsequence. The first challenge of this task is to determine the length of discords. Besides, detecting top-*k* discords in streaming time series poses another challenge that is fast response when new data points arrive at high speed. To handle these challenges, we propose two novel methods, TopK-EP-ALeader and TopK-EP-ALeader-S, which combine segmentation and clustering for detecting top-*k* discords in static and streaming time series, respectively. Moreover, a circular buffer is built to store the local segment of a streaming time series and calculate anomaly scores efficiently. Along with this circular buffer, a delayed update policy is defined for achieving instant responses to overcome the second challenge. The experiments on nine datasets in different application domains confirm the effectiveness and efficiency of our methods for top-*k* discord discovery in static and streaming time series.

Keywords: Anomaly detection · Top-*k* discords · Segmentation · Clustering · Streaming time series

1 Introduction

A streaming time series is an unbounded sequence of data points. In this sequence, new data points are continuously appended as time progresses. Recently, anomaly detection in streaming time series has emerged as an attractive topic because more applications need to be processed in real time rather than in batches. Such applications that include the anomaly detection task on streaming time series are listed as follows: detecting unusual patterns in flowing electrocardiograms (ECG) data from patients [11] and detecting anomalous patterns in streaming sensor data [1].

© ICST Institute for Computer Sciences, Social Informatics and Telecommunications Engineering 2021
Published by Springer Nature Switzerland AG 2021. All Rights Reserved
P. Cong Vinh and A. Rakib (Eds.): ICCASA 2021, LNICST 409, pp. 147–163, 2021.
https://doi.org/10.1007/978-3-030-93179-7_12

Compared to static time series, streaming time series have their own characteristics: (1) Data elements are frequently appended in streaming time series. (2) The size of a streaming time series is potentially unlimited. (3) Data synopsis and one-pass algorithms are often required to achieve a real time response as it is difficult to store all the data in memory or on disk with their frequent fast updates. Because of these three characteristics, several previous methods that were developed for static time series may not work in the streaming time series scenario.

On the other hand, discord detection in streaming time series is more difficult than similarity search in streaming time series. The major challenges for the existing anomaly detection methods on streaming time series are how to determine the length of anomalous subsequences and how to incrementally update the top-k discords whenever a new data point arrives.

Furthermore, finding top-k discords in time series is more important than only finding the most unusual subsequence since the set of top-k discords contains not only the most unusual subsequence but also some other important unusual subsequences. It makes the result more informative and complete.

In this paper, we devise two effective and efficient methods, named TopK-EP-ALeader and TopK-EP-ALeader-S, for detecting top-k discords in static and streaming time series, respectively, dealing with the aforementioned challenges. The main contributions of our paper are highlighted as follows.

The first contribution is TopK-EP-ALeader, our novel top-k discords detection algorithm in static time series under Euclidean distance. In TopK-EP-ALeader, a segmentation method based on the major extrema method proposed by Fink and Gandhi [4] is used to divide a time series into subsequences. After that, an incremental clustering method is applied to group similar subsequences into the same cluster and at the same time, dissimilar subsequences into different clusters. These subsequences in the resulting clusters are processed to return top-k discords. Through an empirical evaluation, TopK-EP-ALeader outperforms TopK-EP-ILeader, which is a variant of EP-ILeader [16] used for top-k discords detection in static time series.

The second contribution of our work is TopK-EP-ALeader-S, our extended version of TopK-EP-ALeader for detecting top-k discords in a more challenging scenario: streaming time series. TopK-EP-ALeader-S is a new algorithm that can find top-k discords immediately after one new pattern appears in the streaming time series. This remarkable feature of TopK-EP-ALeader-S is defined from the online property of the segmentation algorithm and the incrementality of the clustering algorithm. Indeed, the experimental results on various streaming time series show that TopK-EP-ALeader-S can bring out accurate top-k discords on the fly.

Furthermore, at the center of the two aforementioned contributions is the third contribution of our work. For this contribution, we propose A-Leader, an efficient subsequence clustering method used in TopK-EP-ALeader and TopK-EP-ALeader-S. A-Leader is defined as an improved version of I-Leader in our previous work [17] by speeding up Euclidean distance computation so that the subsequence clustering process can be accelerated.

The remainder of this paper is structured as follows. Section 2 introduces some background and related works. Section 3 describes supporting techniques to our proposed algorithms. Section 4 introduces our two proposed algorithms: TopK-EP-

ALeader and TopK-EP-ALeader-S for detecting top-k discords in static time series and streaming time series. The experimental results of our proposed algorithms TopK-EP-ALeader and TopK-EP-ALeader-S are reported in Sect. 5. Finally, Sect. 6 gives some conclusions and remarks on future works.

2 Background and Related Works

2.1 Background

Time series anomaly detection means finding the unusual (anomalous, novel, deviant, *discord*) subsequences in a time series. A time series discord is a subsequence that is maximally different from its closest matching subsequence. However, generally, the best matches of a given subsequence (apart from itself) tend to be very close to the subsequence under consideration. Such matches are called *trivial matches*. When detecting anomaly subsequences, we should discard trivial matches which can hinder our anomaly detection process. So, we define a non-trivial match (non-self match) as follows. Using this definition, discord-related concepts are presented.

Definition 1. (*Non-self match*) Given a time series T, containing a subsequence C of length n starting at position p and a matching subsequence M starting at position q, we say that M is a non-trivial match to C if $|p - q| \geq n$.

Definition 2. (*1-discord*) Given a time series T, the subsequence C in T is considered as the most important discord (also called 1-discord or top-anomaly) in T if C has the largest distance to its nearest non-trivial match.

In fact, detecting top-k discords in time series is more important than just only finding the most unusual subsequence. We are therefore interested in finding top-k discords in time series.

Definition 3. (k^{th} - *discord*) Given a time series T and the subsequence D of length n beginning at position p is the kth-discord in T if it has the kth largest distance to its nearest non-trivial match, with no overlapping region to the ith discord beginning at position p_i, for all $1 \leq i \leq k$. That is, $|p - p_i| \geq n$.

These above definitions which are commonly-used in time series discord detection, are from the work by Keogh et al. [8]. The problem of 1-discord detection can be solved by the brute-force algorithm which is given in [8]. In the brute-force algorithm, using a sliding window, we extract all possible candidate subsequences in the outer loop and then find the distance to the nearest non-self match for each candidate subsequence in the inner loop. The candidate subsequence with the largest distance to its nearest non-self match is the 1-discord. Since the brute-force algorithm is a window-based method for detecting discords in a time series with a nested loop, it incurs high complexity. Its complexity is $O(m^2)$, where m is the length of the time series.

Notice that we can modify the brute-force algorithm to obtain the algorithm which can detect top-k discords in time series.

2.2 Related Works on Anomaly Detection in Static Time Series

Bu et al. [2] proposed WAT algorithm for finding top-k discords in static time series. This algorithm needs to predetermine the discord length. It is based on a sliding-window approach for time series discord discovery. The discord length parameter setting is not easy to be done and the sliding window approach gives WAT algorithm a high computational cost. So, it might be very complicated to adapt WAT for detecting top-k discords in streaming time series.

Linardi et al. [9] proposed a variable-length motif and discord discovery framework. In this framework, the subsequence pairs with the largest Euclidean distances of each length in the user-defined range are returned as discords. This framework can find top k-discords with variable length in a time series.

Compared to our work, [9] is an interesting work for finding top k-discords with variable length in a time series. However, this algorithm requires complex parameter settings. Moreover, it is hard to determine which discord and which subsequence length are appropriate among many returned variable-length discords in user's applications. Above all, this algorithm aims to detect discords in static time series, while ours are dedicated to top-k discords detection from both static and streaming time series.

2.3 Related Works on Anomaly Detection in Streaming Time Series

For anomaly detection on streaming time series, a few research works have been proposed as briefly reviewed below.

Liu et al. [10] proposed a framework for anomaly detection in streaming time series called Detection of Continuous Discords (DCD). DCD can detect continuous 1-discords from local segments of a streaming time series which reside in a buffer with a predefined size. One major technique in DCD framework is that it limits the search space to further enhance the efficiency of the discord detection process. Since DCD framework is a window-based method in anomaly detection, DCD still has a high computational cost.

Sanchez and Bustos [14] presented a method for 1-discord detection in static time series which employed bounding rectangles and R-tree to establish two ordering heuristics for the two loops in the 1-discord detection process. Sanchez and Bustos extended this idea for discord detection in streaming time series. However, the detected anomalous subsequence is not really the top-discord of the whole streaming time series in the buffer. In other words, the algorithm can detect any approximate anomalous subsequence from a streaming time series rather than the top discord from the streaming time series in the buffer.

SKDIS method proposed by Giao and Anh [5] is a window-based method for detecting top-k discords in streaming time series. SKDIS is the incremental version of the brute-force algorithm for detecting top-k discords in static time series. SKDIS has to maintain and update the historic information of the interim top-k discords detected from the current buffer whenever a new data point arrives. To improve the efficienc of anomaly detection process, SKDIS applies some techniques from the suite of techniques UCR-ED [13] to speed up Euclidean distance computation.

All the aforementioned methods for discord detection in streaming time series belong to the window-based category which is often costly in terms of processing time. So, a new effective and efficient method is thus needed for detecting top-k discords in streaming time series.

3 Supporting Techniques

Before presenting the two proposed methods for finding top-k discords in static and streaming time series, we describe some supporting techniques for these two methods.

3.1 Accelerating Euclidean Distance Calculation in Clustering Algorithm

Euclidean distance (ED) calculates the distance between the two subsequences $C_1 = x_1$, $x_2, \ldots, x_m$} and $C_2 = \{y_1, y_2, \ldots, y_m\}$ with the same length m by taking the square root of the sum of squares of differences of the two corresponding points in two subsequences as shown in the following formula.

$$ED(C_1, C_2) = \sqrt{\sum_{i=1}^{m} (x_i - y_i)^2}$$

Since computing the distance between two time-series subsequences is time-consuming, in this work, we apply two techniques to accelerate ED calculation in I-Leader clustering algorithm. These two techniques are inspired from the UCR-ED suite introduced by Rakthanmanon et al. [13]. The two techniques are described as follows:

- *Using the Squared Distance.* ED uses a square root calculation. However, if we omit this step, the relative ranking of comparative subsequences is not changed, since the ED function is monotonic and concave. Furthermore, the absence of the square root function makes the ED computation faster.
- *Early Abandoning of ED.* During the ED computation, if the current sum of the squared differences between each pair of corresponding data points $(x_i - y_i)$ $(i = 1..$ k, $k < m)$ exceeds a given threshold in the Leader clustering algorithm, then the computation is stopped. In other words, early abandoning technique can be used to prune the dissimilar subsequences from the set of subsequences so as to retain the candidates for further measuring their similarity with direct ED. Figure 1 illustrates the idea of early abandoning.

Fig. 1. An illustration of early abandoning in calculating Euclidean distance between C_1 and C_2.

When we apply these two techniques to improve I-Leader clustering algorithm [17], we obtain the new variant of I-Leader clustering and name it A-Leader algorithm (abbreviated for Accelerated variant of Leader).

3.2 A-Leader Clustering Algorithm

A-Leader is an improved version of I-Leader. I-Leader, proposed by [17], is also a variant of Leader algorithm, a well-known incremental clustering algorithm proposed by Hartigan [6]. I-Leader uses "*centroid*" as cluster representative rather than "*leader*" proposed in the original Leader algorithm.

In I-Leader, the distance between G_m and C_j is the distance between C_j and the centroid of cluster G_m. I-Leader computes the centroids of clusters in an incremental manner. Whenever a new subsequence t is put into a cluster, a technique is used to calculate a new centroid incrementally.

I-Leader clustering algorithm is described as follows.

- **Input**: A list C of subsequences and a user-specified distance threshold ε.
- **Output**: A list G of clusters.
- **Process**:
    Step 1: Assign the first subsequence, C_1, to the cluster G_1; set $i = 1$ and $j = 1$.
    Step 2: Set $j = j + 1$; consider clusters G_1 to G_i in ascending order of the index and assign C_j to cluster G_m ($1 \leq m \leq i$) if the distance between G_m and C_j is the smallest distance and this distance is less than a distance threshold ε. Otherwise, set $i = i + 1$ and assign C_j to a new cluster G_i.
    Step 3: Refine the clustering result of *Step 2* by merging the subsequences in *under-filled*" clusters to their nearest "*good*" clusters.
    Step 4: Repeat *Step 2* and *Step 3* until all of the subsequences in the list C are assigned to clusters.

Definitions of "*under-filled*" and "*good*" clusters are detailed in [17]. Here, we explain briefly about them. Clusters with few instances are called "*under-filled*" clusters and clusters with more instances are called "*good*" clusters. The number of instances in the cluster considered as "under-filled" or "good" is based on the distribution ratio of the instances in the clusters. So, Step 3 in I-Leader aims to improve the quality of the resultant clusters in terms of the distribution of the instances in the clusters. In Step 3, I-Leader merges the subsequences in "under-filled" clusters to their nearest "good" clusters. More details about I-Leader algorithm, interested readers can refer to [17].

In A-Leader, we apply some techniques to accelerate the computation of ED (as mentioned in the first part of Sect. 3) when we have to calculate the distance between the subsequence and the centroid of a particular cluster to decide whether the subsequence is pushed into the cluster or not. The threshold value for speeding up ED calculation here is the threshold ε of I-Leader algorithm. Thus, A-Leader differs from I-Leader in the way of calculating ED while all the other steps of A-Leader are the same as those of I-Leader.

3.3 EP-ALeader

EP-ALeader algorithm is an improved version of EP-ILeader by using A-Leader clustering instead of I-Leader clustering. EP-ILeader (abbreviated for Extreme Points and Improved Leader) is an anomaly detection algorithm in static time series proposed in our previous work [16].

For our approach, we do not use any sliding window to extract subsequences. Instead we use a segmentation method for extracting subsequences in time series and a clustering method to cluster the extracted subsequences. Then, based on the result of the clustering step, we can calculate the anomaly score of each subsequence. In order to calculate an anomaly score of each subsequence, we use the two following definitions given by [7].

Definition 4. (*Large and Small Clusters*). Given a set of patterns D that has been grouped into a set of clusters $C = \{C_1, C_2, ..., C_k\}$ such that $|C_1| \geq |C_2| \geq ... \geq |C_k|$. Given two parameters α and β, if $|C_1| + |C_2| + ... + |C_b|)$ is greater than $|D| * \alpha$ and $|C_b| / |C_{b+1}| \geq \beta$ then clusters $C_1, C_2, ..., C_b$ are large clusters and clusters $C_{b+1}, C_{b+2}, ..., C_k$ are small ones, in which b is an integer from 1 to k.

The set of large clusters is defined as $LC = \{C_i \mid i \leq b\}$ and the set of small clusters is defined as: $SC = \{C_j \mid j > b\}$.

Definition 5. (*Anomaly score*). Given a time series T that has been segmented into the set of subsequences and this set of subsequences has been grouped into a set of clusters $C = \{C_1, C_2, ..., C_k\}$ such that $|C_1| \geq |C_2| \geq ... \geq |C_k|$. The meanings of LC and SC are the same as they are defined in Definition 4. For each subsequence t of time series T, an anomaly score of t is defined as follows:

$$Score(t) = \begin{cases} |C_i| * \min\big(dist(t, C_j)\big), if \ t \in C_i, C_i \in SC \ and \ C_j \in LC(j = 1..b) \\ |C_i| * dist(t, C_i), if \ t \in C_i, C_i \in LC \end{cases}$$

where $dist(t, C_i)$ is the distance from subsequence t to cluster C_i. In the context of EP-ALeader and EP-ILeader, the distance from subsequence t to cluster C_i is the distance from subsequence t to the centroid of cluster C_i.

EP-ALeader differs from EP-ILeader only in Step 3. In Step 3, EP-ILeader uses ordinary Euclidean distance computation while EP-ALeader uses Euclidean distance with the two speeding up techniques previously presented.

The pseudo code of EP-ALeader is describes as follows.

- **Input**: A time series T with length m; compression rate R.
- **Output**: The pattern and position of the top anomaly.
- **Process**:

    Step 1: Divide the time series T into subsequences (pattern candidates) using the major extreme point method proposed by Fink and Gandhi [4].

    Step 2: Transform the extracted subsequences to those with the same length by using homothetic transformation [18].

    Step 3: Cluster the pattern candidates using the A-Leader algorithm and calculate the anomaly scores of all the candidates.

    Step 4: Identify the pattern candidate with the largest anomaly score as the top anomaly pattern of the time series.

4 Proposed Methods

In this section, we describe two proposed methods: TopK-EP-ALeader and TopK-EP-ALeader-S for detecting the top k-discords in static time series and streaming time series, respectively.

4.1 TopK-EP-ALeader for Finding Top k-discords in Static Time Series

For top-k discords detection in static time series, we propose TopK-EP-ALeader, which is an extension of EP-ALeader previously introduced. In our method, the definition of time series discords given by Keogh et al. [8] is used.

TopK-EP-ALeader is different from EP-ALeader only in Step 4. In Step 4, TopK-EP-ALeader returns the top-k discords which are the subsequences with the k-th largest anomaly scores while EP-ALeader returns only the 1-discord which is the subsequence with the largest anomaly score. Thanks to the existence of anomaly scores, top-k discords detection in a time series is straightforward and thus incurs no overhead.

4.2 TopK-EP-ALeader-S for Finding Top k-discords in Streaming Time Series

For detecting top-k discords in streaming time series, we propose TopK-EP-ALeader-S as an extended version of our TopK-EP-ALeader algorithm. The extended features of TopK-EP-ALeader-S are determined to overcome the challenges in finding top-k discords over streaming time series.

Compared to TopK-EP-ALeader, TopK-EP-ALeader-S is defined with a *moving window* to store time series in the streaming time series context. In this window, a local segment of streaming time series is stored as time goes by. Only the most recent data points are included in the moving window.

In addition, TopK-EP-ALeader-S works with a delayed update policy instead of an instant update policy for more efficiency.

4.2.1 The Circular Buffer

In our work, the moving window is implemented as a *circular buffer*. Indeed, this circular buffer stores a segment of a streaming time series that contains the most recent data points of the streaming time series. In addition, this buffer operates its contents in a circular fashion.

The working of the circular buffer is illustrated in Fig. 2. When handling streaming time series, after the buffer is full, a newly incoming data point will *overwrite* the oldest point in the current circular buffer.

The length of the buffer might have an impact on the efficiency of the top-k discords detection in streaming time series. In this work, the buffer length is estimated based on the *period* of the time series under consideration. The buffer length should be a multiple of the period of the time series in order that for periodic time series, the newly incoming data point and the obsolete data point will have some similar variation. There have been a few methods for periodicity detection in a time series.

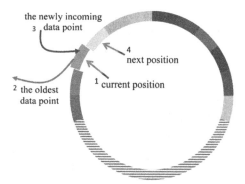

Fig. 2. Circular buffer.

To detect the period of a time series, we can apply a time series motif discovery method. Here we apply a method for estimating the length of the 1-motif in a time series, proposed by Phien [12]. This method is based on a variable-length motif discovery approach which uses grammar induction algorithm at its core.

4.2.2   The Delayed Update Policy

In the streaming time series context, as data points arrive continuously, it takes time to execute every process for detecting top-k discords with each new data point. For example, with our segment-based method, the Major Extrema method, A-Leader, and TopK-EP-ALeader need to be invoked to find top-k discords whenever a new data point arrives. Therefore, for more efficiency, we define a delayed update policy to determine when we should segment the time series again and then activate the anomaly detection process. In this delayed update policy, instead of the arrival of each new data point, we use the arrival of each new major extreme point to trigger the process of TopK-EP-ALeader-S. That is whenever a new major extreme point is found from newly incoming data points, a process of detecting new top-k discords in the current buffer is activated. At that time, we obtain a new subsequence that contains new data points. This subsequence is assigned to the nearest cluster. Furthermore, if the oldest data point in the buffer has not been the right end point of the oldest subsequence, the oldest subsequence is still kept in its certain cluster. The oldest subsequence is removed from its certain cluster if the oldest data point in the buffer is the last data point of the oldest subsequence.

4.2.3   TopK-EP-ALeader-S Algorithm

Using the circular buffer and the delayed update policy, TopK-EP-ALeader-S is described as follows. At first, when the circular buffer is full with the data points from a streaming time series, TopK-EP-ALeader-S invokes TopK-EP-ALeader to detect the top-k discords in the first buffer. After that starting history point, TopK-EP-ALeader-S begins to apply the delayed update policy for detecting more new top-k discords continuously from the remaining part of the streaming time series. From now on, TopK-EP-ALeader-S detects more top-k discords in the current buffer whenever the latest data point in the buffer is identified as a major extreme point. The pseudo code of TopK-EP-ALeader-S is presented in Algorithm 1.

Algorithm 1   *TopK-EP-ALeader-S algorithm*

Input: - y: a streaming time series
            - k: the number of the desired top-k discords
            - R: Compression rate
            -*Threshold*: Threshold for cluster assignment

Output:- The top-k discords and positions of the top-k discords

1: Read the time series data points into buffer B /* Initialize the buffer */
2:   Call   TopK-EP-ALeader($B,R,Threshold,Sub$-$List,Cluster,Positions$-of-top-k-
                                                                            $discords$)
      /* Detect the top-k discords in the current buffer;
      Sub-List is the list of the extracted subsequences. */
3: Print out the top-k discords found in the current buffer and their positions
4: **Repeat**
5:   **if** Type(Last Extreme Point) = Max **then**
6:      Find the next major minimum point in the newly incoming data points

7:   **else**   /* Last extreme point is minimum*/
8:      Find the next major maximum point in the newly incoming data points
9:   **endif**
10: ExtractNewSubsequence(B, *Sub*) /* *Sub* is the new extracted subsequence. */
11: Homothety(Sub, *NewSub*) /**NewSub* is the new transformed subsequence*/
12: Insert(Newsub, *NewSub-List*, *Cluster*)
      /* Insert the Newsub into *Cluster*;
      NewSub-List is the *Sub-List* after the Newsub is inserted. */
13: **if** all the data points in the first subsequence *FirstSub* in *NewList*
                                                    are out of buffer B **then**
14:     Delete(FirstSub, *NewSub-List*, *Cluster*)
            /* Remove the FirstSub out of *Cluster* and the *NewSub-List*} */
15: **endif**
16: Calculate anomaly scores for all the subsequences in *Cluster*
17: Print out the top-k discords corresponding to k subsequences with the greatest
                                                    anomaly scores and their positions
18: **Until** Stop

In Algorithm 1, on lines 1–3, TopK-EP-ALeader-S invokes TopK-EP-ALeader to detect the first top-k discords in the full buffer at the first time. From that moment, on lines 4–18, its process is executed repeatedly whenever a new major extreme point is obtained. In particular, on lines 5–9, TopK-EP-ALeader-S checks the arrival of a new major extreme point incrementally. On lines 10–12, a new subsequence is extracted, transformed with homothety, and then inserted into its nearest cluster. After that, on lines 13–15, the content of the circular buffer is checked for up-to-date data and the clusters are updated accordingly. On line 16, an anomaly score of each subsequence in the clusters is calculated as described previously. Finally, the top-*k* discords are returned from *k* subsequences with the greatest anomaly scores and their corresponding positions. It is also noted for the termination condition on line 18 of the loop **repeat.. until**. Normally this stop condition is true whenever the entire dataset has been processed. In reality, this iterative process keeps working if new data points still come.

5   Empirical Evaluation

To evaluate our proposed methods, we conduct an empirical evaluation study with two experiments as follows:

- Experiment 1: Evaluate TopK-EP-ALeader for detecting top-*k* discords in static time series.
- Experiment 2: Evaluate TopK-EP-ALeader-S for detecting top-*k* discords in streaming time series.

In our experiments, we use 9 datasets including *ECG5000, ECG, AEM, ERP, POWER, STOCK, Power_demand_Italy, AHA_0001_ECG*, and *AF_learning-set-n01*. The datasets *AF_learning-set-n01*, and *AHA_0001_ECG* are from The Research Resource for Complex Physiologic Signals [15]. The rest datasets are downloaded from the UCR Time series Classification/Clustering [3]. These datasets are from different domains: finance, medicine and industry. Table 1 describes all the datasets used in our experiments.

Table 1. Descriptions of all datasets in experiments.

No	Dataset	Source	Domain	Length	Period	Experiment
1	ECG5000	[3]	Medicine	5000	33	2
2	ECG	[3]	Medicine	20000	60	1, 2
3	AEM	[3]	Industry	17000	80	1, 2
4	ERP	[3]	Industry	10000	50	1,2
5	POWER	[3]	Industry	20000	226	1,2
6	STOCK	[3]	Finance	20000	100	1,2
7	Power_demand_Italy	[3]	Industry	1000	80	2
8	AHA_0001_ECG_2500	[15]	Medicine	2500	106	2
9	AF_learning-set-n01	[15]	Medicine	1280	433	2

We implemented the comparative methods in Visual C#. The experiments were conducted on an HP Intel(R) Core i7–3630 QM CPU with 2.40 GHz processor, 8 GB RAM.

Before conducting Experiment 1 and Experiment 2, we empirically evaluate A-Leader in comparison with I-Leader for the clustering process in our proposed methods. The experimental results on five datasets show that the clustering results of

A-Leader are similar to those of I-Leader, but on average, the clustering process of A-Leader is about 1.37 times faster than that of I-Leader.

Besides, we empirically evaluate EP-ALeader in comparison with EP-ILeader for the anomaly detection process. The experimental results on five datasets show that the 1-discord results of EP-ALeader match with those detected by Brute-Force and EP-ILeader, but on average, the execution of EP-ALeader is about 19.1 times faster than that of EP-ILeader.

We do not need to compare the efficiency of EP-ALeader with that of HOT SAX [8] since we already compared the efficiency of EP-ILeader to that of HOT SAX in our previous work [16] and knew that EP-ILeader could perform much faster than HOT SAX.

5.1   Experiment 1: Evaluation of TopK-EP-ALeader

This subsection reports the experimental results on TopK-EP-ALeader, a method for detecting top-k discords in static time series.

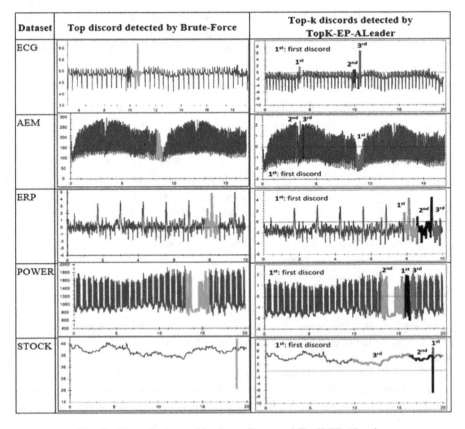

Fig. 3. Discords detected by Brute Force and TopK-EP-ALeader.

For checking the effectiveness of TopK-EP-ALeader, we check if top-*k* discords detected by TopK-EP-ALeader contain the top discord annotated by experts or not. Figure 3 shows that the top-*k* discords detected by TopK-EP-ALeader on each dataset include the top discord detected by Brute-Force. For example, Fig. 3 shows that with ECG dataset, Brute-Force only detects one top discord close to position 10000 and it ignores the 2nd discord and 3rd discord close to position 10000. Meanwhile, TopK-EP-ALeader exactly detects all three top discords in ECG dataset annotated by experts which are displayed in Fig. 5. This result shows that TopK-EP-ALeader is effective in finding top-*k* discords accurately from static time series.

For checking the efficiency of TopK-EP-ALeader, we compare the running time of TopK-EP-ALeader to that of TopK-EP-ILeader on five datasets. Since EP-ILeader is the algorithm that can detect the top discord in static time series [16], we have to modify EP-ILeader so that it can detect top-*k* discords in time series and name it TopK-EP-ILeader.

Table 2 depicts the running times (in seconds) of TopK-EP-ALeader and TopK-EP-ILeader over five test datasets. We can see that the runtime of TopK-EP-ALeader is less than that of TopK-EP-ILeader. In average, TopK-EP-ALeader can run faster than TopK-EP-ILeader about 1.9 times. This is obvious because TopK-EP-ALeader uses A-Leader clustering method and A-Leader is faster than I-Leader clustering method which is used in TopK-EP-ILeader.

Table 2. Running times (in seconds) of TopK-EP-ILeader and TopK-EP-ALeader.

Dataset	Length	Running time		TopK-EP- ILeader/ TopK-EP- ALeader
		TopK-EP- ILeader	TopK-EP- ALeader	
ECG	20,000	0.275	**0.234**	1.2
AEM	17,000	1.706	**0.508**	3.4
ERP	10,000	0.019	**0.011**	1.7
POWER	20,000	1.133	**0.661**	1.7
STOCK	20,000	0.016	**0.010**	1.6
			Average	**1.9**

5.2   Experiment 2: Evaluation of TopK-EP-ALeader-S

For TopK-EP-ALeader-S, we have to set one parameter: the buffer length which is based on the period of the time series. The period and buffer length used by TopK-EP-ALeader-S for each dataset are reported in Table 3. For example, as for POWER dataset, with its found period of 226, we set the buffer length to 452 (452 = 2*226).

Recall that TopK-EP-ALeader-S does not require the length of top-*k* discords as a parameter. The number *k* of top-*k* discords in our experiments is set to 3, the same value used in SKDIS method by Giao and Anh [5].

Table 3 describes nine datasets used in the evaluation of TopK-EP-ALeader-S for detecting top-k discords in streaming time series. Here, we set buffer length to a multiple of the period of each time series dataset.

Table 3. Buffer length for each dataset used in the experiments of detecting top-k discords in streaming time series.

Dataset	Length of dataset	Period	Buffer length
ECG	20000	60	12000
AEM	1000	80	480
ERP	10000	50	5000
POWER	1000	226	452
STOCK	20000	100	10000
Power_demand_Italy	1000	80	480
AHA_0001_ECG_2500	2500	106	1272
AF_learning-set-n01	1280	433	866
ECG5000	5000	33	2310

5.2.1   Effectiveness of TopK-EP-ALeader-S

For an illustration, we test the effectiveness of TopK-EP-ALeader-S in one dataset: ECG (electrocardiogram). Figure 4 shows the shapes of discords (in bold) in ECG dataset after TopK-EP-ALeader-S identifies some major extreme points in the streaming time series context. Figure 4 displays a view of the local segment of the time series after pushed into the buffer. The positions of discords in this case are about 4000, 10000, and 10500. It can be seen that our discord results over ECG dataset match those found by HOT SAX reported in [8] which are shown in Fig. 5. These three discords reported in [8] have also been detected as time progresses by TopK-EP-ALeader-S in our experiment. So, we can conclude that our discords detected by TopK-EP-ALeader-S match the top-3 discords in ECG dataset annotated by experts.

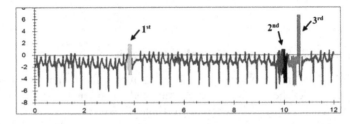

Fig. 4. Images of the top-3 discords detected by TopK-EP-ALeader-S.

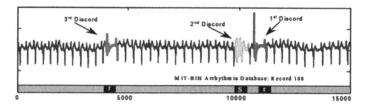

Fig. 5. Images of the top-3 discords in ECG dataset annotated by experts [8].

5.2.2   Efficiency of TopK-EP-ALeader-S

Table 4 shows the execution time (in seconds) of TopK-EP-ALeader-S after each new subsequence arrives over each of the nine datasets simulated as streaming time series. Moreover, we skip comparing the efficiency of TopK-EP-ALeader-S with those of the existing works like SKDIS [5] because of different approaches. SKDIS used the window-based approach while TopK-EP-ALeader-S uses the segmentation-based approach.

Table 4. Execution times (in seconds) of TopK-EP-ALeader-S after each new subsequence arrives.

No	Dataset	Execution time
1	ECG	0.006
2	AEM	0.005
3	ERP	0.004
4	POWER	0.007
5	STOCK	0.003
6	Power_demand_Italy	0.006
7	AHA_0001_ECG_2500	0.005
8	AF_learning-set-n01	0.007
9	ECG5000	0.005
Average		0.0053

To test the ability of immediate response of our proposed algorithm for streaming time series, we measure the execution time from the time point when a new major extreme point appears to the time point when the corresponding top-*k* discords are obtained. The response times for nine streaming time series are reported in Table 4. Table 4 shows that on average, TopK-EP-ALeader-S algorithm can respond immediately in about 5.3 ms whenever a new major extreme point appears.

Now, we answer the question how our online anomaly detection method meets the requirements of real world applications. Consider one experimented dataset: ECG (electrocardiogram data). As for ECG dataset, the full period of a heartbeat is about one second. Each extreme point will mark a half of the heartbeat (i.e. 0.5 s). Our TopK-EP-ALeader-S can detect top-*k* discords in about 6 ms (see Table 4). So, the speed of TopK-EP-ALeader-S is about 83 times faster than the transfer rate of ECG data. So, the above analysis shows that TopK-EP-ALeader-S, our proposed algorithm for discovering top-k discords in streaming time series, can meet the practical requirement for real time anomaly detection on streaming power consumption data and ECG data.

6 Conclusions and Future Works

In this paper, we have proposed two effective and efficient methods for detecting top-k discords in static and streaming time series, TopK-EP-ALeader and TopK-EP-ALeader-S, respectively. These two methods hinge on major extrema-based segmentation and incremental subsequence clustering. In terms of effectiveness, the discords found by our two methods on several benchmark datasets match those annotated by the experts. In terms of efficiency, our two methods give fast response to discover top-k discords in both static and streaming time series via the experimental results on several time series in various application domains. Such better performance of our two methods is from a significant contribution of A-Leader clustering algorithm for incremental subsequence clustering and EP-ALeader algorithm for anomaly detection. As a result, our two methods can meet the practical requirements of time-critical real-world applications in both static and streaming time series contexts.

In the future, we plan to utilize TopK-EP-ALeader-S in some various real-world applications. Parallelizing the process of TopK-EP-ALeader on GPU is also of our interest for more efficiency.

References

1. Ahmad, S., Lavin, A., Purdy, S., Agha, Z.: Unsupervised real-time anomaly detection for streaming data. Neurocomputing **262**, 134–147 (2017)
2. Bu, Y., Leung, T.W., Fu, A.W.C., Keogh, E., Pei, J., Meshkin, S.: WAT: Finding top-k discords in time series database. In: Proceedings of the 2007 SIAM International Conference on Data Mining, pp. 449–454 (2007)
3. Chen, Y., et al.: The UCR Time series Classification/Clustering. https://www.cs.ucr.edu/~eamonn/time_series_data/. Accessed 2017
4. Fink, E., Gandhi, H.S.: Important extrema of time series. In: Proceedings of IEEE International Conference on System, Man and Cybernetics, pp. 366–372. Montreal, Canada (2007)
5. Giao, B.C., Anh, D.T.: Efficient search for top-k discords in streaming time series. Int. J. Bus. Intell. Data Min. **16**(4), 397–417 (2020)
6. Hartigan, J.A.: Clustering Algorithms. Wiley, New York (1975)
7. He, Z., Xu, X., Deng, S.: Discovering cluster-based local outliers. Pattern Recogn. Lett. **24**(9–10), 1641–1650 (2003)
8. Keogh, E., Lin, J., Fu, A.: HOT SAX: efficiently finding the most unusual time series subsequence. In: Proceedings of the Fifth IEEE International Conference on Data mining, pp. 226–233. Houston, Texas (2005)
9. Linardi, M., Zhu, Y., Palpanas, T., Keogh, E.: Matrix profile goes MAD: variable-length motif and discord discovery in data series. Data Min. Knowl. Disc. **34**(4), 1022–1071 (2020). https://doi.org/10.1007/s10618-020-00685-w

10. Liu, Y., Chen, X., Wang, F., Yin, J.: Efficient detection of discords for time series stream. In: Li, Q., Feng, L., Pei, J., Wang, S.X., Zhou, X., Zhu, Q.-M. (eds.) APWeb/WAIM -2009. LNCS, vol. 5446, pp. 629–634. Springer, Heidelberg (2009). https://doi.org/10.1007/978-3-642-00672-2_62

11. Ngo, D.H., Veeravalli, B.: Design of a real-time morphology-based anomaly detection methods from ECG streams. In: Proceedings of IEEE International Conference on Bioinformatics and Biomedicine (BIBM), pp. 829–836 (2015)

12. Phien, N.N.: An efficient method for estimating time series motif length using sequitur algorithm. In: Meng, L., Zhang, Y. (eds.) MLICOM 2018. LNICSSITE, vol. 251, pp. 531–538. Springer, Cham (2018). https://doi.org/10.1007/978-3-030-00557-3_52

13. Rakthanmanon, T., et al.: Searching and mining trillions of time series subsequences under dynamic time warping. In: Proceedings of the 18th ACM SIGKDD International Conference on Knowledge Discovery and Data Mining, pp. 262–270, Beijing, China (2012)

14. Sanchez, H., Bustos, B.: Anomaly detection in streaming time series based on bounding boxes. In: Traina, A.J.M., Traina, C., Cordeiro, R.L.F. (eds.) SISAP 2014. LNCS, vol. 8821, pp. 201–213. Springer, Cham (2014). https://doi.org/10.1007/978-3-319-11988-5_19

15. The Research Resource for Complex Physiologic Signals. https://www.physionet.org. Accessed 22 Oct 2020

16. Thuy, H.T.T., Anh, D.T., Chau, V.T.N.: A novel method for time series anomaly detection based on segmentation and clustering. In: 2018 10th International Conference on Knowledge and Systems Engineering (KSE), pp. 276–281. IEEE (2018)

17. Thuy, H.T.T., Anh, D.T., Chau, V.T.N.: Incremental Clustering for time series data based on an improved leader algorithm. In: 2019 IEEE-RIVF International Conference on Computing and Communication Technologies (RIVF), pp. 1–6. IEEE (2019)

18. Truong, C.D., Anh, D.T.: An efficient method for motif and anomaly detection in time series based on clustering. Int. J. Bus. Intell. Data Min. **10**(4), 356–377 (2015)

Hardware/Software Co-design for Convolutional Neural Networks Acceleration: A Survey and Open Issues

Cuong Pham-Quoc[1,2]([✉]), Xuan-Quang Nguyen[1,2], and Tran Ngoc Thinh[1,2]

[1] Ho Chi Minh City University of Technology (HCMUT),
Ho Chi Minh City, Vietnam
{cuongpham,nxquang,tnthinh}@hcmut.edu.vn
[2] Vietnam National University - Ho Chi Minh City (VNU-HCM),
Ho Chi Minh City, Vietnam

Abstract. In this paper, we survey hardware/software co-design approaches in the literature to accelerate Convolutional neural networks, one of the two successful forms of Deep Neural Networks. We classify these approaches according to target platforms used to accelerate CNNs, including FPGA-based and ASIC-based. Due to the flexibility of FPGAs, we mainly focus on FPGA-based designs. These designs are categorized into sub-classes according to optimization techniques used. We then analyze in detail to compare FPGA-based hardware accelerator systems for CNNs regarding working frequency and performance efficiency. Through the survey, we also identify open issues for this research topic. These challenges can be research directions for optimizing performance, accuracy, and energy consumption of hardware accelerator systems for CNN using the hardware/software co-design approach.

Keywords: Hardware/software co-design · Convolutional neural networks · FPGA · ASIC

1 Introduction

Convolutional Neural Networks (CNNs), one of the two most successful forms of Deep Neural Networks (DNNs) along with Recurrent Neural Networks [14] (RNNs), are becoming a dominant approach in machine learning for different applications such as image classification, voice recognition, or natural languages processing. In recent years, many researchers focus on improving the accuracy of DNN models that make these models require high computing power, consume much energy, and use a large amount of memory [15]. For example, the VGG19 CNN model image classification with 224×224 input pixels may take up to

P. Cong Vinh and A. Rakib (Eds.): ICCASA 2021, LNICST 409, pp. 164–178, 2021.
https://doi.org/10.1007/978-3-030-93179-7_13

39B+ floating-point operations (FLOPs) and need more than 500 MB of memory storage parameters [35]. Therefore, executing the inference phase of CNN models in suitable platforms is non-trivial work. With the current technology, traditional CPUs can offer up to ~100GFLOPs per second while using more than 1 J (J) of energy per 1GOP. Hence, traditional CPUs cannot meet the requirements of high-performance and low power for CNNs-based applications.

Meanwhile, to continue improving the performance of computing systems, including embedded and edge computing, at the end of Moore's Law and Dennard scaling [42], system architects develop a new paradigm that concurrently optimizes both software and hardware for application domains. The most promising approach in this paradigm is to design specialized high-performance and energy-efficient hardware-based computing cores to perform a hefty workload. Two well-known instances of this approach are general-purpose graphic processor units (GPGPUs) and hardware accelerator systems. Although GPGPUs offer tremendous potential for the training and inference phases of DNNs [36], they suffer from energy inefficiency. Therefore, both academia and industry have already applied fully specialized hardware accelerators for DNNs such as neural processing units (NPUs), in which the Tensor processing unit is an excellent example [6]. It is also crucial to develop software support when developing specialized hardware accelerators because systems usually cannot fully utilize them without appropriate software support. These software supports include operating-system-level supports such as direct memory access supports and compiler-level supports such as forming new instructions in ISA (instruction set architecture). Therefore, to accelerate DNNs, we need a hardware/software co-design approach to develop both hardware and software for better optimization.

This paper surveys the cutting-edge systems designed and implemented with the hardware-software co-design approach for accelerating CNNs-based applications. We categorize these systems according to the hardware technologies, including Field Programmable Gate Arrays (FPGAs) and Application Specific Integrated Circuits (ASICs). Although in the literature, there exist some related surveys recently [10,23,43], they mainly focus on analyzing techniques used to optimized hardware accelerator cores such as pruning, quantization, or data reuse. In contrast, we focus on the co-design approach to eventually resulting in system performance and energy consumption. We also identify open issues for accelerations of CNNs with the hardware/software co-design approach so that researchers can consider them as future work.

The rest of the paper is organized as follows. Section 2 gives an overview of the CNN architecture and the background of the hardware/software co-design approach. A survey of CNN accelerations with HW/SW co-design is presented and analyzed carefully in Sect. 3. Based on the study, we deliver open issues for future work of the research topic in Sect. 4. Finally, we conclude our paper in Sect. 5.

2 Preliminary

This section presents an overview of the CNN architecture upon which many studies in the literature try to accelerate with the hardware/software (HW/SW) co-design approach. To clarify the co-design approach, we also introduce the HW/SW co-design approach background in this section.

2.1 Convolutional Neural Networks

Figure 1 illustrates a traditional simple CNN. Typically, a CNN consists of Convolution layers and Fully connected layers. Convolution layers usually calculate two main operators, including 2D convolutions (2D Conv) and subsampling ($X-$pooling). The input, e.g., a 32×32 pixels color image with three red, green, and blue channels, is convoluted with convolutions kernels, e.g., 5×5 to create $C1$ feature maps, e.g., 9 28×28 feature maps. Consequently, these feature maps are sampled with different pooling functions (max-pooling or average-pooling) to reduce the redundancy of feature maps. For example, a 2×2 max-pooling function in Fig. 1 reduces 9 28×28 feature maps to 9 14×14 feature maps. The two operations can be repeated several times depending on application domains and experts. Outputs of the Convolution layers (2D feature maps) are converted to a 1D vector. Each vector element is connected to a neuron of a traditional neural network in the Fully connected layers for classification.

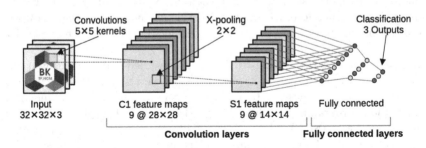

Fig. 1. An overview of convolution neural network

In CNN models, the Convolution layers are the most critical operations and contribute more than 99% of processing time [10]. The 2D Conv operation is given by Eq. 1.

$$F(x,y) = f(\sum_{j=0}^{k-1}\sum_{i=0}^{k-1} I(x - \frac{k-1}{2} + i, y - \frac{k-1}{2} + j) \times W(i,j) + b) \quad (1)$$

where $F(x,y)$ is the convolution value of the point (x,y) in the output feature maps, f is the activation function used for CNN (e.g., Tanh, Sigmoid, etc.), k is the size of the kernel W (odd number), $I(x - \frac{k-1}{2} + i, y - \frac{k-1}{2} + j)$ is a pixel value in the input feature maps, and b is the bias.

2.2   Hardware Software Co-design

Figure 2 presents the flow of the hardware/software co-design approach. Hardware/software co-design exploits trade-offs between hardware and software to achieve system-level goals such as performance, time-to-market, or faster and better integration by designing both hardware and software concurrently [3]. Hardware/software co-design approaches can be classified into three categories. Those are co-design of embedded systems, co-design of application-specific instruction set processors (ASIPs), and co-design for reconfigurable computing (FPGAs). Compared to the first former one, the two latter ones offer more performance and suitable for accelerating computationally-intensive applications like CNNs. The co-design of ASIPs targets ASIC technologies that are not flexible and able to optimize after manufactured. In contrast, the co-design of reconfigurable computing offers more rooms to personalize for a particular application. Therefore, many studies in the literature mainly exploit the latest approach.

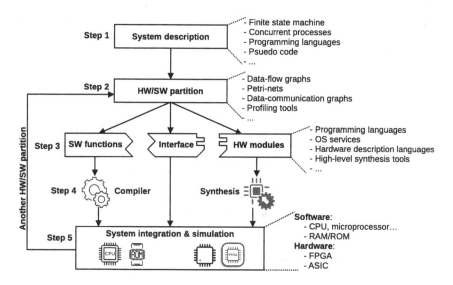

Fig. 2. The hardware/software co-design flow

3   CNN Accelerations with the HW/SW Co-design Approach

This section analyzes hardware accelerator systems for CNNs based on the hardware/software co-design in the literature. We categorize these proposals into classes FPGA-based acceleration and ASIC-based acceleration.

3.1 FPGA-Based Acceleration

Nowadays, FPGAs play an essential role in data sampling and processing industries due to their flexibility in custom hardware, highly parallel architecture,
and low power consumption. Most FPGA-based accelerations are based on the
general architecture of the FPGA-based HW accelerator, as shown in Fig. 3. At
the same time, there is a soaring demand for high-energy efficiency hardware
implementations in the artificial intelligence field and massively parallel computing capacity for training and inference CNNs. Some advantages of FPGAs
can be listed, such as good power and performance, efficiency in parallel processing, supporting customized architecture, high on-chip memory bandwidth,
low latency, high reliability, high accuracy, and a relatively short time to market. However, FPGAs usually suffer from low working frequency compared to
ASIC or GPU designs. Therefore, hardware system architects can use several
optimization techniques to improve the throughput of proposed systems. The
surveys below are categorized according to optimization techniques used, including **increasing parallelism**, **reducing the complexity of computing**, and
exploiting data reuse. Although a single proposal may deploy multiple optimization techniques, we classify them according to the method that contributes
most to performance improvement.

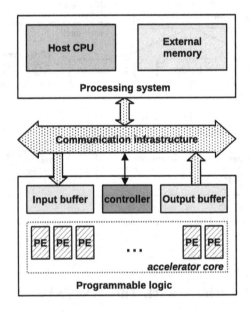

Fig. 3. The generic architecture of FPGA-based HW accelerator

Increasing Parallelism: Due to many hardware resources, FPGAs offer a
high level of parallelism. This optimization technique builds several processing

elements (PEs) or exploits the loop unrolling approach to accelerate the system performance. Kaiyuan Guo et al. [8] (**K. Guo**) proposed an FPGA-based Aristotle architecture for accelerating CNNs. In this proposed architecture, an array of PEs deployed in reconfigurable fabrics calculates multiple 2D convolution operations. The PEs can process convolutions in a pipeline model to achieve the 1 pixel per cycle throughput. The entire computing systems include a CPU, external memory, and FPGA fabrics for convolution operations. A shared memory performs data communication between the host processor and PEs in the FPGA fabrics. Other works exploiting this optimization technique in the literature as follows. Research in [17] (**H. Li**) introduced a hardware accelerator CNN with all layers concurrently working in a pipeline model. Xinhan Lin et al. proposed an FPGA-based CNN with the layer clusters paralleling mapping method [19] (**X. Lin**). Parallel structures for CNNs on FPGA were suggested in [20] (**Z. Liu**). Yufei Ma et al. introduced their FPGA-based CNN architecture, fully utilizing hardware resources to achieve higher performance [22] (**Y. Ma**). The novel parallel convolution binarized architecture was proposed in [44] (**Y. Li**). Research in [48] (X. Zhang) suggested a fine-grained layer-based pipeline architecture for FPGA-based CNN's acceleration. A highly parallelized Winograd convolution computing engine was developed in [31] (**A. Podili**). Mohammad Motamedi et al. exploited exploiting all sources of parallelism in a deep CNN [26] (**M. Mota**). There may exist other works in the literature that apply the increasing parallelism technique. However, we only focus on research published in high-ranked conferences and journals and reporting detailed parameters for comparison. Figure 4 compares the proposals for maximum working frequency (MHz) and performance efficiency (Giga-operations-per-second per Watt - GOPS/W).

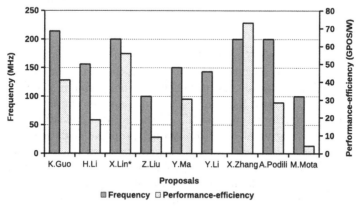

* this work did not provide power consumption; we used the experiment FPGA device to estimate. Y.Ma's proposal mentioned performance in term of frames per second instead of GOPS

Fig. 4. Maximum working frequency and performance-efficiency comparison of the parallelism proposals

Reducing the Complexity of Computing: By reducing the complexity of convolution operations, for example, pruning, multiplexer-free, shift-operator, or Binarized Neural Network (BNN), this optimization can improve the performance. Yifan Yang et al. [45] proposed the **Synetgy** FPGA-based accelerator and a novel ConvNet model for accelerating 1×1 convolutions. Due to 1-bit weight and 4-bit input, output, and activation function, the proposed system achieved an impressive improvement in performance when compared to other works. M. Ghasemzadeh et al. proposed **ReBNet** [5] for the FPGA design that uses Binary CNN with the standard Xnor operation. The low-bit-width computing module for FPGA was introduced in [12] (**L. Jiao**). Authors in [25] (**D. Moss**) presented their FPGA-based accelerators with both binary weights and binary activation functions. The FPGA-based BNN architecture with the XNOR-MAC circuit streaming operation was proposed in [27] (**N. Hiroki**). Eriko Nurvitadhi et al. [28] (**N. Eriko**) proposed a hardware accelerator architecture for BNNs. Research in [32] (**B. Prost**) introduced the architecture of an FPGA-based accelerator for convolutional ternary neural networks. **FINN**, a novel optimizations for mapping BNNs onto FPGAs, was presented in [38]. FPGA-based accelerators for very low precision were proposed in [49] (**Z. Ritchie**). S. Liang et al. introduced their **FP-BNN** architecture [18] with multipliers replaced by XNOR and shift operators. The Bank-Balanced Sparsity, which is a novel and efficient FPGA accelerator implementation, was presented in [1] (**S. Cao**). S. Kala et al. introduced CNN FPGA-based processing units for computing both general element-wise matrix multiplications and Winograd filtering algorithm [13] (**S. Kala**). Research in [40] proposed the FPGA-based acceleration of hybrid extremely low-bit-width CNNs called (**ELB-NN**). Caiwen Ding et al. presented their REQ-YOLO framework to implement efficient FPGA-based object detection [4] (**C. Ding**). Figure 5 compares the working frequencies and performance efficiency of the proposals.

Exploiting Data Reuse: Due to the limitation of on-chip buffer size (Block RAM), the data reuse optimization technique helps the system to reduce communication overhead when transferring data between the on-chip buffer and external memory. In an FPGA-based hardware accelerator system, data communication overhead usually contributes up to 50% of the entire application's execution time [30]. Jichen Wang et al. [39] (**J. Wang**) proposed a data reuse scheme called ping-pong to avoid data transfer between external memory and buffers. Research in [21] (**L. Lu**) introduced an FPGA-based architecture for employing line-buffer structure to accelerate matrix multiplication in CNNs. The FP-DNN framework was designed in [7] (**Y. Guan**) to optimize communication bandwidth used for FPGA-based CNN implementations. Qiu Jiantao et al. proposed an FPGA-based design for CNNs that reduced memory footprint to improve the performance [33] (**Q. Jiantao**). Research in [41] (**X. Wei**) implemented a systolic array architecture for low global data transfer to accelerate CNNs. Yongming Shen et al. proposed the **Escher** architecture [34] for FPGA-based CNNs acceleration focusing on data buffered on-chip. Kaiyuan Guo et al. introduced

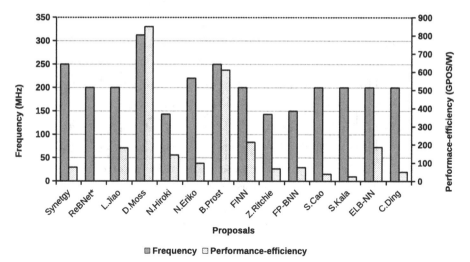

Fig. 5. Maximum working frequency and performance-efficiency comparison of the reducing complexity proposals

the **Angle-Eye** architecture [9] for FPGA-based CNNs to fully utilize the on-chip buffer. Similar to other optimization techniques, there may exist some other related work in the literature. However, we only focus on studies published by top conference publications and reporting detailed parameters for comparison. We compare proposals that use this technique in Fig. 6.

Figure 7 compares the three above optimization techniques in terms of average operational frequency and performance efficiency. Due to the reduction of complexity, computing cores in this technique usually require fewer hardware resources. Therefore, they often function at a higher frequency and provide better performance than computing cores in other techniques. However, they typically suffer from lower accuracy. However, they usually suffer from lower accuracy. The two approaches, exploiting data reuse and increasing parallelism, offer the same operating frequency and performance. Although they are not as good as the reducing complexity technique, they provide higher accurate results.

3.2 ASIC-Based Acceleration

Compared to FPGA design, ASIC-based acceleration suffers from longer time-to-market, higher design effort, and implementation cost. However, ASIC-based acceleration systems offer higher performance and energy efficiency than FPGA accelerators. Different from FPGA-based HW accelerator architecture, ASIC-based accelerations for CNNs can exploit different architectures. Moreover, instead of developing only hardware-based convolution cores, ASIC-based approaches usually implement entire systems, including general-purpose host processors and convolution cores.

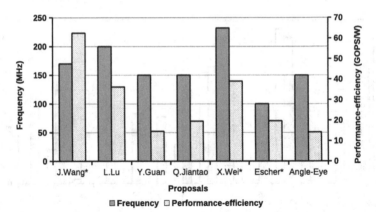

* These works did not provide power consumption; we used the experiment FPGA
devices to estimate.

Fig. 6. Maximum working frequency and Performance-efficiency comparison of the
data-reuse technique proposals

Hokchhay Tann et al. [37] presented their MF-DFP accelerator for CNN models. The architecture includes an array of neural processing units (NPUs) and
three independent buffers for inputs, outputs, and kernels. Each NPU contains
some processing units for processing 16 neurons. 8-bit quantizations are used
to eliminate multipliers resulting in only ∼1.1% accuracy reduction. Table 1
summarize details of some well-known and latest ASIC-based CNN hardware
accelerator systems in the literature.

Table 1. Comparison of the ASIC-based accelerators for CNNs

Proposals	Throughput	Max. Freq.	Technology	Area	Power
MF-DFP [37]	N/A	250 MHz	65 nm	1.99 mm^2	138.96 mW
Eyeriss [2]	42 GOPS	250 MHz	65 nm	12.25 mm^2	332 mW
Envision [24]	408 GOPS	200 MHz	28 nm	1.87 mm^2	300 mW
UNPU [16]	345.6 GOPS	200 MHz	65 nm	16 mm^2	297 mW
Sticker [46]	5,638 GOPS	200 MHz	65 nm	7.8 mm^2	248.4 mW
D.Han [11]	51.2 GOPS	200 MHz	65 nm	3.52 mm^2	126 mW
SNAP [47]	7,884 GOPS	480 MHz	16 nm	2.4 mm^2	364 mW

4   Open Issues for FPGA-Based Hardware/Software Co-design

As mentioned above, although ASIC-based designs offer higher performance and
energy efficiency, they suffer from several obstacles, exceptionally long time-to-

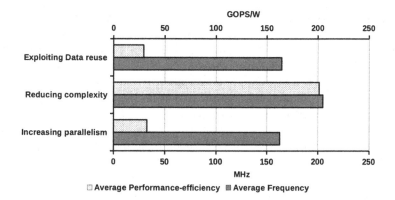

Fig. 7. Comparison of the three optimizations mentioned above

market. Therefore, we mainly focus on the FPGA-based approach only because there exists more room for optimization with different methods. Although many have proposed several FPGA-based hardware accelerator systems in the literature and industry, future research should consider multiple open issues when working with this approach. To the best of our knowledge, we recognize five different possible problems compared to other accelerator approaches.

1. **Low-frequency:** As shown in the previous section, FPGA-based accelerator cores function at a lower frequency than ASIC. Hence, peak throughputs of these cores are also worst than ASIC. Therefore, future research should focus on pipeline design or critical datapath optimization to enhance FPGA-based computing core working frequency. Besides, modern FPGA architecture should offer more complex configurable logic blocks and equip higher performance multiplication units inside.
2. **Design time:** Although design time and time-to-market of FPGA-based accelerator cores generally are better than ASIC, these periods are much more extended than GPU. Therefore, high-level synthesis design tools that directly synthesize high-level programming language CNN-based applications to hardware description language modules should be used more frequently. In addition, FPGA vendors and researchers should focus on the performance optimization of these tools and support more high-level programming languages instead of only C/C++ and Python.
3. **Low buffer size:** One of the most critical issues of FPGA-based convolution computing cores is the limited size of on-chip buffers. It, in turn, increases processing time when processing more and more data. While designers or architects can configure the size of memory in ASIC and GPU's internal memory is enormous, FPGAs suffer from a low amount of on-chip memory. Therefore, FPGA-based CNN computing cores should be equipped with a better memory hierarchy. Distributed memory can also be a solution for the low buffer issue. However, this may increase the complexity of the design. This problem, in turn, can reduce the working frequency of the system.

4. **Data communication overhead:** As discussed in [30], the communication overhead of a generic FPGA-based accelerator system contributes to half of system processing time. Therefore reducing data communication overhead is an essential demand for future research, especially in CNN-based applications due to enormous data. Furthermore, researchers should investigate high-performance communication infrastructure for host and cores in CNNs such as hybrid interconnect or reconfigurable on-chip interconnection networks [29].

5. **Design space exploration:** Finally, one of the most critical requirements to achieve to most optimized systems in terms of performance and energy efficiency is design space exploration. Compared to GPU designs, FPGA-based designs suffer from longer design time. Therefore, it is much difficult for us to explore the design space of FPGA-based systems than GPU. Hence, researchers should develop estimation tools or design space exploration tools for CNNs-based applications for FPGAs. Researchers must have much knowledge in both deep neural networks and FPGA design to cope with this issue.

Figure 8 compares the difficulty levels of the five open issues in hardware/software co-design for CNNs. To the best of our experience, the **design space exploration** is the most challenging issue since researchers need to be experts in both deep neural networks and FPGA design. Meanwhile, **design time** is the most straightforward issue due to many high-level synthesis tools released in the past years.

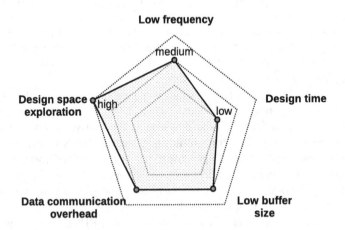

Fig. 8. The difficulty level of the five open issues

5   Conclusion

In this paper, we present one of the most promising approaches for accelerating the performance of convolutional neural networks computing, the hardware/software co-design. We survey proposals submitted in high-ranking journals and conferences for this approach. We categorize these proposals into two classes, FPGA-based and ASIC-based accelerators. The former accelerators offer more room to optimize than the latter one. Therefore, we mainly analyze and compare proposed systems with the first category. We finally introduce five different research open issues for future work on this topic. These hardware/software co-design challenges for accelerating CNNs are research directions for further optimizing the performance and energy of CNN-based applications.

Acknowledgment. This research is funded by Vietnam National University - Ho Chi Minh City under grant number B2021-20-02.

References

1. Cao, S., et al.: Efficient and effective sparse LSTM on FPGA with bank-balanced sparsity. In: Proceedings of the 2019 ACM/SIGDA International Symposium on Field-Programmable Gate Arrays, FPGA 2019, pp. 63–72. Association for Computing Machinery (2019)
2. Chen, Y.H., Krishna, T., Emer, J.S., Sze, V.: Eyeriss: an energy-efficient reconfigurable accelerator for deep convolutional neural networks. IEEE J. Solid-State Circ. **52**(1), 127–138 (2017)
3. DeMicheli, G., Sami, M.: Hardware/Software Co-design. Nato Science Series E. Springer, Netherlands (1996). https://www.springer.com/gp/book/9780792338833
4. Ding, C., Wang, S., Liu, N., Xu, K., Wang, Y., Liang, Y.: REQ-YOLO: a resource-aware, efficient quantization framework for object detection on FPGAs. In: Proceedings of the 2019 ACM/SIGDA International Symposium on Field-Programmable Gate Arrays, FPGA 2019, pp. 33–42. Association for Computing Machinery, New York (2019). https://doi.org/10.1145/3289602.3293904
5. Ghasemzadeh, M., Samragh, M., Koushanfar, F.: ReBNet: residual binarized neural network. In: 2018 IEEE 26th Annual International Symposium on Field-Programmable Custom Computing Machines (FCCM), pp. 57–64. IEEE Computer Society, Los Alamitos, May 2018
6. Google Inc.: Cloud tensor processing units. https://cloud.google.com/tpu/docs/tpus. Accessed 2 June 2021
7. Guan, Y., et al.: FP-DNN: an automated framework for mapping deep neural networks onto FPGAs with RTL-HLS hybrid templates. In: 2017 IEEE 25th Annual International Symposium on Field-Programmable Custom Computing Machines (FCCM), pp. 152–159 (2017)
8. Guo, K., Han, S., Yao, S., Wang, Y., Xie, Y., Yang, H.: Software-hardware codesign for efficient neural network acceleration. IEEE Micro **37**(2), 18–25 (2017)
9. Guo, K., et al.: Angel-eye: a complete design flow for mapping CNN onto embedded FPGA. IEEE Trans. Comput. Aided Des. Integr. Circ. Syst. **37**(1), 35–47 (2018)
10. Guo, K., Zeng, S., Yu, J., Wang, Y., Yang, H.: [DL] a survey of FPGA-based neural network inference accelerators. ACM Trans. Reconfigurable Technol. Syst. **12**(1), 1–26 (2019)

11. Han, D., Lee, J., Lee, J., Yoo, H.J.: A low-power deep neural network online learning processor for real-time object tracking application. IEEE Trans. Circ. Syst. I Regul. Pap. **66**(5), 1794–1804 (2019)
12. Jiao, L., Luo, C., Cao, W., Zhou, X., Wang, L.: Accelerating low bit-width convolutional neural networks with embedded FPGA. In: 2017 27th International Conference on Field Programmable Logic and Applications (FPL), pp. 1–4 (2017)
13. Kala, S., Jose, B.R., Mathew, J., Nalesh, S.: High-performance CNN accelerator on FPGA using unified winograd-GEMM architecture. IEEE Trans. Very Large Scale Integr. (VLSI) Syst. **27**(12), 2816–2828 (2019). https://doi.org/10.1109/TVLSI. 2019.2941250
14. Khan, A., Sohail, A., Zahoora, U., Qureshi, A.S.: A survey of the recent architectures of deep convolutional neural networks. Artif. Intell. Rev. **53**(8), 5455–5516 (2020). https://doi.org/10.1007/s10462-020-09825-6
15. Lacey, G., Taylor, G.W., Areibi, S.: Deep learning on FPGAs: past, present, and future (2016). https://arxiv.org/abs/1602.04283
16. Lee, J., Kim, C., Kang, S., Shin, D., Kim, S., Yoo, H.J.: UNPU: a 50.6 TOPS/W unified deep neural network accelerator with 1b-to-16b fully-variable weight bit-precision. In: 2018 IEEE International Solid - State Circuits Conference - (ISSCC), pp. 218–220 (2018)
17. Li, H., Fan, X., Jiao, L., Cao, W., Zhou, X., Wang, L.: A high performance FPGA-based accelerator for large-scale convolutional neural networks. In: 2016 26th International Conference on Field Programmable Logic and Applications (FPL), pp. 1–9 (2016)
18. Liang, S., Yin, S., Liu, L., Luk, W., Wei, S.: FP-BNN: binarized neural network on FPGA. Neurocomputing **275**, 1072–1086 (2018)
19. Lin, X., Yin, S., Tu, F., Liu, L., Li, X., Wei, S.: LCP: a layer clusters paralleling mapping method for accelerating inception and residual networks on FPGA. In: 2018 55th ACM/ESDA/IEEE Design Automation Conference (DAC), pp. 1–6 (2018)
20. Liu, Z., Dou, Y., Jiang, J., Xu, J.: Automatic code generation of convolutional neural networks in FPGA implementation. In: 2016 International Conference on Field-Programmable Technology (FPT), pp. 61–68 (2016)
21. Lu, L., Liang, Y., Xiao, Q., Yan, S.: Evaluating fast algorithms for convolutional neural networks on FPGAs. In: 2017 IEEE 25th Annual International Symposium on Field-Programmable Custom Computing Machines (FCCM), pp. 101–108 (2017)
22. Ma, Y., Cao, Y., Vrudhula, S., Seo, J.S.: Optimizing loop operation and dataflow in FPGA acceleration of deep convolutional neural networks. In: Proceedings of the 2017 ACM/SIGDA International Symposium on Field-Programmable Gate Arrays, FPGA 2017, pp. 45–54. ACM, New York (2017)
23. Mittal, S.: A survey of FPGA-based accelerators for convolutional neural networks. Neural Comput. Appl. **32**(4), 1109–1139 (2020)
24. Moons, B., Uytterhoeven, R., Dehaene, W., Verhelst, M.: 14.5 envision: a 0.26-to-10TOPS/W subword-parallel dynamic-voltage-accuracy-frequency-scalable convolutional neural network processor in 28nm FDSOI. In: 2017 IEEE International Solid-State Circuits Conference (ISSCC), pp. 246–247 (2017)
25. Moss, D.J.M., et al.: High performance binary neural networks on the xeon+FPGA^{TM} platform. In: 2017 27th International Conference on Field Programmable Logic and Applications (FPL), pp. 1–4 (2017)

26. Motamedi, M., Gysel, P., Akella, V., Ghiasi, S.: Design space exploration of FPGA-based deep convolutional neural networks. In: 2016 21st Asia and South Pacific Design Automation Conference (ASP-DAC), pp. 575–580 (2016)
27. Nakahara, H., Fujii, T., Sato, S.: A fully connected layer elimination for a binarizec convolutional neural network on an FPGA. In: 2017 27th International Conference on Field Programmable Logic and Applications (FPL), pp. 1–4 (2017)
28. Nurvitadhi, E., Sheffield, D., Sim, J., Mishra, A., Venkatesh, G., Marr, D.: Accelerating binarized neural networks: Comparison of FPGA, CPU, GPU, and ASIC. In: 2016 International Conference on Field-Programmable Technology (FPT), pp. 77–84 (2016)
29. Oveis-Gharan, M., Khan, G.N.: Reconfigurable on-chip interconnection networks for high performance embedded SOC design. J. Syst. Architect. **106**, 101711 (2020)
30. Pham-Quoc, C., Al-Ars, Z., Bertels, K.: Heterogeneous hardware accelerators interconnect: an overview. In: 2013 NASA/ESA Conference on Adaptive Hardware and Systems (AHS-2013), pp. 189–197 (2013)
31. Podili, A., Zhang, C., Prasanna, V.: Fast and efficient implementation of convolutional neural networks on FPGA. In: 2017 IEEE 28th International Conference on Application-specific Systems, Architectures and Processors (ASAP), pp. 11–18 (2017)
32. Prost-Boucle, A., Bourge, A., Pétrot, F., Alemdar, H., Caldwell, N., Leroy, V.: Scalable high-performance architecture for convolutional ternary neural networks on FPGA. In: 2017 27th International Conference on Field Programmable Logic and Applications (FPL), pp. 1–7 (2017)
33. Qiu, J., et al.: Going deeper with embedded FPGA platform for convolutional neural network. In: Proceedings of the 2016 ACM/SIGDA International Symposium on Field-Programmable Gate Arrays, FPGA 2016, pp. 26–35. ACM, New York (2016)
34. Shen, Y., Ferdman, M., Milder, P.: Escher: A CNN accelerator with flexible buffering to minimize off-chip transfer. In: 2017 IEEE 25th Annual International Symposium on Field-Programmable Custom Computing Machines (FCCM), pp. 93–100 (2017)
35. Simonyan, K., Zisserman, A.: Very deep convolutional networks for large-scale image recognition (2015). https://arxiv.org/abs/1409.1556
36. Strigl, D., Kofler, K., Podlipnig, S.: Performance and scalability of GPU-based convolutional neural networks. In: 2010 18th Euromicro Conference on Parallel, Distributed and Network-based Processing, pp. 317–324 (2010)
37. Tann, H., Hashemi, S., Bahar, R.I., Reda, S.: Hardware-software codesign of accurate, multiplier-free deep neural networks. In: 2017 54th ACM/EDAC/IEEE Design Automation Conference (DAC), pp. 1–6 (2017)
38. Umuroglu, Y., et al.: FINN: a framework for fast, scalable binarized neural network inference. In: Proceedings of the 2017 ACM/SIGDA International Symposium on Field-Programmable Gate Arrays, FPGA 2017, pp. 65–74. ACM, New York (2017)
39. Wang, J., Lin, J., Wang, Z.: Efficient hardware architectures for deep convolutional neural network. IEEE Trans. Circ. Syst. I Regul. Pap. **65**(6), 1941–1953 (2018)
40. Wang, J., Lou, Q., Zhang, X., Zhu, C., Lin, Y., Chen, D.: Design flow of accelerating hybrid extremely low bit-width neural network in embedded FPGA. In: 2018 28th International Conference on Field Programmable Logic and Applications (FPL), pp. 163–1636 (2018). https://doi.org/10.1109/FPL.2018.00035
41. Wei, X., et al.: Automated systolic array architecture synthesis for high throughput CNN inference on FPGAs. In: 2017 54th ACM/EDAC/IEEE Design Automation Conference (DAC), pp. 1–6 (2017)

42. Williams, R.: What's next? [The end of Moore's law]. Comput. Sci. Eng. **19**(02), 7–13 (2017)

43. Wu, R., Guo, X., Du, J., Li, J.: Accelerating neural network inference on FPGA-based platforms-a survey. Electronics **10**(9), 1025 (2021)

44. Yang, L., He, Z., Fan, D.: A fully onchip binarized convolutional neural network FPGA impelmentation with accurate inference. In: Proceedings of the International Symposium on Low Power Electronics and Design, ISLPED 2018. ACM, New York (2018)

45. Yang, Y., et al.: Synetgy: Algorithm-hardware co-design for convnet accelerators on embedded FPGAs. In: Proceedings of the 2019 ACM/SIGDA International Symposium on Field-Programmable Gate Arrays, FPGA 2019, pp. 23–32. ACM, New York (2019)

46. Yuan, Z., et al.: Sticker: a 0.41-62.1 TOPS/W 8bit neural network processor with multi-sparsity compatible convolution arrays and online tuning acceleration for fully connected layers. In: 2018 IEEE Symposium on VLSI Circuits, pp. 33–34 (2018)

47. Zhang, J.F., Lee, C.E., Liu, C., Shao, Y.S., Keckler, S.W., Zhang, Z.: SNAP: a 1.67—21.55TOPS/W sparse neural acceleration processor for unstructured sparse deep neural network inference in 16nm CMOS. In: 2019 Symposium on VLSI Circuits, pp. C306–C307 (2019)

48. Zhang, X., et al.: DNNBuilder: an automated tool for building high-performance DNN hardware accelerators for FPGAs. In: Proceedings of the International Conference on Computer-Aided Design, ICCAD 2018. ACM, New York (2018)

49. Zhao, R., et al.: Accelerating binarized convolutional neural networks with software-programmable FPGAs. In: Proceedings of the 2017 ACM/SIGDA International Symposium on Field-Programmable Gate Arrays, FPGA 2017, pp. 15–24. ACM, New York (2017)

Image Segmentation and Transfer Learning Approach for Skin Classification

Hiep Xuan Huynh[1]([✉]), Cang Anh Phan[2], Loan Thanh Thi Truong[3], and Hai Thanh Nguyen[1]

[1] College of Information and Communication Technology, Can Tho University, Can Tho 900000, Vietnam
{hxhiep, nthai.cit}@ctu.edu.vn

[2] Faculty of Information Technology, Vinh Long University of Technology Education, Vinh Long, Vietnam
cangpa@vlute.edu.vn

[3] Cai Nhum Town High School, Vinh Long, Vietnam

Abstract. Skin problems are not only detrimental to physical health but also cause psychological. Especially for patients with damaged or even disfigured faces. In recent years, the incidence of skin diseases has increased rapidly. The medical examination of skin lesions is not a simple task. There are similarities among skin lesions where the doctor's experience with a little inattention can give an inaccurate diagnosis. The automatic classification of skin lesions is expected to save effort, time, and human life. This work has deployed a method using the pre-trained MobileNet model on about 1,280,000 images from the 2014 ImageNet challenge and refined over 25,331 images of the International Skin Imaging Collaboration (ISIC) 2019 dataset. Transfer learning was applied, replacing the classifier with an active softmax layer with three or eight types of skin lesions. An accuracy measure is used to evaluate the performance of the proposed method.

Keywords: Skin lesions · Segmentation · Classification · Transfer learning

1 Introduction

Screening and early diagnosing are decisive issues to the effectiveness of treatment for patients, especially cancer. Modern medicine has researched and applied many methods to help early diagnosis with high accuracy, in which diagnostic imaging plays an important role. If the test serves as an indirect "sighting" of the disease, abnormalities can be detected through blood and urine tests (sometimes with a check of stool and other secretions), and then diagnostic imaging is to see

© ICST Institute for Computer Sciences, Social Informatics and Telecommunications Engineering 2021
Published by Springer Nature Switzerland AG 2021. All Rights Reserved
P. Cong Vinh and A. Rakib (Eds.): ICCASA 2021, LNICST 409, pp. 179–191, 2021.
https://doi.org/10.1007/978-3-030-93179-7_14

the injury "directly", even while still a source of danger. However, understanding and applying imaging techniques for screening are not easy. Doctors will depend on age, sex, personal history, and family history to screen and precisely diagnose the disease. Image classification is essential in the medical to determine the class labels of test images based on knowledge gathered from training data. The authors [1] propose a new Large Local Margin Estimate classification model with a sparse representation based on a subcategory. The authors [2] propose a new prediction model that classifies skin lesions into benign or malignant lesions using Convolutional Neural Network with Novel Regularizer. The authors [3] propose a fully automatic calculation method for skin lesion classification using optimized depth features from many well-established CNNs and some abstraction levels. However, medical imaging presents not only large differences but also similarities among classes in object space. This affects the accuracy of the classification.

Some skin lesions resemble melanoma. Tumors develop when cells reproduce too quickly. It can be seen or felt, in other cases, it will only be detected on imaging tests. However, using human vision to detect melanoma in images can be inaccurate as it depends on the physician's experience. In lesion detection, image classification is the ultimate goal of medical image analysis to differentiate among diseases. One of the main challenges of image classification is the large differences among classes. Establishing the medical image classification model is a big step forward in the field of disease diagnosis.

In this paper, we propose a new approach with transfer learning [4] for skin lesions classification. Use weights and features of the pre-trained MobileNet model [5] in the ImageNet dataset [6]. According to the previous research, MobileNet is a good extraction feature for imaging classification, object detection, and segmentation. The contributions of the proposed system can be summarized as follows: Image segmentation based on the Superpixels method to divide normal skin and skin lesions and Skin classification with transfer learning.

The remainder of this work is presented as follows. Section 2 introduces the details about the skin lesions. Section 3 introduces the proposed method for skin classification with Transfer learning. Section 4 presents processing. We give a short description of the dataset, tools, and experiment results in Sect. 5. Finally, we conclude in Sect. 6.

2   Skin Lesions

Skin lesions [7] is a part of the skin that has unusual growth or appearance relative to the skin around it. There are two types of skin lesions, primary and secondary. Primary skin lesions are abnormal skin conditions present at birth, with skin color changes called macules, which are flat lesions on the skin surface, neither raised nor infiltrated. A liquid lesion is a bulging sack of the epidermis, which contains fluid: vesicles, pustules, or firm lesions: papules, nodules, warts, keratosis. Secondary skin lesions are lesions that have been deformed during the pathological process, as a result of the disease or as a result of treatment.

Secondary skin lesions include scale, crust, excoriation, erosion, fissure, ulcer, atrophy, skin spots, scarring, fibrosis, lichenification.

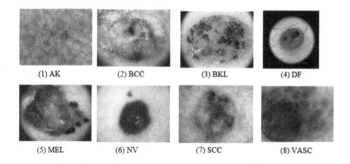

Fig. 1. One sample of each class from the ISIC 2019.

Skin lesions come in many different shapes such as linear lesions with the shape of a straight line, annular lesions, nummular lesions with a circular or coin shape, and target lesions (bull's eye or iris) appearing as rings with central opacity, Serpiginous lesions with linear, branching, and curvilinear elements, reticular lesions with a thread or lattice pattern, Verrucous lesions with irregular surfaces, stones, or rough, ... The basic types of skin lesions (Fig. 1 - One sample of each class from the ISIC 2019): Actinic Keratosis [8,9], Basal cell carcinoma [10], Benign keratosis [11–13], Dermatofibroma [14], Melanoma [15,16], Melanocytic nevus [17], Squamous cell carcinoma[1] and The vascular lesion [18,19]. The basic types of skin lesions are shown in Table 1.

3   Skin Lesions Classification with Transfer Learning

3.1   Segmentation with Superpixels

Segmentation is the identity of specific pixels that make up the object of interest. For example, Superpixels [20] are introduced by Ren and Malik [21] in 2003, superpixels group the same pixels in color and other low-level attributes. In this regard, superpixels solve two problems inherent to digital image processing. First, pixels are merely the result of arbitrariness. Second, the high number of pixels in a large image causes many algorithms that are not computationally feasible. Therefore, Ren and Malik introduced superpixels as more natural entities - grouping pixels that belong to each other while significantly reducing the number of primitives for subsequent algorithms.

A superpixel can be defined as a group of pixels with common characteristics (such as pixel intensity). Superpixel is becoming useful in image processing algorithms and computer vision, such as image segmentation, semantic labeling, object detection, and tracking.

---

[1] https://www.skincancer.org/skin-cancer-information/squamous-cell-carcinoma/.

Table 1. The basic types of skin lesions.

Skin lesions	Cause	Characteristics
Actinic Keratosis	- It is considered precancerous or an early form of cutaneous - A scaly spot found on sun-damaged skin	- A flat or thickened papule or plaque-White or yellow; scaly, warty or horny surface - Skin coloured, red or pigmented - Tender or asymptomatic - 1cm to 2cm in size
Benign keratosis	A harmless warty spot that appears during adult life as a common sign of skin ageing	- Flat or raised papule or plaque - Skin coloured, yellow, grey, light brown, dark brown, ... - Smooth, waxy or warty surface - 1 mm to several cm in diameter
Basal cell carcinoma	- Common form of skin cancer - DNA mutations in the patched (PTCH) tumour suppressor gene - exposure to ultraviolet radiation	- Slowly growing plaque or nodule - Skin coloured, pink or pigmented - Spontaneous bleeding or ulceration - a few mm to several cm in diameter
Squamous cell carcinoma	- A common type of keratinocytecancer or non-melanoma skin cancer - Associated with numerous DNA mutations in multiple somatic genes	- Grow over weeks to months - May ulcerate - Tender or painful - Located on sun-exposed sites - a few mm to several cm in diameter
Melanoma	- A potentially serious type of skin cancer - An uncontrolled proliferation of melanocytic stem cells that have undergone a genetic transformation	- An unusual looking freckle or mole - A variety of colours: tan, dark brown, black, blue, ... - Itchy or tender, bleed easily or crust over - a few mm-cm in diameter
Dermatofibroma	- A common benign fibrous nodule usually found on the - Minor trauma including insect bites, injections, or a rose thorn injury	- Occur anywhere on the skin - Skin dimples on pinching - Pink to light brown (white skin dark brown to black (dark skin) - Sometimes painful, tender, itchy - 0.5–1.5 cm diameter
Melanocytic nevus	- Benign skin lesion due to a local proliferation of pigment cells - Bepends on genetic factors, on sun exposure	- Any part of the body - Flat or protruding - Pink or flesh tones to dark brown steel blue, or black - A few mm-cm in diameter
Vascular lesion	- Abnormalities of the skin and underlying tissues	- Infants and children and underlying tissues - Tumors and malformations - Red or purple - Solid structure, called a red lump or lacune

3.2   Transfer Learning with MobileNet

MobileNet's [5] integrated neural network has pre-trained over 1,280,000 images containing 1,000 object layers from the 2014 ImageNet challenge. The weights and features of the MobileNet model are pre-trained in the source domain ImageNet dataset. Then, they are transferred to the target domain for skin lesion classification.

The MobileNet architecture was adapted to classify skin images by replacing the last layer with a new fully connected, SoftMax, and classification output layer. The size of the output fully connected layer is $N \times 2048$, where N refers to the class number. Softmax is a common learning algorithm for multiple linear classification functions. The softmax value for output z_j is calculated by the Eq. 1:

$$\sigma(z_j) = \frac{e^{z_j}}{\sum_{k=1}^{K} e^{z_k}} \qquad (1)$$

where $\sigma(z_j)$ is the softmax value, z is a vector of inputs to the output layer and j indexes the output units from 1, 2, 3, ..., K.

We use the MobileNet model for the following advantages: MobileNet is one of the most popular and widely used architectures because of its computational accuracy and performance. MobileNet has fewer parameters than some others, so it is easy to train. MobileNet applies depth-separated convolution, eliminating the dependence on depth when convolution. Using a pre-trained encoder helps the model converge faster than the untrained model.

3.3   Evaluation

The performance of the proposed model was evaluated using accuracy. Accuracy is the measure/indicator to evaluate the accuracy of the model by the ratio of the number of correctly detected skin images (with skin lesions and no skin lesions) to the total number of skin images, by the Eq. 2:

$$Accuracy = \frac{TP + TN}{TP + TN + FP + FN} \qquad (2)$$

where: TP (True Positive): the number of skin images bearing the lesion label correctly classified into the lesion class. FP (False Positive): number of skin images bearing the non-lesion label correctly classified into the lesion class. FN (False Negative): number of skin images with lesion labels incorrectly classified into the non-lesional class. TN (True Negative): number of skin images bearing the non-lesion label correctly classified into the non-lesional class.

4   Processing

The skin lesion detection system model consists of three phases: Pre-processing, Segmentation, and Classification. Figure 2 shows the proposed system that is used in this research. We will describe experimental methods in each phase.

Phase 1: Pre-processing: The dataset contains images of skin lesions at different resolutions. However, the resolution of some high-resolution skin lesion images requires high computation costs. Therefore, it is necessary to resize the lesion image for the deep learning network.

Pre-processing of skin lesion images was performed by using the Keras[2] image_data_generator. Samples in the dataset have been scaled down to 224 ×

---

[2] https://keras.io/.

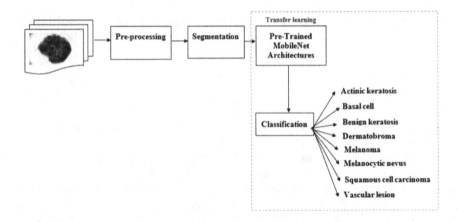

Fig. 2. Classification framework of skin lesions.

224 pixels from the different resolutions to make the images MobileNet compatible.

Phase 2: Segmentation: The segmentation must be efficient so that lesion information can be extracted with high confidence. Besides, the precision of this process directly affects the step of extraction characteristics. Therefore, an appropriate segmentation technique is crucial to obtain good classification results for the problem in question.

Image segmentation is the process of dividing an image into several segments (a set of pixels, also known as superpixels). The goal of image segmentation is to simplify the image for easy analysis. Image segments are often used to locate objects and boundaries. More precisely, image segmentation is a process of labeling every pixel in a sample so that pixels with the same label share fixed characteristics. The result of superpixels segmentation on a skin lesion image is shown in Fig. 3.

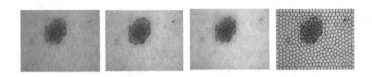

Fig. 3. Image segmentation based on Superpixels.

Phase 3: Classification: We classify the inlet test image into layers of skin lesions using the MobileNet model to reduce space and time to classify skin lesions. In image classification, the dataset is divided into training and testing on an 80:20 scale. The classification model is developed based on training templates using transfer learning. In the experiment, the accuracy of the learned model is measured with the test dataset. We also use weights of the MobileNet network model trained on the ImageNet dataset. Dimensions of all images are determined by resizing to 224 × 224 for width, height. Table 2 shows the trainable and non-trainable parameters of the customized and fine-tuned models.

Table 2. Trainable and non-trainable parameters

Model	Total parameters	Trainable
Customized Model	2,268,232	10,248
Fine Tuned Model	2,268,232	2,257,984

5 Experiment

In our experiments, we identified three classification scenarios. In the first scenario, skin cancer classification, this study uses the image three categories: Melanoma, Basal cell carcinoma, and Squamous cell carcinoma. The second scenario, skin lesions classification, can classify the image into eight categories: Melanoma, Basal cell carcinoma, Squamous cell carcinoma, Actinic keratosis, Benign keratosis, Dermatofibroma, Melanocytic nevus, and Vascular lesion. In the third scenario, we change the learning rate.

In this section, Sect. 5.1 description the dataset. We present the tools used in Sect. 5.2. Section 5.3 presents the training and test dataset .We formulate scenarios to test the results and discussion in Sect. 5.4, Sect. 5.5, Sect. 5.6 and 5.7 respectively.

5.1 Dataset

International Skin Imaging Collaboration (ISIC) 2019[3] dataset provides 25,331 skin lesion images for training data shown in Table 3.

The ISIC 2019 dataset contains the HAM10000 [22] and BCN_20000 [23] and MSK [24]. HAM10000 contains 600 × 450 samples that are centered and cut around the lesion. This dataset is the older challenge of ISIC 2018. Whereas BCN_20000 contains samples of various sizes such as 600 × 450, 1024 × 671, 1024 × 679, 1024 × 680, 1024 × 682, 1024 × 685, 1024 × 764, 1024 × 768, 1024 × 1024, ... This dataset is difficult to classify because many samples have not been cropped, and lesions are in confusing and uncommon locations. Finally, the MSK dataset contains images of various sizes. Skin samples that are color swatches in JPG format are divided into eight classes shown in Fig. 1.

---

[3] https://challenge.isic-archive.com/data.

Table 3. The number of samples for each class in the dataset

Diagnostic	Acronym	Sample
Actinic keratosis	AK	867
Basal cell carcinoma	BCC	3,323
Benign keratosis	BKL	2,624
Dermatofibroma	DF	239
Melanocytic nevus	NV	12,875
Melanoma	MEL	4522
Squamous cell carcinoma	SCC	628
Vascular lesion	VASC	253

5.2   Tools

Our method has been deployed on an R [25] platform together with the tfhub, Keras library packages. RStudio is a free and open-source integrated development environment (IDE) for R. Using the tfhub library package provides R wrappers for the Tensorflow Hub. Tensorflow Hub is a library for reusable machine learning modules. Modules are an independent part of the Tensorflow Hub diagram and, together with weights, can be reused for different tasks in a process known as transfer learning.

5.3   Training and Test

The dataset is divided into two parts: 80% equivalent to 20,265 images for training and 20% with 5,066 images for test dataset shown in Table 4.

Table 4. The table describes the number of images per class of the training and test dataset.

Diagnostic	Training	Test
Actinic keratosis	694	173
Basal cell carcinoma	2,658	665
Benign keratosis	2,099	525
Dermatofibroma	191	48
Melanocytic nevus	10,300	2,575
Melanoma	3,618	904
Squamous cell carcinoma	502	126
Vascular lesion	203	50

5.4   Scenario 1: Skin Cancer Classification (3 Classes)

The classification was conducted experimentally on three cancer layers: Melanoma, Basal cell carcinoma, and Squamous cell carcinoma with a training sample number of 6,778 and a test dataset of 1,695. The scenario helps to classify cancer group in the dataset.

The pre-trained MobileNet delivered learning with the modified softmax to accommodate the three classes of skin lesions. When the number of epoch = 5, the model reached an accuracy of 0.7177, then increased epoch = 10, the accuracy reached 0.8179. The results experiment in Scenario 1 are shown in Table 5.

Table 5. Table comparing the results of three classes.

Results	Epoch = 5	Epoch = 10
Training	0.8146	0.8589
Testing	0.7177	0.8179

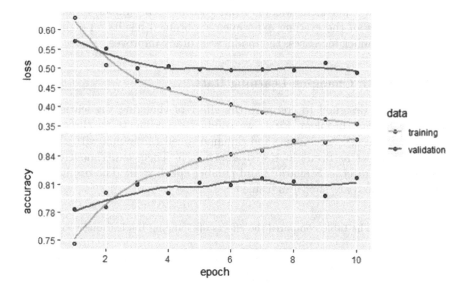

Fig. 4. Accuracy and loss with epoch = 10 (three-class classification).

Skin lesions classification performance in training and testing phases of the model for Scenario 1 with epoch = 10 shown in Fig. 4. Accuracy increases with the number of iterations along with the symmetrical downward slope of the loss curve. The average precision for ten runs is calculated as the overall accuracy of the model. The training loss is 0.358. The validation loss is 0.489.

5.5   Scenario 2: Skin Lesions Classification (8 Classes)

The second scenario can classify the image into eight categories: Melanoma, Basal cell carcinoma, Squamous cell carcinoma, Actinic keratosis, Benign keratosis, Dermatofibroma, Melanocytic nevus, and Vascular lesion. Similar to the three-tier classification, transfer learning is applied to pre-trained MobileNet, where the softmax is modified to work with eight classes. The number of epochs is trained 10, 20, and 40, respectively.

Table 6. Table comparing the results of eight classes.

Results	Epoch = 10	Epoch = 20	Epoch = 40
Training	0.7361	0.7583	0.7679
Testing	0.6426	0.6604	0.6626

We conducted the classification on eight data classes with epoch = 10. The results achieved the accuracy on the Test set is 0.6426. Then, we increase the number of epochs = 20, the performance on the test set increases to 0.6604. Finally, the third experiment was performed with epoch number = 40. Table 6 gives an overview of the grading experiments' obtained results on eight layers. As the epoch number increases, the model's accuracy improves.

5.6   Scenario 3: Changing Learning Rate

This scenario is designed to compare the effect of changing the learning rate in the classification problem. First, we conduct experiments on three classes: Melanoma, Basal cell carcinoma, and Squamous cell carcinoma with the same number of samples as Scenario 1 with epoch = 5. Then, experiment on eight classes with a dataset as Scenario 2 and number epoch = 10. The results experiment in Scenario 3 are shown in Table 7.

Table 7. The table compares the effects of changing the learning rate.

Results	Epoch = 5	Epoch = 10
Scenario 1	0.7177	
Scenario 2		0.6426
Scenario 3	0.8011	0.6737

Table 7 shows the same training model. Again, when we change the learning rate to 0.0001, the classification results increase.

A comparative study was done with the ISIC 2019 rankings. In [26], the authors explore multi-resolution EfficientNets for skin lesion classification, combined with extensive data augmentation, loss balancing, and ensembling, achieving an accuracy rate of 63%. Our proposed method with accuracy is 66%. Furthermore, the accuracy of the proposed method increased when we changed the learning rate.

5.7   Discussion

The efficiency of transfer learning in multilayered CNN architecture with the MobileNet model is verified on a total of 25,331 skin lesions images from the ISIC 2019[4] dataset.

From the experimental results, the classification results in the three classes are always higher than the classification results in the eight classes. When we increase the classes to classify, the complexity of the scenario also increases. The factors that make it difficult for the classification are the similarity of the skin lesions, the uneven distribution of data among classes. Several images in the dataset are considered too homogeneous, which affects the accuracy of the classification.

The use of MobileNet in the classification of skin lesions to assist physicians in medical imaging tasks has improved. However, classification systems often require much time in training and need the hardware to have a GPU graphics card.

6   Conclusion

Detecting skin lesions is an area of great interest due to its importance in skin cancer prevention and early diagnosis of skin diseases.

First, we learn the characteristics of different skin lesions types from the ISIC 2019 dataset. Second, we apply the fractionation technique basing on superpixels to generate the lesion segmentation on the skin images. Third, we grasp transfer learning techniques and perform transfer learning under three scenarios basing on the MobileNet network model to predict skin images. Experimental results show that using transfer learning technology can help us train multitier CNN networks with only a limited set of data and satisfactory results. For image classification problems with small training datasets, transfer learning is one of the first solutions to use. When we use transfer learning, depending on the dataset, we choose an appropriate approach.

With the achieved results, classifying skin lesions by transfer learning method is expected to support doctors in diagnosing skin lesions, especially melanoma.

---

[4] https://challenge.isic-archive.com/data.

References

1. Song, Y., et al.: Large margin local estimate with applications to medical image classification. IEEE Trans. Med. Imaging **34**(6), 1362–1377 (2015). https://doi.org/10.1109/tmi.2015.2393954
2. Albahar, M.A.: Skin lesion classification using convolution neural network with novel regularizer. IEEE Access **7**, 38306–38313 (2019). https://doi.org/10.1109/access.2019.2906241
3. Mahbod, A., Schaefer, G., Wang, C., Ecker, R., Ellinge, I.: Skin lesion classification using hybrid deep neural networks. In: IEEE International Conference on Acoustics, Speech and Signal Processing (ICASSP) (2019). https://doi.org/10.1109/icassp.2019.8683352
4. Pan, S.J., Yang, Q.: A survey on transfer learning. IEEE Trans. Knowl. Data Eng. **22**(10), 1345–1359 (2010). https://doi.org/10.1109/tkde.2009.191
5. Howard, A.G., et al.: MobileNets: efficient convolutional neural networks for mobile vision applications (2017). http://arxiv.org/abs/1704.04861
6. Deng, J., Dong, W., Socher, R., Li, L.-J., Li, K., Fei-Fei, L.: ImageNet: a large-scale hierarchical image database. In: IEEE Conference on Computer Vision and Pattern Recognition (2009). https://doi.org/10.1109/cvpr.2009.5206848
7. Sumithra, R., Suhil, M., Guru, D.S.: Segmentation and classification of skin lesions for disease diagnosis. Proc. Comput. Sci. **45**, 76–85 (2015). https://doi.org/10.1016/j.procs.2015.03.090
8. Akay, B.N., Kocyigit, P., Heper, A.O., Erdem, C.: Dermatoscopy of flat pigmented facial lesions: diagnostic challenge between pigmented actinic keratosis and lentigo maligna. Br. J. Dermatol. **163**(6), 1212–1217 (2010). https://doi.org/10.1111/j.1365-2133.2010.10025.x
9. Cameron, A., Rosendahl, C., Tschandl, P., Riedl, E., Kittler, H.: Dermatoscopy of pigmented Bowen's disease. J. Am. Acad. Dermatol. **62**(4), 597–604 (2010). https://doi.org/10.1016/j.jaad.2009.06.008
10. Lallas, A., et al.: The dermatoscopic universe of basal cell carcinoma. Dermatol. Pract. Conceptual **4**(3), 11–24 (2014). https://doi.org/10.5826/dpc.0403a02
11. Zaballos, P., et al.: Studying regression of seborrheic keratosis in lichenoid keratosis with sequential dermoscopy imaging. Dermatology **220**(2), 103–109 (2010)
12. Moscarella, E., et al.: Lichenoid keratosis-like melanomas. J. Eur. Acad. Dermatol. Venereol. **65**(3), e85–e87 (2011)
13. Braun, R.P., et al.: Dermoscopy of pigmented seborrheic keratosis: a morphological study. Arch. Dermatol. **138**(12), 1556–1560 (2002)
14. Zaballos, P., Puig, S., Llambrich, A., Malvehy, J.: Dermoscopy of dermatofibromas. Arch. Dermatol. **144**(1), 75–83 (2008). https://doi.org/10.1001/archdermatol.2007.8
15. Tschandl, P., Rosendahl, C., Kittler, H.: Dermatoscopy of flat pigmented facial lesions. J. Eur. Acad. Dermatol. Venereol. **29**(1), 120–127 (2014). https://doi.org/10.1111/jdv.12483
16. Schiffner, R., et al.: Improvement of early recognition of lentigo maligna using dermatoscopy. J. Am. Acad. Dermatol. **42**(1), 25–32 (2000). https://doi.org/10.1016/s0190-9622(00)90005-7
17. Rosendahl, C., Cameron, A., McColl, I., Wilkinson, D.: Dermatoscopy in routine practice - 'chaos and clues'. Aust. Fam. Phys. **41**(7), 482–487 (2012)
18. Zaballos, P., et al.: Dermoscopy of solitary angiokeratomas. Arch. Dermatol. **143**(3), 318–325 (2007). https://doi.org/10.1001/archderm.143.3.318

19. Zaballos, P., et al.: Dermoscopy of pyogenic granuloma: a morphological study. Br. J. Dermatol. **163**(6), 1229–1237 (2010). https://doi.org/10.1111/j.1365-2133.2010.10040.x
20. Stutz, D., Hermans, A., Leibe, B.: Superpixels: an evaluation of the state-of-the-art. Comput. Vis. Image Underst. **166**, 1–27 (2018). https://doi.org/10.1016/j.cviu.2017.03.007
21. Ren, X., Malik, J.: Learning a classification model for segmentation. In: Proceedings Ninth IEEE International Conference on Computer Vision (2003). https://doi.org/10.1109/iccv.2003.1238308
22. Tschandl, P., Rosendahl, C., Kittler, H.: The HAM10000 dataset, a large collection of multi-source dermatoscopic images of common pigmented skin lesions. Sci. Data **5**, 180161 (2018). https://doi.org/10.1038/sdata.2018.161
23. Combalia, M., et al.: BCN20000: dermoscopic lesions in the wild (2019). arXiv:1908.02288
24. Codella, N.C.F., et al.: Skin lesion analysis toward melanoma detection: a challenge at the 2017 international symposium on biomedical imaging (ISBI), hosted by the international skin imaging collaboration (ISIC) (2017). arXiv:1710.05006
25. Ihaka, R., Gentleman, R.: R: a language for data analysis and graphics. J. Comput. Graph. Stat. **5**(3), 299–314 (1996). https://doi.org/10.2307/1390807
26. Gessert, N., Nielsen, M., Shaikh, M., Werner, R., Schlaefer, A.: Skin lesion classification using ensembles of multi-resolution EfficientNets with meta data. MethodsX 100864 (2020). https://doi.org/10.1016/j.mex.2020.100864

Blockchain and Identity Management

Xin Yang and Johnny Chan[(✉)]

The University of Auckland, Auckland, New Zealand
jh.chan@auckland.ac.nz

Abstract. On one end of the world, we have a billion people who do not have any registered identity or bank account. On the other end, there are billions of people registered with multiple digital identities, who are having their personal information and privacy being invaded on a daily basis. The objective of this paper is to explore opportunities in addressing both problems through the application of blockchain-based identity management. A systematic review is conducted, and 53 papers are summarised and analysed. It discusses how blockchain technology could process sensitive and large identity dataset among different domains.

Keywords: Blockchain · Identity · Privacy · Identity management · Cyber-security · IoT · Healthcare

1 Introduction

On one end of the world, we have a billion people who do not have any registered identity [1], and 1.7 billion adults are living without a bank account [2]. Most of them reside in rural areas or war zones that lack the means for persistent and trustworthy identity management [3, 4]. On the other end, there are billions of people registered with multiple identities for numerous digital services, worrying about their identity-associated information and privacy could be invaded by hackers, corporations and governments [5]. This problem will always be there if identities are managed by a single institution at the centre. We desperately need a solution to solve the identity crises on both ends.

Blockchain, the underlying technology behind Bitcoin [6], has shown some promises by replacing traditional centralised systems with decentralised and distributed systems and networks [7]. The decentralised structure offers two main benefits: tamper-proof data immutability and disintermediation. Blockchain is a technology that combines cryptography, mathematical algorithms and peer-to-peer networking [8]. The objective of this paper is to explore the opportunities of blockchain-based identity management through a systematic review of the existing literature [9].

© ICST Institute for Computer Sciences, Social Informatics and Telecommunications Engineering 2021
Published by Springer Nature Switzerland AG 2021. All Rights Reserved
P. Cong Vinh and A. Rakib (Eds.): ICCASA 2021, LNICST 409, pp. 192–204, 2021.
https://doi.org/10.1007/978-3-030-93179-7_15

2   Literature Review

2.1   Search String

To select the relevant papers from the literature systematically, a series of keywords in identity management and blockchain technology are considered for composing a search string. As it turns out, "identity" is not an ideal search phrase on its own, because research publication databases often equate that with "identify" in which the context is usually irrelevant to personal identity or identity management. After a few trial-and-error attempts, this issue could be remedied by adding the word "privacy" with "identity" as a combined keyword to search for identity management. Therefore, the finalised search string is composed as [(Identity AND Privacy) AND Blockchain].

2.2   Screening Process

The screening process is carried out in two steps. The first step aims to eliminate papers associated with irrelevant fields. An abstract and keyword screening is applied to all selected papers. Some relevant papers could be identified by abstract screening alone. However, when the abstract does not remotely correspond to blockchain and identity management, a keyword screening is followed to minimise the chance of eliminating papers with valuable information. Some of these papers do not focus on blockchain-based identity management systems, but they have some detailed description of such a system as part of the project, product or service they study or propose. For instance, a paper on Internet of Things (IoT) may include a full description of a blockchain-based identity management system for secured identity data storage, even though its abstract does not mention anything about it.

The second step is a full-text screening of all papers considered relevant from the first step, and it removes any paper that does not discuss blockchain-based identity management systems within the body of the article. Through the full-text screening, the final list of papers is classified into different research areas.

2.3   Result

After applying the composed search string, 267 papers are initially collected from six databases including ABI/Inform, Business Source Premier, Emerald Insight, IEEE, JSTOR and ScienceDirect. Only studies published in academic and practitioner journals are selected for quality control reasons [10]. It is worth noting that a significant portion of the literature is collected from ABI/Inform and Science Direct, including 74 and 162 papers, respectively. All papers are separated into two categories. Category A represents the candidate papers of the systematic review, and Category B stores the filtered papers at the end of the screening process. During the abstract and keyword screening, 77 papers are placed in Category A and 190 papers are placed in Category B. The majority of papers from Category B are associated with network security which contains the keywords "privacy" and "identity". However, they do not discuss identity management and hence are categorised as irrelevant. The full-text screening stage further moves 24 papers from Category A to Category B. Most of them are associated with the security improvement of the cryptocurrency ecosystem, or reviews of popular blockchain technologies. Although these papers have mentioned blockchain-based identity management, they do not provide enough detail to be part of the knowledge base built from the systematic review. Figure 1 captures the screening process and the resulting Review Knowledge Base.

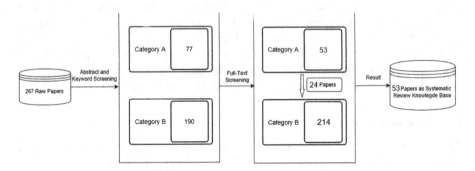

Fig. 1. Screening process and review knowledge base

Based on the Screening Process, there are 214 identity management irrelevant papers, and most of these papers discuss the identity and privacy problems in cryptocurrency. Compared to cryptocurrency, blockchain-based identity management is significantly under explored, even though it might be one possible solution to the severe identity management problem.

3 Analysis of Existing Solutions

The knowledge base of the systematic review contains 53 papers with 10 primary domains emerging as shown in Table 1. Even a paper could be related to multiple domains, they are being classified by their strongest association. The 10 primary domains are: IoT (19), healthcare (9), cyber-identity (8), data management (5), energy (3), cloud service (3), manufacturing (2), social network (2), cybersecurity (1) and financial service (1).

The top three primary domains are IoT, healthcare and cyber-identity, and they represent almost 70% of the knowledge base from the study. All papers from the IoT and healthcare domains also associate with the identity management domain. The proportionally large number of papers from the IoT domain indicates the role and importance of smart devices and connectivity to our identity management in the future, centralised or decentralised. The stronger thematic association to healthcare among those papers shows that identity management in this specific context is the most critical one being studied by researchers and scholars. The following subsections would focus on these three primary domains, to discuss the identity management problems they are facing, and how blockchain technology was integrated and enhanced their identity management.

Table 1. The knowledge base

No	Title	Reference	Primary domain
1	Trustworthy data-driven networked production for customer-centric plants	[11]	IoT
2	E-residency and blockchain	[12]	Cyber-Identity
3	A Blockchain Ecosystem for Digital Identity: Improving Service Delivery in Canada's Public and Private Sectors	[13]	Cyber-Identity
4	Designing microgrid energy markets	[14]	Energy
5	BIDaaS: Blockchain Based ID As a Service	[15]	Cyber-Identity
6	Blockchain's roles in strengthening cybersecurity and protecting privacy	[16]	IoT
7	Toward open manufacturing	[17]	Manufacturing
8	OmniPHR: A distributed architecture model to integrate personal health records	[18]	Healthcare
9	Hitching Healthcare to the Chain: An Introduction to Blockchain Technology in the Healthcare Sector	[19]	Healthcare
10	Cecoin: A decentralized PKI mitigating MitM attacks	[20]	Cybersecurity
11	Access control in the Internet of Things: Big challenges and new opportunities	[21]	IoT
12	Ancile: Privacy-preserving framework for access control and interoperability of electronic health records using blockchain technology	[22]	Healthcare
13	A medical records managing and securing blockchain based system supported by a Genetic Algorithm and Discrete Wavelet Transform	[23]	Healthcare
14	CreditCoin: A Privacy-Preserving Blockchain-based Incentive Announcement Network for Communications of Smart Vehicles	[24]	IoT
15	Decentralized privacy preserving services for Online Social Networks	[25]	Social Network
16	A Social-Network-Based Cryptocurrency Wallet-Management Scheme	[26]	Social Network
17	An OpenNCP-based Solution for Secure eHealth Data Exchange	[27]	Healthcare
18	A Privacy-Preserving Trust Model Based on Blockchain for VANETs	[28]	IoT
19	Digital identity – From emergent legal concept to new reality	[29]	Identity Management
20	Internet of things security: A top-down survey	[30]	IoT
21	Toward a blockchain cloud manufacturing system as a peer to peer distributed network platform	[31]	Cloud Service

(continued)

Table 1. (*continued*)

No	Title	Reference	Primary domain
22	A Case Study for Blockchain in Manufacturing: "fabRec": A Prototype for Peer-to-Peer Network of Manufacturing Nodes	[32]	Manufacturing
23	Blockchain for digital rights management	[33]	Cyber-Identity
24	Decentralized enforcement of document lifecycle constraints	[34]	Data Management
25	A Survey on Anonymity and Privacy in Bitcoin-Like Digital Cash Systems	[35]	Cyber-Identity
26	Block-secure: Blockchain based scheme for secure P2P cloud storage	[36]	Cloud Service
27	Bubbles of Trust: A decentralized blockchain-based authentication system for IoT	[37]	IoT
28	Blockchain technology for security issues and challenges in IoT	[38]	IoT
29	Blockchain mechanisms for IoT security	[39]	IoT
30	A blockchain future for internet of things security: a position paper	[40]	IoT
31	A Survey on Essential Components of a Self-Sovereign Identity	[41]	Cyber-Identity
32	A first look at identity management schemes on the blockchain	[42]	Cyber-Identity
33	FHIRChain: Applying Blockchain to Securely and Scalably Share Clinical Data	[43]	Healthcare
34	Blockchain Technology for Healthcare: Facilitating the Transition to Patient-Driven Interoperability	[44]	Healthcare
35	Authenticating Health Activity Data Using Distributed Ledger Technologies	[45]	Healthcare
36	Privacy-Preserving and Efficient Aggregation Based on Blockchain for Power Grid Communications in Smart Communities	[46]	Energy
37	A Blockchain-Based Notarization Service for Biomedical Knowledge Retrieval	[47]	Healthcare
38	Blockchain and the future of energy	[48]	Energy
39	A TISM modeling of critical success factors of blockchain based cloud services	[49]	Cloud Service
40	Towards decentralized IoT security enhancement: A blockchain approach	[50]	IoT
41	A remote attestation security model based on privacy-preserving blockchain for V2X	[51]	IoT
42	Smart-toy-edge-computing-oriented data exchange based on blockchain	[52]	Data Management

(*continued*)

Table 1. (*continued*)

No	Title	Reference	Primary domain
43	On blockchain and its integration with IoT. Challenges and opportunities	[53]	IoT
44	Multi-tier blockchain framework for IoT-EHRs systems	[54]	IoT
45	IoT security: Review, blockchain solutions, and open challenges	[55]	IoT
46	Machine learning based privacy-preserving fair data trading in big data market	[56]	Data Management
47	Controllable and trustworthy blockchain-based cloud data management	[57]	Data Management
48	Blockchain's adoption in IoT: The challenges, and a way forward	[58]	IoT
49	A survey on internet of things security from data perspectives	[59]	IoT
50	A secure versatile light payment system based on blockchain	[60]	Financial Service
51	Renovating blockchain with distributed databases: An open source system	[61]	Data Management
52	A blockchain-based location privacy-preserving crowdsensing system	[62]	IoT
53	MOF-BC: A memory optimized and flexible blockchain for large scale networks	[63]	IoT

3.1 IoT

The rapid growth of smart devices and high-speed internet have made the IoT become one of the most popular topics recently. As more devices like smartwatches and smart surveillance cameras are being connected, more identity data would be generated and flowing through the web, creating new challenges for identity management among IoT systems [58].

A common architecture of an IoT system has smart devices collecting data in a distributed manner, and they report to a centralised cloud service through multiple network layers. However, this setting is vulnerable and susceptible to malicious attacks. For example, an attacker could pretend to be one of the smart devices, monitor the instructions from the centralised server, and steal the backup data. Additionally, the centralised server itself could also become a victim from cyberattacks [55].

Many researchers have investigated the integration of the IoT system with blockchain technology. They discuss the possibility, and they develop and evaluate new IoT models by adopting blockchain technologies. Most of the review papers discuss the scalability and robustness of the centralised and the decentralised systems. Makhdoom et al. [58] have constructed a table to compare the differences between the system structures of a centralised cloud and a decentralised blockchain. Cloud service is under the centralised control of one trusted entity. If that trusted entity encounters an accident or a malicious attack, the entire IoT system could break down. However, the blockchain technology provides an edge storage feature with each miner node containing a full copy of the blockchain. So even if one node is taken down, the other nodes will become its back up to ensure the IoT system will stay functional.

Many papers discuss different consensus protocols among blockchain-based systems. A consensus protocol can reduce the data communication overhead between the nodes and the centralised server by allowing node to node activities, such as data exchange and authentication, to be carried out in a distributed manner. In addition, decision-making programmes can be embedded as smart contracts in a blockchain to allow the nodes of an IoT system to make decisions without a server, and hence enabling a rapid data exchange among all the nodes. Ouaddah et al. [21] point out that a decentralised blockchain authentication system for identity management in an IoT system would be less dependent on a trusted entity.

However, system performance could become an issue. Reyna et al. [53] explain that as the data stored in each node increases and the size of the blockchain grows, the nodes would consume more resources and affect system performance. For instance, the synchronisation time of adding a new node will increase. There could be gigabytes of data generated by IoT systems within an hour, but many current blockchain-based systems could only process a few transactions per second. Hammi et al. [37] present a decentralised blockchain-based authentication system called the Bubble of Trust. One of the issues they identify is that their system could not be adapted to real time application because the consensus time for validating one transaction would take 14 s from the Ethereum main chain.

Some researchers try to integrate a decentralised blockchain with the traditional centralised IoT system to tackle the performance issue. Xu et al. [51] develop a remote attestation security model with a blockchain for IoT systems in vehicles. Each node of this blockchain stores the access control information and its current status. As the nodes take over the access control and status monitoring, the workload of the server is reduced. Also, the security risks are now distributed to all the nodes and therefore the possibility of the entire system being compromised drops. The performance evaluation of their system shows a 97% success rate of updating their status with a confirmation time of 3 s on real vehicles. Similarly, Lu et al. [28] propose a blockchain-based anonymous reputation system for Vehicle ad hoc Networks (VANET) which stores the authentication keys for the access control of the VANET system to avoid the escrow problem in centralised IoT authentication systems with a decentralised blockchain identity storage.

3.2   Healthcare

With the traditional centralised systems, the management and exchange of health records and identities have been raised as a common problem in the healthcare domain. One reason is that health records and identities are often distributed among various third parties, including the hospitals, the clinics, and the insurance companies, who do not have a shared data repository. Therefore, when applying a medical treatment to a patient, certain data exchanges among the third parties may be required to gather the necessary health data. However, the health identities of patients are private, and it is important for them to be informed where, when and who their health identities are stored, exchanged and accessed.

Gordon and Catalini [44] propose that the current institute-driven health identity management should be transformed to patient-driven. The concept of patient-driven identity management encourages third parties to hand over the health identity sovereignty back to the individuals. For instance, in a case where an institute needs the health identity of a patient for medical treatment, the institute will ask the patient for permission to access the data. The patient can choose to authorise the institute and give them a key to the other third parties' databases to access his entire health record and identity. The institute is only allowed to access, update or transfer the health identity based on the level of permissions it has been given by the patient. Dagher et al. [22] create a framework for the access control and data exchange of health identity called Ancile. In this framework, a blockchain is used to store the permissions of different institutes for a patient. Once an institute requests an access to the patient's health identity, the blockchain will first check its permission level. If the institute does not hold the permission to access, the blockchain will ask the patient for authorisation. As only the patient has the right to alter the permission level, the health identity management is now driven by the patient. Additionally, the framework has a transaction log to record all the institutes' activities, therefore a patient can monitor any activities to their health record and identity.

Beside the issue of sovereignty, others have proposed new channels for the data exchange to happen between different institutes. For instance, Zhang et al. [43] introduce a framework called FHIRChain to store the encrypted database addresses of patients' health identities. For one institute requesting to exchange a patient's health identity with another, the digital keys from both institutes are required to decrypt the database addresses. Hence, the institute can review, retrieve or update the data by accessing the database through the decrypted addresses.

The data exchange between different institutes could also bring security challenges. The traditional unsecured data exchange channels may be attacked and result in data leakage. Blockchain-based systems could provide a more secure data exchange channel with lowered network overhead [43]. Even if data is leaked, the encrypted addresses still leave the attackers a formidable challenge. Furthermore, because of the lowered network overhead, that could benefit health identity management in rural areas. The health identity of the patients living in rural areas can therefore be transferred to a place with better internet infrastructures. For the health institutes in rural areas, instead of updating or downloading the full documents, they can visit or update a patient's health identity directly from a remote database. By exchanging the lightweight database addresses, the health identity management in rural areas will become more accessible.

Compared to IoT, the healthcare domain only manages a relatively smaller amount of identity data. However, the identity management in healthcare still needs to store the patients' health records and identities in the databases off-chain, and it cannot avoid the involvement of the third parties. Therefore, the identity management could not be fully decentralised.

3.3   Cyber-Identity

Contrary to the research from domains of IoT and healthcare, papers from cyber-identity focus mainly on systems aiming to manage individual identity in a more secure and convenient way without a specific context.

Lee [15] proposes a framework called BIDaaS to support the identity verification process. BIDaaS has three entities, namely the BIDaaS provider, the partner and the user. The BIDaaS provider stores the identity information of users off-chain and manages a Virtual ID generator on-chain. The partners are the trusted third parties which may require a user's identity information. They can be any legal entity like the banks, the hospitals, and the councils, which require the identity of a user for social services; or small-sized institutions such as online shopping providers which require the identity information of a user for subscription. The users hold a digital key for authentication and Virtual ID generation. Traditionally, a user provides his identity information directly to the partners for verification. However, with the support of BIDaaS, the user can use the digital key to generate a Virtual ID on the blockchain and send it to the partners. The partners can then obtain the identity information from the BIDaaS provider by sending this Virtual ID to the BIDaaS server. The users can specify which identity information is shared during the key generation so that they are still in control of the shared content. This framework provides convenience to both the partners and the users. For the partners, instead of maintaining an identity verification system, they can now retrieve verified identity information directly from the BIDaaS system. For the users, without the need of managing various identity documents, they only need to bring a digital key for the identity verification from any third parties.

The capability of a blockchain-based cyber-identity system is not limited to identity verification. For instance, Estonia has established an e-residency program with Bitnation [12]. The purpose of this program is to encourage the e-resident to access social and commercial activities and services in Estonia, including banking services, and company formation and taxation services. Bitnation, as the e-residency provider, issues an e-identity and a series of documents storage services based on the blockchain technology. Therefore, the Bitnation users can create their new identity and store their documents such as marriage certification, insurance policy and land title on-chain to access the public services.

The blockchain-based identity management in healthcare reveals a pattern of having both a decentralised decision-making structure and a centralised data storage. A similar trend could also be observed among general blockchain-based cyber-identity system design as well, dealing with all kinds of identities including financial records, vehicle registrations or criminal records.

4   Discussion and Conclusion

To conclude, the decentralised blockchain-based system has shown significant potentials in fast authentication, secured data exchange and improved self-sovereignty with user identity. These potentials can benefit the management of the large quantity of identity data from IoT, as well as the sensitive and private records such as healthcare records and cyber-identity. Unfortunately, as a potential solution to many identity management problems among different domains, blockchain-based identity management is still under explored. It is the time to shift some focus from cryptocurrency to blockchain-based identity management. The future works for blockchain-based identity management can be concluded into two aspects. The first aspect is to increase the level of decision-making from the decentralised nodes, and the node functions should not be limited to authentication and data exchanges but including a registration system to let users create new identities. The second aspect is to introduce the current blockchain-based identity management frameworks to more domains and areas.

References

1. The World Bank Group: Identification for Development (ID4D) Global Dataset. https://datacatalog.worldbank.org/dataset/identification-development-global-dataset
2. Demirguc-Kunt, A., Klapper, L., Singer, D., Ansar, S., Hess, J.: The Global Findex Database 2017 - Measuring Financial Inclusion and the Fintech Revolution: Overview. The World Bank (2018). https://doi.org/10.1596/978-1-4648-1259-0
3. Harbitz, M., del Carmen Tamargo, M.: The Significance of Legal Identity in Situations of Poverty and Social Exclusion: The Link between Gender, Ethnicity, and Legal Identity (2009)
4. Williams, R., Drury, J.: Personal and collective psychosocial resilience: implications for children, young people and their families involved in war and disasters. In: Cook, D.T., Wall, J. (eds.) Children and Armed Conflict. SCY, pp. 57–75. Palgrave Macmillan UK, London (2011). https://doi.org/10.1057/9780230307698_5
5. Samarati, P., di Vimercati, S.D.C.: Data protection in outsourcing scenarios: issues and directions. In: The 5th ACM Symposium on Information, Computer and Communications Security, pp. 1–14. ACM, New York, USA (2010). https://doi.org/10.1145/1755688.1755690
6. Nakamoto, S.: Bitcoin: A Peer-to-Peer Electronic Cash System (2008). https://doi.org/10.1007/s10838-008-9062-0
7. Underwood, S.: Blockchain beyond bitcoin. Commun. ACM. **59**, 15–17 (2016). https://doi.org/10.1145/2994581
8. Lin, I.-C., Liao, T.-C.: A survey of blockchain security issues and challenges. IJ Netw. Secur. **19**, 653–659 (2017)
9. Tranfield, D., Denyer, D., Smart, P.: Towards a methodology for developing evidence-informed management knowledge by means of systematic Review. Br. J. Manage. **14**, 207–222 (2003). https://doi.org/10.1111/1467-8551.00375
10. Crossan, M.M., Apaydin, M.: A multi-dimensional framework of organizational innovation: a systematic review of the literature. J. Manage. Stud. **47**, 1154–1191 (2010). https://doi.org/10.1111/j.1467-6486.2009.00880.x
11. Preuveneers, D., Joosen, W., Ilie-Zudor, E.: Trustworthy data-driven networked production for customer-centric plants. Ind. Manage. Data Syst. **117**, 2305–2324 (2017). https://doi.org/10.1108/IMDS-10-2016-0419
12. Sullivan, C., Burger, E.: E-residency and blockchain. Comput. Law Secur. Rev. **33**, 470–481 (2017). https://doi.org/10.1016/j.clsr.2017.03.016

13. Wolfond, G.: A blockchain ecosystem for digital identity: improving service delivery in Canada's public and private sectors. Technol. Innov. Manage. Rev. **7**, 35–40 (2017). https://doi.org/10.22215/timreview/1112

14. Mengelkamp, E., Gärttner, J., Rock, K., Kessler, S., Orsini, L., Weinhardt, C.: Designing microgrid energy markets. Appl. Energy. **210**, 870–880 (2017). https://doi.org/10.1016/j.apenergy.2017.06.054

15. Lee, J.H.: BIDaaS: blockchain based ID as a service. IEEE Access. **6**, 2274–2278 (2017). https://doi.org/10.1109/ACCESS.2017.2782733

16. Kshetri, N.: Blockchain's roles in strengthening cybersecurity and protecting privacy. Telecomm. Policy. **41**, 1027–1038 (2017). https://doi.org/10.1016/j.telpol.2017.09.003

17. Li, Z., Wang, W.M., Liu, G., Liu, L., He, J., Huang, G.Q.: Toward open manufacturing. Ind. Manage. Data Syst. **118**, 303–320 (2017). https://doi.org/10.1108/imds-04-2017-0142

18. Roehrs, A., da Costa, C.A., da Rosa Righi, R.: OmniPHR: a distributed architecture model to integrate personal health records. J. Biomed. Inform. **71**, 70–81 (2017). https://doi.org/10.1016/j.jbi.2017.05.012

19. Engelhardt, M.A.: Hitching healthcare to the chain: an introduction to blockchain technology in the healthcare sector. Technol. Innov. Manage. Rev. **7**, 22–34 (2017). https://doi.org/10.22215/timreview/1111

20. Qin, B., Huang, J., Wang, Q., Luo, X., Liang, B., Shi, W.: Cecoin: a decentralized PKI mitigating MitM attacks. Futur. Gener. Comput. Syst. (2017). https://doi.org/10.1016/j.future.2017.08.025

21. Ouaddah, A., Mousannif, H., Abou Elkalam, A., Ait Ouahman, A.: Access control in the Internet of Things: big challenges and new opportunities. Comput. Networks. **112**, 237–262 (2017). https://doi.org/10.1016/j.comnet.2016.11.007

22. Dagher, G.G., Mohler, J., Milojkovic, M., Marella, P.B.: Ancile: privacy-preserving framework for access control and interoperability of electronic health records using blockchain technology. Sustain. Cities Soc. **39**, 283–297 (2018). https://doi.org/10.1016/j.scs.2018.02.014

23. Hussein, A.F., ArunKumar, N., Ramirez-Gonzalez, G., Abdulhay, E., Tavares, J.M.R.S., de Albuquerque, V.H.C.: A medical records managing and securing blockchain based system supported by a genetic algorithm and discrete wavelet transform. Cogn. Syst. Res. **52**, 1–11 (2018). https://doi.org/10.1016/j.cogsys.2018.05.004

24. Lun, L., Jiqiang, L., Lichen, C., Shuo, Q., Wei, W., Xiangliang, Z.: CreditCoin: a privacy-preserving blockchain-based incentive announcement network for communications of smart vehicles. IEEE Trans. Intell. Transp. Syst. **19**, 2204–2220 (2018). https://doi.org/10.1109/TITS.2017.2777990

25. Bahri, L., Carminati, B., Ferrari, E.: Decentralized privacy preserving services for online social networks. Online Soc. Networks Media. **6**, 18–25 (2018). https://doi.org/10.1016/j.osnem.2018.02.001

26. He, S., et al.: A social-network-based cryptocurrency wallet-management scheme. IEEE Access. **6**, 7654–7663 (2018)

27. Staffa, M., et al.: An OpenNCP-based solution for secure eHealth data exchange. J. Netw. Comput. Appl. **116**, 65–85 (2018). https://doi.org/10.1016/j.jnca.2018.05.012

28. Liu, W., Lu, Z., Liu, Z., Wang, Q., Qu, G.: A privacy-preserving trust model based on blockchain for VANETs. IEEE Access. **6**, 45655–45664 (2018). https://doi.org/10.1109/access.2018.2864189

29. Sullivan, C.: Digital identity – from emergent legal concept to new reality. Comput. Law Secur. Rev. **34**, 723–731 (2018). https://doi.org/10.1016/j.clsr.2018.05.015

30. Kouicem, D.E., Bouabdallah, A., Lakhlef, H.: Internet of things security: a top-down survey. Comput. Networks. **141**, 199–221 (2018). https://doi.org/10.1016/j.comnet.2018.03.012

31. Li, Z., Barenji, A.V., Huang, G.Q.: Toward a blockchain cloud manufacturing system as a peer to peer distributed network platform. Robot. Comput. Integr. Manuf. **54**, 133–144 (2018). https://doi.org/10.1016/j.rcim.2018.05.011

32. Angrish, A., Craver, B., Hasan, M., Starly, B.: A case study for blockchain in manufacturing: "fabRec": a prototype for peer-to-peer network of manufacturing nodes. Procedia Manuf. **26**, 1180–1192 (2018). https://doi.org/10.1016/j.promfg.2018.07.154

33. Ma, Z., Jiang, M., Gao, H., Wang, Z.: Blockchain for digital rights management. Futur. Gener. Comput. Syst. **89**, 746–764 (2018). https://doi.org/10.1016/j.future.2018.07.029

34. Hallé, S., Khoury, R., Betti, Q., El-Hokayem, A., Falcone, Y.: Decentralized enforcement of document lifecycle constraints. Inf. Syst. **74**, 117–135 (2018). https://doi.org/10.1016/j.is.2017.08.002

35. Khalilov, M.C.K., Levi, A.: A survey on anonymity and privacy in bitcoin-like digital cash systems. IEEE Commun. Surv. Tutorials. **20**, 2543–2585 (2018). https://doi.org/10.17654/cs017010035

36. Li, J., Wu, J., Chen, L.: Block-secure: blockchain based scheme for secure P2P cloud storage. Inf. Sci. (Ny) **465**, 219–231 (2018). https://doi.org/10.1016/j.ins.2018.06.071

37. Hammi, M.T., Hammi, B., Bellot, P., Serhrouchni, A.: Bubbles of trust: a decentralized blockchain-based authentication system for IoT. Comput. Secur. **78**, 126–142 (2018). https://doi.org/10.1016/j.cose.2018.06.004

38. Kumar, N.M., Mallick, P.K.: Blockchain technology for security issues and challenges in IoT. Procedia Comput. Sci. **132**, 1815–1823 (2018). https://doi.org/10.1016/j.procs.2018.05.140

39. Minoli, D., Occhiogrosso, B.: Blockchain mechanisms for IoT security. Internet of Things. **1–2**, 1–13 (2018). https://doi.org/10.1016/j.iot.2018.05.002

40. Banerjee, M., Lee, J., Choo, K.K.R.: A blockchain future for internet of things security: a position paper. Digit. Commun. Networks. **4**, 149–160 (2018). https://doi.org/10.1016/j.dcan.2017.10.006

41. Mühle, A., Grüner, A., Gayvoronskaya, T., Meinel, C.: A survey on essential components of a self-sovereign identity. Comput. Sci. Rev. **30**, 80–86 (2018). https://doi.org/10.1016/j.cosrev.2018.10.002

42. Dunphy, P., Petitcolas, F.A.P.: A first look at identity management schemes on the blockchain. IEEE Secur. Priv. **16**, 20–29 (2018). https://doi.org/10.1109/MSP.2018.3111247

43. Zhang, P., White, J., Schmidt, D.C., Lenz, G., Rosenbloom, S.T.: FHIRChain: applying blockchain to securely and scalably share clinical data. Comput. Struct. Biotechnol. J. **16**, 267–278 (2018). https://doi.org/10.1016/j.csbj.2018.07.004

44. Gordon, W.J., Catalini, C.: Blockchain technology for healthcare: facilitating the transition to patient-driven interoperability. Comput. Struct. Biotechnol. J. **16**, 224–230 (2018). https://doi.org/10.1016/j.csbj.2018.06.003

45. Brogan, J., Baskaran, I., Ramachandran, N.: Authenticating health activity data using distributed ledger technologies. Comput. Struct. Biotechnol. J. **16**, 257–266 (2018). https://doi.org/10.1016/j.csbj.2018.06.004

46. Zhang, X., et al.: Privacy-preserving and efficient aggregation based on blockchain for power grid communications in smart communities. IEEE Commun. Mag. **56**, 82–88 (2018). https://doi.org/10.1109/mcom.2018.1700401

47. Kleinaki, A.S., Mytis-Gkometh, P., Drosatos, G., Efraimidis, P.S., Kaldoudi, E.: A blockchain-based notarization service for biomedical knowledge retrieval. Comput. Struct. Biotechnol. J. **16**, 288–297 (2018). https://doi.org/10.1016/j.csbj.2018.08.002

48. Brilliantova, V., Thurner, T.W.: Blockchain and the future of energy. Technol. Soc. (2018). https://doi.org/10.1016/j.techsoc.2018.11.001

49. Prasad, S., Shankar, R., Gupta, R., Roy, S.: A TISM modeling of critical success factors of blockchain based cloud services. J. Adv. Manage. Res. **15**, 434–456 (2018). https://doi.org/10.1108/JAMR-03-2018-0027

50. Qian, Y., et al.: Towards decentralized IoT security enhancement: a blockchain approach. Comput. Electr. Eng. **72**, 266–273 (2018). https://doi.org/10.1016/j.compeleceng.2018.08.021

51. Xu, C., Liu, H., Li, P., Wang, P.: A remote attestation security model based on privacy-preserving blockchain for V2X. IEEE Access. **6**, 67809–67818 (2018). https://doi.org/10.1109/ACCESS.2018.2878995

52. Yang, J., Lu, Z., Wu, J.: Smart-toy-edge-computing-oriented data exchange based on blockchain. J. Syst. Archit. **87**, 36–48 (2018). https://doi.org/10.1016/j.sysarc.2018.05.001

53. Reyna, A., Martín, C., Chen, J., Soler, E., Díaz, M.: On blockchain and its integration with IoT. Challenges and opportunities. Futur. Gener. Comput. Syst. **88**, 173–190 (2018). https://doi.org/10.1016/j.future.2018.05.046

54. Badr, S., Gomaa, I., Abd-Elrahman, E.: Multi-tier blockchain framework for IoT-EHRs systems. Procedia Comput. Sci. **141**, 159–166 (2018). https://doi.org/10.1016/j.procs.2018.10.162

55. Khan, M.A., Salah, K.: IoT security: review, blockchain solutions, and open challenges. Futur. Gener. Comput. Syst. **82**, 395–411 (2018). https://doi.org/10.1016/j.future.2017.11.022

56. Zhao, Y., Yu, Y., Li, Y., Han, G., Du, X.: Machine learning based privacy-preserving fair data trading in big data market. Inf. Sci. (Ny) **478**, 449–460 (2019). https://doi.org/10.1016/j.ins.2018.11.028

57. Zhu, L., Wu, Y., Gai, K., Choo, K.K.R.: Controllable and trustworthy blockchain-based cloud data management. Futur. Gener. Comput. Syst. **91**, 527–535 (2019). https://doi.org/10.1016/j.future.2018.09.019

58. Makhdoom, I., Abolhasan, M., Abbas, H., Ni, W.: Blockchain's adoption in IoT: the challenges, and a way forward. J. Netw. Comput. Appl. **125**, 251–279 (2019). https://doi.org/10.1016/j.jnca.2018.10.019

59. Hou, J., Qu, L., Shi, W.: A survey on internet of things security from data perspectives. Comput. Networks. **148**, 295–306 (2019). https://doi.org/10.1016/j.comnet.2018.11.026

60. Zhong, L., Wu, Q., Xie, J., Li, J., Qin, B.: A secure versatile light payment system based on blockchain. Futur. Gener. Comput. Syst. **93**, 327–337 (2019). https://doi.org/10.1016/j.future.2018.10.012

61. Muzammal, M., Qu, Q., Nasrulin, B.: Renovating blockchain with distributed databases: an open source system. Futur. Gener. Comput. Syst. **90**, 105–117 (2019). https://doi.org/10.1016/j.future.2018.07.042

62. Yang, M., Zhu, T., Liang, K., Zhou, W., Deng, R.H.: A blockchain-based location privacy-preserving crowdsensing system. Futur. Gener. Comput. Syst. **94**, 408–418 (2019). https://doi.org/10.1016/j.future.2018.11.046

63. Dorri, A., Kanhere, S.S., Jurdak, R.: MOF-BC: a memory optimized and flexible blockchain for large scale networks. Futur. Gener. Comput. Syst. **92**, 357–373 (2019). https://doi.org/10.1016/j.future.2018.10.002

Binary Classification for Lung Nodule Based on Channel Attention Mechanism

Khai Dinh Lai[1,2,3], Thai Hoang Le[1,2(✉)], and Thuy Thanh Nguyen[4]

[1] Faculty of Information Technology, University of Science,
Ho Chi Minh City 70000, Vietnam
laidinhkhai@sgu.edu.vn, lhthai@fit.hcmus.edu.vn
[2] Vietnam National University, Ho Chi Minh City 70000, Vietnam
[3] Faculty of Information Technology, Saigon University,
Ho Chi Minh City 70000, Vietnam
[4] VNU University of Technology, Ha Noi City, Vietnam
nguyenthanhthuy@vnu.edu.vn

Abstract. In order to effectively handle the problem of tumor detection on the LUNA16 dataset, we present a new methodology for data augmentation to address the issue of imbalance between the number of positive and negative candidates in this study. Furthermore, a new deep learning model - ASS (a model that combines Convnet sub-attention with Softmax loss) is also proposed and evaluated on patches with different sizes of the LUNA16. Data enrichment techniques are implemented in two ways: off-line augmentation increases the number of images based on the image under consideration, and on-line augmentation increases the number of images by rotating the image at four angles (0°, 90°, 180°, and 270°). We build candidate boxes of various sizes based on the coordinates of each candidate, and these candidate boxes are used to demonstrate the usefulness of the suggested ASS model. The results of cross-testing (with four cases: case 1, ASS trained and tested on a dataset of size 50×50; case 2, using ASS trained on a dataset of size 50×50 to test a dataset of size 100×100; case 3, ASS trained and tested on a dataset of size 100×100 and case 4, using ASS trained on a dataset of size 100×100 to test a dataset of size 50×50) show that the proposed ASS model is feasible.

Keywords: Attention convolutional network · Nodules detection · SE block

1 Introduction

Lung cancer is a form of cancer that occurs in the lungs, often known as a malignant tumor of the respiratory tract [1]. The condition develops when a malignant tumor starts in the lung and rapidly grows in size, causing invasion and pressing on surrounding organs. Furthermore, benign lung tumors can still occur in some circumstances. Benign tumors vary fundamentally from malignant tumors (cancerous cells). However, proper scientific diagnostic methods from doctors and medical professionals are still required to precisely detect the nature of the tumor. Lung cancer progresses via four stages, the first of which is the detection of lung lesions via general examination or CT scan. The earliest symptoms of lung cancer, however, are quite similar to those of common

© ICST Institute for Computer Sciences, Social Informatics and Telecommunications Engineering 2021
Published by Springer Nature Switzerland AG 2021. All Rights Reserved
P. Cong Vinh and A. Rakib (Eds.): ICCASA 2021, LNICST 409, pp. 205–218, 2021.
https://doi.org/10.1007/978-3-030-93179-7_16

pneumonia and flu, and the features on small CT scans are not obvious, which can easily confuse clinicians [2]. Over the last two decades, computer-aided diagnosis (CAD) systems have been proposed as a viable solution [3]. These systems have strongly developed high performance as well as diagnostic accuracy. Especially, groundbreaking researches when there is the birth of deep learning networks, typically convolutional deep learning networks (CNNs) [4]. The convolutional deep learning network has handled image processing and classification challenges with excellent results, such as medical image analysis and emotional face classification [5]. CAD's primary goals are candidate screening and false positive reduction. These two tasks correspond to the two challenges set by LUNA to research groups in order to develop a full lung nodule detection system based on data provided by LIDC/IDRI [6–8]. Problem 1: Pulmonary nodule detection is a candidate detection stage, which is designed to simplify lung imaging. That is, ignoring the unimportant components such as the lung wall, keeping only the element with great potential is called the nodule candidate. Problem 2: false positive reduction. This aims to remove false positive candidates from the candidate group collected during the candidate detection step. Therefore, the false-positive reduction process needs to be equipped with a classifier with strong discriminant ability to separate nodule and non-nodule objects. In this study, we focus on the second problem of reducing false positives, or in other words, the binary classification problem: nodule class and non-nodule class. Many researches have carried out this work with good outcomes; we would like to refer only a few works that use the CNN methodology on 2D or 3D models.

2D Models
The DIAG CONVNET model, developed by Setio and colleagues [9], is a multi - view convolutional network that incorporates three node detectors for small, medium, and large notes (depending on diameter). For each option, the scientists collected nine 65×65 patches of size 50×50 pixels from distinct viewpoints corresponding to distinct planes of symmetry in the cuboid. These images are processed using a stream of 2D convolutional networks comprised of three integration layers and a max-pooling layer. The sizes of the convolutional layers are as follows: 24 kernels of size 5×5; 32 kernels of size 3×3; and 48 kernels of size 3×3.

3D Models
Dou and colleagues [10] use the multi-context 3D convolutional network concept called CUMedVis as the foundation to build 3 deep learning network architectures (Archi-1, Archi-2, Archi-3) to solve challenges due to differences in node size, shape and geometrical features. Each network uses a different input image to incorporate different levels of contextual information around lung nodules. In the final stage, these three architectures are merged with a weighted linear combination to obtain the final classification result for the candidates.

Ding [11] proposed a pulmonary lymph node detection system based on CNNs. Their system involves applying region-based CNNs to detect nodules on image slices and using 3-D CNNs to reduce the false positive rate. The method was evaluated on the LUNA16 dataset and achieved a high sensitivity (94.4%). The authors have taken advantage of VGG 16 and used the proposed network to achieve high performance, but the cost of building the proposed network by region is not small.

Rushil Anirudh et al. [12] present a tumor search strategy based on Convolution neural networks (CNN), with pre-labeled dataset, using 5 Convolution and ReLU convolution layers, 2 max-pooling and 2 softmax layers, 2 fully connected (FC) layers for classification of 1×1 kernels. The author offers a tumor notation model in which the doctor just needs to make notes about the nodule's center and size. Then, they can use CNN to pinpoint the tumor's location with high accuracy, even if the labels are inaccurate.

We found that most of the research groups performed the combination of multiple models on original size CT images. The results are appreciated but the training process is quite expensive. In addition, the authors have not exploited the specificity of CT images to have appropriate weights. Therefore, we approach the method of dividing the image into small patches around the candidates, and at the same time apply the Attention mechanism to keep the important features and ignore the less important features.

Our main contributions to this study can be summarized as follows:

(1) Data preparation: (a) Propose technique for creating the candidate box on CT images; (b) Propose a data enrichment technique for CT images containing tumors in the training data set with the aim of solving the problem of imbalanced data.
(2) Propose an image classification system, with or without a nodule, that is integrated with a deep learning network model and an attention mechanism.

2 Background

2.1 Attention Mechanism with SE Block

Jie Hu proposes the Squeeze-and-Excitation block (SE Block) to improve the quality of representations of complex neural networks [13]. This SE block consists of two main steps. In the "Squeeze" step, the author uses the global mean to aggregate feature maps of the size $H \times W$ to create a channel descriptor. In the "excitation" step, the author uses fully-connected layers corresponding to the output neurons after the "squeeze" step to give weights to each channel. This weight will be used for feature maps to select the important feature that is also the final result of the SE block (Fig. 1).

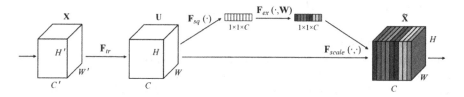

Fig. 1. Squeeze-and-Excitation (SE Block)

The implementation of the SE block is detailed below. We assume that the input image X is of size $H' \times W' \times C'$, where H' and W' are the height and width of the image, respectively, and C' is the number of channels. F_{tr} is the convolutional multiplication X with the filters $V = [v_1, v_2, \ldots, v_C]$ where v_c is the parameter value corresponding to the Cth kernel to generate the feature map $U \in \mathbb{R}^{H \times W \times C}$. So for C filter we have $U = [u_1, u_2, \ldots, u_c]$ với

$$u_c = v_c * X = \sum_{s=1}^{C'} v_c^s * x^s \tag{1}$$

In the "squeeze" step, we aggregate feature maps across their spatial dimensions H × W to create a channel descriptor using global average pooling. With the C feature map, we have a vector $z \in \mathbb{R}^C$, with the cth component of z determined using a formula:

$$z_c = F_{sq}(u_c) = \frac{1}{H \times W} \sum_{i=1}^{H} \sum_{j=1}^{W} u_c(i, j) \tag{2}$$

In the "excitation" step, two fully-connected layers are used to get vector s via the formula:

$$s = F_{ex}(z, W) = \sigma(W_2 RELU(W_1 z)) \tag{3}$$

where $W_1 \in \mathbb{R}^{\frac{C}{r} \times C}$ và $W_2 \in \mathbb{R}^{C \times \frac{C}{r}}$ is the weights of the fully-connected layers, The parameter r is defined as the "reduction ratio." The smaller the intermediate representations are, the higher the r-value. σ is the sigmoid function to map the component values of s to the range [0, 1]. In this case, s is a gate with an Attention mechanism, Specifically, each component s_i corresponds to a channel U_i. If the value s_i is close to 1 then the U_i corresponding channel is significant and vice versa. In the last step, the output of the SE block is performed by multiplied the feature map U by the vector s.

$$\hat{X} = s \times U \tag{4}$$

By this multiplier, less important channels will be ignored, while other critical channels will be retained.

2.2 Revisiting ASS Model

a. Attention Sub-Convnet

The squeeze-and-excitation block acts as a plugin that may be added to any CNN network architecture. In our research, we just apply the Attention mechanism to build us a distinct subnet namely Attention sub-Convnet [14]. Specifically, an Attention sub-convnet is made up of many components. The first is that the convolutional layer accepts an image of size H × W with initial channels C'. Then, use convolutional multiplication with a Kernel of size K × K to get feature maps of size H × W with C channels. Second, the average pooling layer averages the values of the channels' components on each feature map of size H × W and form a vector z of length C. Third, the fully-connected layer on the z vector produces vector s with C components. Next, the sigmoid function is used to normalize the components of the vector s to the corresponding values of the value domain [0; 1]. Finally, the Attention sub-convnet network performs vector multiplication s with feature maps of size H × W × C where C is the number of channels to get the output of feature maps with selected channels (Table 1).

Table 1. An overview of the Attention sub-Convnet architecture included: layers, input size, output size and parameters

Layer	Input size	Output size	Parameter
Input	H × W × C′		
Convolution	H × W × C′	H × W × C	Kernel K × K
Average Pooling	H × W × C	1 × 1 × C	Kernel H × W
Fully connected	1 × 1 × C	1 × 1 × C	
Sigmoid	1 × 1 × C	1 × 1 × C	
Multiply	H × W × C, 1 × 1 × C	H × W × C	
Output		H × W × C	

b. ASS Model

In [14], we integrates Attention sub-convnet networks into what we call ASS. ASS combines 3 Attention sub-convnet networks interspersed with max pooling layers to reduce feature map size. At the flatten layer we get a vector of size 10816. This vector is passed through two fully-connected layers with output sizes of 512 and 2 respectively. Finally, to determine if a candidate is a nodule or not, we apply the softmax-loss function for binary classification.

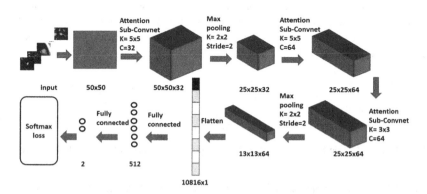

Fig. 2. Architecture of ASS model in [14]

3 Proposal Nodule Detection System

We propose a lung nodule classification system that integrates the ASS model shown in Fig. 3.

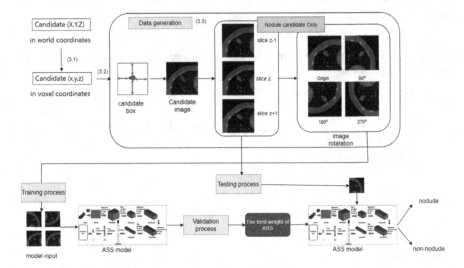

Fig. 3. Proposal nodule detection system with (3.1, 3.2, 3.3) will be explained in next section.

3.1 Convert World Coordinates into Voxel Coordinates

For the first challenge, LUNA encourages research groups to build systems for identifying lung nodules, and the results of this challenge are collected by LUNA in an excel file candidate_v2. In this file, each nodule candidate is placed on a row with data about the nodule's X, Y, and Z coordinates in the real world coordinate system and labeled data as 0 or 1 corresponding to the tumor or non-tumor classification. Therefore, in step 1, we convert the candidate coordinates in the real world coordinate system to the voxel coordinate system. (see in Fig. 4).

```
def worldToVoxelCoord(worldCoord, origin, spacing):
    stretchedVoxelCoord = np.absolute(worldCoord - origin)
    voxelCoord = stretchedVoxelCoord / spacing
    return voxelCoord
```

Fig. 4. Pseudocode for converting world coordinate system to voxel coordinate system

While the worldCoord parameter is an array of candidate values received from the file candidate_v2, origin parameter is the origin representing the position of the first voxel (0, 0, 0) in the anatomical coordinate system, and spacing is the distance that defines the distance between the voxels along each axis (units in mm). These parameters are read from the mhd file in the LUNA16 database.

3.2   Candidate Box

Once the candidates appear in the voxel coordinate system, we perform candidate framing by considering the candidate coordinates to be the center of a square with sides of the desired size. From this box, we get an image containing the candidate whose size is equal to the box size with the formula (x $\pm$ size/2, y $\pm$ size/2, z_0). For example, a candidate with coordinates (x_0, y_0, z_0) and the box is 100 $\times$ 100 pixels, we determine the height and width of the candidate box by using the formula (x $\pm$ 50, y $\pm$ 50, z_0). Figure 2 shows pseudocode that captures the frame surrounding a candidate. From the candidate envelope, we crop the image to the box size and get the image containing the candidate (Figs. 5 and 6).

```
def crop_patch(img_file, out_file, X, Y, size=100):
    # read image from file
    img = cv2.imread(img_file)
    H, W = img.shape[:2] # get image height and width

    # get coordinates for cropping patch
    i_min, i_max = max(Y-size, 0), min(Y+size+1, H)
    j_min, j_max = max(X-size, 0), min(X+size+1, W)
    patch = img[i_min:i_max, j_min:j_max]

    # resize patch to expected size
    patch = cv2.resize(patch,(size, size))

    # save patch to output file
    cv2.imwrite(out_file, patch)
```

Fig. 5. Pseudocode for creating a candidate box.

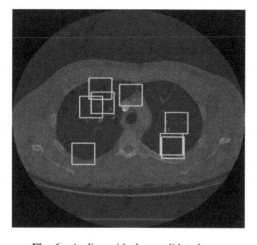

Fig. 6. A slice with the candidate boxes

3.3   Data Augmentation

The number of positive candidates in the LUNA16 database is quite modest in comparison to the number of negative candidates. Therefore, in order to reduce the impact of data imbalance during the learning process, we augment the data in two ways based on the positive candidates.

Off-line Data Augmentation
As shown in Sect. 3.2, from a candidate box we take an image sized according to the size of the box. The LUNA16 dataset is another format derived from LIDC_IDRI collections, which have all cases with slice thickness <2 mm [6]. This ensures that the appearance of the nodule with a diameter >3 mm is represented by three contiguous slices [15]. As a result, we can take two more patches, one each from the front and rear slices that contain the candidate under consideration and are labeled as positive candidates. Thus, for a positive candidate whose coordinates (x_0, y_0, z_0), a candidate box is determined by the formula $(x \pm size/2, y \pm size/2, z_0)$, the formula $(x \pm size/2, y \pm size/2, z_0 -1)$; $(x \pm size/2, y \pm size/2, z_0 + 1)$ finds the two more candidate boxes to make 2 patches with positive labels (Fig. 7).

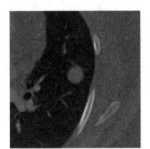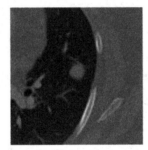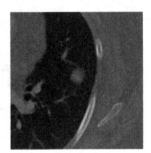

Fig. 7. Three patches in three consecutive slices with minor differences

On-line Data Augmentation
Based on the analysis of how the doctor places the CT image when observing, we discover that the doctor can orient the image horizontally or vertically and that even if the image is accidentally inverted, the doctor can still determine whether the image has a nodule or not. Aside from placing the image in a standard view, the doctor can also place it in the 90°, 180° or 270° right rotation. Therefore, we take advantage of this feature to enrich the data during training. When an image is supplied, we select one of three the right rotations 90°, 180°, 270° at random, or we preserve the original form (0° rotation). We guarantee that from an initial image, we will generate three additional images with three separate rotations at each learning time without saving any images on our device (Fig. 8).

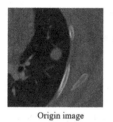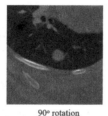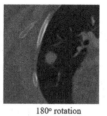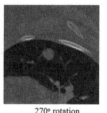

| Origin image | 90° rotation | 180° rotation | 270° rotation |

Fig. 8. The origin image and its three different rotation

4   Experimental Results

4.1   Datasets

From the dataset LUNA16 and the file candidate v2, which contains candidate coordinates and class labels. We utilize an algorithm to define the candidate box and off-line data augmentation to produce two databases with varying image sizes, which we call data50 and data100 matching image data with dimensions of 50 × 50 pixels and 100 × 100 pixels. These two sets of images were created in collaboration with a number of picked candidates differed only in the size of their candidate box. These two sets have the same number of images. The ratio of positive to negative groups is 20:80 (Table 2).

Table 2. The number of candidates were classed as positive or negative.

Dataset type	Positive samples	Negative samples
Train	1200	4800
Val	400	1600
Test	400	1600

4.2   ASS_w50 and ASS_w100

We undertake sequential training on two data sets, data50 and data100, using the ASS model provided in Sect. 2.2, and get two different sets of weights. As a result, we termed the model ASS_w50 after the ASS model that was trained on data50. The ASS model trained on data100 is represented by the ASS_w100 model and we obtain the weight ASS_w100.

4.3   Environment for Experiments

Models are built in the same computing environment. Setting up a set of weights based on a Gaussian distribution with a mean of zero, a standard deviation of 0.02, and a bias of zero. The gradient-based optimization technique of stochastic objective functions, Adam was selected based on adaptive lower-order moments estimations. We have a learning rate of 1e−4 and a weight decay rate of 1e−6. We run roughly 50 epochs for each scenario, with a batch size of 8 images. For training process, we used an early stopping strategy. This not only saves us time training after the performance converged, but also helps us prevent overfitting.

4.4   Evaluation

We used the Holdout method to evaluate models. To get objective results, we split the data into three independent directories with ratio between training set, validating set and testing set, respectively 60%, 20% and 20%.

When we performed the test step, we identified that the outcomes were divided into four groups in the confusion matrix. They were, in order, true positive (TP), false positive (FP), true negative (TN), and false negative (FN). Precision, recall, specificity, and AUC were the measures we used in our comparative analysis [16].

$$\text{Precision} = \frac{TP}{(TP + FP)} \tag{5}$$

$$\text{Recall} = \frac{TP}{(TP + FN)} \tag{6}$$

The specificity is the measurement which is distinctive in that it represents the percent of correctly defined negatives. Properly defined as the proportion of segmented slices free of nodule cancer.

$$\text{Specificity} = \frac{TN}{(TN + FP)} \tag{7}$$

5   Experimental Results

Case 1: ASS_w50 performs training, evaluating and testing on data50.

In this case, we use ASS model to train and validate on data50 to get w50 weight set (Fig. 9 and Table 3).

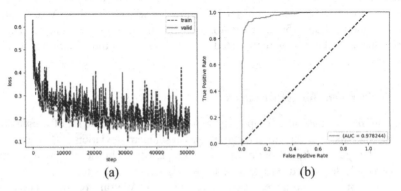

(a)   (b)

Fig. 9. ASS_w50 performs training, evaluating and testing on data50. (a) the value of loss parameter during training and validating. (b) the ROC curve of case 1.

Table 3. Displays results for Precision, Recall, Specificity of ASS_50 on data50

Model	Precision	Recall	Specificity
ASS_50/Data50	0.917	0.840	0.984

Case 2: ASS_w50 performs a cross-testing on data100.

In this scenario, we employ ASS trained on data50 to cross-test against data100 (Fig. 10 and Table 4).

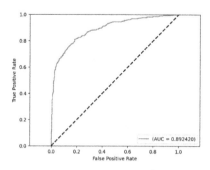

Fig. 10. The diagrams show the ROC curve of case 2.

Table 4. Displays results for Precision, Recall, Specificity of ASS_50 on data100

Model/Data	Precision	Recall	Specificity
ASS_50/Data100	0.853061	0.522500	0.977500

Case 3: ASS_w100 performs training, evaluating and testing on data100.

The same as in case 1, but we use ASS model to train and validate on data100 to get ASS_w100 weight set (Fig. 11 and Table 5).

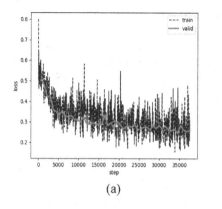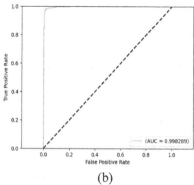

(a)　　　　　　　　　(b)

Fig. 11. ASS_w100 performs training, evaluating and testing on data100. (a) the value of loss parameter during training and validating. (b) the ROC curve of case 4.

Table 5. Displays results for Precision, Recall, Specificity of ASS_100 on data100

Model	Precision	Recall	Specificity
ASS_100/Data100	0.962500	0.996250	0.973451

Case 4: ASS_w100 performs a cross-testing on data50.

In this time, we train the ASS on data100 and use this model with its weight which is obtained to conduct to test on data50 (Fig. 12 and Table 6).

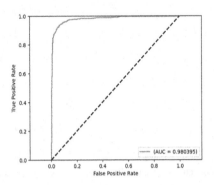

Fig. 12. The diagrams show the ROC curve of case 4.

Table 6. Displays results for Precision, Recall, Specificity of ASS_100 on data50

Model/Data	Precision	Recall	Specificity
ASS_100/Data50	0.929539	0.857500	0.983750

We make some observations, with two cases having similarity in the size of the data during training, evaluating and testing (case 1 and 3), the model achieves positive results, such as using ASS for training and testing on data50. When using a set of weights trained from a set of 50 × 50 size, testing data with size of 100 × 100 gives lower results than the rest of the cases. However, the specificity result of case 2 is still above 90%. In the opposite case, ASS with w100 weight set to test on data50 produces acceptable results. Consequently, it demonstrates that the proposed ASS model is effective when tested on various LUNA16 data sets.

6 Conclusions

In this paper, we offer a new data augmentation strategy to deal with the problem of imbalanced data in the training process. This method is based on the characteristic of lung nodules screening with computed tomography and the doctor's visual angle while observing the CT scan. Furthermore, we present a method for generating candidate boxes based on candidate coordinates in order to generate patches of varying sizes (50 × 50, 100 × 100). The techniques of augmenting and building candidate box allow us to assess the usefulness and feasibility of the ASS model presented in [14] on datasets of various sizes. The data enrichment strategy is not restricted in this study; it may also be used to produce rich data sources in imbalanced data problems.

Acknowledgements. This research is funded by University of Science, VNU-HCM under grant number CNTT 2021-09.

References

1. Bray, F., Ferlay, J., Soerjomataram, I., Siegel, R.L., Torre, L.A., Jemal, A.: Global cancer statistics 2018: GLOBOCAN estimates of incidence and mortality worldwide for 36 cancers in 185 countries. CA: A Cancer J. Clin. **68**(6), 394–424 (2018)
2. Grippi, M.A., et al.: Fishman's Pulmonary Diseases and Disorders, 5th edn. McGraw-Hill, New York (2015)
3. Ignatious, S., Joseph, R.: Computer aided lung cancer detection system. In: Global Conference on Communication Technologies (GCCT), Thuckalay, pp. 555–558 (2015)
4. Lecun, Y., Bengio, Y., Hinton, G.: Deep learning. Nature **521**(7553), 436 (2015)
5. Vo, D.M., Le, T.H.: Deep generic features and SVM for facial expression recognition. In: 3rd National Foundation for Science and Technology Development Conference on Information and Computer Science (NICS), Danang, pp. 80–84 (2016). https://doi.org/10.1109/NICS.2016.7725672
6. Armato III, S.G., et al.: Data from LIDC-IDRI (2015). https://doi.org/10.7937/K9/TCIA.2015.LO9QL9SX
7. LIDC-IDRI. https://wiki.cancerimagingarchive.net/display/Public/LIDC-IDRI
8. LuNa. https://luna16.grand-challenge.org/
9. Setio, A.A.A., et al.: Pulmonary nodule detection in CT images: false positive reduction using multi-view convolutional networks. IEEE Trans. Med. Imaging **35**(5), 1160–1169 (2016)
10. Dou, Q., Chen, H., Yu, L., Qin, J., Heng, P.A.: Multilevel contextual 3-D CNNs for false positive reduction in pulmonary nodule detection. IEEE Trans. Bio-medical Eng. **64**(7), 1558–1567 (2017). https://doi.org/10.1109/TBME.2016.2613502. https://ieeexplore.ieee.org/document/7576695. Print ISSN 0018-9294. Electronic ISSN 1558-2531
11. Ding, J., Li, A., Hu, Z., Wang, L.: Accurate pulmonary nodule detection in computed tomography images using deep convolutional neural networks. In: Descoteaux, M., Maier-Hein, L., Franz, A., Jannin, P., Collins, D.L., Duchesne, S. (eds.) MICCAI 2017. LNCS, vol. 10435, pp. 559–567. Springer, Cham (2017). https://doi.org/10.1007/978-3-319-66179-7_64
12. Anirudh, R., Thiagarajan, J.J., Bremer, T., Kim, H.: Lung nodule detection using 3D convolutional neural networks trained on weakly labeled data. In: SPIE Medical Imaging (2016). https://doi.org/10.1117/12.2214876
13. Hu, J., Shen, L., Albanie, S., Sun, G., Wu, E.: Squeeze-and-excitation networks. In: The IEEE Conference on Computer Vision and Pattern Recognition (CVPR), pp. 7132–7141 (2018)
14. Lai, K.D., Cao, T.M., Thai, N.H., Le, T.H.: The combination of attention sub-convnet and triplet loss for pulmonary nodule detection in CT images. In: Miraz, M.H., Excell, P.S., Ware, A., Soomro, S., Ali, M. (eds.) iCETiC 2020. LNICSSITE, vol. 332, pp. 227–238. Springer, Cham (2020). https://doi.org/10.1007/978-3-030-60036-5_16

15. Brown, M.S., Lo, P., Goldin, J.G., et al.: Correction to: toward clinically usable CAD for lung cancer screening with computed tomography. Eur. Radiol. **30**, 1822 (2020). https://doi.org/10.1007/s00330-019-06512-1
16. Branco, P., Torgo, L., Ribeiro, R.: A survey of predictive modeling on imbalanced domains. ACM Comput. Surv. **49**(2), Article no. 31 (2016)

Design Cloud-Fog Systems Using Heuristic Solutions on the Energy of IoT Devices

Nguyen Thanh Tung$^{(\boxtimes)}$

International School, Vietnam National University, Hanoi, Vietnam
tungnt@isvnu.vn

Abstract. In the Cloud-Fog system paradigm, the IoT services take an important role. It is a service layer upper from the shared physical infrastructure layer. The actual implementation of service functions is a key aspect of increasing service operation. Deployment decisions need to address the resource requirements of the services, ensure that the services meet its QoS constraints while reducing the overall operating cost. Allocating resources in an inefficient operation will lead to less efficient of services and increase the number of physical servers to use while some of these having very low utilization rates.

In this paper, we investigate the problem of IoT devices deployment in Cloud-Fog system to provide the maximum operation time under the battery constraint of IoT devices. Although we can use Linear Programming (LP) to calculate the solution, we cannot run the LP in small IoT device, therefore heuristic algorithms are needed. Our trial shows that the approximate solution is far better than the random solution.

Keywords: IoT · Cloud-Fog system · Battery constraint · Operation time · Linear programming

1 Introduction

The Cloud-Fog system is very efficient for IoT services to guarantee QoS. However, IoT devices are too small to handle jobs for computation due to its limitations on power source [1, 2, 7] (Fig. 1).

The optimal implementation of IoT networks on Cloud-Fog system faces many challenges even though the core of the system have been deployed in many places. The IoT device operations are located near fog nodes but not cloud for low latency and location tracking. However, the fog nodes can only have low capability of operation. Contrary to fog nodes, cloud is a powerful and unlimited capacity of operation. As a result, developers must optimize resource usage while meeting strict latency constraints of IoT system.

When more resources are allocated than required, virtualizing services will be expensive, but under-allocation of resources will result in service inefficiencies. Cloud-Fog system is a multi-layer design in which each device has its own functions, the deployment implementation determines the cost of services. Our designs must research the capacity and energy efficiency of computing and transmission sources to lower the power cost.

© ICST Institute for Computer Sciences, Social Informatics and Telecommunications Engineering 2021
Published by Springer Nature Switzerland AG 2021. All Rights Reserved
P. Cong Vinh and A. Rakib (Eds.): ICCASA 2021, LNICST 409, pp. 219–225, 2021.
https://doi.org/10.1007/978-3-030-93179-7_17

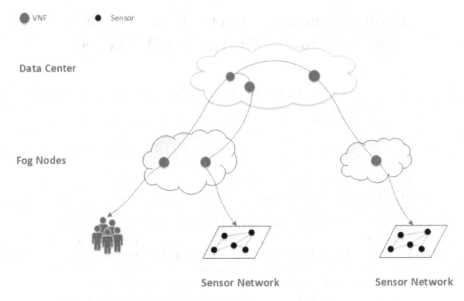

Fig. 1. Three-layer Cloud-Fog system paradigm.

2 Related Work

In [5], based on CISCO's IoT model proposes a cloud-fog architecture to provide IoT data efficiently and reliably for corresponding IoT applications while guaranteeing time delay. They use the LEACH-Centralized protocol, a modified version of LEACH, for sensor networks and estimating the power consumption of m-proxy servers and other IoT nodes. These devices are normal for the first time and keep the remaining power level for the next rounds to remove unnecessary communications power from the LEACH-C. The test results show that the total network delay and utilization are lowered.

In [6] also proposes an IoT-based fog computing model to efficiently allocate tasks to fog nodes (FNs) in a way that preserves total energy consumption. The model is called IoT-FCM (Fog Computing Model), which is made up of two components: the cloud-fog layer part and the terminating layer part. In the cloud-fog layer part, they use three criteria: latency, energy, and distance. They show that IoT-FCM is more energy efficient than some other algorithms. For the terminal layer part, IoT-FCM modified LIBP (Least Noise Signaling Protocol) by adding more sink nodes. Simulation results also show that IoT-FCM saves more energy than original LIBP and the device can operate longer.

3 Proposed Heuristic Algorithm

Linear Programming is not suitable for sensor-IoT networks because if a network changes the topology then we have to design again. Each time there is a change in the network, the solution needs to be recalculated. Also, IoT devices are too small to handle jobs for computation due to its limitations on power source [3, 4].

The energy needs to be balanced among sensor nodes and the FNs roles are also rotated to maximize the remaining energy of sensor nodes.

Therefore, the FNs position needs to be reallocated among the IoT nodes so that the remaining energy of all IoT nodes is maximized. The heuristic method is called RA-LEACH (Random LEACH) and can be stated as below.

RA-LEACH (Random LEACH):

In every round, We chose k_ Fog Node from N_ Fog Nodes

Input:

$N\_$: The number of FNs indexed from 1 to $N\_$

$s\_$: The present FN solution

For every round of operation

we chose $k\_$ different Fog Node randomly from $N\_$ FNs.

Result: the set $s\_$ becomes the FNs solution for the round obtained from the algorithm.

Repeat until the first IoT device has none of energy.

(End of code)

RE-LEACH (Remaining Energy):

In every round, We chose k_ Fog Node from N_ Fog Nodes

Input:

$N\_$: The number of FNs indexed from 1 to $N\_$

$s\_$: The current CH solution

For every round of operation

we chose $k\_$ different Fog Node randomly from $N\_$ FNs.

$$\sum_{i=1..k} \frac{1}{E_i} = min$$

Result: the set $s\_$ becomes the FNs solution for the round obtained from the algorithm.

Repeat until the first IoT device has run none of energy.

(End of code)

Ave-LEACH (Average Energy):

In every round, We chose k_ Fog Node from N_ Fog Nodes

Input:

$N\_$: The number of FNs indexed from 1 to $N\_$

$s\_$: The current CH solution

For every round of data transmission

we chose k_ different Fog Node randomly from N_ FNs.

$$E_i \geq \frac{\Sigma_{k=1..N} E_k}{N}$$

Result: the set $s\_$ becomes the FNs solution for the round obtained from the algorithm.

Repeat until the first IoT device has run none of energy.

(End of code)

4   Simulation Results

We test performances of RA- LEACH, RE-LEACH and Ave-LEACH. We create hundreds of 100-node IoT networks in simulation, starting with 10,000,000 battery units at each device. The algorithm RA-LEACH, RE-LEACH and Ave-LEACH are test over the networks while the number of Fog Nodes is set to 3 and the total nodes is set to 5. The location of the cloud center is at (50, 1000). IoT device location and FN location are determined as shown in Fig. 2 and Fig. 3.

Figure 4 shows that RE-LEACH and Ave-LEACH performs nearly the same and far better than RA-LEACH. Figure 5 shows that RE-LEACH and Ave-LEACH spend much more energy than RA-LEACH. Therefore, RE-LEACH and Ave-LEACH balance the energy of nodes better than RA-LEACH.

Network size $(100\ m \times 100\ m)$

Fog Nodes (0.0,120.0);
(50.0,120.0);(100.0,120.0);(120.0,50.0);(120.0,0.0)

Cloud location (50.0,1000.0)

Number of devices   one hundred devices

Position of devices: Uniformly distributed

Power consumption: square model

Fig. 2. IoT devices and Fog Nodes

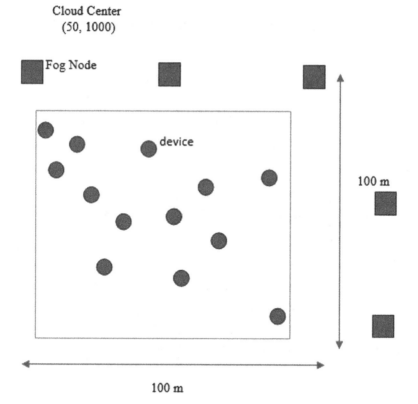

Fig. 3. Network topologies with Cloud center

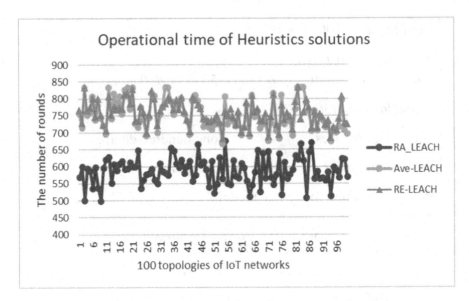

Fig. 4. The lifetime of RA-LEACH, RE-LEACH and Ave-LEACH

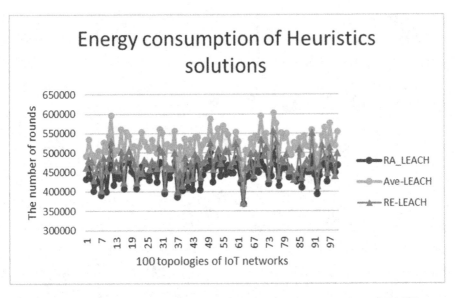

Fig. 5. The energy consumption of RA-LEACH, RE-LEACH and Ave-LEACH

5   Conclusion

Although we can use Linear Programming (LP) to calculate the solution, we cannot run the LP in small IoT device, therefore heuristic algorithms are needed. Our trial shows that the approximate solution is far better than the random solution. Simulation shows that RE-LEACH and Ave-LEACH performs nearly the same and far better than RA-LEACH and RE-LEACH and Ave-LEACH spend much more energy than RA-LEACH.

References

1. Barcelo, M., Correa, A., Llorca, J., Tulino, A.M., Vicario, J.L., Morell, A.: IoT-cloud service optimization in next generation smart environments. IEEE J. Sel. Areas Commun. **34**(12), 4077–4090 (2016)
2. Hajibaba, M., Gorgin, S.: A review on modern distributed computing paradigms: cloud computing, jungle computing and fog computing. J. Comput. Inf. Technol. **22**(2), 69–84 (2014)
3. Tung, N.T., Duc, N.V.: Optimizing the operating time of wireless sensor network. EURASIP J. Wirel. Commun. Netw. (2013). https://doi.org/10.1186/1687-1499-2012-348. ISSN 1687-1499
4. Tung, N.T., Thanh Binh, H.T.: Base station location-aware optimization model of the lifetime of wireless sensor networks. Mob. Netw. Appl. **21**(1), 10–17 (2015). https://doi.org/10.1007/s11036-015-0614-3
5. Cha, H.-J., Yang, H.-K., Song, Y.-J.: A study on the design of fog computing architecture using sensor networks. Sensors **18**(11), 3633 (2018)
6. Ma, K., Bagula, A., Nyirenda, C., Ajayi, O.: An IoT-based fog computing model. Sensors **19**(12), 2783 (2019)
7. Nguyen, T.D., Trinh, H.T., Nguyen, N.T., Nguyen, T.T., Koichiro, W.: A new evaluation of particle filter algorithm and apply it to the wireless sensor networks. In: 2013 International Conference on Computing, Management and Telecommunications (ComManTel) (2013)

An International Overview and Meta-analysis for Using the Mechanical Ventilation in the Medical Treatment

Ha Quang Thinh Ngo[1,2(✉)]

[1] Department of Mechatronics, Faculty of Mechanical Engineering, Ho Chi
Minh City University of Technology (HCMUT), 268 Ly Thuong Kiet Street,
District 10, Ho Chi Minh City, Vietnam
nhqthinh@hcmut.edu.vn
[2] Vietnam National University Ho Chi Minh City, Linh Trung Ward, Thu Duc
District, Ho Chi Minh City, Vietnam

Abstract. There are a lot of injuries in lung that makes unique clinical challenges. Mechanical ventilator is considered as an useful solution to treat the respiratory patients. Especially, some of them become so serious that they must stay in Intensive Care Unit during a long time. It causes the overload status in order to take care all patients at the same time. Therefore, the better treatment by using the mechanical ventilator in the initial stage could reduce the rising number of patients and release the burden works for doctors and nurses. The purpose of this investigation is to examine various patterns of the mechanical ventilators and to determine potential opportunities for further development. Many research topics have been revised and synthesized during a long time, from January 2010 to present time, so that our results could provide a systematic overview and brief summary along the historical progress. In addition, a number of different resources which are available in the internet, is mentioned to offer a practical view. Most of these ventilators are classified into several sub-categories according to their technical specifications, usage and working principle. Pressure support and volume assist control are the most common signal for the initial mode in mechanical ventilator that used with or without the inhalation injury. All comments in these articles report in the affirmative that there are certain situations where the early intervention is essential. Target readers consist of doctors, nurses and medical staff who only concentrate on clinical factors and ignore the related technologies.

Keywords: Ventilation system · Respiratory patient · Infectious disease · Artificial inhalation · Home-based treatment

1 Introduction

In the field of medicine, the mechanical ventilation is one of the key methods for breathing aid when the respiratory failure occurs suddenly. The patients who suffer the respiratory diseases, could not breathe in the natural manner. Hence, the artificial ventilation support is a life-saving technique to deal with respiratory failures as soon as

P. Cong Vinh and A. Rakib (Eds.): ICCASA 2021, LNICST 409, pp. 226–235, 2021.
https://doi.org/10.1007/978-3-030-93179-7_18

possible. In general, there are two kinds of the respiratory support system, positive and negative pressure ventilation. However, the positive pressure mechanical ventilation [1] which is applied in various modalities [2], is superior and common. In recent time, to response to the larger requirements of patients [3–6], more investigations on technical ventilators are fully studied. The most important technique is to match the adaptive performance of airflow from artificial machine to human's breath. Obviously, it should be aware that any missing or problem during the respiratory process could cause the severe results for patients. Besides, the over-usage of sedatives or prolongation is able to take place during the medical therapy. To ensure the synchronization in breathing, the lung-like model which is simulated to track human's pattern. It is considered as an component in the control scheme for the type of adaptive support ventilation (ASV) in order to adjust robustly the deep breath and rate of airflow [7–9]. The control design is to maintain the lowest threshold of breathing rate and estimate the frequency of human's breath. In contrary way, the trigger signal from the neural ventilation system is fed to the machine of neutrally adjusted ventilatory assist (NAVA). This signal is activated by electrodes mounted on a naso-gastric tube located at the lower esophagus [10, 11]. Belong to this category, the proportional assist ventilation (PAV) provides the proportionally supplementary pressure to support patient as the additional efforts. In [12–14], the weaning technique could be noticed through the curing process [12–14].

In the last few months ago, there is an increased demand for ventilators during the treatment process of COVID-19 (coronavirus disease 2019) patients [15]. In fact, it is really catastrophic for humankind in those days. Even well-equipped hospitals have many efforts to meet the great increase in the number of sick persons such sharing the same air supply between two patients [16], they could not satisfy all requirements at the same time. To deal with the worldwide trouble of ventilator shortage, developers have innovated to release the low-cost, open-source ventilators [17, 18] for numerous patients. Basically, these developments are able to provide the instantaneous responses in hospital or healthcare service. It is agreed that this approach might be potentially one of the best solutions for poor nations or emergency case [19].

In fact, mechanical ventilator is a device which support human to breath in order to maintain their blood oxygenated. Once, a breathing regularly starts with inspiratory activity when air enters the lung, and ends with exhalation of breath when air is expiratory. The inspiration is prompted by differences of pressure which naturally exerted by diaphragm and the chest motion as well as by machine-driven mechanism, in human's airway that launches a flow of air. Whenever expiration, it is passive and motivated by the elastic force of tissues in lung. Generally, this machine is complicated and expensive in large.

Despite a change to non-invasive respiratory support, mechanical ventilation still becomes an essential tool for the medical care of critically ill patients. A variety of advanced techniques on medical devices with available modes and data fusion presents the potential solutions. Since various manufacturers utilize different nomenclature to depict relative modes of ventilation, communication among users of different machines has turned into challenges. The working modes of mechanical ventilation are often categorized into the act of breathing. Breaths could be started by a timing mechanism in spite of person's inspiratory efforts. Alternatively, breaths might be prompted by the patient's inspiration named as synchronization or patient-triggered ventilation.

2 Materials and Methods

2.1 Purpose

We conducted a survey to determine the development, usage and applications of potential strategies for medical treatment by ventilator-based therapy. Our targets are to synthesize, analysis and release the statistic evaluation in order to provide an overview of present status. The questionnaire consists of items about the purposes of using the ventilation system for clinical applications such:

– Where the ventilator is employed
– What diseases need the ventilator-based solution
– How the ventilator could be solved
– Why this machine is necessary to treat
– When the ventilation system is useful

2.2 Materials

It is important to investigate a large number of articles during the long period, from January 2010 to present time. The other sources such post-graduate dissertations, news, bulletins and so on are also cited in this work. Most of them are available in the cyber space where everyone could access freely and easily. Owing to these evidences, the historical development and the medical procedure to cure which patients are better, are demonstrated clearly. Besides, the advanced functions were added to response the newly adaptive ability of diseases. The progression of serious illness also affects on the health of patients, for instance a respiratory disease patient often suffers the rapid evolution comparing to their responses.

2.3 Target Readers

In our intention, the reader-oriented maxim is obviously integrated into the content of this work. Doctor or nurses could refer to this article to extend their knowledge which is only encapsulated in the medical field. Furthermore, it is similarly useful for the staff who are technical maintenance or operators, to discuss according to their jobs in hospital or healthcare center. Especially, it is considered as the valuable source for both medical students and mechanical learners.

3 Results of Research

In fact, a mechanical ventilator is a machine that helps a patient breathe (ventilate) when they are having surgery or cannot breathe on their own due to a critical illness. The patient is connected to the ventilator with a hollow tube (artificial airway) that goes in their mouth and down into their main airway or trachea. They remain on the ventilator until they improve enough to breathe on their own. Thus, this ventilator is used to decrease the work of breathing until patients improve enough to no longer need it. The machine makes sure that the body receives adequate oxygen and that carbon dioxide is removed. This is necessary when certain illnesses prevent normal breathing.

It is important to note that mechanical ventilation does not heal the patient. Rather, it allows the patient a chance to be stable while the medications and treatments help them to recover. The main benefits of mechanical ventilation are the following:

- The patient does not have to work as hard to breathe – their respiratory muscles rest
- The patient's as allowed time to recover in hopes that breathing becomes normal again
- Helps the patient get adequate oxygen and clears carbon dioxide
- Preserves a stable airway and preventing injury from aspiration

On the whole, Table 1 describes the summary reviews of previous articles in the interest topics. The first category named as the self-adjusted ventilation system or automated reimbursement ventilation, plays as a typical prototype for synchronization between human and machine. It mainly assists the burden work of patient's lung through the additional airflow. Usually, from the dynamical computation of mathematical model, the control rule is derived to manipulate the system parameters such pressure, airway and inspiratory inflow. The inspiration of patient initially triggers and cycles according to the natural breath. Furthermore, an operator must provide the initial coefficients such size and mode of the appropriate airway. Later, the automated search engine is activated and checks the data table to determine the airway resistance. At this time, the smart control scheme would order the driving commands based on the set-up model. Maybe, this machine must reveal the powerful abilities in computation and interpolation during short period.

Table 1. The review of the state-of-the-art researches.

Classification	Author(s)	Purpose	Advantage(s)	Disadvantage(s)
Adaptive Support Ventilation (ASV)	Claure, N. et al. [20]	Randomized crossover comparative study in a 12-bed ICU (intensive care unit)	In passive patients with acute respiratory failure, the proposed approach is safe and able to ventilate patients with less pressure while producing the same results in terms of oxygenation	Because of the diversity of patients treated, one algorithm might not fit all patients. The most severe and unstable patients or very specific patients require the tuned parameters
	Beijers, A. J. et al. [21]	Observational comparative study with automatically settings selected by ventilator	It is safe to utilize for ventilated patients with various lung conditions	Data is collected once a day and not continuously. Numbers of severe patients are too small to draw definite conclusions on safety

(*continued*)

Table 1. (*continued*)

Classification	Author(s)	Purpose	Advantage(s)	Disadvantage(s)
	Malli, F. et al. [9]	This systematic review provides the principle, algorithm and accuracy of closed-loop controlled oxygen device	The closed-loop controller maintain higher saturation levels, spend less time below the target saturation and save oxygen resources	Fail-safe mechanism, limited reliability of sensors and the need for standardized evaluating method of assessing risk are mentioned
	Hamama, K. M. et al. [22]	For a subgroup of patients, driving pressure and mechanical power are observed to predict the medical risk	In short term, this ventilator could choose the proper driving pressure and mechanical power in safe ranges for lung protection	Only one measurement is made per patient at a given time. Hence, the results do not reflect the average value over a longer period of time
Neutrally Adjusted Ventilatory Assist (NAVA)	De La Oliva, P., et al. [23]	Prospective study in spontaneously breathing patients intubates for acute respiratory failure	This ventilator reduces trigger delay, inspiratory time in excess and the number of patient-ventilator asynchronies in intubated patients	The clinical impact of this improved synchrony should be determined
	Yonis, H. et al. [24]	Comparative study between conventionally lung-protective mechanical ventilation (MV) and lung-protective MV with NAVA	This method decreases the medical risks although it does not improve survival in ventilated patients	The study by its very nature is unblinded, hence it could bias the decisions made by nursing service. Moreover, patient severity of illness is greater than expected
	Gross-Hardt, S. et al. [25]	Respiratory control by extracorporeal CO_2 removal on non-invasive NAVA	This investigation firstly introduces the usefulness of the electrical activity in diaphragm to monitor and guide patients with severe acute exacerbation	Randomized controlled trials in patients with severe acute exacerbations are needed to confirm
Proportional Assist Ventilation (PAV)	Lewis, K. A. et al. [26]	To synthesize the randomized controlled trials of PAV between invasive and non-invasive in critically ill patients	The systematic review and meta-analysis is novel in synthesizing current best evidence for clinical applications of PAV	This study does not support the clinical evidences for the usage of invasive or non-invasive PAV

(*continued*)

Table 1. (*continued*)

Classification	Author(s)	Purpose	Advantage(s)	Disadvantage(s)
	Sindelar, R. et al. [27]	The competitive effect on oxygenation between PAV and NAVA	The results indicate that there is no significant difference in oxygenation indices but NAVA is better in the alveolar arterial oxygen gradient	Whilst arterial samples might have been more precise, the use of capillary blood samples would have substantially influenced these results
	Rebelo, T. et al. [28]	The research of assisted parameters affecting on synchronization and inspiratory workload in PAV	This ventilator could reduce the work of breathing but it brings the asynchrony if the settings are not correct	All tests are performed on lung simulator and, under one typical lung mechanics setting
Noninvasive Open-source Mechanical Ventilator (NOMV)	Arcos Legarda, J. et al. [29]	Low-cost, open-source mechanical ventilator with pulmonary monitoring	The method considers pressure measurements from the inspiratory limb and alerts clinicians in real-time whether the patient is under a healthy situation or not	Alarms using either screen or speaker should be included for further safety cautions
	Zivcak, J. et al. [30]	Mechanical ventilator for baby	The ventilator prototype that produced by continuous positive airway pressure method, is for transferring intensive care between medical institutions	The working ability of long-time process is not ensured
	Borges, E. F. et al. [31]	Pediatric home mechanical ventilator after hospitalization	It allows earlier transition out of the pediatric ICU and with increasing disposition to enhance nursing facilities	The translation of acute-care ventilator management method to those with chronic respiratory failure is unclear
	Nguyen, J., et al. [32]	Mechanical ventilator milano for rapid, large-scale and low-cost production	It is designed to support the long-term invasive ventilation and operate in pressure-regulated ventilation modes	It needs to be verified under the international medical use instead of ISO standards

(*continued*)

Table 1. (*continued*)

Classification	Author(s)	Purpose	Advantage(s)	Disadvantage(s)
	Tharion, J. et al. [33]	A simple, low-cost alternative ventilator using a novel pressure-sensing approach and control algorithm	This technique is potential to provide safe emergency ventilation without any complicated sensors and control software while its construction enables reduction in cost and complexity	The study should be justified in progressing this technology to clinical trials
	Vivas, F. et al. [18]	A low-cost ventilator with readily-available hospital equipment for use in emergency or low-resource settings	This novel ventilator is able to safely and reliably ventilated patients with a range of pulmonary disease in a simulated setting	The current model offers only intermittent mandatory pressure-controlled ventilation
	Tsuzuki, M. S. et al. [34]	The enhanced version of MIT E-Vent in rapidly scalable ventilator prototype	A manual resuscitator, an external compression mechanism and a control system for adjusting tidal volume, inspiration-to-expiration ratio and respiratory rate are included	More advanced sensing modules, adaptive control scheme and stable software are additionally implemented

For the second group, in order to guarantee the high performance of the neutrally adjusted ventilatory assist, the servo control scheme must be taken account into the model of the first one. Nevertheless, this ventilator involves several extra-developments because of its complex platform. For the target of patient-ventilator synchrony, the mechanical ventilator aids either resistive or elastic component for the breathing process due to the respiratory reaction. Customarily, via the inflow, the proposed controller could symmetrically estimate the airway pressure depending on the data possessed from diaphragmatic breathing. Doctor or nurse feeds the fraction between pressure and voltage so as to control the airway pressure. Eventually, the third ventilation system, termed as proportional assist ventilation, often consists of advanced strategy such a servo targeting circuit. In reality, this kind of machine utilizes the more innovative model and difficult computation than the others. Similarly, the third ventilator takes care both resistive and elastic work of breath related to the patient's respiratory effort. This system collects various feedback signals in term of patient-ventilator synchrony. Besides, the operating principle is to regulate pressure based on the equation of air motion. To trigger the operating mode, an operator must insert the desired settings for elastance and resistance to be maintained.

In recent time, the concept of open-source hardware is commonly risen in our community, especially for the mechanical ventilator. To aim at the treatment and prevention of COVID-19, modern microprocessor-based electronic devices have been embedded such that the complexity of control scheme, advanced functions and powerful resources are allowed to implement. In [35], researchers has studied a microcontroller-driven mechanical ventilator using AmbuBag which is pressed by the arm mechanism. The trajectory of mechanical components is planned by camshaft (CAM) generation. The output results presents the time-varying characteristic of tidal volume. In the same method but different mechanism, authors [36] developed a low-cost, open-source ventilator that was initialized by the global shortage of mechanical ventilator for COVID-19 patients. The driving motor which is controlled by Raspberry Pi, provides the maximum pressure up to 70 cm H_2O. Additionally, although the design is simple but efficient, the experimental device for ventilation satisfies the desired volume and pressure in respect to clinical requirements [37]. For future steps, developers discusses about reliability of the mechanisms and software, mass production with appropriate standards and regulatory approval or exemption. With portable purpose, investigators in [38] introduce an ease-to-use and mobile version of AmbuBag-based compression machine. This system is manipulated by Arduino and offers various breathing modes with varying tidal volumes. The rate for breathing is from 5 to 40 breaths/minute and max ratio between inhalation and exhalation is 1:4. The repeatability and precise exceeding personal capabilities in this design are proved in experiments. Although the original design consisting of two paddles is actuated by an electric motor [39], there are still several efforts to represent the pressure-controlled ventilation. It is noted that the usage of electromechanical actuators to press AmbuBag is an excellent solution. Whether the supplies of compressed air is available or not, the tidal volume could increase linearly [40].

4   Conclusion

This work has documented a hugely potential development for mechanical ventilator in clinical therapies. There is wide variation in the diagnosis, inside structure, working principle and management among ventilation systems. The data presented suggest that both doctors and nurses should decide a proper treatment based on the actual condition of the respiratory patients. Many researchers and developers ought to focus on which type is necessary to implement for our community in present-day.

Some results, such as the methodical classifiers, might be beneficial for future work. Although the mechanical ventilators are either the commercial product or not, their motivations still need to encourage owing to public health. Particularly, the open-source design should be promoted to extend for common knowledge so that each patient could build it by themselves. As a result, the solution for home-based treatment is efficient and feasible in the overload of hospital or healthcare center.

Acknowledgements. We acknowledge the support of time and facilities from Ho Chi Minh City University of Technology (HCMUT), VNU-HCM for this study.

References

1. Pham, T., Brochard, L.J., Slutsky, A.S.: Mechanical ventilation: state of the art. In: Mayo Clinic Proceedings, vol. 92, no. 9, pp. 1382–1400. Elsevier, September 2017
2. Gattinoni, L., et al.: The future of mechanical ventilation: lessons from the present and the past. Crit. Care 21(1), 1–11 (2017)
3. Yoshida, T., et al.: Volume-controlled ventilation does not prevent injurious inflation during spontaneous effort. Am. J. Respir. Crit. Care Med. 196(5), 590–601 (2017)
4. Holanda, M.A., Vasconcelos, R.D.S., Ferreira, J.C., Pinheiro, B.V.: Patient-ventilator asynchrony. J. Bras. Pneumol. 44, 321–333 (2018)
5. Shen, D., Zhou, Y., Shi, Y.: Coupling effects of double lungs on dynamic characteristics of volume-controlled mechanical insufflation-exsufflation secretion clearance system. J. Dyn. Syst. Measur. Control 140(7), 071008 (2018)
6. Krause, H., Kraemer, J.F., Penzel, T., Kurths, J., Wessel, N.: On the difference of cardiorespiratory synchronisation and coordination. Chaos: Interdisc. J. Nonlinear Sci. 27(9), 093933 (2017)
7. De Bie, A.J., et al.: Fully automated postoperative ventilation in cardiac surgery patients: a randomised clinical trial. Br. J. Anaesth. 125(5), 739–749 (2020)
8. Bayram, B., Şancı, E.: Invasive mechanical ventilation in the emergency department. Turkish J. Emerg. Med. 19(2), 43–52 (2019)
9. Malli, F., Boutlas, S., Lioufas, N., Gourgoulianis, K.I.: Automated oxygen delivery in hospitalized patients with acute respiratory failure: a pilot study. Can. Respir. J. (2019)
10. Chen, C., Wen, T., Liao, W.: Neurally adjusted ventilatory assist versus pressure support ventilation in patient-ventilator interaction and clinical outcomes: a meta-analysis of clinical trials. Ann. Transl. Med. 7(16) (2019)
11. Vaporidi, K.: NAVA and PAV+ for lung and diaphragm protection. Curr. Opin. Crit. Care 26(1), 41–46 (2020)
12. Ou-Yang, L.J., Chen, P.H., Jhou, H.J., Su, V.Y.F., Lee, C.H.: Proportional assist ventilation versus pressure support ventilation for weaning from mechanical ventilation in adults: a meta-analysis and trial sequential analysis. Crit. Care 24(1), 1–10 (2020)
13. Wilcox, M.E., Vaughan, K., Chong, C.A., Neumann, P.J., Bell, C.M.: Cost-effectiveness studies in the ICU: a systematic review. Crit. Care Med. 47(8), 1011–1017 (2019)
14. Sklar, M.C., et al.: Duration of diaphragmatic inactivity after endotracheal intubation of critically ill patients. Crit. Care 25(1), 1–15 (2021)
15. Qiu, J., Shen, B., Zhao, M., Wang, Z., Xie, B., Xu, Y.: A nationwide survey of psychological distress among Chinese people in the COVID-19 epidemic: implications and policy recommendations. Gen. Psychiatry 33(2) (2020)
16. Beitler, J.R., et al.: Ventilator sharing during an acute shortage caused by the COVID-19 pandemic. Am. J. Respir. Crit. Care Med. 202(4), 600–604 (2020)
17. Pearce, J.M.: Distributed manufacturing of open source medical hardware for pandemics. J. Manuf. Mater. Process. 4(2), 49 (2020)
18. Vivas Fernández, F.J., et al.: ResUHUrge: a low cost and fully functional ventilator indicated for application in COVID-19 patients. Sensors 20(23), 6774 (2020)
19. Acho, L., Vargas, A.N., Pujol-Vázquez, G.: Low-cost, open-source mechanical ventilator with pulmonary monitoring for COVID-19 patients. In: Actuators, vol. 9, no. 3, p. 84. Multidisciplinary Digital Publishing Institute, September 2020
20. Claure, N., Bancalari, E.: Automated closed loop control of inspired oxygen concentration. Respir. Care 58(1), 151–161 (2013)
21. Beijers, A.J.R., Roos, A.N., Bindels, A.J.G.H.: Fully automated closed-loop ventilation is safe and effective in post-cardiac surgery patients. Intensive Care Med. 40(5), 752–753 (2014). https://doi.org/10.1007/s00134-014-3234-7

22. Hamama, K.M., Fathy, S.M., AbdAlrahman, R.S., Alsherif, S.E.D.I., Ahmed, S.A.: Driving pressure-guided ventilation versus protective lung ventilation in ARDS patients: a prospective randomized controlled study. Egypt. J. Anaesth. **37**(1), 261–267 (2021)
23. de la Oliva, P., Schüffelmann, C., Gómez-Zamora, A., Villar, J., Kacmarek, R.M.: Asynchrony, neural drive, ventilatory variability and COMFORT: NAVA versus pressure support in pediatric patients. a non-randomized cross-over trial. Intensive Care Med. **38**(5), 838–846 (2012). https://doi.org/10.1007/s00134-012-2535-y
24. Yonis, H., et al.: Patient-ventilator synchrony in Neurally Adjusted Ventilatory Assist (NAVA) and Pressure Support Ventilation (PSV): a prospective observational study. BMC Anesthesiol. **15**(1), 1–9 (2015)
25. Gross-Hardt, S., et al.: Low-flow assessment of current ECMO/ECCO 2 R rotary blood pumps and the potential effect on hemocompatibility. Crit. Care **23**(1), 1–9 (2019)
26. Lewis, K.A., et al.: Comparison of ventilatory modes to facilitate liberation from mechanical ventilation: protocol for a systematic review and network meta-analysis. BMJ Open **9**(9), e030407 (2019)
27. Sindelar, R., McKinney, R.L., Wallström, L., Keszler, M.: Proportional assist and neurally adjusted ventilation: clinical knowledge and future trials in newborn infants. Pediatr. Pulmonol. **56**(7), 1841–1849 (2021)
28. Rebelo, T., et al.: ATENA–a novel rapidly manufactured medical invasive ventilator designed as a response to the COVID-19 pandemic: testing protocol, safety, and performance validation. Front. Med. 1312 (2021)
29. Arcos-Legarda, J., Tovar, A.: Mechatronic design and active disturbance rejection control of a bag valve-based mechanical ventilator. J. Med. Dev. **15**(3), 031006 (2021)
30. Živčák, J., et al.: A portable BVM-based emergency mechanical ventilator. In: 2021 IEEE 19th World Symposium on Applied Machine Intelligence and Informatics (SAMI), pp. 000229–000234. IEEE, January 2021
31. Borges, E.F., Borges-Júnior, L.H., Carvalho, A.J.L., Ferreira, H.M., Hattori, W.T., de Oliveira Azevedo, V.M.G.: Invasive home mechanical ventilation: 10-year experience of a pediatric home care service. Respir. Care **65**(12), 1800–1804 (2020)
32. Nguyen, J., et al.: Repurposing CPAP machines as stripped-down ventilators. Sci. Rep. **11**(1), 1–9 (2021)
33. Tharion, J., Kapil, S., Muthu, N., Tharion, J.G., Kanagaraj, S.: Rapid manufacturable ventilator for respiratory emergencies of COVID-19 disease. Trans. Indian Nat. Acad. Eng. **5**, 373–378 (2020)
34. Tsuzuki, M.S.G., et al.: Mechanical ventilator VENT19. Polytechnica **4**(1), 33–46 (2021). https://doi.org/10.1007/s41050-021-00031-z
35. Marzetti, S., et al.: Low cost artificial ventilator embedding unsupervised learning for hardware failure detection [society news]. IEEE Circuits Syst. Mag. **21**(3), 73–79 (2021)
36. Ramos-Paz, S., Belmonte-Izquierdo, R., Inostroza-Moreno, L.A., Velasco-Rivera, L.F., Mendoza-Villa, R., Gaona-Flores, V.: Mechatronic design and robust control of an artificial ventilator in response to the COVID-19 pandemic. In: 2020 IEEE International Autumn Meeting on Power, Electronics and Computing (ROPEC), vol. 4, pp. 1–6. IEEE, November 2020
37. Domènech-Mestres, C., Blanco-Romero, E., de la Fuente-Morató, A., Ayala-Chauvin, M.: Design for the automation of an AMBU Spur II manual respirator. Machines **9**(2), 45 (2021)
38. Skrzypczak, N.G., Tanikella, N.G., Pearce, J.M.: Open source high-temperature RepRap for 3-D printing heat-sterilizable PPE and other applications. HardwareX **8**, e00130 (2020)
39. MIT E-Vent. MIT emergency ventilator project. https://e-vent.mit.edu/
40. AndalucíaRespira. https://www.andaluciarespira.com/en/andalucia-respira-en

Blockchain-Based Governance in Fractional Ownership: Mitigating Zero-Sum Games Through Decentralized Autonomous Agents

Mina Cu$^{(\boxtimes)}$, Johnny Chan, Gabrielle Peko, and David Sundaram

The University of Auckland, Auckland 1010, New Zealand
{mina.cu, jh.chan, g.peko, d.sundaram}@auckland.ac.nz

Abstract. The sharing economy is a mega-trend in the world and fractional homeownership is on the rise. When each transaction is a high-stake bargaining game involving multiple stakeholders, maintaining a harmonious and friction-less fractional ownership in real estate is challenging. While academics and practitioners have been focusing on nascent technology like blockchain application in this domain, their potential in supporting the governance of fractional ownership is not fully understood. Using a design science research approach, this paper studies the conflicts of interests in fractional ownership real estate transactions through the lens of zero-sum game and three dimensions of full, equal, and trustful participations. It then proposes a novel, blockchain-based governance ecosystem built on a decentralized autonomous organization.

Keywords: Blockchain · Governance · Risk, and compliance · Decentralized autonomous organization · Fractional ownership

1 Introduction

More and more, we need to share our place in a very open way. Some symbolic examples of the sharing economy mega-trend are the Airbnb model or the property unit ownerships and fractional house ownerships. The current situation of the real estate market in developed countries, including the US, is that people who can afford to buy a house individually are getting older. Owning only a shared building unit or one fraction of a house becomes a preferable choice for individuals to get onto the housing ladder [1]. In the context of this study, the fractional ownership real estate transaction (FORET) is referred to as the housing transactions of people who could not afford or own a house individually but desire to buy a fraction of a place to live. This definition of fractional ownership is purposefully distinguished from other investment ownership such as real estate investment trusts (REITs), shares, or tokenized assets. Agents play an essential role in this type of real estate transaction. Without an agent, the consumer becomes a less protected and more vulnerable party [2]. As FORET is one of the most complex types of real estate transaction [3], the time required to finish a FORET might be counted by years if it involves a mortgage or loan. Prior research revealed that the dilemma of a real estate transaction is often rooted from the incomplete information

P. Cong Vinh and A. Rakib (Eds.): ICCASA 2021, LNICST 409, pp. 236–254, 2021.
https://doi.org/10.1007/978-3-030-93179-7_19

condition of joint-ownership agreement [1, 4]. FORET involves multiple owners and intermediaries such as lawyers, banks, insurance companies, sales agents, and so on. This means the conflicts of interests in a FORET are multiple and multilayers. Solving the conflicts of interest in a FORET to achieve harmonious and successful ownership is challenging. Transaction participants need to rely on an optimal search strategy based on the information they have. Once the demand and supply match, buyer and seller will start engaging in a series of bargaining games that are usually chaotic with interwoven strategies [4]. Thus, it often results in not achieving a FORET match. For example, to maximize the benefits, both agent and principle would hide some part of information regarding the property. Or more seriously, an agent might work for two sellers on the same real estate with different fractions without their knowing. On the other hand, if the bargaining is successful, buyer and seller will need to deal with several arrangements with agents, which often become a puzzle. The full ownership real estate transaction has been proven as a highly complex process, especially in the high value low frequency transactions [5]. In FORET, the complex of communication and interaction between participants is shifted to a higher level due to the assemble of multiple agents and multiple owners (Fig. 1). Motivated by these issues, this paper desires to shed light on the principal-agent problems in a FORET from zero-sum game perspectives aiming to provide a solution to mitigate the relevant conflict of interests. The paper first seeks answers to the research questions "what are the zero-sum games of principal-agent problems in a FORET? And how to use information tools to mitigate these conflicts of interests?". Prior studies have looked at principal-agent problems in real estate transactions under game perspectives such as the transactional game by Berne [6], Patron and Roskelley's bargaining game [7], Lulu and Zhi multi-agents' game [8]. Nevertheless, these studies mostly focus on the bargaining game. Moreover, none of the previous works has converted the real estate game into three subcategories to analyze its principal-agent problems. By answering the research questions, this paper shows a need for solutions that move beyond business-as-usual using evidence from science to reassess the relationships between agent and principal. Such solutions can help governing transaction execution and mitigating conflict of interests between involved parties. One of the potential solution is the emerging technology of blockchain, which is growing attention in supporting fractional ownership transactions. Several studies have proposed blockchain solutions to resolve transactional verification, transparency, and governance [9, 10]. It is notable that even though blockchain remains in its nascent years, it is predicted to be a potential decentralized governance framework for real estate property [11, 12].

Design science research (DSR) is a methodology that is motivated by the desire to improve the environment by the introduction of innovative artifacts and the processes for building these artifacts [13]. Using DSR as the methodology, this paper aims to (i) identify problems of FORET using the agency theory approach with the support of online experiment platform, (ii) Develop a novel governance, risk, and compliance (GRC) framework typically for fractional ownership real estate transactions that benefits involved parties, (iii) improve transaction transparency to mitigate conflict of interest in the multi-owned property, and (iv) fulfill the knowledge gaps of fractional ownership research domain. The following discussion reviews the relevant extent literature. Next, the adopted design science research methodology is explained. Then the conceptual artefacts, proof of concept, and the system artefact will be described in the discussion and evaluation plan.

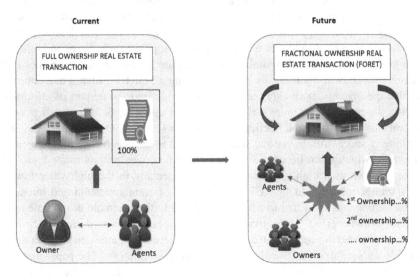

Fig. 1. Full and fractional ownership real estate transactions.

2   Literature Review

2.1   Real Estate Transactional Games

The transactional game emphasizes using transactions to discover information [6]. In the context of Berne's [6] study, a game is an ongoing series of complementary ulterior transactions progressing to a predictable outcome. A game is generally established by a set of repetitious and plausible transactions with a concealed motivation. One of the typical transactional games is the "insurance game", in which no matter what type of interaction, the agents will perform as a hard player as they aim for the highest outcome of the game – the clients sign the insurance contracts. This principle also applies to other games and occupations such as "the real estate game", "the panama game", and the "balance Sheet" game. In the transactional game, how individuals interact with one another, and how the ego states affect each set of transactions would be fully focused. By which, the transactional game believes that the change of these interactions would be the path to solve the problems by providing solutions rather than just the understanding. The unproductive or counterproductive transactions would be considered as the signs of problems at the ego state. Berne [6] believes that virtually everyone has something problematic about their ego states. Hence, the negative behaviors cannot be solved by giving the treatment to the problematic behaviors only but by analyzing individual's developmental history to adjust their behaviors from the root. Berne [6] purports that the most important aspects of transactional game is the contract, which is an agreement made by both players to pursue specific goals that each of the player desires.

In terms of principal-agent problem in a transactional game, Grohman [2] identified the elements that are necessary for an agency relationship to exist between the selling broker and the purchaser. As a result, the purchaser usually reveals to the broker material information which the broker is obligated to disclose to the seller. Following this perspective, Clauretie and Daneshvary [14] conducted a quantitative study in exploring the volatility of property price impact on principal-agent problem during the transaction timelines. The study suggested that bargaining power is a factor that impacts the successful outcome of real estate transactions. By estimating the effects of the changes that agent made on selling timeline and transaction price, the findings showed that except for the high amount of agency costs, the agent-consumer tactics changed when it was closer to the expired date of listing contract. The discrepancy between agent and consumer's expectations regarding listed transaction fees would create principal-agent conflict. This conflict usually resulted in a change of agent before the transaction finishes, which is equivalent to the weakening bargaining power of the consumer. Specifically, prices are lower if the property is sold near the expiration of the listing contract, indicating that the price-reduction effect dominates the broker-efforts. By using multi methodological approach, Yavas [4] identified that broker played a more prominent role during a real estate transaction than any other third party, and the principal-agent problem engaged in the seller-broker relationship. Patron and Roskelley [7] analyzed the two-period bargaining game between buyers, sellers, and real estate agents which were selected to determine the sales price of a house. The results showed that agents seemed to pay less effort on bargaining when receiving commissions or working for buyer. Agents perform similarly with little effort on bargaining advice in the less market competition condition. While when the potential returns were large or the second agent appear, agents likely bargained aggressively. The same scenario appeared when the house's sales price is closely related to the agent's reputation and future business opportunities.

Lulu and Zhi [8] figured out that investment process of decision-making in the real estate market is a multi-agent-stage dynamic process. In this process, the ultimate equilibrium is an outcome of most of the games that the participants adjusted themselves under certain conditions. Based on Berne's [6] perspective, Ricks and Egbert [15] discovered that applications mostly relied on simulated crowds to populate games and system architecture resulting in the issue that agents did not socialize naturally with each other. The study thus proposed an expressive algorithm for adding a new dimension of realism into simulations. This architecture allowed agents to have multiple social interactions with other agents evolving multiple stages extracted from the psychological area of transactional analysis. Remarkably, the presented algorithm had a flexible architecture that will run with almost any obstacle avoidance algorithm. It included bi-modal crowds and social environments that can be changed in real-time. The results showed that the social crowd algorithm tested in real-time with up to 4,000 agents were far more realistic behaviors than previously simulated. Kim, Bang, and Ko [16] emphasized that inter-agent interactions played an important role in digital space for social interactions between agents and people. The study developed a simulation that replaced human communication by a card game. This card game was corresponded to the ego state model of transactional game. The agent communication module represented the agent-agent transactions based on the ego state model. The agents, the attacker, and defender, then participated in a game simulation with the cards that have messages and personalities. To win the game, the agents firstly needed to identify the intentions of their opponent – other agents. Then showing a card that matched their opponent's sample word or personality. Transactional games are believed that they could be applied to investigate economic decision-making process of principal and agent [6]. As individual economic actors in markets interaction might be influenced by subconscious cognitive processes and transactional games, there may exist an historical component that could adjust these principal-agent' behaviors. The study tried to seek evidence that showed the impact of subconscious social transaction games played between individuals on outcomes of the decision strategy in the context of a marketplace.

Using agency theory as an approach to research conflicts of interests between transaction participants has long been conducted ubiquitously. Nevertheless, there is only a limited amount of research has framed the principal-agent problem into games. Notably, among these studies, the principal-agent problem hasn't been studied in a specific domain of fractional ownership and included three dimensions of full, equal, and trustful participations in order to propose a solution via improvement of governance, risk, and compliance (GRC).

2.2   Blockchain-Based Governance

Blockchain Governance, Risk, and Compliance (GRC) in Real Estate. The effectiveness of GRC in adjusting strategic decisions of transactions' participants has been proven in prior research. It is believed that IT GRC provides a framework of decision rights and accountabilities that provoke the desirable behavior of participants [17]. From this perspective, Butler and McGovern [18] build a conceptual model and information system (IS) framework for the design and adoption of an environmental compliance management system. With the focus on environmental compliance and risk, this study explores the problems of GRC in dealing with regulations and to identify how these problems are being solved using the compliance management system. Furthermore, the study proposes a process-based conceptual model and related IS framework on the design and adoption of this compliance management system. Surujnath [19] proves that blockchain could radically reinvent the existing market infrastructure, hence the current body of derivatives laws and regulations would need to be amended to adapt to these changes. By analyzing scholarly articles and the opinions of actively engaged entrepreneurs, Sulklowski [20] identifies that distributed electronic ledgers will only be realized in the context of effective GRC. The current capacity of real estate management provided by a tech tycoon in Blockchain-as-a-service (BaaS) such as SAP or IBM includes object management, contract management, credit management, space optimization, and business process management. Nevertheless, it remains a lack of comprehensive transaction governance framework built on blockchain for fractional real estate transaction. Several academic studies have been carried on the applications of blockchain for real estate management: Wang and Kogan [21] employed DSR to build up a confidentiality-preserving Blockchain-based transaction processing system; Study by Chong et al. [22] presented a comparative case study of five blockchain-based business models to prove that blockchain is effective in improving business processes governance; Ziolkowski, Miscione, and Schwabe [23] used the qualitative method to study decision problems in blockchain governance. The findings of these studies provided a better understanding of how blockchain governance links to existing concepts and how it is enacted in practice. In terms of using DSR methodology, Wouda and Opdenakker [24] proposed a framework to improve the quality of the data by using the decentralized mechanism though which enhance the transaction process of an office building. The study also presented an application that was built up alongside the design. Hoksbergen et al. [5] employed DSR to propose a hash table database with a blockchain backbone for knowledge management of high value low frequency real estate transactions. Aiming to resolve the conflicts of interest between agent and consumer in real estate transaction, Huh and Kim [25] used blockchain to validate algorithms that could secure real estate transactions through encryption. Notably, Huh and Kim [25] built up a research model to compare and verify the practical Byzantine fault tolerance (PBFT) algorithm of hyperledger through the blockchain agreement process. The authors then implemented a virtual machine (VM) research methodology to propose a verification process for real estate contracts. This finding represented that the main functions of the smart contract could be included in the elastic models. However, this study mainly focused on rental aspects of real estate transactions that have been popularly provided by BaaS companies recently. The current research and BaaS services showed that there is a gap in bridging blockchain and governance for real estate transactions, specifically for FORET. Nevertheless, the flourishing services of blockchain-based GRC in building management, as well as the current research framework proved that there is a possibility of constructing a comprehensive blockchain-based GRC for a typical type of real estate transaction including FORET. A qualitative study by Kim [12] in analyzing fractional ownership in blockchain-enabled asset tokenization figured out that blockchain is expected to resolve problems of centralization, inefficiency, and information asymmetry in the innovative market. Whitaker and Kräussl proposed a conceptual framework for retained fractional equity that might potentially have broad implications for compensation of early-stage creative work in any field [26]. Graglia and Mellon [27] examined that blockchain is a novel technology in its characteristics as a social technology. It thus can be designed to govern the behaviour of groups of people through social and financial incentives. Konashevych [28] presented a concept of real estate tokenization, which includes legal, technological, and organizational aspects. The study proposed a theory of a title token which can be a basis for developing a new type of property registries. Current research on tokenization assets built on blockchain shows the possibility of employing such technology to develop a GRC framework for fractional ownership transactions, of which FORET would be a sample that has a reasonable scale to build up a pilot study.

The Decentralized Autonomous Organization as Autonomous Agent. The concept of Decentralized Autonomous Organization (DAO) was originally derived from Bitcoin, which also can be concerned as the initial prototype of DAO. The appearance of DAO has shifted GRC to a new level [11]. The DAO, which acts as the manager of smart contracts, is operated autonomously in a decentralized network architecture [10, 29]. By which, it significantly transforms the traditional ways of payment, transaction structure, ledger, protocol, ownership, and information verification into a brand-new type of governance recognition [9]. Based on DAO functions, Merkle described DAO as an entity that owns internal property that can update its internal state, is responsive to the members, and run the smart contracts [10]. These are some of the most basic functions which DAOs can perform through its organs provided by the Ethereum blockchain. Nevertheless, there are no compliance standards (like the ERC20 for tokens) for DAO. Motivated by this issue, Buterin [30] published a series of codes to program DAO that contains the assets and encodes the bylaws of smart contracts. This white paper suggested that Ethereum provides blockchain with a built-in fully-fledged Turing-complete programming language by which smart-contracts can be utilized to encode arbitrary state transition functions. However, DAO remains constraints in its technical design, typically in the security issues. Forward and Dhillon explained a DAO is a blockchain entity built on a consensus of decisions by its members which is presented in the form of DAO tokens usually [31]. There are only two entities participating in a DAO, including an executive (company) and members (smart contracts). Forward and Dhillon thus denoted DAO's significant steps in running a crowdfunding project such as setting up DAO, creating a wallet, creating stocks, assigning shares, issuing new stocks, and assigning shares to the other entity under the bylaws. Following this research stream, Norta [32] built up the electronic community of business collaborating DAOs to the point of consensually agreed upon smart contracts. The study resolved the problem of currently existing smart-contract solutions that equip the protocol layer on top of blockchains with Turing-complete programming languages by introducing the agent-based negotiation into DAO. This negotiation is a semi to fully automated negotiation. The agent-based coordinated-negotiation architecture allows conducting complex cross-organizational collaborations. Due to DAO is programmed to be an optimal system, without inefficient human negotiations where all policies were defined by program code [29], it allows investors to finance and manage new companies on the Ethereum blockchain directly.

3   Design Science Research Methodology

As DSR examines the problems through an inherent awareness of existing problems rather than by primarily an observation method for example. It generally guides the study design for the development of a new system [13, 33]. Owing to this paper seeks for the problems between participants of a FORET in order to develop a GRC system as a solution, it thus is suitable to follow DSR framework. The multi methodological approach is included to give a deeper understanding of research problems and propose solutions by the full or partial integration of more than one methodology [34]. In a real estate game, both agent and consumer are rational, thus they always try to maximize the payoffs. Hence, their strategy might change during the bargaining process depending on the actual situation. Due to the adjustable nature of strategic decisions of agent and consumer in the real estate games, it's insufficient to observe the negotiation process by only one experiment. This paper thus included the design of the experiment (DOE) approach to the DSR methodology framework. The integration of the DOE approach is to execute the experiments of three levels of games. The DOE approach propounds experimenters doing a sequence of small experiments instead of relying on one big experiment to give the answers [35, 36]. DOE emphasizes that while one big experiment might provide a valid result, it is more general to perform multiple experiments before attaining the final answer. In other words, repeatedly conduct small experiments might give more insights into the research subjects. The sequential or iterative approach of DOE thus works best as the logical move through stages of experiments. Each stage of the experiment provides insight as to how should the next experiment get done. Based on the cyclic multi-methodological approach by Nunamaker et al. [33], this paper implemented the DOE approach to construct an experimental design science research (EDSR) framework (Fig. 2).

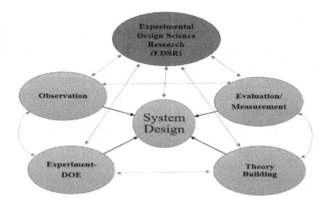

Fig. 2. The EDSR framework.

The significance of the EDSR is, by including the DOE approach, it builds up the artefacts and systems based on the results obtained through a series of small experiments. It thus can be considered as a unique approach to the DSR methodology. In the context of this research, following the EDSR framework, the strategic decisions of agent and consumer were tested repeatedly throughout game sessions. It thus can reflect comprehensively the conflicts of interests between agent and consumer with a higher reliability of test results. Hence, the choice of integrating DOE into the DSR cycle is appropriate. Anderson and Whitcomb [39] argue that the DOE is a crucial element in the success of process development and improvement. In contrast to traditional experimental methods, DOE delivers a more effective and scientific approach to achieve meaningful results. DOE thus has been widely acknowledged as a foundational work in experimental design. Up to now, DOE has been applied across research domains including information systems (IS) areas [39].

4 Conceptual Artifact

This paper focuses on conflict of interests in FORET. By proposing a blockchain-based GRC system framework, it expects to mitigate the zero-sum games between agents and consumers by implementing decentralized autonomous agents. The theoretical framework underlying the establishment of Fig. 3 revolves around agent and consumer's conflicts of interests and is a linkage of relevant studies on real estate zero-sum games from agency theory perspective. This theoretical framework established a foundation for constructing conceptual and system artefacts. The conceptual artefacts, which were constructed by using the EDSR framework, include the concept of participation dimensions in a FORET reflected in the zero-sum games between agent and consumer. These dimensions include:

- The search game – the "full" dimension. This game refers to the efforts of obtaining the entire body of information. This game reflects the principal-agent problem in the early stage of FORET.
- The bargaining game – The "equal" dimension. This game reflects the efforts to negotiate the agency costs meanwhile guarantee equal rights and responsibilities of both agent and consumer.
- The trust game – The trustful dimension. This game refers to finding the optimal "Nash equilibrium" in trust of both sides to avoid risks accompanied by violable contracts (see Fig. 3).

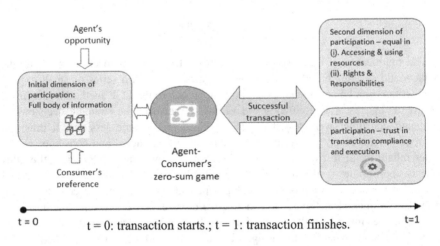

Fig. 3. Dimensions of agent-consumer's participations.

While the problems in FORET, which are zero-sum games between participants, lay on GRC framework, the blockchain technology would serve as a potential solution. The implication of agency theory approach performs as a bridge to deliver the solutions to resolve these problems. This interconnection created multidisciplinary research in the context of information systems.

5 Proof of Concept

This paper provides the proof of concept for the proposed conceptual artefacts by using the DOE approach integrated into DSR methodology to executing experiments on the oTreehub. oTree is an open-source and online platform for implementing interactive experiments in the visual laboratory. By using oTree, this paper simulates three levels of conflict of interest between agent and consumer in a FORET. The experimental factors include agent and consumer. Three levels of experiments include search game, bargaining game, and trust game.

5.1 Search Game Experimental Design

A search game is a zero-sum game with two players that occurs in a search place [37]. It can also be expanded to the business domain that contains representative dilemmas such as the principal-agent problem. In the context of this experiment, the search game is converted to become an online experimental game on the oTreehub website, for instance the Matching Pennies game. The Matching Pennies game is a zero-sum game as one's gain is the other's loss (Fig. 4). The probability of choosing "Heads" or "Tails" is distributed between players, and there is no Nash equilibrium. The asymmetric payoffs of the Matching Pennies game can represent the full dimension of participations – the whole body of information. For example, to get higher interest, the agent might have to decide whether to disclose or not the full information to the consumer and vice versa.

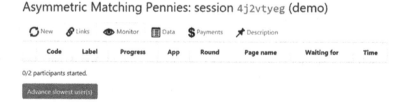

Fig. 4. Matching pennies game configuration.

The experiment has three stages each session. Each stage has four rounds. The player will be matched with another one in the room and play four rounds with the same player. After each stage, the player will be matched with a new player. In each stage, the agent will be the Row player, and the consumer will be the Column player. Both agents and consumers simultaneously choose between "Heads" and "Tails". If their choices match, the Row player (consumer) earns 0, while the Column player (agent) earns 1. If the choices mismatch, the Row player (consumer) earns 1, while the Column player (agent) earns 0. Adopting this simulation to be the principal-agent problem in the context of FORET can be denoted as below: (i) "Heads" and "Tails" can represent the strategy of agent and consumer separately for provide full information or hide part of the information, (ii) when the choices match, whether both provide complete information or conceal information, the agent earns the point for getting the transaction done. The consumer earns 0 for paying fees for a fair service, no gain no loss, (iii) when the choices mismatch, it means there is asymmetric information between agent and consumer. The agent then earns zero for failing to acquire the consumer. The consumer earns 1 for not paying fees but gains a certain amount of knowledge or experience, (iv) in the case both agent and consumer earning 0, the transaction can still be considered as complete as the consumer pays fees to gain a fair service, agents get the number of costs which is equivalent to expense without earning.

5.2   Bargaining Game Experimental Design

The bargaining game is the most popular type of principal-agent problem in a real estate transaction [14]. This experiment is designed typically for the bargaining game in the context of FORET. In this game, two players will perform the role of agent and consumer separately. They will be matched with each other to conduct bargaining over the distribution of lottery tickets. There are 100 lottery tickets that can be divided between agent and consumer. Each player's payoffs are based on the outcome of a lottery conducted at the end of the game. It will define who the winner is. Each player will be in a different lottery, and the value of cash prizes might be varied. This design is to match with the fact that even though a FORET can be established, the consumer and agent will face uncertainties after signing the agreements. This type of issue is similar to drawing a lottery at the end of the game. Nevertheless, it might not always be the result that one is the winner, and one is the loser. It might instead be that both agents and consumers win the respective lotteries, or both lose the lotteries. The likelihood of winning relied on the numbers of lottery tickets that the player has. In other words, the bigger number, the higher possibility to win. For instance, if the player has 10 tickets, the probability of winning is 0.10; if the player has 50 tickets, the probability of winning the cash prize is 0.50, and so on. Once the game begins, two players have up to five minutes to bargain with each other regarding how to divide the 100 lottery tickets. The agent and the consumer can each make an unlimited number of proposals. These proposals are in the form of: I receive [BLANK] tickets, and you receive [BLANK] tickets. The total number of proposed tickets cannot be larger than 100. Each time each player makes a proposal, the amount is showed on the other person's screen. If the player accepts the proposal at any time within five minutes, the game is successfully completed, and each player received the number of tickets as proposed. If two players cannot reach an agreement, the game is failed, and both receive zero tickets. The cash prize is distributed separately between two players with different amounts. Both players do not know the cash prize that the other person would receive if he/she wins and vice versa (Fig. 5).

Cooperative Bargaining Game: session `ars60fmu` (demo)

Code	Label	Progress	App	Round	Page name	Waiting for	Time

0/2 participants started.

Advance slowest user(s)

Fig. 5. Bargaining game configuration.

5.3   Trust Game Experimental Design

The Trust Game or the investment game, which was initially designed by Berg et al. is an experiment of choice to measure trust in economic decisions [36]. The concept of trust in the study by Berg et al. referred to the confidence in an economic primitive. In other words, trust is the principle of the player's interest per se in an economic transaction [38]. The conflicts of interest between agent and consumer in a trust game lay on the fact that both consumers and agents cannot completely trust each other. For example, the consumer would not entirely trust the intermediaries in sending money. On the contrary, the agent might suspect the consumer in payment compliance. In the context of real estate transactions, it might be less stressful because of the appearance of intermediaries such as the licensed lawyers, property advisers, and city councils. Nevertheless, due to the high level of human involvements, consumer and agent might still concern about the moral risks in executing a violable contract. In FORET, the problems that aggravate trust is more complicated. The factors that need to be considered include agent reputation issue, financial leverage issue, sharing space issue, legislation, and so on. For example, the consumer might use financial leverage to gain the mortgage while their actual assets and income are much lower than the criteria, or the satisfaction in sharing common space, and so on. As the players are rational, it might result in each player are not willing to take risks. Hence, the Nash equilibrium in the trust game is zero. In this experiment, the two players act separately as an agent and a consumer to play a game in perfect information condition. Each player has a project timeline and relative payoffs. The player also knows the other player's project timeline and payoffs. Based on the information each player has, they need to decide which period they want to launch their project (Fig. 6).

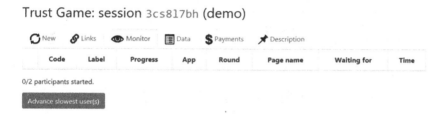

Trust Game: session `3cs817bh` (demo)

Code	Label	Progress	App	Round	Page name	Waiting for	Time

0/2 participants started.

Advance slowest user(s)

Fig. 6. Trust game configuration.

The period is distributed from 0 to 20, with the relative payoff counts from 0% to 100%. Each player's decision will reflect their trust in the information they have, that is, trust or not the data of project timeline and payoffs that was provided by another player. This experiment is set up with the purpose to represent the trust issues of both players.

5.4   Execution

The experiments were conducted by the participations of two players at two separate locations. The players cannot interact with each other during the experiments. The experiment executor was responsible for results recording and coding. Total time of experiments: three to four hours for running five sessions of each game. Device: PC/laptop, internet protocols. Platform: cloud, oTreehub. Instruction: oTreehub.-com → public project → game theory_sim; trustgame1.

5.5   Findings

Data collected from the experiments showed that the results are consistent with proposed conceptual artefacts. The game scores after five sessions of the experiment suggested that: (i) it was difficult to have a match in the search game. For instance, in the matching pennies game the change of payoffs led to changes in the optimal strategy of the two players. When both players chose "Heads", the consumer receives maximum payoffs of only 0.5. The agent then has a more significant advantage when choosing more "Heads" while the consumer tended to choose "Tails" (see Fig. 7 and Table 1).

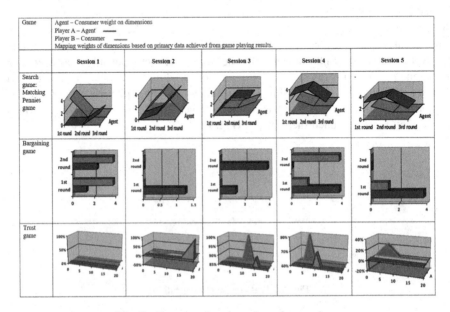

Fig. 7. Game scoring throughout five sessions

(ii). The bargaining game and trust game were hard to achieve a Nash equilibrium, which was the optimal situation for both agent and consumer. In the bargaining game, the number of proposals the players offered to each other throughout five sessions sequentially as 5, 18, 9, 8, 9, to gain the proportions of tickets. However, even with more tickets, the game might still have 0 payoffs for both players (see results of sessions 2 and 3 of bargaining game), (iii) in the trust game, both players showed a divergence in trust in each other. Both the agent and the consumer tried to be the winner, seeking maximum benefits throughout the sessions, resulted in failing in getting payoffs (see results of session 1).

The total number of choices in search games for each player throughout five sessions was calculated as 4 stages $\times 3$ rounds $\times 5$ sessions = 60 times. The results of three games, which represent the tendency of three dimensions of full, equal, and trust, are presented in Fig. 8. The results of each dimension in each session were calculated as population mean (expected value) of its stages' scores using formula 1.

$$\mu = \frac{\sum_{i=1}^{N} x_i}{N} \tag{1}$$

In the formula 1, x_i is the session of the game, with i value from 1 to 5. N is the number of stages in the game session that the players played. This calculation represents the central tendency of the dimensions.

Table 1. "Heads" and "Tails" in matching pennies game

	Heads	Tails	Total
Row	22	38	60
Column	45	15	60

The final scoring is a measurement of central tendency of each dimension. Agent-consumer's game scoring was different in three dimensions of full, equal, and trust throughout five sessions (S1 to S5). It shows a divergence and fluctuated tendency of the full, equal, and trustful participations between agent and consumer even in the same game. These results are reasonable to lead to further tests using DOE in a larger sample scale (minimum 30 samples) for the quantitative analysis that was mentioned in the methodology section.

6 System Artifact

To mitigate the conflicts of interest between agent and consumer, which was reflected on the above experiments, a novel blockchain-based GRC framework for FORET is proposed herein. The system framework includes three layers, i.e., user/service, database, and governance. The system employs both private blockchain and consortium blockchain from a BaaS provider to construct the decentralized apps (dApps) and the DAO. In the BaaS blockchain, users can access the virtual table to verify data and

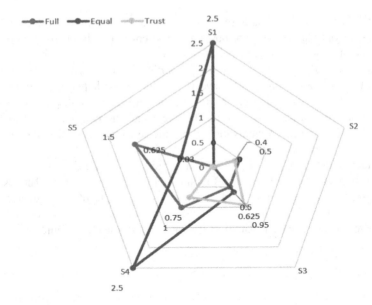

Fig. 8. Final scoring.

integrate it to multichain. In this system, token performs as a tool for verification rather than for trading purposes. The system will then transfer transaction records to a BaaS cloud platform and integrate them into BaaS blockchain via a service adapter.

Moreover, the decentralized verification mechanism of this system could be integrated into executive processes of FORET. The distributed governance framework allows participants to validate the transaction, manage the contract processes, and conduct the real-time audit. This design enables the DAO to govern smart contracts and execute FORET within peer-reviewed, transparent, and secured settings. By which, we expect this blockchain-based GRC system to empower the controlled user group and reduce the conflicts of interest between participants.

7 Discussion and Evaluation Plan

As blockchain is an emerging technology that has sparked arguments over its effectiveness, security, and legislation [11, 19, 26], the blockchain-based system artifact proposed in this paper is in the initial design phase. In future research, a qualitative analysis will be carried out using a case study to examine the systematic concepts at the early stage of the experiments. Additionally, for a more effective evaluation, a quantitative measurement with a sample size of 40 to 50 players will be carried on. This would support more sequential interactive experiments between games, thus might provide deeper insights. Furthermore, an accomplished dApps will be built up alongside this design using blockchain services offered by BaaS firms such as SAP or Microsoft Azure. In terms of the validation plan, the system artefacts will be validated using DSR guidelines of evaluation [13, 33]. In particular, field study, testing, and description methods will be implemented. The field study will provide a full range of experiments and simulations to discover facts, test hypotheses, and demonstrate findings. The prototype can be deployed and obtain feedbacks within six months. Meanwhile, testing methods such as Black box, White box, and Grey box would be practical tools to validate the solution. The description method will allow the artefacts to be evaluated based on existing knowledge obtained through reviews of experts such as Property experts/managers, Lawyers, IS experts, Banking experts. Solutions to improve DAO security will also be taken into consideration when constructing the prototype in the future. The proposed system will also be developed and generalized to apply to other types of fractional ownership transactions rather than FORET (Fig. 9).

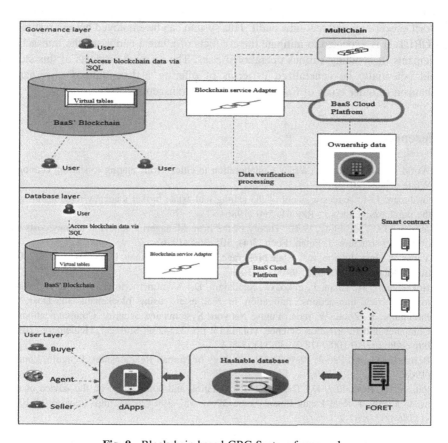

Fig. 9. Blockchain-based GRC System framework.

8 Conclusion

This study is a discovery of the principal-agent problem in FORET under the lens of zero-sum games. The principal-agent problem in FORET has raised concerns of compliance management as well as transparency of transaction execution. From the agency theory perspective, these conflicts of interest in FORET involve the agency costs, principal-agent problem, and risks accompanied by violable contracts. The experiment results showed that it is difficult to have a match in providing a full body of information between agent and consumer, the trust between agent and consumer is divergence, and the Nash equilibrium, which stands for the optimal situation for both two players, is hard to achieve. To mitigate these conflict of interests, this study uses DSR methodology along with the agency theory to propose a systematic design of a framework built on blockchain technology. The purpose is to mitigate the agent-consumer problems in FORET. In future research, a prototype of the framework will be built up alongside this design using blockchain technology. This blockchain-based architecture can be integrated into the executive processes of FORET. It works as a decentralized governance center allowing participants to conduct the transaction, contract executions, and real-time audit. This system can be employed but not restricted to FORET. It is expected to mitigate the conflicts of interest and assist the transaction participants in avoiding various operational risks. The research artefacts of this study would potentially be generalized in terms of offering a decentralized governance mechanism to other types of fractional ownership transactions.

References

1. World Economic Forum (WEF): Collaboration in cities: from sharing to sharing economy. White papers (2017)
2. Grohman, J.M.: A reassessment of the selling real estate broker's agency relationship with the purchaser. John's L. Rev **61**, 560 (1986)
3. Jensen, M.C., Meckling, W.H.: Theory of the firm: Managerial behavior, agency costs and ownership structure. J. Finan. Econ. **3**(4), 305–360 (1976)
4. Yavas, A.: Introduction: real estate brokerage. J. Real Estate Finan. Econ. **35**(1), 1–5 (2007). https://doi.org/10.1007/s11146-007-9030-1
5. Hoksbergen, M., Chan, J., Peko, G., Sundaram, D.: Asymmetric information in high-value low-frequency transactions: mitigation in real estate using blockchain. In: Doss, R., Piramuthu, S., Zhou, W. (eds.) Future Network Systems and Security. Communications in Computer and Information Science, vol. 1113, pp. 225–239. Springer, Heidelberg (2019). https://doi.org/10.1007/978-3-030-34353-8_17
6. Berne, E.: Games People Play: The Psychology of Human Relationships. Penguin, London (1968)
7. Patron, H., Roskelley, K.: The effect of reputation and competition on the advice of real estate agents. J. Real Estate Finan. Econ. **37**(4), 387–399 (2008). https://doi.org/10.1007/s11146-007-9082-2
8. Lulu, S., Zhi, C.: Centipede game network model of investment in real estate market based on grey integration and forwards induction. In: Proceedings of 2013 IEEE International Conference on Grey systems and Intelligent Services (GSIS), pp. 421–424 (2013)
9. Beck, R., Müller-Bloch, C., King, J.L.: Governance in the blockchain economy: a framework and research agenda. J. Assoc. Inf. Syst. **19**(10), 1 (2018)
10. Merkle, R.: DAOs, democracy and governance. Cryon. Mag. **37**(4), 28–40 (2016)
11. Tapscott, D., Tapscott, A.: Blockchain Revolution: How the Technology BEHIND BITCOIN is Changing Money, Business, and the World. Penguin, US (2016)

12. Kim, S.: Fractional ownership, democratization and bubble formation-the impact of blockchain enabled asset tokenization. In: AMCIS 2020 Virtual Conference (2020)

13. Hevner, A., Ram, S.: Design science in information system research. MIS Q. **28**(1), 75–105 (2004)

14. Clauretie, T., Daneshvary, N.: Principal–agent conflict and broker effort near listing contract expiration: The case of residential properties. J. Real Estate Finan. Econ. **37**(2), 147–161 (2008). https://doi.org/10.1007/s11146-007-9045-7

15. Ricks, B., Egbert, P.: Social crowds using transactional analysis. In: Plemenos, D., Miaoulis, G. (eds.) Intelligent Computer Graphics 2012, pp. 147–168. Springer, Heidelberg (2013). https://doi.org/10.1007/978-3-642-31745-3_8

16. Kim, Mi-Sun., Bang, G., Ko, Il.-Ju.: The agent communication simulation based on the ego state model of transactional analysis. In: Park, J.J (Jong Hyuk)., Pan, Yi., Yi, Gangman, Loia, Vincenzo (eds.) CSA/CUTE/UCAWSN -2016. LNEE, vol. 421, pp. 360–365. Springer, Singapore (2017). https://doi.org/10.1007/978-981-10-3023-9_55

17. Weill, P.: Don't just lead, govern: how top-performing firms govern IT? MIS Q. Exec. **3**(1), 1–17 (2004)

18. Butler, T., McGovern, D.: A conceptual model and IS framework for the design and adoption of environmental compliance management systems. Inf. Syst. Front. **14**(2), 221–235 (2012). https://doi.org/10.1007/s10796-009-9197-5

19. Surujnath, R.: Off the chain: a guide to blockchain derivatives markets and the implications on systemic risk. Fordham J. Corpor. Finan. Law **22**(2), 257 (2017)

20. Sulkowski, A.: Blockchain, business supply chains, sustainability, and law: The future of governance, legal frameworks, and lawyers. Delaware J. Corpor. Law **43**, 303 (2018)

21. Wang, Y., Kogan, A.: Designing confidentiality-preserving blockchain-based transaction processing systems. Int. J. Account. Inf. Syst. **30**, 1–18 (2018)

22. Chong, A.Y.L., Lim, E.T., Hua, X., Zheng, S., Tan, C.W.: Business on chain: a comparative case study of five blockchain-inspired business models. J. Assoc. Inf. Syst. **20**(9), 9 (2019)

23. Ziolkowski, R., Miscione, G., Schwabe, G.: Decision problems in blockchain governance: old wine in new bottles or walking in someone else's shoes? J. Manag. Inf. Syst. **37**(2), 316–348 (2020)

24. Wouda, H.P., Opdenakker, R.: Blockchain technology in commercial real estate transactions. J. Proper. Invest. Finan. **37**(6), 570–579 (2019)

25. Huh, J.H., Kim, S.K.: Verification plan using neural algorithm blockchain smart contract for secure P2P real estate transactions. Electronics **9**(6), 1052 (2020)

26. Whitaker, A., Kraussl, R.: Blockchain, fractional ownership, and the future of creative work. Center for Financial Studies (CFS) (594). SSRN 3100389 (2019)

27. Graglia, J.M., Mellon, C.: Blockchain and property in 2018: at the end of the beginning. Innov. Technol. Govern. Global. **12**(1–2), 90–116 (2018)

28. Konashevych, O.: General concept of real estate tokenization on blockchain: the right to choose. Eur. Prop. Law J. **9**(1), 21–66 (2020)

29. DuPont, Q.: Experiments in algorithmic governance: a history and ethnography of the DAO, a failed decentralized autonomous organization. In: Bitcoin and Beyond, pp. 157–177 (2017)

30. Buterin, V.: A next-generation smart contract and decentralized application platform. White Paper, **3**(37) (2014)

31. Forward, C., Dhillon, V.: Decentralized Organizations in the DAO Hacked in Blockchain Enabled Applications. Apress, Berkeley (2017)

32. Norta, A.: Creation of smart-contracting collaborations for decentralized autonomous organizations. In: Matulevičius, R., Dumas, M. (eds.) Perspectives in Business Informatics Research, vol. 229, pp. 3–17. Springer, Heidelberg (2015). https://doi.org/10.1007/978-3-319-21915-8_1

33. Nunamaker, J.F., Jr., Chen, M., Purdin, T.D.: Systems development in information systems research. J. Manag. Inf. Syst. **7**(3), 89–106 (1990)
34. Mingers, J.: Realising Systems Thinking: Knowledge and Action in Management Science. Springer, London (2006). https://doi.org/10.1007/0-387-29841-X
35. Fisher, R.A.: Design of experiments. Br. Med. J. **1**(3923), 554 (1936)
36. Berg, J., Dickhaut, J., McCabe, K.: Trust, reciprocity, and social history. Games Econ. Behav. **10**(1), 122–142 (1995)
37. Morgenstern, O., Von Neumann, J.: Theory of Games and Economic Behavior. Princeton University Press, New York (1953)
38. Brulhart, M., Usunier, J.C.: Does the trust game measure trust? Econ. Lett. **115**(1), 20–23 (2012)
39. Anderson, M.J., Whitcomb, P.J.: RSM Simplified: Optimizing Processes Using Response Surface Methods for Design of Experiments. Productivity Press, New York (2016)

A Dynamic Programming Approach for Time Series Discord Detection

Duong Tuan Anh[1(✉)] and Nguyen Van Hien[2]

[1] Department of Information Technology, HCMC University of Foreign Languages and Information Technology, Ho Chi Minh City, Vietnam
anh.dt@huflit.edu.vn
[2] VNG Company, Ho Chi Minh City, Vietnam

Abstract. There have been several methods to search the top anomaly subsequence (1-discord) in a time series. Most of these methods belong to the window-based category which uses a sliding window with a pre-specified length to extract subsequences. However, one of the main shortcomings of these window-based methods for discord detection is that their computational cost is still high in the cases of very large time series data. In this paper, we propose a new dynamic programming approach for discord detection in time series under Euclidean distance in order to improve further its time efficiency. We evaluate our proposed dynamic programming approach on several time series datasets and the results show that our method provides performance up to 25.2 times faster than HOT SAX algorithm.

Keywords: Time series · Discord · Discord detection · Dynamic programming

1 Introduction

Time series discord is the subsequence of a time series which is the most dissimilar to the rest of the subsequences. In [5], Keogh et al. introduced the term *discord* to refine the concept of an anomalous subsequence. The problem of discord (also called anomaly, novelty, deviant pattern) detection in time series has attracted much attention because of the wide diversity of its practical applications. Some typical applications of time series discord discovery in real world can be listed as follows. Nicoli et al. (2013) proposed a method to use anomaly detection in monitoring system's measurements of a hydroelectric dam [1]. Sivaraks and Ratanamahatana (2015) proposed a method for anomaly detection in electrocardiogram (ECG) time series [2]. Ortiz et al. (2019) proposed an anomaly detection approach in electroencephalogram (EEG) time series for dyslexia diagnosis [3]. Munir et al. (2017) proposed a method for anomaly detection on operational time series data of Internet of Things (IoT)- based household devices [4].

There has been several research works on time series discord search in the literature. Various algorithms proposed for this problem will be summarized as follows. Brute-Force, by Keogh, Lin, and Fu (2005) [5], is a simple algorithm for discord detection which comprises two nested loops. HOT SAX, by Keogh et al. (2005) [5], uses Symbolic Aggregate Approximation (SAX) (Lin et al., 2003 [6]) as a

P. Cong Vinh and A. Rakib (Eds.): ICCASA 2021, LNICST 409, pp. 255–266, 2021.
https://doi.org/10.1007/978-3-030-93179-7_20

symbolization transform and utilizes two ordering heuristics for the inner and outer loops to improve the discord search process. Bu et al. (2007) [7] proposed WAT algorithm which searches top k-discords by using Haar Wavelet Transform and augmented trie. Oliveira et al. (2004) [8] found discords in time series by using RBF neural networks. Sanchez and Bustos (2014) [9] proposed a method for time series discord search based on bounding boxes which does not require normalizing the subsequences. Huang et al. (2015) proposed a new discord definition named J-distance discord and a new discord search algorithm which can handle the "twin freak" problem in time series discord discovery [10]. Thuy et al. (2016) proposed some segmentation-based techniques to improve HOT SAX algorithm in time series discord search [11]. Vy and Anh (2016) found discords by using segmentation and anomaly pattern scoring [12]. And Buda et al. (2018) proposed a framework for time series anomaly detection which applies long short term memory (LSTM) network in a prediction-based approach [13].

Time series anomaly detection methods can be categorized into four kinds: window-based methods, segmentation-based methods, prediction-based and classification-based methods. Most of the above-mentioned methods belong to the window-based category which uses a sliding window with a pre-specified length to extract subsequences from a long time series before discord search. However, one of the main shortcomings of these window-based methods for discord detection is that their computational cost is still high in the cases of large scale time series.

In this paper, we propose a new algorithm, called DPDD, which is based on dynamic programming for discord search in time series under Euclidean distance. This dynamic programming algorithm has the same structure as the Brute-Force algorithm for discord discovery and hinges on the data reuse of the distance computations in the first iteration of Brute-Force algorithm for all the rest of iterations in this algorithm. The distance computations for the pairs of subsequences in the Brute-Force algorithm can be seen as overlapping sub-problems in the DPDD algorithm. The DPDD algorithm has time complexity just $O(m)$ where m is the length of the time series. To the best of our knowledge, this algorithm is the first one for time series discord detection which has linear time complexity. We evaluate our proposed dynamic programming approach on eight benchmark datasets and the results show that DPDD can run faster than HOT SAX about 25.2 times while brings out the same accuracy for discord detection.

The rest of the paper is structured as follows. Section 2 reviews some basic backgrounds about discord and Brute-Force algorithm for discord detection. Section 3 introduces the proposed dynamic programming algorithm, called DPDD, for discord detection in time series. Section 4 reports the experiments to evaluate the performance of DPDD in discord detection. Finally, Sect. 5 presents some conclusions and expectations for future work.

2   Background

2.1   Definitions

A time series $T = \{t_1, t_2, ..., t_m\}$ is an ordered list of m data points $t_i \in \Re$, measured at equal intervals.

Definition 1 (*Subsequence*): Given a time series T of length m, a subsequence C of T is a segment of length $n < m$ of consecutive positions from T, that is, $C = t_p, \ldots, t_{p+n-1}$ for $1 \leq p \leq m-n+1$.

We can denote the subsequence C as $T_{p:p+n-1}$.

Definition 2. (*Non-trivial match*): Given a time series T, including a subsequence C of length n beginning at position p and a matching subsequence D beginning at the position q. D is called as a non-trivial match to C if $|p - q| \geq n$.

Definition 3. (*Discord*): Given a time series T, the subsequence D in T is called the most significant discord (1-discord) in T if it has the largest distance to its nearest non-trivial match.

2.2 Brute-Force Algorithm

The problem of finding 1-discord can be solved by the Brute-Force algorithm (called BFDD) is given in [5]. In Brute-Force algorithm, using a sliding window, all possible candidate subsequences can be extracted in the outer loop, and then the algorithm finds the distance to the nearest non-trivial match for each candidate subsequence in the inner loop. The candidate subsequence with the largest distance to its nearest non-trivial match is the 1-discord.

Since the brute-force algorithm is a window-based method for searching discords in a time series with a nested loop, it incurs high complexity. Its complexity is $O(m^2)$, where m is the length of the time series.

3   A Dynamic Programming Approach for Time Series Discord Detection

3.1 The Main Idea

Euclidean distance is the most widely-used distance measure in time series data mining. Given two time series $X = x_1, x_2, .., x_n$ and $Y = y_1, y_2, .., y_n$, the Euclidean distance between X and Y is given as in the following formula:

$$Dist(X, Y) = \sqrt{\sum_{i=1}^{n} (x_i - y_i)^2} \tag{1}$$

In the context of time series discord detection, if we do not use square root in the above formula, this does not change the relative rankings of nearest matches, since Euclidean function is monotonic and concave [14].

The main idea of dynamic programming approach for time series discord search is that we have to compute directly the distances between the pairs of subsequences in the first iteration (in the BFDD) only and store them in a table and reuse these values to compute the distances between the pairs of subsequences for all the rest of iterations. In a time series T, the distance between the subsequence at position p and the subsequence at position q of the same length n is denoted as $D(p, q)$. Here we index the elements in T as the integers $0,.., |T| - 1$. So the distance between two subsequences which is denoted as $D(p, q)$ is computed as:

$$\left(T_p-T_q\right)^2 + \left(T_{p+1}-T_{q+1}\right)^2 + .. + \left(T_{p+n-1} - T_{q+n-1}\right)^2$$

And $D(p + 1, q + 1)$, the distance between the subsequence at position $p + 1$ and the subsequence at position $q + 1$ of the same length n, is computed as:

$$\left(T_{p+1}-T_{q+1}\right)^2 + \left(T_{p+2}-T_{q+2}\right)^2 + .. + \left(T_{p+n} - T_{q+n}\right)^2$$

We can see that the distance $D(p+1, q+1)$ is different from $D(p, q)$ at only the first and the last quantity in the computing formula. So we can view computing $D(p, q)$ and $D(p + 1, q + 1)$ as overlapping subproblems. Basing on this finding, we compute $D(p + 1, q + 1)$ by using the stored value of $D(p, q)$ as in the following formula.

$$D(p+1, q+1) = D(p,q) - \left(T_p-T_q\right)^2 + \left(T_{p+n} - T_{q+n}\right)^2 \qquad (2)$$

Now consider a toy example. Given a time series T with length 11, we index T with the values 0, 1, 2,..., 10. Assume that the length of sliding window is 3. Based on the above mentioned dynamic programing idea, we can compute the distances between pairs of subsequences in the Brute-Force algorithm for this example by using a table which is illustrated in Fig. 1. Remember that $D(1, 4)$ means $Dist(T_{1:3}, T_{4:6})$.

In Fig. 1, we store the computed distances in a table which is implemented as a one-dimensional array. We can used $D(0, 3)$ (i.e. $Dist(T_{0:2},T_{3:5})$) to compute $D(1, 4)$ (i.e. $Dist(T_{1:3},T_{4:6})$) and all these data reuses are highlighted by the arrows between two adjacent cells in the table in Fig. 1. So we have to compute only the distances between the pairs of subsequences in the first iteration of the Brute-Force algorithm. In all the other iterations, we can derive the distances from the stored distances in the table rather than computing them from the scratch.

Besides, in the cases that p is greater than q, we can derive $D(p, q)$ from $D(q, p)$ due to the *symmetry* of the Euclidean distance $(Dist(X,, Y) = Dist(Y, X))$. Therefore, in Fig. 1 we do not have to compute $D(6, 1)$, $D(6, 2)$, $D(6, 3)$ since $D(1, 6)$, $D(2, 6)$, $D(3, 6)$ are already available in the table at that iteration. In Fig. 1 for all the distances in the iterations 6,.., 8 we can refer to the stored distance values in the table basing on the symmetry of Euclidean distance. All these distances are highlighted in bold in Fig. 1 and we do not have to store them in the table. As for the case of a time series of the length 11 and the sliding window of the length 3, we need a one-dimensional array of length $(11–2*3 + 1)* (11–2*3 + 2)/2 = 21$ to store necessary distance values.

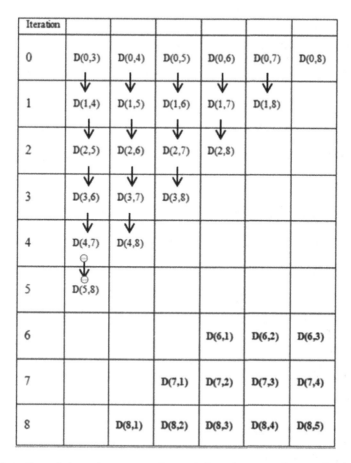

Iteration						
0	D(0,3)	D(0,4)	D(0,5)	D(0,6)	D(0,7)	D(0,8)
1	D(1,4)	D(1,5)	D(1,6)	D(1,7)	D(1,8)	
2	D(2,5)	D(2,6)	D(2,7)	D(2,8)		
3	D(3,6)	D(3,7)	D(3,8)			
4	D(4,7)	D(4,8)				
5	D(5,8)					
6				D(6,1)	D(6,2)	D(6,3)
7			D(7,1)	D(7,2)	D(7,3)	D(7,4)
8		D(8,1)	D(8,2)	D(8,3)	D(8,4)	D(8,5)

Fig. 1. Illustration of dynamic programming technique in computing Euclidean distances between pairs of subsequences for BFDD algorithm.

3.2 Dynamic Programming Algorithm for Discord Detection

Based on the main idea explained in the above subsection, we come with the dynamic programming algorithm for time series discord detection, which is called DPDD (abbreviated for Dynamic Programming for Discord Detection). The pseudo code for DPDD algorithm is described as follows:

Algorithm 1: (DPDD)
Input: T is a time series and n is discord length
Output: discord_dist and discord_loc: distance and location of the found 1-discord.
1. discord_dist = infinity;
2. discord_loc = NaN
3. k = 0;
4. **for** j = n **to** |T|- n
5.   dist = Dist($T_{0:n-1}$, $T_{j:j+n-1}$]
6.   a[k] = dist
7.   k = k+1
8.   **if** dist < discord_dist
9.   discord_dist = dist
10 **endif**
11 **endfor**
12 discord_loc = 0
13 **for** p = 1 **to** |T| - n
14   nearest_match_dist = infinity
15   **for** q = 0 **to** |T| - n
16   **if** abs(p − q) ≥ n
17   **if** q ≥ p
18   index = (|T| - n*2)*(p-1) − (p-1)*(1+ (p-1))/2 +q − n
19   dist = a[index] − (T_{p-1}- T_{q-1})^2 + (T_{p-1+n} − T_{q-1+n})^2
20   **else**
21   index = (|T| - n*2)*q − q*(1+q)/2 + p −n
22   dist = a[index]
23   **endif**
24   a[k] = dist
25   k = k+1
26   **if** dist < nearest_match_dist
27   nearest_match_dist = dist
28   **endif**
29   **endif**
30   **endfor**
31   **if** nearest_match_dist > discord_dist
32   discord_dist = nearest_match_dist
33   discord_loc = p
34   **endif**
35 **endfor**
36 **return** <discord_dist, discord_loc>

Even though the table in Fig. 1 looks like a matrix data structure, in DPDD, for saving memory space, we use a one-dimensional array a to implement this table for storing the computed distances. The length of array a for a time series T with a sliding window of length n is computes as follows:

$$l = (|T| - 2 * n + 1)(|T| - 2 * n + 2)/2 \tag{3}$$

In Algorithm 1, the first *for* loop (lines 4–11) performs the direct distance computations for the pairs of subsequences in the first iteration of the algorithm. All the distances computed in the first iteration are stored in the array a. The next *for* loop (lines 13–35) performs the distance computations in all the rest of iterations for finding the 1-discord in the time series T. Notice that $D(p, q)$ is stored in array a at the element with the index $(|T| - n * 2) * (p - 1) - (p - 1) * ((p - 1) + 1)/2 + q - n$.

If the basic operation in the DPDD is the distance computation for a pair of subsequences, it is obvious that the time complexity of DPDD is about $O(m)$ where m is the length of the time series. But DPDD requires an array to store intermediate values and this space complexity is $O(m^2)$ due to Formula (3). So, dynamic programming approach always exhibits the trade-off between time and space cost in a given algorithm. However, with large capacity of RAM in current computers, all the data involved in the computations in DPDD for a given time series can fit into the main memory.

4 Empirical Evaluation

For empirical evaluation, we investigate the performance of two algorithms, DPDD and HOT SAX. The comparative methods are implemented with C++ and the experiments are conducted on MacBook Pro 2015 - MJLQ2, 2.2 GHz Quad-Core Intel Core i7, RAM: 16 GB.

The experiments aim to compare DPDD, the proposed dynamic programming approach for discord search with HOT SAX in two perspectives: effectiveness and computational efficiency. The HOT SAX is selected as the baseline algorithm due to its popularity in time series discord detection.

4.1 Datasets and Parameter Setting

The test datasets used in our experiments are obtained from the UCR time series archive for discord detection [15]. These 8 test datasets are from different domains (finance, health care, industry). Table 1 shows the description and the length of each tested dataset. Figure 2 shows the plots of some time series out of eight tested time series.

Table 1. Description and length of eight datasets

Dataset	Description	Length
TEK16	Industry	4992
TEK17	Industry	5000
TEK14	Industry	5000
ECG	Medicine	21600
stock_20_0	Finance	5000
Power_demand_italy	Industry	29931
Power_data	Industry	35040
memory	Industry	6875

We have set some parameters for HOT SAX as follows: size of the alphabet is 3 and the SAX word length is 8.

For all the eight test datasets and for both HOT SAX and DPDD, we select the sliding window length (i.e. the length of 1-discord) as 128. These parameter selections are based on the experiments from several previous works in time series discord detection which used the same benchmark datasets.

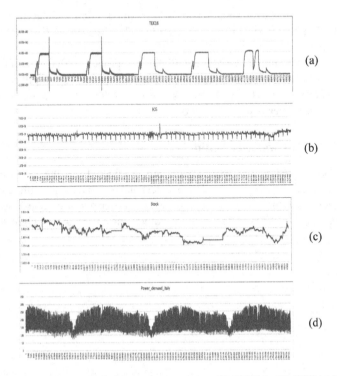

Fig. 2. Some time series out of eight test time series: (a) TEK16, (b) ECG, (c) Stock, and (d) Power_demand_italy

4.2   Experimental Results

From our experiments, through human inspection, we found out that the resultant 1-discord subsequence detected by DPDD for each test dataset matches with the one found by HOT SAX. As for TEK16, TEK17, TEK14 and ECG datasets, the resultant 1-discord subsequence detected by DPDD for each test dataset also matches with the one annotated by experts [5]. Besides, for each test dataset, the start location of the 1-discord detected by DPDD is exactly the same as that of the 1-discord found by HOT SAX. Table 2 reports the start locations of the 1-discords found by DPDD and HOT SAX on eight test datasets. Figure 3 shows the test dataset TEK16 and the 1-discord found in the dataset by DPDD which matches with the one found by HOT SAX.

Table 2. Locations of discords detected by DPDD and HOT SAX

Dataset	DPDD	HOT SAX
TEK16	4253	4253
TEK17	2101	2101
TEK14	1091	1091
ECG	10864	10864
stock_20_0	122	122
Power_demand_italy	26343	26343
power_data	4594	4594
memory	6260	6260

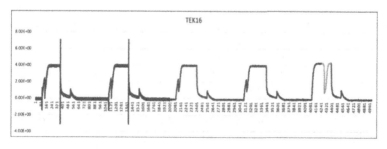

Fig. 3. Time series TEK16 and the 1-discord found by DPDD (in red) in this time series.

Table 3 reports the running times in milliseconds of DPDD and HOT SAX on eight datasets. The speed-up rates of DPDD over HOT SAX on each test dataset are reported in the 4th column of Table 3. This speed-up rate depends on the characteristics of each time series and the size of this time series. The experimental results in Table 3 show that in average, DPDD can execute faster than HOT SAX about 25.2 times.

Table 3. Execution times (in milliseconds) of DPDD and HOT SAX on eight test datasets

Dataset	DPDD	HOT SAX	Speed-up
TEK16	1392	7962	5.720
TEK17	1402	61402	43.796
TEK14	1393	58464	41.790
ECG	32626	124782	3.824
stock_20_0	1408	13968	9.920
Power_demand_italy	67392	3980000	59.057
power_data	82953	2374770	28.627
memory	2753	24250	8.809

4.3   Discussion

In comparison to HOT SAX, DPDD algorithm brings out remarkably higher time efficiency since the time complexity of DPDD is linear. But one more important fact is that a higher efficiency can still be obtained if this dynamic programming algorithm is properly adapted to the GPU programming environment [16, 17]. There have been some research works which proposed some efficient parallelization strategies for dynamic programming algorithms on GPUs, for example, the work [18] by Wani and Quadri in 2013 and the work [19] by Berger et al. in 2013. These research works suggest some guidelines which can be used in designing a parallel implementation for DPDD algorithm on GPU environment.

5   Conclusion and Future Work

This paper has introduced a new dynamic programming algorithm, called DPDD, for discord detection in time series under Euclidean distance. This algorithm has the same structure as the Brute-Force algorithm for discord discovery and hinges on the data reuse of the distance computations in the first iteration for all the rest of iterations. The DPDD algorithm has time complexity just $O(m)$ where m is the length of the time series and memory complexity $O(m^2)$. We evaluate our proposed dynamic programming approach on eight benchmark datasets and the results show that DPDD can run faster than HOT SAX about 25.2 times while brings out the same accuracy for discord detection.

This work is just the first part of our ongoing research project. As for future work, we intend to improve DPDD algorithm to address the "twin freak" problem in time series discord detection [10, 20]. Besides, we plan to accelerate DPDD algorithm further by implementing this algorithm as a parallel version on GPU computing [16, 17].

References

1. Sivaraks, H., Ratanamahatana, C.A.: Robust and accurate anomaly detection in ECG artifacts using time series motif discovery. In: Computational and Mathematical Methods in Medicine, vol. 2015, 20 p. (2015)
2. Nicoli, S., Jargini, J.A., Magrini, L.G., Miranda, C.D.M.: Detection of nonconformities in monitoring system's measurements. In: IEEE PES Conference on Innovative Smart Grid Technologies - Latin America (ISGT LA), Sao Paulo, 15–17 April (2013)
3. Ortiz, A., López, P.J., Luque, J.L., Martínez-Murcia, F.J., Aquino-Britez, D.A., Ortega, J.: An anomaly detection approach for dyslexia diagnosis using EEG signals. In: Vicente, J.M. F., Álvarez-Sánchez, J.R., de la Paz, F., López, J.T., Moreo, H.A. (eds.) Understanding the Brain Function and Emotions. LNCS, vol. 11486, pp. 369–378. Springer, Cham (2019). https://doi.org/10.1007/978-3-030-19591-5_38
4. Munir, M., Erkel, S., Dengel, A., Ahmed, S.: Pattern based contextual anomaly detection in HVAC systems. In: Proceedings of IEEE International Conference on Data Mining Workshops (ICDMW), pp. 1066–1073 (2017)
5. Keogh, E., Lin, J., Fu, A.: HOT SAX: efficiently finding the most unusual time series subsequence. In: Proceedings of the Fifth IEEE International Conference on Data mining, Houston, Texas, pp. 226–233 (2005)
6. Lin, J., Keogh, E., Lonardi, S., Chiu, B.: Symbolic representation of time series, with implications for streaming algorithms. In: Proceedings of the 8th ACM SIGMOD Workshop on Research Issues in Data Mining and Knowledge Discovery, San Diego, CA, 13 June (2003)
7. Bu, Y., Leung, T.W., Fu, A.W.C., Keogh, E., Pei, J., Meshkin, S.: WAT: finding top-k discords in time series database. In: Proceedings of the 2007 SIAM International Conference on Data Mining, April, pp. 449–454 (2007)
8. Oliveira, A.L.I., Neto, F.B.L. and Meira, S.R.L.: A method based on RBF-DAA neural network for improving Novelty detection in time series. In: Proc. of 17th International FLAIRS Conference, AAAI Press, Miami Beach (2004)
9. Sanchez, H., Bustos, B.: Anomaly detection in streaming time series based on bounding boxes. In: Traina, A.J.M., Traina, C., Cordeiro, R.L.F. (eds.) Similarity Search and Applications. LNCS, vol. 8821, pp. 201–213. Springer, Cham (2014). https://doi.org/10.1007/978-3-319-11988-5_19
10. Huang, T., Zhu, Y. Wu, Y. and Shi, W.: J-distance discord: an improved time series dis-cord definition and discovery method. In: Proceedings of 15th International Conference on Data Mining Workshops, pp. 303–310 (2015)
11. Thuy, H.T.T., Anh, D.T., Chau, V.T.N.: Some efficient segmentation-based techniques to improve time series discord discovery. In: Vinh, P.C., Barolli, L. (eds.) Nature of Computation and Communication. LNICSSITE, vol. 168, pp. 179–188. Springer, Cham (2016). https://doi.org/10.1007/978-3-319-46909-6_17
12. Vy, N.D.K., Anh, D.T.: Detecting variable length anomaly patterns in time series data. In: Tan, Y., Shi, Y. (eds.) Data Mining and Big Data. Lecture Notes in Computer Science, vol. 9714, pp. 279–287. Springer, Heidelberg (2016). https://doi.org/10.1007/978-3-319-40973-3_28
13. Buda, T.S., Caglayan, B., Assem, H.: DeepAD: a generic framework based on deep learning for time series anomaly detection. In: Phung, D., Tseng, V.S., Webb, G.I., Ho, B., Ganji, M., Rashidi, L. (eds.) PAKDD 2018. LNCS (LNAI), vol. 10937, pp. 577–588. Springer, Cham (2018). https://doi.org/10.1007/978-3-319-93034-3_46

14. Rakthanmanon, T., et al.: Addressing big data time series: Mining trillions of time series subsequences under dynamic time warping. ACM Trans. Knowl. Discov. Data (TKDD) **7** (3), 10 (2013)
15. The UCR Time Series Dataset Archive for Discord Detection. https://www.cs.ucr.edu/ ~eamonn/discords/. Accessed 2019
16. NVIDIA: CUDA Programming Guide Version 8.0 (2017). https://docs.nvidia.com/cuda/ index.html
17. NVIDIA: CUDA Toolkit Documentation Version 8.0 (2017). https://docs.nvidia.com/cuda/ index.html
18. Wani, M.A., Quadri, S.M.K.: Accelerated dynamic programming on GPU: a study of speed up and programming approach. Int. J. Comput. Appl. **69**(3), 18–21 (2013)
19. Berger, K.E., Galea, F.: An efficient parallelization strategy for dynamic programming on GPU. In: Proceedings of IEEE 27th International Symposium on Parallel and Distributed Processing Workshops and PhD Forum, pp. 1797–1806 (2013)
20. Zhang, C., Liu, H., Yin, A.: Research of detection algorithm for time series abnormal subsequence. In: Proceedings of International Conference of Pioneering Computer Scientists, Engineers and Educations, 16 September, pp. 12–26 (2017)

Recent Researches on Human-Aware Navigation for Autonomous System in the Dynamic Environment: An International Survey

Ha Quang Thinh Ngo[1,2]([✉])

[1] Department of Mechatronics, Faculty of Mechanical Engineering, Ho Chi Minh City University of Technology (HCMUT), 268 Ly Thuong Kiet Street, District 10, HCMC, Vietnam
nhqthinh@hcmut.edu.vn
[2] Vietnam National University Ho Chi Minh City, Linh Trung Ward, Thu Duc District, Ho Chi Minh City, Vietnam

Abstract. The basic instinct of autonomous robot is to navigate in the unstructured environment. In several decades, the human-machine interaction has significantly developed and gained many greater achievements of the interesting fields such as perception, reasoning mechanism, manipulation, learning ability and navigation. In these topics, navigation becomes one of the most attractive studies for investigators to explore. Especially, the novel approached with the constraints of human comfort together with social rules are newly proposed. This paper provides a survey of past and present researches for human-aware navigation framework and synthesizes the potential solutions for the existing challenges in related fields.

Keywords: Autonomous system · Human-aware navigation · Human-centered planning · Mobile robot · Motion planning

1 Introduction

In the early stage of robotics, there are two key streams which attracted many researchers all over the world. The first one is manipulation and the rest is navigation. It could be momentarily explained that manipulation [1] is mainly focused on a robot arm control. Usually, robotic manipulator is working on the assembling line in a wide range of industries. They need to pick various objects in complex environments. Although the workspace for the manipulation is restricted, the hardware architecture of the robot arm is too complicated [2]. Hence, the requirements of planning schemes are often sophisticated to do the manipulating jobs. In the other manner, navigation [3] is the main role in an autonomous robot control. Its observation in the surrounding space includes the feedback signals from cameras, laser scanners and the other sensors, then it builds the environmental model [4]. With the achieved data, it schedules the robot's trajectory to move from the starting point to target point. Based on the artificial intelligence, if possible, robot could become more and more useful.

P. Cong Vinh and A. Rakib (Eds.): ICCASA 2021, LNICST 409, pp. 267–282, 2021.
https://doi.org/10.1007/978-3-030-93179-7_21

In many years ago, the applications for navigation and manipulation were primarily in industry. In other words, robotic system served in the industries. Recently, many robots are working instead of labor force [5]. Several developers solved main research issues for the industrial robots and implemented the practical systems [6, 7]. Though, they have not completely solved the research issues. It is quite important and necessary to deeply study the issue and improve the developed algorithms. However, on the other hand, robotics needs a new research issue.

Industrial robotics developed key components for building more human-like robots, such as sensors and motors. From 1990 to 2000, Japanese companies developed various animal-like and human-like robots as Fig. 1. Sony developed AIBO [8] which is a dog-like robot and QRIO [9] which is a small human-like robot. Mitsubishi Heavy Industries, LTD developed Wakamaru [10]. Honda developed a child-like robot called ASIMO [11]. Unfortunately, Sony and Mitsubishi Heavy Industries, LTD have stopped the projects but Honda is still continuing.

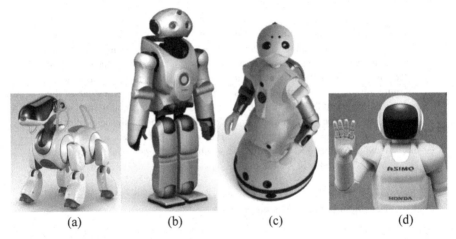

(a)   (b)   (c)   (d)

Fig. 1. The initial generations of service robot, (a) AIBO, (b) QRIO, (c) Wakamaru and (d) ASIMO.

The most considerable difference between industrial robots and robots works in the daily environments is an interactive activities. In the regular environments, robots encounter with humans, and they have to interact with them before doing the task. Rather, the interaction will be the main task of the robots. These robots developed by the companies had various functions with the animal-like or human-like appearance to interact with people. Nevertheless, most of the current versions in service robot are wheeled robots or vehicle-type platforms which are flexible to move any location. The rest of this article is organized as follows: Sect. 2 briefly summarizes the historical development of human-aware navigation framework. It also provides an introduction of service robot in both academic researches and commercial products. In Sect. 3, several challenges of human-aware navigation theme in either the past time or present are synthesized the effective solutions and the existing problems. Section 4 mentions the potential approaches to solve these challenges. Finally, some conclusions are carried out in Sect. 5.

2 Historical Background

The term social robot or sociable robot was coined by Aude Billard and Kerstin Dautenhahn [12, 13]. The field of social robotics concentrates on the development and design of robots which interact socially with humans, but sociality between robots (e.g., in multirobot systems) is not part of the field. They can be distinguished between a weak and a strong approach in social robotics. While the strong approach wants to motivate robots which have the capabilities to display social and emotional behavior, the weak approach researches in the imitation of social and emotional behavior only. Social robots need to show the human-like social characteristics for instance the expression of emotions, the ability to conduct high-level dialogue, to learn, to develop personality, to use natural cues, and to develop social competencies [14–16]. In the last years, the term human-robot interaction (HRI) became more prominent than that of social robotics.

Nowadays, a social robot is an intelligent platform that integrated socially and cleverly human-aware behaviors in order to communicate with persons and other robots. In the office or factory, they are potential to handle tasks by themselves, for example reception and basic guide. For home-based application, social robots are able to serve and manipulate as a private duenna, and flexibly behave according to personal characteristics. In Fig. 2, some of them are listed as below:

- hitchBOT [16] - a social robot that attempted to hitchhike across the United States in 2014
- Kismet [17] - a robot head that understands and exhibits emotion when interacting with humans
- Tico [18] - a robot developed to improve children's motivation in the classroom
- Bandit [19] - a social robot designed to teach social behavior to autistic children
- Jibo [20] is a consumer-oriented social robot. Jibo understands speech and facial expressions, is able to find out relations with family, and match with them that characterizes it.

Additionally, a social robot might be monitored from far distance, possibly handling as a TelePresence agent at a business meeting [21] or at home [22], or as a nurse in healthcare center [23]. The other ones that are autonomous systems, are implemented with locally artificial intelligence in order to communicate independently in respect to human's response and object's occurrence in workplace [24]. Occasionally, this robot is considered as an autonomously smart robot. The awareness of intelligent robot naturally depends on a perceptive computing model which imitates human's actions and thoughts. Cognitive computing [25] comprises various models of machine learning approach which employ the techniques of data mining, pattern recognition and natural language processing (NLP) to simulate what the human brain acts.

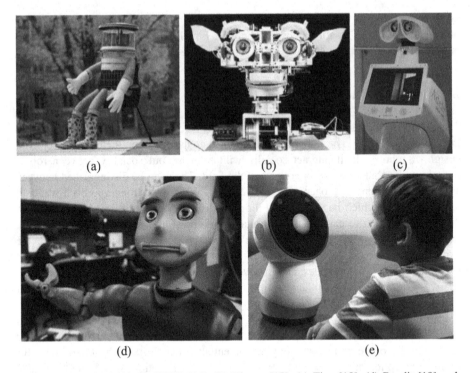

Fig. 2. Social robots, (a) hitchBOT [16], (b) Kismet [17], (c) Tico [18], (d) Bandit [19] and (e) Jibo [20].

Although social robots employ leading modern technology in any research, they're really not persons and lack sympathy, feeling and reasoning mechanism. They proceed their missions from which they are planned to do, but then they might perform unexpectedly to circumstances for which they were not taught. Above all, every robot is sensitive to any malfunction and failure, and potentially suffers an expensive repair and maintenance. Furthermore, developers who investigate a dependence to an excessive degree on social robots, such emotional closeness, could be ignored when interacting among humans that are the necessities of the human characters.

3   Challenges and Opportunities

In general, the interest topics in human-aware robot navigation involves the interactive optimization of annoyance and stress to be more comfortable, the integration of cultural knowledge in robot's awareness or the improvement of robot's behavior to be more natural. All of them have the same goal to acquire the acceptance from community or society. To be considered as human-like factor, the human comfort should be taken into account. When a robot moves toward to target position, it can cause the discomfort feeling for human observers. The reasons are that too closed-distance, too fast or slow movement in respect to human must be avoided to reduce discomfort. The larger part of researches focuses on the avoidance of negative emotional responses such as fear or anger. The report indicates various strategies ranging from sustaining appropriate distance, proper strategy and precise control scheme to prevent being noisy, and planning to prevent interference (Figs. 3 and 4).

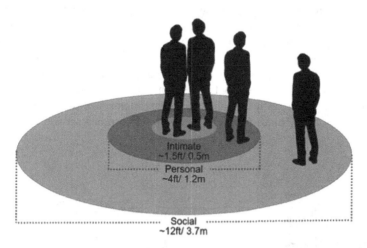

Fig. 3. The virtual zones of social interaction for various situations in proxemics [26].

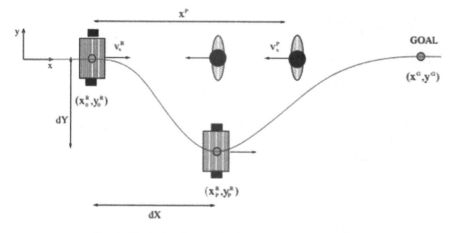

Fig. 4. Desired trajectory for the passage maneuver [27].

4 Toward Modern Human-Aware Navigation

4.1 Observing Human's Reactions

The purpose is to realize real services by the robot through the interactions. These researches have mainly focused on the development of the general functions and behavior of the robot [32, 33]. They would include moving to a destination and greeting as Fig. 5. The service robot should have situated behaviors to the environment, and they should follow contexts. In a complicated environment, it is quite difficult to design robot behaviors a priori. Thus, a tele-robot was introduced to develop: an operator remotely controlled the robot, and robot recorded the sensory data and visual data from the tags and cameras installed in the environment. Basically, this prototype obtains the robot autonomous functions based on the recorded sensory data.

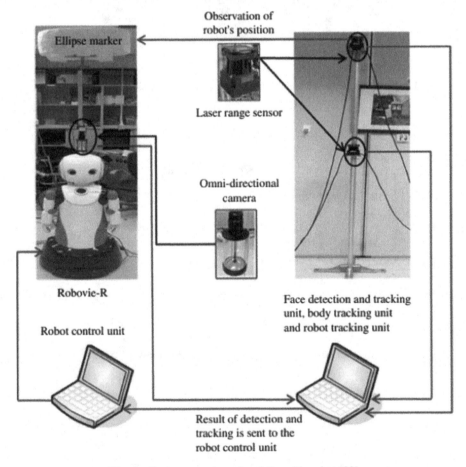

Fig. 5. System overview of mobile guide robot [32].

However, the merit of the tele-operated system was not only for developing robot autonomous behaviors in a complicated environment. The sensory data from both of the robot and environment indicated many things about how people react to robot behavior. It provided the rich information about human interactive behaviors, but there is a limitation to the psychological studies done in laboratories. They cannot provide enough variety of human interactive behaviors since there is no rich context in the laboratory environment. It is a rather assumed situation and not real. However, some field tests [34] with the tele-operated robot can induce real and rich interactive behavior among people as Fig. 6. Thus, the tele-operated systems and the sensor network in the field test enable to deeply study the psychological and cognitive aspect of people's behaviors.

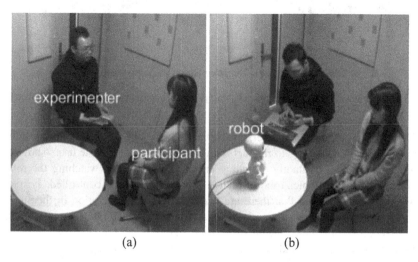

(a)   (b)

Fig. 6. Scenario in the practical implementation, (a) direct interview and (b) remoted interview [34].

4.2   User's Attitude and Expectations

In the study between human and robot, a lot of articles have focused on users' expectations. Most of persons also have their prospects about robots' jobs and missions, and in what way robots were developed. It could be seen clearly that user desires human-like presence for applications which require communal skills [35]. To response these requirements, human prefers to deliver missions acting as human-like robots rather than machine-like robots [36]. Related to human as Fig. 7, an operator wishes robot to co-work for such service-oriented duties or jobs which needs the deeply cognitive thinking [37], and challenged tasks [38]. Besides, the impact of culture was also noticed that in some special situations, human tends from accepting robot's attitude to cultural behavior [39]. Likewise, differences in culture cause an alternative way for robot to communicate with people [40].

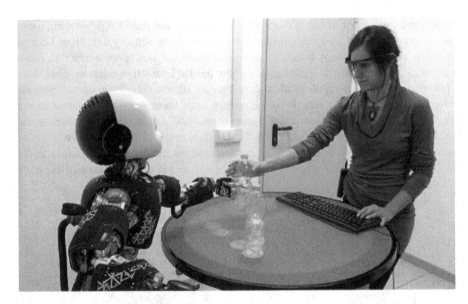

Fig. 7. Experimental validation of a gaze cueing protocol by integrating in action sequence [36].

These studies reported how users interacted with social robots. Some users showed very positive attitudes trying to interact with robots repeatedly; some users showed an intermediate attitude, hesitantly crowding around the robot and watching the robot's behavior. In the first topic, robot which is known to be tele-controlled, is mainly discussed. It is considered that there are needs of remotely operation in the stage of utilization, operators do not know their impacts clearly. In the other manner, humans prefer to directly communicate with social robot and they are not interested in the tele-operated robot. For the second approach, user's attitude is addressed as the key factor. In the case that a lot of articles concentrate on the robot design and evaluate user's acceptance attitude, there are not many studies to indicate the possible reason that human reveals negative attitude toward social robot. The contents of these studies match with mentioned problems. As a result, a novel idea for psychological indicators to estimate user's attitude, and discovers the reasonable answers why there exists some negative attitudes from human toward robots.

4.3 Framework of Naturally and Comfortably Behaviors in Social Interaction

In reality, a given robot which situates the directional position of its body and displays both pose and gesture, is completely demonstrated in meaningful track [33]. Whenever an user is speaking to a robot, it has been clearly stated that this robot which non-verbally answers to a human's speech, makes several deep feelings such listening to, understanding, and sharing a story with spoken man [41]. In the coworking-attention task, it was denoted that user observe a robot's nonverbal cues to predict its internal state [42] (Fig. 8).

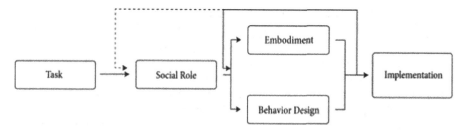

Fig. 8. A characterization for manipulating the socially interactive robot for various tasks [33].

Likewise, the interactive performance of nonverbal behaviors has been validated as following. From the user's gaze, the feedback information has been effectively reflected [43], preserve engagement [44, 45], and regulate the conversation flow [46, 47]. As well, the other gestures such pointing is usefully indicated as a conversation's target objects [48, 49]. Most of those researches largely concentrate on estimating natural behavior of a human-like robot. In the first approach, a work related to deictic interaction, was introduced. When talking about objects, people naturally engage in deictic interaction, associating with pointing gestures. Since deictic interaction frequently occurs, it indicates about new signals that are outside our mutual knowledge [50]. Whenever robots are driven in a public place, the usage of deictic interaction as Fig. 9 becomes one of the relevantly interactive features in natural manner. Via these visual expression, human can rapidly understand what robot refers. In [51], authors have successfully simulated the use of conventional reference gestures such as kore, sore, and imitated human behaviors in deictic interactions.

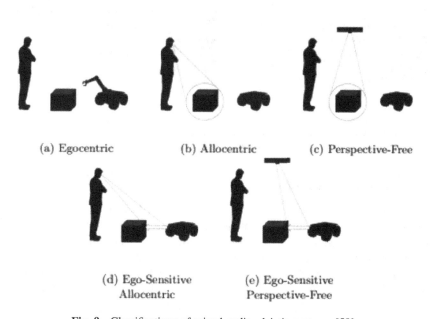

(a) Egocentric   (b) Allocentric   (c) Perspective-Free

(d) Ego-Sensitive   (e) Ego-Sensitive
Allocentric   Perspective-Free

Fig. 9. Classifications of mixed-reality deictic gestures [50].

In the second approach, the zones around human was mentioned as the proxemics. During conversations, people adjust their distance to others based on their relationship and the situation. When discussing about objects, their formation is an O-shaped space that stand around the target object [52]. In this method, each member can see both the central object and other members in the conversation as Fig. 10. Such contributions in human communication have been replicated in human–robot interaction. Because robots are mobile platform, it is essential to manage its position during interaction. In the earlier stage [53], it discussed to achieve control based on a standing position, and robot is enabled to stand in a queue. Lately, developers in [54] have studied that people tend to concern about appropriate distance between them and a robot when interacting.

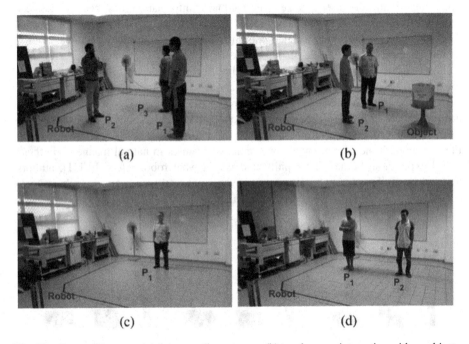

Fig. 10. Group of humans, (a) three standing persons, (b) two humans interacting with an object, (c) walking human and (d) group of two walking people [52].

4.4   Data Fusion Approach

Sensing system is the fundamental components in most of robotic systems. In present time, people lives in the world with ubiquitous sensors, and access to the Internet via smart phones and computers to refer to information in distant locations. In similar metaphor, as robots are networked, large part of sensing can be done with ubiquitous sensors in network robot system. There is a large number of sensing devices for the network robot operating in the unstructured environment such floor sensors, active tags or passive tags, laser-based scanner and digital camera.

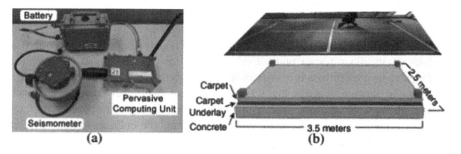

Fig. 11. Setting of floor sensor, (a) sensing unit and (b) testbed for footstep or fall down recognition [55].

The floor sensor [55] is defined as a kind of pressure sensor which has a wide range. Usually, this equipment could sense the occurrence of both human and robot for using in indoor environment as Fig. 11. The active tags as well as passive tags are employed to determine humans around the robot [56, 57]. These tags are attached on humans, and the tag reader is located onboard as Fig. 12. While active tag has a wider range of detection than passive tag, it still needs a battery. The existing problem in this case is that time using battery is not as long as desired working time, and depends on how robot utilizes. However, battery needs to be regularly charged. Alternatively, there is no battery source in the passive tag, although the effective range to detect is only 10 mm. The most inconvenient thing is that human must put the tag on reader correctly. Subsequently, the selection for proper type of tag would be motivated by the purpose and situation of research.

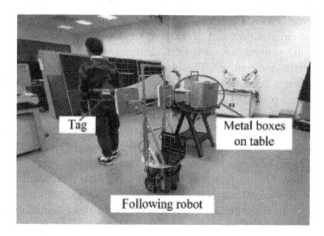

Fig. 12. Experimental demonstration of following a tagged human [56].

One of the most powerful sensors is lidar and camera. In [58], the benefits of digital cameras are small size, compact and easy to use, especially in an indoor environment since they are often attached on mobile platform. Though, they are not so good as required specifications for an outdoor environment for the reason that the dynamic adaptation against brightness is restricted. In the very bright zones and very dark zones co-existing in the same scene as Fig. 13, camera cannot identify any target for instance human and robot. In contrast, lidar is moderately unchanging in respect to the fluctuation of brightness. Recently, there is a trend to combine both sensors in order to achieve the best performance. If several lidars are sourced, the tracking performance is stably ensured. Then, multi cameras to detect whether face or facial emotion according to the detected positions by lidars, the tracking results are obviously improved.

Fig. 13. Data fusion between 2D lidar and digital camera for human detection [58].

In recent years, these sensors could be integrated to launch the different kinds of sensor networks. In the field of navigation control, the sensor network is regularly classified into three classes, improving the sensor performance onboard, observing for safe events in the environment and developing the augmented autonomy for robot. In the first group, the sensing network must distribute sensors to cover densely and precisely both robots and humans. These onboard sensors are not strong enough and not intelligent enough because robot is not able to attach an appropriate number of sensing devices, and provide sufficiently computational abilities. Accordingly, active and passive tags are alternatively explored. In the other articles, the modern network including lidar and cameras, is mentioned. This sensor network can surely identify and follow both robots and humans simultaneously. Hence, dangerous situations as well as emergency case could be detected. Last but not least, the third category is to build the robot autonomously. Owing to the precisely sensory data that attained by sensing networks, it motivates investigators to create the highly autonomous robots in the real-world environment. Besides, the advanced algorithms are also essential to integrate into hardware level.

5   Conclusion

The scope of this review is to represent the state-of-the-art methodologies that related to human-aware navigation in the dynamic environment. The conceptual model as well as the historical development were re-drawn in order to provide the systematic overview in this field. Later, the respective methodologies were clustered accordingly by both traditional researches and modern topics so that the features of the human-aware navigation method are summarized and analyzed completely. Each category of specifications and a diversity of methods were synthesized and exploited for a variety of problems. The progress developed so far permits establishing the robot navigation system to be more autonomous and intelligent in social manner.

The publications found in this paper, deals with individual domains and challenges. It still remains the existing troubles which require more researches and investigations such that the adaptive performance of single service robot is mandatory in front of crowded including both humans and mobile vehicles. The autonomy of swarm system should be studied and mapped into the human-aware navigation planning.

Acknowledgements. We acknowledge the support of time and facilities from Ho Chi Minh City University of Technology (HCMUT), VNU-HCM for this study.

References

1. Billard, A., Kragic, D.: Trends and challenges in robot manipulation. Science, **364** (6446) (2019)
2. Johannsmeier, L., Gerchow, M., Haddadin, S.: A framework for robot manipulation: Skill formalism, meta learning and adaptive control. In: 2019 International Conference on Robotics and Automation (ICRA), pp. 5844–5850. IEEE (2019)
3. Pandey, A., Pandey, S., Parhi, D.R.: Mobile robot navigation and obstacle avoidance techniques: a review. Int. Rob. Auto. J. 2(3), 00022 (2017)
4. Ravankar, A., Ravankar, A.A., Kobayashi, Y., Hoshino, Y., Peng, C.C.: Path smoothing techniques in robot navigation: state-of-the-art, current and future challenges. Sensors **18**(9), 3170 (2018)
5. Kim, W., et al.: Adaptable workstations for human-robot collaboration: a reconfigurable framework for improving worker ergonomics and productivity. IEEE Robot. Autom. Mag. **26**(3), 14–26 (2019)
6. Koch, P.J., et al.: A skill-based robot co-worker for industrial maintenance tasks. Procedia Manuf. **11**, 83–90 (2017)
7. Liu, H., Wang, L.: An AR-based worker support system for human-robot collaboration. Procedia Manuf. **11**, 22–30 (2017)
8. Knox, E., Watanabe, K.: AIBO robot mortuary rites in the Japanese cultural context. In: 2018 IEEE/RSJ International Conference on Intelligent Robots and Systems (IROS), pp. 2020–2025. IEEE (2018)
9. Nagasaka, K.: Sony QRIO. In: Humanoid Robotics: A Reference, pp. 187–200 (2019)
10. Porkodi, S., Kesavaraja, D.: Healthcare robots enabled with IoT and artificial intelligence for elderly patients. In: AI and IoT-Based Intelligent Automation in Robotics, pp. 87–108 (2021)

11. Shigemi, S., Goswami, A., Vadakkepat, P.: ASIMO and humanoid robot research at Honda. In: Humanoid Robotics: A Reference, pp. 55, 90 (2018)

12. Billard, A., Dautenhahn, K.: Grounding communication in autonomous robots: an experimental study. Robot. Auton. Syst. **24**(1–2), 71–79 (1998)

13. Breazeal, C.L.: Designing Sociable Robots. MIT Press, Cambridge (2002)

14. Breazeal, C.: Emotion and sociable humanoid robots. Int. J. Hum. Comput. Stud. **59**(1–2), 119–155 (2003)

15. Rahwan, I., et al.: Machine behaviour. Nature **568**(7753), 477–486 (2019)

16. Smith, D.H., Zeller, F.: The death and lives of hitchBOT: the design and implementation of a hitchhiking robot. Leonardo **50**(1), 77–78 (2017)

17. Breazeal, C.: Emotive qualities in robot speech. In: Proceedings 2001 IEEE/RSJ International Conference on Intelligent Robots and Systems. Expanding the Societal Role of Robotics in the the Next Millennium (Cat. No. 01CH37180), vol. 3, pp. 1388–1394. IEEE (2001)

18. Castillejo, E., et al.: Distributed semantic middleware for social robotic services. In: Proceedings of the III Workshop de Robtica: Robtica Experimental, Seville, Spain, vol. 2829 (2011)

19. Luo, X., Zhang, Y., Zavlanos, M.M.: Socially-aware robot planning via bandit human feedback. In: 2020 ACM/IEEE 11th International Conference on Cyber-Physical Systems (ICCPS), pp. 216–225. IEEE (2020)

20. Chen, A.: JiboChat: interactive chatting through a personal robot, Doctoral dissertation, Massachusetts Institute of Technology (2020)

21. Due, B.L.: RoboDoc: semiotic resources for achieving face-to-screenface formation with a telepresence robot. Semiotica **2021**(238), 253–278 (2021)

22. Yang, L., Neustaedter, C.: Our house: living long distance with a telepresence robot. In: Proceedings of the ACM on Human-Computer Interaction, vol. 2, no. CSCW, pp. 1–18 (2018)

23. Koceski, S., Koceska, N.: Evaluation of an assistive telepresence robot for elderly healthcare. J. Med. Syst. **40**(5), 121 (2016)

24. Alers, S., Bloembergen, D., Claes, D., Fossel, J., Hennes, D., Tuyls, K.: Telepresence robots as a research platform for AI. In: 2013 AAAI Spring Symposium Series (2013)

25. Zhang, Y., Tian, G., Chen, H.: Exploring the cognitive process for service task in smart home: a robot service mechanism. Futur. Gener. Comput. Syst. **102**, 588–602 (2020)

26. Hall, E.: The Hidden Dimension. Anchor Books (1966)

27. Pacchierotti, E., Christensen, H.I., Jensfelt, P.: Human-robot embodied interaction in hallway settings: a pilot user study. In: ROMAN 2005. IEEE International Workshop on Robot and Human Interactive Communication, pp. 164–171. IEEE (2005)

28. Smith, T., Chen, Y., Hewitt, N., Hu, B., Gu, Y.: Socially aware robot obstacle avoidance considering human intention and preferences. Int. J. Soc. Robot. 1–18 (2021). https://doi.org/10.1007/s12369-021-00795-5

29. Zardykhan, D., Svarny, P., Hoffmann, M., Shahriari, E., Haddadin, S.: Collision preventing phase-progress control for velocity adaptation in human-robot collaboration. In: 2019 IEEE-RAS 19th International Conference on Humanoid Robots (Humanoids), pp. 266–273. IEEE (2019)

30. Che, Y., Okamura, A.M., Sadigh, D.: Efficient and trustworthy social navigation via explicit and implicit robot–human communication. IEEE Trans. Rob. **36**(3), 692–707 (2020)

31. Ngo, H.Q.T., Tran, A.S.: Using fuzzy logic scheme for automated guided vehicle to track following path under various load. In: 2018 4th International Conference on Green Technology and Sustainable Development (GTSD), pp. 312–316. IEEE (2018)

32. Kuno, Y., Sadazuka, K., Kawashima, M., Yamazaki, K., Yamazaki, A., Kuzuoka, H.: Museum guide robot based on sociological interaction analysis. In: Proceedings of the SIGCHI Conference on Human Factors in Computing Systems, pp. 1191–1194 (2007)
33. Deng, E., Mutlu, B., Mataric, M.: Embodiment in socially interactive robots. arXiv preprint arXiv:1912.00312 (2019)
34. Shimaya, J., Yoshikawa, Y., Kumazaki, H., Matsumoto, Y., Miyao, M., Ishiguro, H.: Communication support via a tele-operated robot for easier talking: case/laboratory study of individuals with/without autism spectrum disorder. Int. J. Soc. Robot. 11(1), 171–184 (2019). https://doi.org/10.1007/s12369-018-0497-0
35. Edwards, A., Edwards, C., Westerman, D., Spence, P.R.: Initial expectations, interactions, and beyond with social robots. Comput. Hum. Behav. 90, 308–314 (2019)
36. Wykowska, A.: Social robots to test flexibility of human social cognition. Int. J. Soc. Robot. 12(6), 1203–1211 (2020). https://doi.org/10.1007/s12369-020-00674-5
37. Wang, L., Törngren, M., Onori, M.: Current status and advancement of cyber-physical systems in manufacturing. J. Manuf. Syst. 37, 517–527 (2015)
38. Hayashi, K., Shiomi, M., Kanda, T., Hagita, N.: Are robots appropriate for troublesome and communicative tasks in a city environment? IEEE Trans. Auton. Ment. Dev. 4(2), 150–160 (2011)
39. Kumm, A.J., Viljoen, M., de Vries, P.J.: The digital divide in technologies for autism: feasibility considerations for low-and middle-income countries. J. Autism Dev. Disorders, 1–14 (2021). https://doi.org/10.1007/s10803-021-05084-8
40. Bröhl, C., Nelles, J., Brandl, C., Mertens, A., Nitsch, V.: Human–robot collaboration acceptance model: development and comparison for Germany, Japan, China and the USA. Int. J. Soc. Robot. 11(5), 709–726 (2019). https://doi.org/10.1007/s12369-019-00593-0
41. Van Pinxteren, M.M.E., Pluymaekers, M., Lemmink, J.: Human-like communication in conversational agents: a literature review and research agenda. J. Serv. Manag. 31(2), 203–225 (2020). https://doi.org/10.1108/JOSM-06-2019-0175
42. Yang, Y., Williams, A.B.: Improving human-robot collaboration efficiency and robustness through non-verbal emotional communication. In: Companion of the 2021 ACM/IEEE International Conference on Human-Robot Interaction, pp. 354–356 (2021)
43. Andrist, S., Ruis, A.R., Shaffer, D.W.: A network analytic approach to gaze coordination during a collaborative task. Comput. Hum. Behav. 89, 339–348 (2018)
44. Oertel, C., et al.: Engagement in human-agent interaction: an overview. Front. Robot. AI 7, 92 (2020)
45. Ben-Youssef, A., Clavel, C., Essid, S., Bilac, M., Chamoux, M., Lim, A.: UE-HRI: a new dataset for the study of user engagement in spontaneous human-robot interactions. In: Proceedings of the 19th ACM International Conference on Multimodal Interaction, pp. 464–472 (2017)
46. Chai, J.Y., et al.: Collaborative effort towards common ground in situated human-robot dialogue. In: 2014 9th ACM/IEEE International Conference on Human-Robot Interaction (HRI), pp. 33–40. IEEE (2014)
47. Iio, T., Satake, S., Kanda, T., Hayashi, K., Ferreri, F., Hagita, N.: Human-like guide robot that proactively explains exhibits. Int. J. Soc. Robot. 12(2), 549–566 (2020)
48. Neto, P., Simão, M., Mendes, N., Safeea, M.: Gesture-based human-robot interaction for human assistance in manufacturing. Int. J. Adv. Manuf. Technol. 101(1–4), 119–135 (2018). https://doi.org/10.1007/s00170-018-2788-x
49. Du, G., Chen, M., Liu, C., Zhang, B., Zhang, P.: Online robot teaching with natural human–robot interaction. IEEE Trans. Ind. Electron. 65(12), 9571–9581 (2018)
50. Williams, T., Tran, N., Rands, J., Dantam, N.: Augmented, mixed, and virtual reality enabling of robot deixis. In: Chen, J.Y.C., Fragomeni, G. (eds.) Virtual, Augmented and

Mixed Reality: Interaction, Navigation, Visualization, Embodiment, and Simulation, pp. 257–275. Springer, Cham (2018). https://doi.org/10.1007/978-3-319-91581-4_19

51. Kanda, T., Shiomi, M., Miyashita, Z., Ishiguro, H., Hagita, N.: A communication robot in a shopping mall. IEEE Trans. Rob. **26**(5), 897–913 (2010)

52. Truong, X.T., Ngo, T.D.: Toward socially aware robot navigation in dynamic and crowded environments: a proactive social motion model. IEEE Trans. Autom. Sci. Eng. **14**(4), 1743–1760 (2017)

53. Savino, M.M., Mazza, A.: Kanban-driven parts feeding within a semi-automated O-shaped assembly line: a case study in the automotive industry. Assem. Autom. (2015)

54. Hong, S.W., Schaumann, D., Kalay, Y.E.: Human behavior simulation in architectural design projects: an observational study in an academic course. Comput. Environ. Urban Syst. **60**, 1–11 (2016)

55. Clemente, J., Song, W., Valero, M., Li, F., Liy, X.: Indoor person identification and fall detection through non-intrusive floor seismic sensing. In: 2019 IEEE International Conference on Smart Computing (SMARTCOMP), pp. 417–424. IEEE (2019)

56. Wu, C., Tao, B., Wu, H., Gong, Z., Yin, Z.: A UHF RFID-based dynamic object following method for a mobile robot using phase difference information. IEEE Trans. Instrum. Meas. **70**, 1–11 (2021)

57. DeGol, J., Bretl, T., Hoiem, D.: Chromatag: a colored marker and fast detection algorithm. In: Proceedings of the IEEE International Conference on Computer Vision, pp. 1472–1481 (2017)

58. Ngo, H.Q.T., Le, V.N., Thien, V.D.N., Nguyen, T.P., Nguyen, H.: Develop the socially human-aware navigation system using dynamic window approach and optimize cost function for autonomous medical robot. Adv. Mech. Eng. **12**(12), 1687814020979430 (2020)

Recommendation with Subjective Tendency Based on Statistical Implicative Analysis

Hiep Xuan Huynh[1(✉)], Cang Anh Phan[2], Tu Cam Thi Tran[2], and Hai Thanh Nguyen[1]

[1] College of Information and Communication Technology, Can Tho University, Can Tho 900000, Vietnam
{hxhiep,nthai.cit}@ctu.edu.vn
[2] Faculty of Information Technology, Vinh Long University of Technology Education, Vinh Long 85000, Vietnam
{cangpa,tuttc}@vlute.edu.vn

Abstract. The recommendation systems have been investigating and applying in a vast of fields. The core of systems is the similarity measures and the dissimilarity measures. Many scientists have proposed various similarity measurements in different aspects, including the measures between the users and the users, the measures between the items and the items, the measures between users with the items. However, there are not much studies on the effects of statistical implicative in the recommendation system with subjective tendency. We mainly focus on showing the effects of the subjective tendency against the recommendation system's model through the prism of statistics implicative. Three specific approaches, including Independence, Dependence, and Equilibrium combined with the fifteen measures of the statistical bias are considered in our work. The experimental results evaluated on the Jester5k dataset compare the similarity measures and the interestingness measures based on the subjective tendency in recommendation systems.

Keywords: Statistical implicative analysis · Subjective tendency · Collaborative filtering · Interestingness measures · Similarity measures

1 Introduction

Recommendation systems [1–3] uses knowledge and data based on user's benefits and user's interests to provide appropriate advice/recommendations. The system supports and improves quality when the users make decisions to search and choose products online. The subjects that need to be interested in the recommendation system are the users, the items, and the user's feedback (called evaluates or ratings). The recommendation system can predict how a user evaluates an item, predicts the order (ranking) of the items in a list from the most

P. Cong Vinh and A. Rakib (Eds.): ICCASA 2021, LNICST 409, pp. 283–299, 2021.
https://doi.org/10.1007/978-3-030-93179-7_22

attractive to the least attractive for a user or an item (or the list of things) that is suitable.

Recommendation systems are divided into the main groups/forms: Content-Based Recommendation Systems (CBRS) [1,3,4], Collaborative Filtering Systems (CFS) [3,5–7], Knowledge-Based Recommendation Systems (KBRS) [3,4], Hybrid Recommendation System [3,4,8,9] and Context-Based Recommendation Systems (CBRS) [3,4,7]. CFS is commonly used. The collaborative filtering recommendation systems [10–14] suggest users to data items based on those previously rated by the other users (Fig. 1).

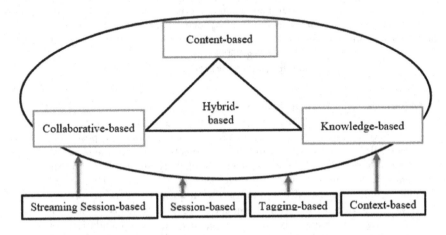

Fig. 1. Recommendation types.

Some other recommendation systems [15] have been developed based on a combination of some of the types listed above and with additional information such as context information, group information, etc. Proposing new consulting models and improving existing consulting methods is a primary research direction. Many methods in data mining and deep learning [16] are used in the consulting problem, such as the problem of classification, clustering [17], association rule mining [18], regression model [19,20]. As for the other methods, the advantage of the recommendation approach based on the association rule is transparency [1] - it can provide an in-depth explanation of the suggestion list for the users. In association rules that have two measures widely applied to evaluate item sets and generate association rule sets are Support and Confidence [14]. However, the quality of association rules and how suggestions are ranked in the recommendation systems should be done through objective similarity measures. The analysis of the effects in implication towards the subjective tendency has demonstrated an proposed approach to give more accurate and relevant recommendations. In this paper we propose a new recommendation model to predict users' missing ratings (ratings) for specific data items and propose items best suited to users based on some essential characteristics (subjective tendency) of statistical implicative analysis approach [12,21]. In the proposed model, the similarity measure is used to filter the set of rules. Through the proposed model, advisory systems will be built.

The article is organized in five parts. The first one introduces about the context and the problems need to be solved by the system as well as the approach should be taken to solve the above issues. The second part briefly describes the subjective tendency and the relevant contents are used for the recommendation system. The next one presents the proposed solutions and it's model to show the feasibility of the recommendation system based on statistical implicative analysis. The fourth part presents the experiments and the discussions, which focuses on presenting the effects of the tendencies of implications on the recommendation model. The finally part of the paper is the conclusion.

2 Subjective Tendency

2.1 Association Rule

Association rules [2,18,22,23] are relationships between the items. Let $T = \{t_1, t_2, t_3, ..., t_n\}$ are n transactions (transaction t_i buy items $I(i_1, i_2, i_3, ..., i_m)$, in which $t_i \subseteq I$). An association rule is implication of the form is $a \to b$ (with: a and b are two sets containing discrete elements so that $a \cap b = \phi$, and $a \subset I$, $b \subset I$). Set a (corresponding b) is associated with a subset of the transactions $A = T(a) = \{t \epsilon T, a \subseteq t\}$ (corresponding $B = T(b)$). Set $\bar{a}$ (corresponding $\bar{b}$) is associated with $\bar{A} = T(\bar{a}) = T - T(a) = \{t \epsilon T, a \not\subseteq t\}$ (corresponding $\bar{B} = T(\bar{b})$). To accept or refuse to have b when appearing a. Normally, we only pay attention to the number of elements $n_{A\bar{B}}$, there is no direction to support law-making $a \to b$.

Each rule is described by parameters: the cardinal n of T is $n = card(T)$, the cardinals n_A of A is $n_A = card(A)$, and the cardinals n_B of B is $n_B = card(B)$, the number $n_{A \cap B} = card(A \cap B)$, and the number $n_{A \cap \bar{B}} = card(A \cap \bar{B})$.

For greater clarity, define the concepts of probability $p(A)$ (corresponding $p(B), p(A \cap B), p(A \cap \bar{B})$)) as the probability value of A (corresponding $B, A \cap B, A \cap \bar{B}$). This probability is calculated by the frequency of occurrence of A : $p(A) = \frac{n_A}{n}$ (corresponding $p(B) = \frac{n_B}{n}, p(A \cap B) = \frac{n_{AB}}{n}, p(A \cap \bar{B}) = \frac{n_{A\bar{B}}}{n}$).

2.2 Statistical Implicative Analysis

Statistical implicative tendency [24] is the attribute showing the relationship between the data (items and items, users and users, users and items). The observations and evaluations for specific situations in the change of interestingness value are a primary method to understand the exciting measures affecting the recommendation systems deeply [24].

Three particular situations including Independence/Dependence [24], Equilibrium [24]. Both the tendencies are called the subject (subjective tendency) of an objective interestingness measure. With n is the total number of occurrences; n_{AB} is the number of occurrences of both A and B; n_A is the number of occurrences of A; n_B is the number of occurrences of B; $n_{A\bar{B}}$ is the number of occurrences of A and $non - B$; $n_{\bar{B}}$ is the number of occurrences of $non - B$ (Fig. 2).

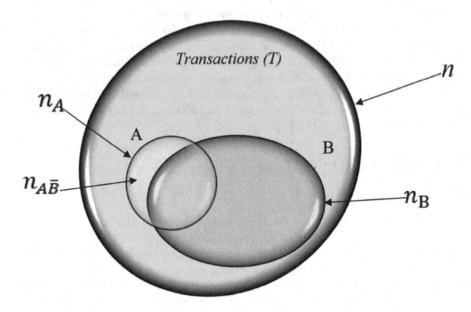

Fig. 2. The Venn diagram for an association rule $a \rightarrow b$ with 4 parameters $(n, n_A, n_B, n_{A\bar{B}})$.

For example of association rule on **Jester transaction** are showed in the Table 1.

Table 1. An example of hand activities

TID	Items
1	{Shaking Hand, Swiping Up}
2	{Thumb Down, Stop Sign, Shaking Hand}
3	{Thumb Down, Thumb Up, Doing other things}
4	{Shaking Hand, Stop Sign}
5	{Thumb Down, Stop Sign, Shaking Hand}
6	{Thumb Down, Doing other things}
7	{Thumb Down, Thumb Up, Shaking Hand, Swiping Up, Stop Sign, Doing other things}
8	{Shaking Hand, Swiping Up, Doing other things}
9	{Swiping Up, Stop Sign}

Corresponding to Table 1, set of transactions $T = \{t_1, t_2, t_3, t_4, t_5,$ $t_6, t_7, t_8, t_9\}$, set of items $I(i_1, i_2, i_3, i_4, i_5, i_6)$ Supposing for an association rule $a \rightarrow b$ with $a = \{Thumb\ Down, Stop\ Sign\}$, $b = \{Thumb\ Up\}$.

Table 2. An example of hand activities represented in a matrix

TID	Thumb down (i_1)	Thumb up (i_2)	Stop sign (i_3)	Shaking hand (i_4)	Swiping up (i_5)	Doing other things (i_6)
t_1	0	0	0	1	1	0
t_2	1	0	1	1	0	0
t_3	1	1	0	0	0	1
t_4	0	0	1	1	0	0
t_5	1	0	1	1	0	0
t_6	1	0	0	0	0	1
t_7	1	1	1	1	1	1
t_8	0	0	0	1	1	1
t_9	0	0	1	0	1	0

Form an example of hand activities in Table 2, $A = \{t_2, t_5, t_7\}$, $B = \{t_3, t_7\}$, $A\bar{B} = \{t_2, t_5\}$. Thus, with the association rule $a \rightarrow b$ in example at Table 1, the result: $n = 9$; $n_A = 3$; $n_B = 2$; $n_{A\bar{B}} = 2$.

2.3   Interestingness Measure

Interestingness measure of an association rule [2, 23–25] is based on an objectively interestingness measure, which will then be calculated based on the number of the rule $f(a \rightarrow b) = f(n, n_A, n_B, n_{A\bar{B}}) \in R$. For the convenience of the calculation process, converting between the numeric parameters of a rule, we can use the transforms as follows:

$$n_{AB} = n_A - n_{A\bar{B}}, n_{\bar{A}} = n - n_A, n_{\bar{B}} = n - n_B, n_{\bar{A}B} = n_B - n_A + n_{A\bar{B}},$$
$$n_{\bar{A}\bar{B}} = n - n_B - n_{A\bar{B}}$$

Example: Interesting value for measure $Lift = \frac{n(n_A - n_{A\bar{B}})}{n_A n_B}$ with the parameters $(n = 9; n_A = 3; n_B = 2; n_{A\bar{B}} = 2)$ are taken from Sect. 2.3

$$f(a \rightarrow b) = f(n, n_A, n_B, n_{A\bar{B}}) = \frac{n(n_A - n_{A\bar{B}})}{n_A n_B} = \frac{9 * (3 - 2)}{3 * 2} = \frac{3}{2} = 1.5$$

2.4   Tendency Evaluating

Subjective tendency [21, 24] were studied in the Independence/Dependence and Equilibrium context. The recommendation system is mainly based on similarity. The similarity measures are influenced by three properties (Independence/Dependence and Equilibrium). The study focuses on the influence of the recommendation system by the similarity measures, according to the subjective tendency.

Independence/Dependence. This tendency can only occur when the premise and outcome of a rule are combined independently. This situation only happens when $n_{AB} = \frac{n_A n_B}{n}$ or $n_{A\bar{B}} = \frac{n_A n_{\bar{B}}}{n}$, if the interestingness value is a constant.

$$f(a \rightarrow b) = f\left(n, n_A, n_B, \frac{n_A n_{\bar{B}}}{n}\right) = constant$$

Example: Interesting value for measure $Lift = \frac{n(n_A - n_{AB})}{n_A n_B}$ is applied by Independence/Dependence tendency.

$$f(a \rightarrow b) = f\left(n, n_A, n_B, \frac{n_A n_{\bar{B}}}{n}\right) = \frac{n\left(n_A - \frac{n_A n_{\bar{B}}}{n}\right)}{n_A n_B} = \frac{n\left(\frac{n n_A}{n} - \frac{n_A n_{\bar{B}}}{n}\right)}{n_A n_B}$$

$$= \frac{n\frac{(n n_A - n_A n_{\bar{B}})}{n}}{n_A n_B} = \frac{n n_A - n_A n_{\bar{B}}}{n_A n_B} = \frac{n_A\left(n - n_{\bar{B}}\right)}{n_A n_B}$$

$$= \frac{\left(n - n_{\bar{B}}\right)}{n_B} = \frac{\left(n - n_{\bar{B}}\right)}{n_B} = \frac{n_B}{n_B} = 1$$

The result of the interestingness measure value of Lift is affected by Independence/Dependence tendency.

Equilibrium. This tendency is the state of an object in which all the values that act on it are balanced. In other words, Equilibrium only can occur when the exciting value of the rule is a constant.

$$f(a \rightarrow b) = f\left(n, n_A, n_B, \frac{n_A}{n}\right) = constant$$

Example: Interesting value for measure $Lift = \frac{n(n_A - n_{A\bar{B}})}{n_A n_B}$ is applied by Equilibrium tendency.

$$f(a \rightarrow b) = f\left(n, n_A, n_B, \frac{n_A}{n}\right) = \frac{n\left(n_A - \frac{n_A}{n}\right)}{n_A n_B} = \frac{n\left(\frac{n n_A}{n} - \frac{n_A}{n}\right)}{n_A n_B}$$

$$= \frac{n\frac{(n n_A - n_A)}{n}}{n_A n_B} = \frac{n n_A - n_A}{n_A n_B} = \frac{n_A\left(n - 1\right)}{n_A n_B} = \frac{\left(n - 1\right)}{n_B}$$

$$= \frac{\left(n - 1\right)}{n_B} \neq constant$$

The result of the interestingness measure value of Lift is not affected by Equilibrium tendency.

Table 3 shows fifteen measures for these criteria, with the value of 1 is satisfied and a value of 0 is unsatisfied. The fifteen measures are considered Collective Strength, Confidence, Conviction, Gini_Index, Implication Index, Laplace, Least Contradiction, Lerman, Sebag & Schoenauer, Lift/Interest Factor, Jaccard, Support, Kappa, Jmeasure, Causal Support to evaluate the variation of interestingness values from Independence value or Equilibrium value. The interestingness measure will be evaluated as the change tendency from Independence/Dependence values or Equilibrium value.

Table 3. Subjective tendency with 15 interestingness measures [24]

Number	Interestingness measures	Independence/dependence	Equilibrium
1	Collective strength	1	0
2	Confidence	0	1
3	Conviction	1	0
4	Gini_Index	1	0
5	Implication index	1	0
6	Laplace	0	1
7	Least contradiction	0	1
8	Lerman	1	0
9	Sebag & Schoenauer	0	1
10	Lift/interest factor	1	0
11	Jaccard	0	0
12	Support	0	0
13	Kappa	1	0
14	J-measure	1	0
15	Causal support	0	0

3   Subjective Tendency Recommendation

3.1   Rating Matrix

The data model can be organized as a table of values in a rating matrix where presents the user's ratings for items. The value which is not rated is denoted as "-". For example, Table 4 exhibits the users with ratings for the products. Based on some computation, a recommendation can provide the rating score for the $user_x$ with the corresponding item column.

Table 4. Rating matrix with users and items

	$item_1$	$item_2$	$item_3$	$item_4$	$item_5$
$user_1$	4	1	-	4	2
$user_2$	-	5	3	-	-
$user_3$	-	2	3	-	3
$user_4$	-	1	4	-	2
$user_x$	4	-	-	-	3

The rating matrix of the dataset is used in a recommendation system model built with the influence of statistical attributes.

Table 5. The rating matrix of the dataset in a recommendation system

	$item_1$	$item_2$	$item_3$	$item_4$	$item_5$
u_{3464}	2.75191	NA	3.58355	NA	NA
u_{15005}	NA	NA	NA	NA	NA
u_{9658}	NA	NA	NA	NA	NA
u_{13396}	NA	NA	NA	NA	NA
u_{9565}	NA	NA	NA	NA	NA

Table 5 shows a rating matrix of 5 (users/rows) × 5 (items/columns) of class 'realRatingMatrix' with 25 ratings are built in the recommendation system.

3.2 Recommendation

A recommendation based on statistical tendency is a recommendation system with the influence of statistical implicative. It is built with statistical tendency and knowledge discovery techniques to make product recommendations [26].

Recommendation based on user's preferences by the similarity measures and interestingness measures [24,27]. Recommendation algorithm with the influence of statistical tendency is presented in Fig. 3 follows.

3.3 Evaluation

To evaluate the recommendation model, we need to build it on the training set and test it on the test set. Therefore, the first step is to prepare the data. In this step, the experimental dataset is divided into two subsets: the training set and the test set [28]. In this paper, we use the k-fold method to divide the dataset to evaluate the recommendation model.

K-fold cross-validation [28]: is a method of cutting experimental data into k subsets of the same size (called k-fold). Then, do k evaluations, with each evaluation using one subset as the test set and the other k − 1 as the training set. Finally, evaluation results are calculated from the results of k tests using the average calculation. This method ensures that all users appear in the test set at least once.

We evaluate the proposed method with the metric of Receiver Operating Characteristic (ROC curve). From the prediction results, we get the predicted variable scores. If we set a cut point for the model, we will have a threshold to evaluate the model that predicts a positive or negative result. The Receiver operating characteristic (ROC) graph exhibits each cut-point corresponding to its sensitivity and False positive rate ratio. The vertical axis corresponds to the Sensitivity rate, and the horizontal axis corresponds to the False positive rate. Based on the ROC curve, one can show whether a model is effective or not. An efficient model has low FPR and high TPR, i.e., a point on the ROC curve close

```
Input:
        - User set U; Itemset I, Rating matrix R;
        - User should be recommended: u_x;
Output:
        Building recommendation for User u_x: I_{u_x} = {i_1, i_2, ..., i_N} with the
    influence of statistical tendency;
```

```
Begin
        Step 1: Identify a list of k users similar to user u_x
            For each user u_i ∈ U perform
                < Determine the similarity between u_x and u_i using the sug-
                gested interestingness measure: SIM(u_x, u_i)>;
                < Sort list of users descending by similarity value>
                < Select the first k users with highest similarity value: N(x)>;
        Step 2: Prediction for products and choose products to recommend for the
    user u_x
        Step 3: Building recommendations with the effects of statistical tendency
                < If the statistical tendency is Independence, recompose them
                as a recommendation with the effects of the independent statis-
                tical tendency >;
                < If the statistical tendency is Dependence, recompose them as
                a recommendation with the effects of the dependent statistical
                tendency >;
                < If the statistical tendency is Equilibrium, recompose them as
                a recommendation with the effects of the Equilibrium statistical
                tendency >;
        Step 4: Model evaluation
End
```

Fig. 3. Subjective tendency recommendation.

to the point with the coordinates (0, 1) on the graph (upper left corner). The closer the curve is, the more efficient the model is.

Also, we select the metrics of Precision, Recall, TPR (True Positive Rate), and FPR (False Positive Rate) for methods comparison.

$$Precision = \frac{Number\ of\ recommendation\ products\ has\ been\ selected}{Total\ number\ of\ products\ introduced}$$

$$Recall = \frac{Number\ of\ recommendation\ products\ has\ been\ selected}{Total\ number\ of\ products\ selected}$$

4 Experiment

4.1 Dataset

The data in this paper is used that is the Jester5k[1] (Jester dataset with 5,000 samples). The data set has 5000 users from the anonymous rating data from the

---

[1] https://rdrr.io/cran/recommenderlab/man/Jester5k,html, accessed on February 01, 2021.

Jester Online Joke Recommendation System collected between April 1999 and May 2003. Moreover, it is used in many types of research around the world. The format of Jester5k is: Formal class 'realRatingMatrix' [package "recommenderlab"].

Jester5k contains a 5000×100 rating matrix (5000 users and 100 jokes) with ratings between -10.00 and $+10.00$. All selected users have rated 36 or more jokes.

4.2   Tool

This model is experimented with by the 'irlba_2.3.3'[2], 'proxy_0.4-26'[3], 'registry_0.5-1'[4], 'kernlab_0.9-29'[5], and 'rimarules' tool is developed by 'arules_1.6-6'[6]. The recommenderLab package develops this tool in the R programming language. Besides, this work also inherited several open-source tools it has researched and has built on the world community. The "rimarules" tool was developed to perform and evaluate the effects of statistical properties according to subjective bias. In addition, this tool can build and run other collaborative filter-based recommendation systems for mutual comparison and evaluation. The fifteen similarity measures were used to build the "rimarules" tool.

Some functions have been built by the system such as: The function displayed the suggestion list for the users and compared the size of the recommendation models with different implications tendencies, the function compared the predicted speeds of the models, the function built data to be evaluated model, and built a recommendation system with statistical implications tendency.

4.3   Scenario 1: Recommendation with Independence Tendency

This scenario discusses the effects of independence tendency obtained from 8 corresponding subjective recommendation models.

Figure 4 shows that the independence tendency positively influences the recommendation model with TRP (true positive rate) and FTP (false positive rate). However, with the Collective Strength measure, the correct predictability is the shortest from about 0.0 to 0.1, opposite the probability of predicting false is height about 0,6. In comparison, Kappa's ability to predict correctly is the highest, about 0,7 (Fig. 5).

Table 6 reveals the results of 8 measures for Equilibrium. Again, Lerman exhibits the best performance at 0.6916667 in Precision, while Collective Strength, Implication index, Gini_index, Kappa are shown the worst, about 0,1.

---

[2] https://cran.r-project.org/web/packages/irlba/.
[3] https://cran.r-project.org/web/packages/proxy/index.html.
[4] https://cran.r-project.org/web/packages/registry/index.html.
[5] https://cran.r-project.org/web/packages/kernlab/index.html.
[6] https://cran.r-project.org/web/packages/arules/arules.pdf.

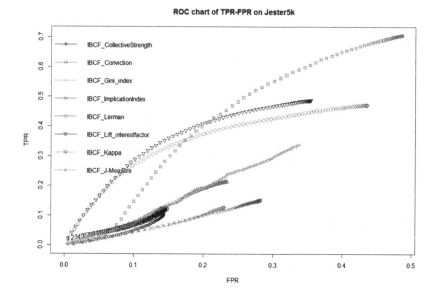

Fig. 4. The ROC chart of TPR-FPR on Jester5k with the eight measures.

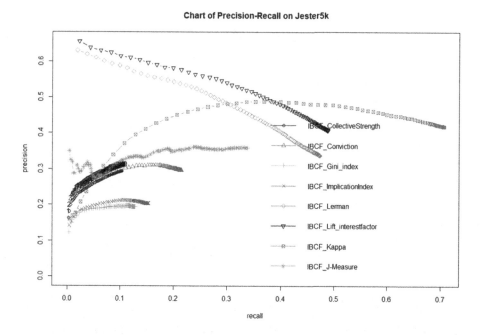

Fig. 5. The chart of Precision-Recall on Jester5k with the eight measures.

Table 6. Recommendation with independence tendency

	Precision	Recall	TPR	FPR
Collective strength	0.145454500	0.001346645	0.001346645	0.005664693
Conviction	0.250000000	0.006371114	0.006371114	0.011342510
Gini_Index	0.138888900	0.004103637	0.004103637	0.014531220
Implication index	0.141844000	0.003823744	0.003823744	0.013962940
Lerman	0.691666700	0.018817320	0.018817320	0.003983070
Lift/interest factor	0.685714300	0.021462830	0.021462830	0.004726987
Kappa	0.151724100	0.003671391	0.003671391	0.013456700
J-measure	0.366987100	0.003461492	0.003461492	0.003691004

4.4   Scenario 2: Recommendation with Dependence Tendency

This scenario presents the effects of the Dependence attribute into the recommendation system (Fig. 7).

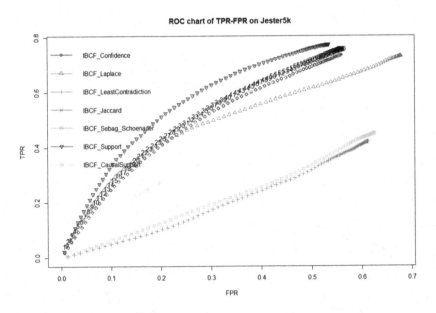

Fig. 6. The ROC of TPR-FPR with the dependence tendency.

Figure 6 shows the dependent attributes on the recommendation system with both TRP and FTP. The ROC chart presents a steady increase between TPR and FPR. However, for two measures (Least Contradiction and Causal Support), the period 0.1 to 0.5 decreased slightly for the value of FPR. In which the value of TPR is relatively increased from 0.0 to 0.3. A comparison between interestingness

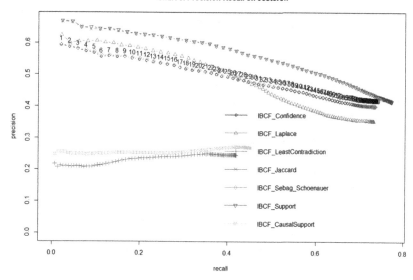

Fig. 7. The Precision-Recall with the dependence tendency.

measures is illustrated in Table 7. As observed, Least Contradiction and Causal Support reveal not better performance in all considered performance measures.

Table 7. Recommendation with dependence tendency.

	Precision	Recall	TPR	FPR
Confidence	0.648275900	0.021474840	0.021474840	0.005511594
Laplace	0.641379300	0.021140840	0.021140840	0.005477616
Least contradiction	0.234482800	0.006757109	0.006757109	0.012850560
Jaccard	0.675862100	0.022506450	0.022506450	0.005006642
Sebag & Schoenauer	0.653793100	0.021644860	0.021644860	0.005422663
Support	0.675862100	0.022455960	0.022455960	0.004997525
Causal support	0.259310300	0.007014131	0.007014131	0.011293410

4.5 Scenario 3: Recommendation with Equilibrium Tendency

In this experimental part, the four measures are used including: Confidence; Laplace; Least Contradiction; Sebag & Schoenauer to describe the influences of equilibrium properties on recommendation model (Fig. 9).

Figure 8 presents Equilibrium attributes on the recommended model. The values of both TPR and FPR increase in the ROC chart. However, the period

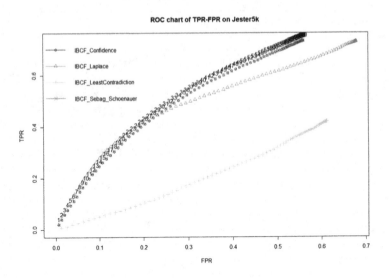

Fig. 8. The ROC of TPR-FPR with the Equilibrium tendency.

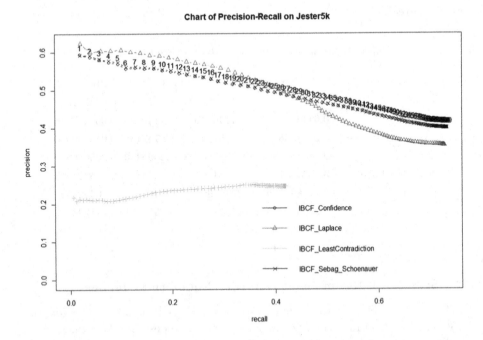

Fig. 9. The Precision-Recall with the Equilibrium tendency.

0.22 to 0.48 is the slow increase rate for Confidence, Laplace, and Sebag & Schoenauer. However, these three measures still offer higher predictability than Least Contradiction.

Table 8. Recommendation with equilibrium tendency.

	Precision	Recall	TPR	FPR
Confidence	0.648275900	0.021474840	0.021474840	0.005511594
Laplace	0.641379300	0.021140840	0.021140840	0.005477616
Least contradiction	0.234482800	0.006757109	0.006757109	0.012850560
Sebag & Schoenauer	0.653793100	0.021644860	0.021644860	0.005422663

Table 8 illustrates the results in detail for four considered interestingness measures. The four measures of the Equilibrium attribute have the positive effects on the recommendation system. As we can see, the gives the lowest predicted value in TPR while Confidence and Sebag & Schoenauer share near the same pattern.

5 Conclusion

In this work, we compared various recommendation models and considered the effects of association law on recommendation systems. Also, we evaluate and compare some tendency including Independence, Dependence, Equilibrium. We investigated the relationships between the user and the user, between the item and the item, and the user with the item with three approaches using three various subjective tendencies (Independence, Dependence, and Equilibrium) along with fifteen popular similarity measures (Collective Strength, Confidence, Conviction, Gini_index, Implication Index, Laplace, Least Contradiction, Lerman, Sebag & Schoenauer, Jaccard, Support, Kappa, j-Measure, CausalSupport) for the comparison.

Experiments were run on Jester5k data set with three scenarios using implications nature-Independence, nature-Dependence, and nature-Equilibrium. The obtained results show that the influence of the attributes on the recommender system is apparent. Each recommender model is affected by private tendency. In particular, Kappa has a tremendous influence on the recommender model of Independence tendency. The recommendation systems with Dependence tendency shows Support and Jaccard are feasible compared to other measures, and confidence presents good influence with Equilibrium tendency. While Least Contradiction shows bad recommendations for both the Dependence and Equilibrium for the recommendation models, Gini_index is also bad for the consulting model with Independence. Most of the cases with various similarity measures of Independence tendency archives better than the others.

References

1. Felfernig, A., Jeran, M., Ninaus, G., Reinfrank, F., Reiterer, S., Stettinger, M.: Basic approaches in recommendation systems. In: Robillard, M.P., Maalej, W., Walker, R.J., Zimmermann, T. (eds.) Recommendation Systems in Software Engineering, pp. 15–37. Springer, Heidelberg (2014). https://doi.org/10.1007/978-3-642-45135-5_2

2. Aggarwal, C.C.: Recommender Systems. Springer, Cham (2016). https://doi.org/10.1007/978-3-319-29659-3

3. Ricci, F., Rokach, L., Shapira, B. (eds.): Recommender Systems Handbook. Springer, New York (2015). https://doi.org/10.1007/978-1-4899-7637-6

4. Adomavicius, G., Tuzhilin, A.: Toward the next generation of recommender systems: a survey of the state-of-the-art and possible extensions. IEEE Trans. Knowl. Data Eng. 17(6), 734–749 (2005)

5. Saqlain, M., Riaz, M., Saleem, M.A., Yang, M.: Distance and similarity measures for neutrosophic hypersoft set (NHSS) with construction of NHSS-TOPSIS and applications. IEEE Access 9, 30803–30816 (2021). https://doi.org/10.1109/ACCESS.2021.3059712

6. Yan, H., Tang, Y.: Collaborative filtering based on Gaussian mixture model and improved Jaccard similarity. IEEE Access 7, 118690–118701 (2019)

7. Huynh, H.X., et al.: Context-similarity collaborative filtering recommendation. IEEE Access 8, 33342–33351 (2020)

8. Mpela, M.D., Zuva, T.: A mobile proximity job employment recommender system. In: 2020 International Conference on Artificial Intelligence, Big Data, Computing and Data Communication Systems (icABCD), pp. 1–6 (2020)

9. Phan, L.P., Huynh, H.H., Huynh, H.X.: Hybrid recommendation based on implicative rating measures. In: International Conference on Machine Learning and Soft Computing, ICMLSC 2018, New York, NY, USA, pp. 50–56. Association for Computing Machinery (2018). https://doi.org/10.1145/3184066.3184076

10. Chirico, R., et al.: Guidelines for reporting of phase equilibrium measurements (IUPAC recommendations 2012). Pure Appl. Chem. 84, 1785–1813 (2012)

11. Goldberg, D., Nichols, D., Oki, B.M., Terry, D.: Using collaborative filtering to weave an information tapestry. Commun. ACM 35(12), 61–70 (1992). https://doi.org/10.1145/138859.138867

12. Huynh, H.X., Phan, N.Q., Duong-Trung, N., Nguyen, H.T.T.: Collaborative filtering recommendation based on statistical implicative analysis. In: Hernes, M., Wojtkiewicz, K., Szczerbicki, E. (eds.) ICCCI 2020. CCIS, vol. 1287, pp. 224–235. Springer, Cham (2020). https://doi.org/10.1007/978-3-030-63119-2_19

13. Banda, L., et al.: Recommender systems using collaborative tagging. Int. J. Data Wareh. Min. 16(3), 183–200 (2020)

14. Nguyen, H.T., Huynh, H.H., Phan, L.P., Huynh, H.X.: Improved collaborative filtering recommendations using quantitative implication rules mining in implication field. In: Proceedings of the 3rd International Conference on Machine Learning and Soft Computing, ICMLSC 2019, New York, NY, USA, pp. 110–116. Association for Computing Machinery (2019). https://doi.org/10.1145/3310986.3310996

15. Huynh, H.X., Cu, G.N., Huynh, T.M., Luong, H.H., et al.: Recommender systems based on resonance relationship of criteria with Choquet operation. Int. J. Data Wareh. Min. (IJDWM) 16(4), 44–62 (2020)

16. Berkani, L., Betit, L., Belarif, L.: A multi-view clustering approach for the recommendation of items in social networking context. In: Senouci, M.R., Boudaren,

M.E.Y., Sebbak, F., Mataoui, M. (eds.) CSA 2020. LNNS, vol. 199, pp. 241–251. Springer, Cham (2021). https://doi.org/10.1007/978-3-030-69418-0_22

17. Nilashi, M., Bagherifard, K., Ibrahim, O., Alizadeh, H., Nojeem, L., Roozegar, N.: Collaborative filtering recommender systems. Res. J. Appl. Sci. Eng. Technol. **5**, 4168–4182 (2013)

18. Osadchiy, T., Poliakov, I., Olivier, P., Rowland, M., Foster, E.: Recommender system based on pairwise association rules. Expert Syst. Appl. **115**, 535–542 (2019). https://www.sciencedirect.com/science/article/pii/S095741741830441X

19. Sarwar, B., Karypis, G., Konstan, J., Riedl, J.: Application of dimensionality reduction in recommender system - a case study (2000)

20. Amatriain, X., Jaimes, A., Oliver, N., Pujol, J.M.: Data mining methods for recommender systems. In: Ricci, F., Rokach, L., Shapira, B., Kantor, P. (eds.) Recommender Systems Handbook, pp. 39–71. Springer, Boston (2011). https://doi.org/10.1007/978-0-387-85820-3_2

21. Gras, R., Kuntz, P.: An overview of the statistical implicative analysis (SIA) development. In: Gras, R., Suzuki, E., Guillet, F., Spagnolo, F. (eds.) Statistical Implicative Analysis. Studies in Computational Intelligence, vol. 127, pp. 11–40. Springer, Heidelberg (2008). https://doi.org/10.1007/978-3-540-78983-3_1

22. Nguyen, H.T., Phan, L.P., Huynh, H.H., Huynh, H.X.: Recommendation with quantitative implication rules. EAI Endorsed Trans. Context-Aware Syst. Appl. **6**(16), e2 (2019)

23. Hills, J., Davis, L.M., Bagnall, A.: Interestingness measures for fixed consequent rules. In: Yin, H., Costa, J.A.F., Barreto, G. (eds.) IDEAL 2012. LNCS, vol. 7435, pp. 68–75. Springer, Heidelberg (2012). https://doi.org/10.1007/978-3-642-32639-4_9

24. Phan, L.P., Phan, N.Q., Phan, V.C., Huynh, H.H., Huynh, H.X., Guillet, F.: Classification of objective interestingness measures. EAI Endorsed Trans. Context-Aware Syst. Appl. **3**(10), e4 (2016)

25. Hills, J., Davis, L.M., Bagnall, A.: Preprint: Interestingness measures for fixed consequent rules (2012)

26. Sarwar, B., Karypis, G., Konstan, J., Riedl, J.: Analysis of recommendation algorithms for e-commerce. In: Proceedings of the 2nd ACM Conference on Electronic Commerce, New York, NY, USA, EC 2000. pp. 158–167. Association for Computing Machinery (2000). https://doi.org/10.1145/352871.352887

27. Mild, A., Reutterer, T.: Collaborative filtering methods for binary market basket data analysis. In: Liu, J., Yuen, P.C., Li, C., Ng, J., Ishida, T. (eds.) AMT 2001. LNCS, vol. 2252, pp. 302–313. Springer, Heidelberg (2001). https://doi.org/10.1007/3-540-45336-9_35

28. Schafer, J.B., Frankowski, D., Herlocker, J., Sen, S.: Collaborative filtering recommender systems. In: Brusilovsky, P., Kobsa, A., Nejdl, W. (eds.) The Adaptive Web. LNCS, vol. 4321, pp. 291–324. Springer, Heidelberg (2007). https://doi.org/10.1007/978-3-540-72079-9_9

Applying Convolutional Neural Network for Detecting Highlight Football Events

Tuan Hoang Viet Le[3], Hoang Thien Van[3], Hai Son Tran[4],
Phat Kieu Nguyen[5], Thuy Thanh Nguyen[6], and Thai Hoang Le[1,2(✉)]

[1] Faculty of Information Technology, University of Science,
Ho Chi Minh City, Vietnam
lhthai@fit.hcmus.edu.vn
[2] Vietnam National University, Ho Chi Minh City, Vietnam
[3] Faculty of Information Technology, Saigon International University,
Ho Chi Minh City, Vietnam
{lehoangviettuan, vanthienhoang}@siu.edu.vn
[4] Faculty of Information Technology, University of Education,
Ho Chi Minh City, Vietnam
haits@hcmup.edu.vn
[5] Department of Academic Affairs, Nguyen Tat Thanh University,
Ho Chi Minh City, Vietnam
nkphat@ntt.edu.vn
[6] VNU University of Technology, Ha Noi, Vietnam
nguyenthanhthuy@vnu.edu.vn

Abstract. Automatic detection of videos with outstanding situations is a practical issue that needs to be studied in many events of different fields with common length and frequency of occurrence for instance: meetings, musicals, sports events that the user uploads regularly, one of the concerned areas is the highlights in football videos. The matches of the annual top leagues and between nations within federations form a huge database in need of different purposes in which requires the specific model assisting in extracting outstanding situations. Besides, building a reliable and accurate model requires an appropriate approach, a large amount of training data (diverse, accurate, clear data), which need to be assigned label correspondingly. The Convolutional Neural Network (CNN) was chosen as an approach to help building a smart system as a foundation, combined with a proposed new method for synthesizing results called the adaptive threshold towards specific data, along with the optimization model to draw a reliable conclusion. The work was proceeded on a video data set of the top four teams of the English Premier League (ELP) 2018–2019 and a randomly selected dataset on the Internet.

Keywords: Key frame · Highlight football events · Convolutional Neural Network (CNN) · Highlight football events classification using CNN · Wrongly-Validated Dataset Re-training (WVDR)

© ICST Institute for Computer Sciences, Social Informatics and Telecommunications Engineering 2021
Published by Springer Nature Switzerland AG 2021. All Rights Reserved
P. Cong Vinh and A. Rakib (Eds.): ICCASA 2021, LNICST 409, pp. 300–313, 2021.
https://doi.org/10.1007/978-3-030-93179-7_23

1 Introduction

Currently, football leagues in general and professional tournaments, in particular, draw great attention from fans, experts in many different fields even from world top companies that recognize football as a promising business field. Their great need is to gather information, collect statistics or simply review the highlights of the football matches. Hundreds of corner kicks, thousands of goals, millions of fouls take place worldwide every weekend when the tournaments occur, hence data explosion is considered a challenge, and working on its solution has highly practical meaning. From this real challenge, the problem of detecting outstanding situations in football videos is proposed as follows: the input as a full video of any match, the output as scenes containing prominent elements. (Corner, Fault, Goal [1]). The overall architecture of an outstanding situation detection system includes: video pre-processing [2–4], extracting and labeling features [5–7], building machine learning models from extracted features [8–10], using it to spot outstanding situations in the input video [11–13].

Therefore, within the scope of this paper, we propose a model based on a convolutional neural network developed from work [14] that was built from the group of authors, in conjunction with adaptive threshold and wrongly-validated dataset retraining and a method for synthesizing the results. The experimental results 95,8% in our EPL dataset showed the feasibility of a proposed model.

2 Background and Related Work

2.1 Background

Machine Learning research has been under serious concern of which Deep Learning is an expansion. To get high degree of accuracy of result in recognition of the vision, speech, and audio; processing and translation of natural language, or filtering of the social network, deep learning architectures have been broadly used.

Yann LeCun introduced an architecture network in 1988 named Convolutional neural networks (CNN), which now has been used in various ranges of activities in problem recognition like translation, medical diagnostics, image classification, and recognition, etc. To get worthwhile information, the inputs are filtered by the layers, which are composed of the CNN. Though no feature selection is needed, useful information extraction relies on automatically filters adjusting. In terms of dealing with problems in image classification, CNN is a better choice in comparison to Normal Neural networks.

In this paper, the authors built an application for training and validating the CNN model by using ConvNetJS. So far, the ConvNetJS has been used within one own browser as an open JavaScript library for training Deep Learning models.

Figure 1. An overview of Convolutional Neural Network architecture for image classification.

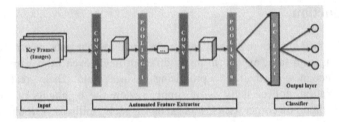

Fig. 1. CNN image classifier model

2.2   Related Work

Identifying highlights in video clips, especially football, is deeply and widely noticed. A demonstration [15], inspired by the model of two-stream CNN, DilateRNN, and long short-term memory (LSTM) units, the authors conducted classification of a data set of SoccerNet. The authors also further investigated the inclusive performance of their best model and achieved significantly improved performance 0.8%–13.6% compared to state of the art, and up to 30.1% accuracy gain in comparison to the baselines. On the other hand [16], the research of ball localization is successfully carried out using several sub-modules to tackle the limitation of using one fixed model. Hence, the authors present an optimized ensemble algorithm for effective and efficient ball tracking. The main module in their proposed design is to localize the ball when it is freely moving on the football pitch with higher accuracy. In [17], the authors also refer to a novel soccer video event detection algorithm based on self-attention. It extracts keyframes through the self-attention mechanism and then obtains the characteristics of time window level through the NetVLAD network. Finally, each video clip is classified into 4 types of events (goals, red/yellow card, substitutions, and others). The experimental results show that with the introduction of the self-attention mechanism, the classification accuracy on the SoccerNet data set has improved from 67.2% to 74.3%.

3   Proposal Methods for Detecting Highlight Football Events

3.1   CNN Model Architecture

As mentioned above, this article proposes a CNN model based on works from [14] to classifying the event of the input video after extracting keyframes, combined with a practical-based evaluation method called "Adaptive threshold" and "Wrongly-validated dataset Re-training" for classifying events.

The model was run on two devices with specification: Local computer (EN1): Intel Core i7 - 4400, 8 GB RAM, Windows 10 pro 64bit; and the second Weak AWS Cloud Computer (EN2): Intel Xeon E5–2686, 8 GB RAM, Windows Server2016 64bit, both surfing Google Chrome browser.

Figure 2. Architectural representation of the model that the authors use to solve the mentioned problem. Each keyframe following through the CNN model leads to a

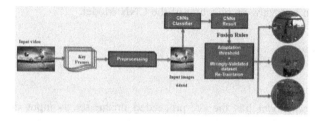

Fig. 2. CNN model architecture

conclusion of belonging or not to the set of highlights. We then apply the proposed evaluation methods and will further present them in Sect. 3.2.

3.2 CNN Model

CNN model, whose architecture is shown as Fig. 3, used to train on 64×64 English Premier League 2018 2019 image dataset (Dataset EPL20182019). This dataset will be mentioned in Sect. 4.3.

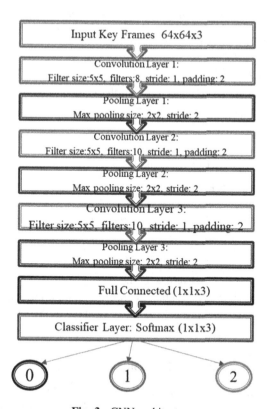

Fig. 3. CNN architecture

Figure 3. An overview architecture of the CNN Model.
With

0 is CORNER
1 is FAULT
2 is GOAL.

The proposed model has the pre-proceeded image set as input data, groups it according to the defined prominent events, then labels them. The proposed model has 3 layers of Conv (The first, second and third layer includes 5, 10, 10 filters each correspondingly), 3 Pooling layers, 1 layer Full connected, and 1 layer Softmax with 3 output results.

3.3   Adaptive Threshold

According to practical experiments, the authors propose a threshold where KF is determined through the training and testing process by the CNN model presented above, it is possible to classify the input data. The term adaptive threshold is developed on the formula:

$$1 - Max(V_{R_C}, V_{R_F}, V_{R_G}) < 0,5 \tag{1}$$

Call $V_{R_x} = \{V_{R_C}; V_{R_F}; V_{R_G}\}$
If (1) is TRUE then result R_x.
If (1) is FAULT then result R_0.
With V_{R_x} is the result of KF after running the CNN model.

R_G means the result of KF is Goal.
R_F means the result of KF is Fault.
R_C means the result of KF is Corner.
R_O means the result of KF is different.

The adaptive threshold, hereby, is determined by:

$$V_{R_{\bar{x}}} = \frac{\sum r_{x1}, r_{x2} \ldots r_{xn}}{n} \tag{2}$$

With R_{xi} mean KFs meet Eq. 1.
$V_{R_{\bar{x}}}$ mean adaptive threshold based on the fact.
Using the above formula, the authors expect to shorten the identification time as well as optimize the outcome through the actual features of the situations occurring in football.

3.4   Wrongly-Validated Dataset Re-training

A wide variety of colors, objects, angles of rotation… in the above features, governs the authors' offer to the *Wrongly-validated dataset Re-training* to improve the structure's accuracy.

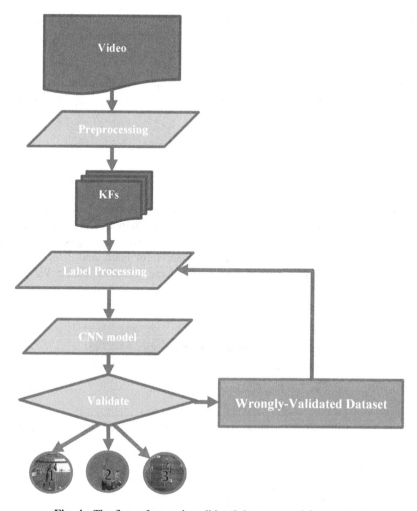

Fig. 4. The flow of wrongly-validated dataset re-training method

With

0 is CORNER
1 is FAULT
2 is GOAL.

Figure 4. The approach and process of the proposed method and are described below:

- **Step 1:** Input videos are pre-proceeded through the conversion system into image frames.
- **Step 2:** Proceed to label the frames by the specialist on the football field.
- **Step 3:** Put the standardized and labeled data into the proposed CNN model to conduct training, then classify the data for the validating set.

- **Step 4:** Proceed to record information of separate validated samples giving false classification results from the validating set (built independently and completely new presented in Sect. 4.3).
- **Step 5:** Synthesize the wrong samples into a set.
- **Step 6:** Apply a label pre-assigned by the specialist into the proposed model for retraining. The results obtained are positive, improved, and presented in Sect. 4.4.

4 Experimental Results

4.1 Dataset

Our primary dataset for the project is Top 4 English Premier League 2018–2019 (ELP20182019) and randomly collected data on the Internet. The dataset contains labeled 600 KFs, which were divided into a training set of 400 images, testing set of 200 images. Each image was marked 0 for Corner, 1 for Fault, and 2 for Goal by a specialist with years of experience in the field of referee in football match. We built 02 datasets from the collected.

Fig. 5. Dataset EPL20182019

Figure 5. The dataset description containing 600 ELP20182019 KFs with dimension 64 × 64.

Fig. 6. Dataset Random_Internet

Figure 6. The dataset 2 description of 200 Random_Collected KFs with dimension 64 × 64.

4.2 Environment for Experiments

Pre-proceeding Image
We scaled each labeled images in Dataset into 64 × 64 size. And then we divided them into two parts of Training and Testing as mentioned previously (Fig. 6). As a result, we have constructed two datasets.

Training CNN Model

With the above CNN architecture, we trained the model with the following parameters:

- Learning Rate: 0.01, Momentum: 0.9,
- Weight decay: 0.0001, Batch size: 1,
- Method for training is Adadelta.

CNN Model Accuracy Evaluation

From our perspective, without Wrongly-Validated dataset Re-training, the assessment of the accuracy of the classification model is essential. To evaluate the proposed model, we have selected any 200 KFs images (consist of 66, 66, 68 labeled Corner, Fault, and Goal images respectively) for proposed model testing, which results in 95.2%. By using Wrongly-Validated dataset Re-training, its accuracy evaluation increases to 95.8% noticeably, which will be presented in detail in the next section.

4.3   CNN Components Accuracy Evaluation

Assessment of the accuracy of the classification is vital because it allows predicting the accuracy of the classification results of future data and participating in the comparison of different classifiers. The CNN classifiers proposed used the Hold-out method for evaluating.

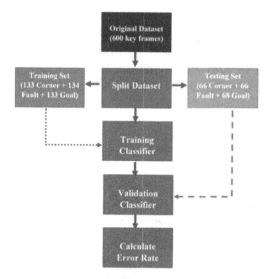

Fig. 7. The structure and flow of operations of the dataset

Figure 7. An overview of the Hold-out method which we had used to evaluate the accuracy of the CNN model.

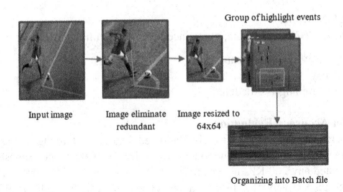

Group of highlight events

Input image   Image eliminate   Image resized to
                     redundant   64x64

Organizing into Batch file

Fig. 8. Keyframe images process flow

Figure 8. The way that the data is proceed in which images are extracted from the video, then stripped of redundant details (do not contain features that influence model decision-making). After being labeled, images will be resized to 64 × 64, and proceed to convert to binary files from the image files into the data set and these binary files form batches of data. This is appropriate input for the proposed CNN model to achieve sufficient performance.

Training Process

Experimenting with the proposed model, the authors used ConvNetJS which is a Javascript library to train deep learning models entirely in the browser, software requirement, compiler, installation, or GPU. This library was designed and built by Karpathy and is used in many research projects because of its high applicability [18] [19]. This is the library realizing the ConvNet model proposed by Yann Lecun.

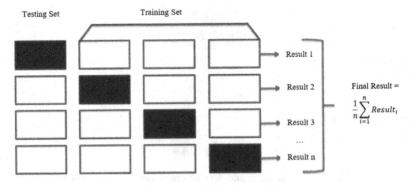

Testing Set   Training Set

Result 1

Result 2   Final Result =
                         $\frac{1}{n}\sum_{i=1}^{n} Result_i$
Result 3

...

Result n

Fig. 9. Experimental progress of the CNN model

Figure 9. During the training and evaluating of the group model, the authors applied the K-Fold evaluation method to conduct experiments.

Evaluation of Validating Process

Table 1. The result of the proposed model in the different environment

Result	Environment	
	EN1	EN2
Training time (minutes)	50	104
Max accuracy on the validate set (%)	95.2	93.6
Classification loss (%)	0.0007	0.0006
L2 Weight loss (%)	0.1346	0.1377

Table 1 shows the result of the proposed in two different environments presented above. It may be observed that the EN2 needs more training time to achieve high results. Besides, the proposed model has proven to work on low-end computers.

In addition, we also prepared a new dataset named EPL20202021 to experiment with the method Wrongly-Validated dataset Re-training of the data organized as follows.

Table 2. Structure of EPL20202021 dataset

Dataset	Corner	Fault	Goal
EPL20202021	500	500	1000

Table 2 shows a structure with a total of 2000 validate samples, we obtained 100 samples that the system misrepresented, then used to retrain the model, and obtained more positive results presented in Sect. 4.4.

4.4   Experimental Results

The Result of CNN Model Testing with Different Environment
The results obtained when experimenting with 2 datasets EPL20182019 on 2 different environments introducced in Sect. 4.2.

Table 3. Result of CNN model different environments

Dataset	EN1	EN2
EPL20182019	95,2%	93,6%
Ramdom_Data	93,4%	91,8%

Table 3 shows that, noticed by the authors, the accuracy differences between the two environments are not significant, demonstrating the compactness, lightness, and feasibility of the proposed model. In addition, the model also achieved a quite high accuracy with the data set randomly selected on the Internet with the feature of images from the camera, which shows good adaptability to different types of data of the model.

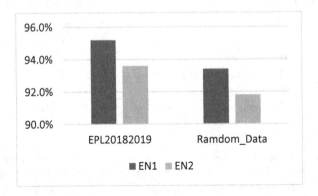

Fig. 10. Result of testing on different environments

Figure 10. The chart depicts the classification results of the proposed model on two different data sets

Table 4. Result of CNN model on different Dataset

Dataset	TOP4_ELP20182019		RANDOM_COLLECT	
Result	Amount	(%)	Amount	(%)
True	190	95	93	93
False	10	5	7	7

Table 4 shows the classification results of the proposed model, the rate of correct recognition, and the number of samples that the system detected wrong. Through a quick review, the authors found that the errors come from the complexity of the GOAL, CORNER situations with a large number of objects and the turbulence of the angle and color in the test cases.

Table 5. Result of CNN model with Adaptive threshold

Fusion rule	CNN Model results			
	Dataset1		Dataset2	
Result	Time(s)	Acc(%)	Time(s)	Acc(%)
Before	55	95.2	63	93.4
After	50	95.2	60	93.4

Table 5. As a result of applying the Adaptive threshold method, the authors found that the training time of the model decreased slightly but still achieved the initial accuracy of the proposed model, is a sign that the effectiveness of the proposed method, as well as suggestions for directions to improve the model in the future.

Table 6. Result of CNN model with Wrongly-Validated dataset Re-training method

WVDR	CNN Model results	
Result	**Dataset1** Acc(%)	**Dataset2** Acc(%)
Before	95.2	93.4
After	95.8	93.6

Table 6. Presenting the improvement of the model's accuracy through retraining the samples that the system recognizes as wrong, through statistics from the validation process, and then aggregated into a new training set. Use the assigned label for this set to train the proposed model to gain more knowledge about difficult false positives.

4.5 Discussion

With the aim of constructing a model with the ability to recognize outstanding situations in football as well as in other sports, then extract outstanding points to serve the needs of a substantial number of fans, experts and also case analysts. The authors also encountered difficulties such as camera angle and distance between stadiums; The dissimilar quality of pictures obtained from broadcasters; Instability in important features such as the color of the player's outfit, accessories; also The stadium design (goal, flagpole, net color...).

Moreover, the challenge of the precision of the standout situation is also noticeable since validity must be taken into account, and the appearance of VAR (Video Assitant Referee) is also noise the statement by the negation of the validity of the situation.

5   Conclusions

In this research, we proposed the CNN model and methods for synthesizing the results of the components of the model which we are called "Adaptive threshold" and "Wrongly-Validated dataset Re-training".

• Propose a suitable CNN network architecture for the highlighted situations as mentioned in football matches.

- Use a combination of the evaluation "Adaptive threshold" and the optimal processing method Wrongly-Validated dataset Re-training
- Validate CNN model with combined evaluation methods to detect two datasets of highlight football events. The accuracy results of 95.2% and up to 95.8% showed the feasibility of the proposed model when it combined these rules.

Acknowledgment. This project would not be posible without the financial means from Sai Gon International University (SIU). Many thanks to my specialist Mr. Nguyen Vo Thuan Thanh, major in Physical Education, for providing expert advice and labeling the dataset. And finally, thanks to numerous friends who endured this process with me, offering me lots of support and effort.

References

1. Vietnam Football Federation: Law of football. The duc the thao Ha Noi Publisher (2013)
2. Shambharkar, P.G., Doja, M.N.: Movie trailer classification using deer hunting optimization based deep convolutional neural network in video sequences. Multimed. Tools Appl. **79**(29), 21197–21222 (2020). https://doi.org/10.1007/s11042-020-08922-6
3. Bastani, F., Madden, S.: MultiScope: efficient video pre-processing for exploratory video analytics. arXiv preprint arXiv:2103.14695 (2021)
4. Del Campo, F.A., et al.: Influence of image pre-processing to improve the accuracy in a convolutional neural network. Int. J. Combin. Optim. Probl. Inform. **11**(1), 88–96 (2020)
5. Stoeve, M., et al.: From the laboratory to the field: IMU-based shot and pass detection in football training and game scenarios using deep learning. Sensors **21**(9), 3071 (2021)
6. Jackman, S.: Football shot detection using convolutional neural networks (2019)
7. Shi, S.: Comparison of player tracking-by-detection algorithms in football videos (2020)
8. Viet, V.H., et al.: Multiple kernel learning and optical flow for action recognition in RGB-D video. In: 2015 Seventh International Conference on Knowledge and Systems Engineering (KSE). IEEE (2015)
9. Bottino, A.G., Hesamian, S.: Deep learning model for 2D tracking and 3D pose tracking of football players (2020)
10. Russo, M.A., Kurnianggoro, L., Jo, K.-H.: Classification of sports videos with combination of deep learning models and transfer learning. In: 2019 International Conference on Electrical, Computer and Communication Engineering (ECCE). IEEE (2019)
11. Sheng, B., et al.: GreenSea: visual soccer analysis using broad learning system. IEEE Trans. Cybern. **51**, 1463–1477 (2020)
12. Tran, D.-S., et al.: Real-time hand gesture spotting and recognition using RGB-D camera and 3D convolutional neural network. Appl. Sci. **10**(2), 722 (2020)
13. Venkatesh, S., Ramachandra, R., Bours, P.: Video based deception detection using deep recurrent convolutional neural network. In: Nain, N., Vipparthi, S., Raman, B. (eds.) CVIP 2019. Communications in Computer and Information Science, vol. 1148, pp. 163–169. Springer, Singapore (2020). https://doi.org/10.1007/978-981-15-4018-9_15
14. Tran, H.S., Le, T.H., Nguyen, T.T.: The degree of skin burns images recognition using convolutional neural network. Indian J. Sci. Technol. **9**(45), 1–6 (2016)
15. Mahaseni, B., Faizal, E.R.M., Raj, R.G.: Spotting football events using two-stream convolutional neural network and dilated recurrent neural network. IEEE Access **9**, 61929–61942 (2021)

16. Perera, D.S., et al.: Ball localization and player tracking using real time object detection. In: International Conference on Advances in Computing and Technology (ICACT–2020) Proceedings. ISSN 2756-9160 (Nov 2020)
17. Ma, S., et al.: Event detection in soccer video based on self-attention. In: 2020 IEEE 6th International Conference on Computer and Communications (ICCC). IEEE (2020)
18. Vo, A.T., Tran, H.S., Le, T.H.: Advertisement image classification using convolutional neural network. In: 2017 9th International Conference on Knowledge and Systems Engineering (KSE). IEEE (2017)
19. Kieu, P.N., et al.: Applying multi-CNN model for detecting abnormal problem on chest x-ray images. In: 2018 10th International Conference on Knowledge and Systems Engineering (KSE). IEEE (2018)

Can Gaming be the Bad Escapism?

Waralak V. Siricharoen[(⊠)] [iD]

Faculty of Information and Communication Technology, Silpakorn University,
Nonthaburi 11120, Thailand
siricharoen_w2@su.ac.th

Abstract. Game (Computer Game) is considered one of entertainment activities for many people. Therefore, several people have used technology to flee from technology as the usage rate has been increasing rapidly because of the emergence of the latest technology as well as the increasing speed of internet. In today's world, technology is considered an essential service, similar to food and alcohol due to several benefits such as for daily activities and work. However, as the usage has been increased, video games or social media can also have advantages, which individuals should also avoid. Although many students use computers for study essentials, building technological skills for work place and learn to combat distraction and procrastination as part of that growth, it is still considered a waste of time especially for those who start to develop an addiction or use as a regular escapism. This paper concluded a number of the researches and facts about taking escapism with gaming too far.

Keywords: Gaming · Escapism · Gamer · Escapist · Technology

1 Escapism Revisited

Several concerns have been developed throughout humans' lifestyles, including work, errands, health problems, etc. The technology has become developed to help solving issues to minimize time as well as assisting with daily activities. It does not only become helpful for individuals, but allow relaxations and experience delight in entertainment or leisure activities like watching movies, hiking, reading, playing games. It is also considered a great escape for individuals as some people use the technology sources to cope with troubles and pressures from daily routine. Considering a healthy amount of using an internet as an escape, it can be a healthy way to shake off from reality especially for a reasonable period. As the COVID-19 pandemic has accelerated several trends to the gaming market, it starts to increase the demands of entertainment sources worldwide. Such contribution has started to cause excessive spending to individuals as well as developing the habits involving gaming especially during the pandemic and lockdowns. Also, it does show that the gaming entertainment industry will keep experiencing its growth for several years without fail.

People start to develop habits in escaping reality using video games more than ever. It is essential to understand that escapism is the reasonable defence reaction, it occurs as a result of people trying to protect themselves from hardships or irritations. Such

P. Cong Vinh and A. Rakib (Eds.): ICCASA 2021, LNICST 409, pp. 314–322, 2021.
https://doi.org/10.1007/978-3-030-93179-7_24

action is also called 'survival mechanism', which is beyond using the source just for relaxation.

This exploitation of this matter may end up being an unhealthy habit because it can develop the condition that makes individuals not able to separate fantasy from the reality. This has become an insecure concept that cause us to deny reality. Laziness or escape behaviour will be interpreted from developing this habit. Even though, being away from reality by using internet can also have positive and negative sides, but living with escapism will produce denial or inability to interact with real life [1].

Gaming has become more popular and mainstream in recent years [2, 3], with a 2016 Roy Morgan report showing that almost a third of Australians aged 14 and older own a gaming console. In the United States, gamers are still detained for committing violence after mass shootings in the country as the media usually have mentioned gaming when the issues have risen. The same report shows that the country's 6.1 million console game owners. Regarding the Digital Australia 2018 report has shown that Australians spend an average of 5–6 h on a daily basis on the Internet and have been increasing during past years. As of now, the Global Games Market Report of Newzoo (https://newzoo.com), a subscription service This includes quarterly trends and forecast update reports, additionally as continuous access to a dashboard with gamer and game revenue forecasts by country and group [3]. The report shows that in 2021 [17], 2.8 billion gamers worldwide helped raising the the global games market generate revenues of over $189.3 billion. In an merging markets, the drive of revenue is considered to be favourable and would also rise infrastructure and economic growth across regions such as in Southeast Asia and the Middle East & Northern Africa. The growth is expected to continue outpacing in the game and entertainment markets as the year 2021, it is expected to exceed over $106.4 billion total revenue with the contribution of 59% total revenue come from smartphone and tablet game applications [3, 17]. Also, the growth of the PUBG Mobile's e-sport have increased rapidly over years and has become the world's fourth-largest esports activity in the year.

Escapism occurs after people try to avoid or procrastinate tasks or issues, which is available in different forms. Some people escape by seeking out alternate activities such as sleeping and outdoor activities. Some have drowned themselves in work or productive activities or substance addictions such as drinking, smoking and drugs. There are two forms of escapism, including positive and negative. The positive form is to feel exposed to new environment and explore new contents which allow individuals to see places to visit in order to cultivate the freedom of adventure. On the other hand, the negative escapism happens when individuals try to get away to feel more secure or as a matter to forget real life's encounters or issues. The type of individuals may feel that living in the fantasy world would help them in forgetting bad thought and rather refuse to grasp or recognize the trouble or pain. It shows that positive escapism helps humans ascend pain and disappointment in this world, while negative escapism prevents humans from doing the exertions necessary that helps in growth. In the Fig. 1 below by Nordby et al. (2019), it shows the main review on the reasons of game playing, which escapism has ranked the first choice among 15 samples out of 393, whereas participants believed that the main advantage for video game playing is rather for entertainment [21].

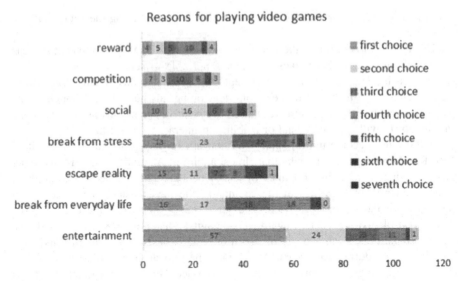

Fig. 1. Reasons for video gaming. (Source: Nordby et al., 2019. Journal of BMC Psychology)

Moreover, there are simple symptoms or signs which individuals with negative escapism many have experienced which are including the desire to quit productive activities such as a job or study, which can lead to a lack of performing such activities. The individuals may also develop the addiction from gaming that can be challenging to stop. They can also start to develop different mindsets by thinking that the world may be a cruel place that can be difficult to handle, and starting to rather procrastinate most real-life activities to perform the routine of gaming without being able to accept the sense of reality. Such signs can create harm to individuals as the intensity of the symptoms have developed to become addiction, which can be challenging for individuals to perform decent lifestyle and may demand a psychological treatment in order to improve mental health and well-being [4].

2 Gaming: The Route to Escape the Reality

> *"Individuals who play games to get away from their lives or to pretend to be other people seem to be those most at-risk for becoming part of a vicious cycle. These gamers avoid their problems by playing games, which in turn interferes with their lives because they're so busy playing games. [5]"*

McGonigal [1] has mentioned that escaping to a better condition is what people have started to seek for especially during hardships without realizing that it can cause harm to individuals, especially in the digital age, gaming has influenced several people's lives as it causes individuals to be less in touch with real life activities than in the past. The statistics showed that people have spent over 300 million minutes a day just on the game Angry Birds and over 170 h a year on Call of Duty. The rate depicted a dramatic increase in the activity, judging from the popular games mentioned. Currently, are not enough psychological studies on downturns of escapism to gaming such as developing mental illnesses, suicidal thoughts, or substance addictions [1]. However, many experts have discussed that gaming can cause negative effects from both physically and mentally to individuals as it is shown to focus on two key issues including mental aggression and postures. McGonigal also stated that these types of issues are considered mild and would not have a high impact towards society as using aggression towards gaming is common, and can help with stress relief, rather causing problems towards others. However, it is undeniable that it can still affect the mood such as creating mood swings and aggression.

Several scientific studies show that competing in gaming with strangers can cause a surge in testosterone, which can make game players to develop traits such as an urge to dominate or to be over-competitive. On another hand, beating someone you are conversant within a game causes testosterone to drop and rather develop a better bond with the person. The sitting disease is common within gamers as it has now been put into an attention as it is considered a complicated issue as sitting for over six hours a day can increase the chance of experiencing death more than moving individuals due to the lack of movement. The only best way to stop individuals from sitting disease is to reduce the screen time. However, it can be troublesome to many individuals to give up on the addiction so suggesting to reduce the screen time can be more beneficial especially at the young age. It helps individuals to become more active in the real world. Also, it is suggested that playing games that takes a short duration to complete or involving physical input can also help solving such issue.

A new study in Comprehensive Psychiatry, published by Elsevier [6, 7], is the first to compare professional electronic sport (e-sport) players with recreational video game players and explores the similarities and differences between what motivates each group. It showed that both esport and recreational gamers run the risk of developing internet gaming disorder when their intense immersion in the activit, which can also lead to escapism. Internet gaming disorder (IGD) is described by leading classification manuals (DSM-5 and ICD-11) as severe behaviour patterns that significantly impair personal, family, social, educational, and occupational functioning [6, 7]. The way in which both esport gamers and recreational gamers escape from reality into virtual worlds could also be the result of different mechanisms and psychological backgrounds. In some pro players, mental health status (stress level, psychosocial well-being, self-esteem) can modify the effect of escapism within the development of gaming disorder [7].

"Escapism can cause negative outcomes and interfere with an esport gamer's career just like any sportsman's career could end with a physical injury or trauma", noted Professor Demetrovics [8]. Escaping to online games and community can create several drawbacks to individuals. As the rate of escapists have increased rapidly, it rather creates a massive community which can cause harm to health and well-being of individuals [9]. Online games have now been commonly played by children, which differs from the past that children used to play more offline community games such as marbles or hide and seek as they are busy playing on their phones or tablets. Such increasing has driven the number of players worldwide.

Overall, problematic life events or stressful situations can motivate individuals to go online and use specific applications, such as video games, to satisfy unhappy needs or to alleviate an unfavourable emotional state [10]. It is noteworthy that this can lead to both positive and negative outcomes, that is, positive when compensation is successful (feel better and when the app is in use for a short time) and negative when this mechanism is constantly on and the intensity of use. Compromise other areas of each person's life can help to balance and prevent the problems from going forward. Moreover, these things are not necessarily mutually exclusive [10, 22]. The interpretations of each problematic used in the gaming habits, which can be categorized into three main types can be shown below (See Fig. 2).

Types	Problematic Causes	Treatments	Measurement Scales
Gaming Disorder	Excessive gaming with reports from self or related on addictions	Self or family reports on the addiction, Clinical treatments	Addiction scales (IGD, PG), Interviews
Internet Addiction	Intensive time spent online, more than average screen-time	Clinical/Professional help on the cause of problem	Scales on internet addiction and IPU, Interviews
Other	Other problematic usages regarding time spent, extension on games	Specific interviews and single-diagnosis on symptoms	Measurement scales on each game or internet usage

Fig. 2. Problematic interpretations on online platform

It is important to notice that the existence of gaming disorder does not mean doctors are saying games are inherently bad or dangerous. Video games can be an effective learning tool, and they can also just be fun [11]. Fun is essential. Nobody wants to take away the fun, and it is good escapism. However, some experts simply feel that addiction is too loaded a term, given the fact that many gaming addicts are children and adolescents. There is concern that classifying such an addiction could lead parents and doctors to classify normal video game use as a pathological behaviour when it suits them, perhaps even leading kids to seek out more dangerous substances when their games are taken away. For now, the sole behavioural addiction in the Diagnostic Statistical Manual (DSM) is gambling addiction. But some argue that addictions to eating, shopping, internet use, sex, and other activities should be included [11, 18].

Addiction does not have to involve drugs or substances as addiction is a chronic disease of brain reward, motivation, memory, and related circuitry or clearly relates to the mental health. Over the past 10 years, scientists have made similar findings of compulsive gaming [12]. Neurological studies have confirmed that video games induce dopamine release in the reward circuitry. However, it also shows that dopamine release does not work in a normal level, but is considered to more excessive when developing addictions. A study in China has found that game players tend to have unusually low activity in the prize circuit once they are expected to receive a monetary reward. Some researchers think that inherently unresponsive reward systems get people hooked by pushing them into the massive excitement pursuit. Others interpret it as an early sign of patience.

On May 25, 2019, the World Health Organization officially voted to adopt the latest edition of its International Classification of Diseasesto include an entry on "gaming disorder" as a behavioural addiction [16]. During the activity, WHO declared that gaming disorder as an official mental illness in the version of draft from International Classification of Diseases (ICD). The information regarding ICD from WHO has the latest 11th edition which provides information in several languages, which serves as inter national standard for diagnosing and treating health conditions [13].

The characteristics were listed by WHO regarding gaming disorders including:

- Impaired control over the onset, frequency, intensity, duration, termination, or context of gaming
- Increasing priority given to gaming to the extent that gaming takes precedence over other life interests and daily activities
- The continuation or escalation of gaming despite the occurrence of negative consequences.

The addition caused by playing games concern two related terms. They are *internet gaming disorder and gaming disorder* [14]. Gaming addiction is described in the American Psychiatric Association's Diagnostic and Statistical Manual of Mental Disorders (DSM-5), which is employed by mental health professionals to diagnose mental disorders.

Internet Gaming Disorder: DSM-5 notes that gaming must cause "significant impairment or distress" in several aspects of a person's life. This proposed condition is limited to gaming and does not include problems with the general use of the internet, online gambling, or use of social media or smartphones. The proposed symptoms of internet gaming disorder include [14]:

- Preoccupation with gaming
- Withdrawal symptoms when gaming is taken away or not possible (sadness, anxiety, irritability)
- Tolerance, the need to spend more time gaming to satisfy the urge
- Inability to reduce playing, unsuccessful attempts to quit gaming
- Giving up other activities, loss of interest in previously enjoyed activities due to gaming
- Continuing to the game despite problems
- Deceiving family members or others about the amount of time spent on gaming
- The use of gaming to relieve negative moods, such as guilt or hopelessness
- Risk, having jeopardized or lost employment or relationship due to gaming.

Gaming disorder is characterised by a pattern of persistent or recurrent gaming behaviour ('digital gaming' or 'video-gaming), which may be online (i.e., over the internet) or offline, manifested by [15, 19]:

1. impaired control over gaming (e.g., onset, frequency, intensity, duration, termina-tion, context);
2. increasing priority given to gaming to the extent that gaming takes precedence over other life interests and daily activities; and
3. continuation or escalation of gaming despite the occurrence of negative consequences.

The pattern of gaming behaviour may be continuous or episodic and recurrent. The pattern of gaming behaviour leads to marked distress or significant impairment in personal, family, social, educational, occupational, or other important areas of func-tioning. The gaming behaviour and other features are normally evident over a period of at least 12 months in order for a diagnosis to be assigned, although the required duration may be shortened if all diagnostic requirements are met and symptoms are severe [20].

3 Conclusion

As escaping reality has become more common in the digital age, it also increases several negative issues for individuals such as increasing in more self-conflicts and are prone to anti-socialism more than individuals without the condition. It is crucial for gamers to consider the time limit in order to prevent the condition or trying to set the limit of time to cease the screen time duration. It can help individuals to have control of game playing and help to cope with addiction better. Escaping to the internet does not only have a negative effect, but also a positive side, which individuals have to consider in order to be able to keep track of reality. Individuals should start applying escapism to other activities including reading, socializing, sports, or outdoor activities which require productivity.

Despites both negative and positive sides from escapism, positive escapism still does lead to more productive activity, which can increase creativity, innovation as well as the sense of adventure whereas negative sides can lead to procrastinating important events as well as denial in reality. If the condition has developed to an extreme intensity or is considered an addiction, individuals are recommended to seek professional health in order to regain the courage to be in touch with reality in the future. As technology has become unavoidable for several individuals, it should be used in the most pro-ductive way in order to prevent negative sides of escapism, especially in gaming activities.

References

1. Kollar, P.: Jane McGonigal on the good and bad of video game escapism (2013). https://www.polygon.com/2013/3/28/4159254/jane-mcgonigal-video-game-escapism
2. Examiner.com.au: Gaming is a form of escapism but when do you know it's too much (2019). https://www.examiner.com.au/story/6330838/balance-in-gaming-is-the-answer-to-health/

3. Wijman, T.: Mobile revenues account for more than 50% of the global games market as it reaches $137.9 billion in 2018 (2018). https://newzoo.com/insights/articles/global-games-market-reaches-137-9-billion-in-2018-mobile-games-take-half/

4. Mistry, M.: 10 signs you're an escapist (both good and bad) (2020). https://www.lifehack.org/articles/productivity/10-signs-youre-escapist-both-good-and-bad.html

5. Kuchera, B.: I play video games to run from my problems (2015). https://www.polygon.com/2015/7/13/8950163/i-play-video-games-to-run-from-my-problems

6. Bányai, F., Mark, D., Griffiths, Z., Demetrovics, O.K.: The mediating effect of motivations between psychiatric distress and gaming disorder among esport gamers and recreational gamers (2019). http://irep.ntu.ac.uk/id/eprint/37462/1/14673_Griffiths.pdf

7. neurosciencenews.com: Escapism: a powerful predictor of internet gaming disorder among video gamers (2019). https://neurosciencenews.com/escapism-internet-gaming-disorder-15107/

8. Debuglies.com: Esport gamers – excessive immersion can indicate mental health issues (2019). https://debuglies.com/2019/10/23/esport-gamers-excessive-immersion-can-indicate-mental-health-issues

9. Mbisasur: Are the online gaming leading to escapism? (2020). http://networkconference.netstudies.org/2019Curtin/2019/05/08/are-the-online-gaming-leading-to-escapism/

10. Melodia, F., Canal, N, Griffiths, M.D.: The role of avoidance coping and escape motives in problematic online gaming: a systematic literature review. Int. J. Ment. Health Addict. (2020). https://doi.org/10.1007/s11469-020-00422-w. https://link.springer.com/content/pdf/10.1007/s11469-020-00422-w.pdf

11. Leaf life radio: Gaming: Just For Fun? (2017). https://www.facebook.com/leafliferadio/posts/1996497357342960

12. Jabr, F.: Can you really be addicted to video games? Newyorktimes magazine (2019). https://www.nytimes.com/2019/10/22/magazine/can-you-really-be-addicted-to-video-games.html

13. Park, A.: 'Gaming disorder' is now an official medical condition, according to the WHO (2019). https://time.com/5597258/gaming-disorder-icd-11-who/

14. Parekh, R.: Internet gaming (2018). https://www.psychiatry.org/patients-families/internet-gaming

15. WHO: ICD-11 for Mortality and Morbidity Statistics (Version: 09/2020): 6C51 Gaming disorder (2020). https://icd.who.int/browse11/l-m/en#/http%3a%2f%2fid.who.int%2ficd%2fentity%2f1448597234

16. Kamenetz, A.: Is 'Gaming disorder' an illness? WHO says yes, adding it to its list of diseases (2019). https://www.npr.org/2019/05/28/727585904/is-gaming-disorder-an-illness-the-who-says-yes-adding-it-to-its-list-of-diseases

17. Newzoo's Games, Esports, and Mobile Trends to Watch in 2021 (2021). https://resources.newzoo.com/hubfs/Reports/2021_Newzoo_Trends_to_Watch_Report.pdf?utm_campaign=Global%20Mobile%20Market%20Report%202020&utm_medium=email&_hsmi=1130815
65&_hsenc=p2ANqtz-95D0XIfqPPpk7mNSMFQtvgHgTDq7ocK0G9mIFuZCBM9AYuunt
YAfXrEPGgG4fGPMQj5UldqUR_Fy7TG4D9T0CI3FcXmw&utm_content=113081565
&utm_source=hs_automation

18. Mayer, I.: Press enter of escape to play deconstructing escapism in multiplayer gaming (2009). https://d1wqtxts1xzle7.cloudfront.net/32050604/09287.04129-with-cover-page-v2.pdf?Expires=1631387763&Signature=cMB8QLWKavoae88OCvBti5Uhk9HqcTUm7x1a
WlEdC0srMNDvp5cefbdYSbKsylDNyzu0s7gtBKBf4izkV9PqmvSrFzgqkG~ElwR6Li3
EyiEW1vf-RoBog6FPp1nUfZ~UpL58dvmgwgMevnoZ9-hCeWXM-aePjYLYU9d-tum
NZmPXNcP~zUmjZ-42hvcZVj1DhmpkfMcrn-XcN78NYwl2roxJpUlmcIDL077wO8d
KVHARG2mQsekXbBe-23LkuyUCnedCDYF9LP7n1D5mbiy7MPXhjkkWMwZfCPxDu

Lh2JVZjeZxlbYqMdd6oEGWzQKRivgdu-IBgULO64w90qN8lng__&Key-Pair-Id=APKAJ
LOHF5GGSLRBV4ZA

19. Kardefelt-Winther, D.: The moderating role of psychosocial well-being on the relationship between escapism and excessive online gaming (2014). https://doi.org/10.1016/j.chb.2014.05.020
20. Li, D., Liau, A., Khoo, A.: Examing the influence of actual-ideal self-discrepancies, depression, and escapism on pathological gaming among massively multiplayer online adolescent gamers (2011). https://doi.org/10.1089/cyber.2010.0463
21. Nordby, K., Løkken, R.A., Pfuhl, G.: Playing a video game is more than mere progcrastination (2019). https://doi.org/10.1186/s40359-019-0309-9
22. Carras, M.C., Shi, J., Hard, G., Saldanha, I.J.: Evaluating the quality of evidence for gaming disorder: a summary of systematic reviews of associations between gaming disorders and depression or anxiety (2020). https://doi.org/10.1371/journal.pone.0240032

Applying CoKriging Method for Air Pollution Prediction PM10 in Binh Duong Province

Nguyen Cong Nhut$^{(\boxtimes)}$ [iD]

Faculty of Information Technology, Nguyen Tat Thanh University,
Ho Chi Minh City, Vietnam
ncnhut@ntt.edu.vn

Abstract. Geostatistics is a branch of statistics that focuses on spatial data sets. Geostatistics is used for prediction in many fields such as ore mining, petroleum geology, climate, geography, environment. CoKriging can be seen as a point interpolation, which requires a point map as input and which returns a raster map with estimations and optionally an error map. CoKring is a prediction method for problems with two or more parameters, including one main parameter. Tthe costs of installing new observational stations to observe metropolitan air pollution sources, as PM10 (Particulate Matter), CO (Cacbon monoxit), SO_2 (Dioxit Sunfua) and NO_2 (oxit Nito) concentrations are high. In this study, analysis of air pollution of 16 stations monitored in 2018 year was carried out. Geostatistics have been used by many researchers to effectively predict air pollution, ore mining, and groundwater levels.

Keywords: Air pollution · Cokriging · Prediction · PM10

1 Introduction

The information from the monitoring center - technical resources and environment of Binh Duong province, network quality monitoring air environment of Binh Duong has 16 stations. This number is still too small compared to a province with a large population and large area. However, the investment cost for a monitor is too expensive, and the preservation in tropical climates like Vietnam is also very difficult. The problem is based on existing stations, forecasting for areas that have not been installed.

Vietnam is a developing country with many effective activities for economic growth. However, in parallel with economic development, development activities are also sources of emissions causing environmental pollution in general and air environment in particular. In which, the main sources of air pollution include: transportation; Industrial production; construction and people living; agriculture and craft villages; landfilling and waste treatment. The main air pollutants include: total suspended dust (TSP), PM10 dust (dust $\leq$ 10 μm), lead (Pb), ozone (O_3); inorganic

---

In this article, author use the recorded PM10 concentrations at several observational stations in Binh Duong province, employ the CoKriging interpolation method to find suitable models, then predict PM10 concentrations at some unmeasured stations in the city. From the data set, author found the best forecast model with the smallest forecast error to predict PM10 concentration.

P. Cong Vinh and A. Rakib (Eds.): ICCASA 2021, LNICST 409, pp. 323–335, 2021.
https://doi.org/10.1007/978-3-030-93179-7_25

substances such as carbon monoxide (CO), sulfur dioxide (SO_2), nitrous oxide (NOx), hydrochloride (HCl), hydrofluoride (HF)...; organic substances such as hydrocarbons (CnHm), benzene (C_6H_6)...; unpleasant odors such as ammonia (NH_3), hydrosulfide (H_2S)...; heat, noise.

The study area is Binh Duong in Southeastern of Vietnam. It is located between $10°51'46''-11°30'$ northing and $106°20'-106°58'$ easting and has the following administrative boundaries: the East borders on Dong Nai province; the West borders on Tay Ninh province and Ho Chi Minh City; to the South, it borders on Ho Chi Minh City; the North borders on Binh Phuoc province. And the area has more than 2694.4 km^2. Binh Duong has a fairly flat terrain. Binh Duong is located in a tropical monsoon climate, subequatorial in nature. There are two seasons in a year, the rainy season from May to November, the dry season from December to April of the following year. Figure 1 shows the study area.

Fig. 1. Air monitoring network in Binh Duong province.

Figure 2 shows the geographical location of the monitoring with pollution levels.

2 Materials and Methods

Dust is a common name for solid and liquid particles, a few micrometres to half a millimeter in diameter, settle on their own by their weight but can remain suspended in the air for a while. PM10 dust: is dust particles with kinetic diameter ≤ 10 μm. Figure 2 shows the air quality monitoring stations PM10 in Binh Duong (see Table 1). Physical noises are vibrations of sound waves of varying magnitudes and frequencies,

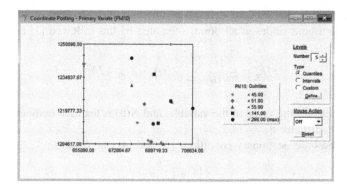

Fig. 2. Map of air quality monitoring stations with pollution levels.

arranged out of order and propagated in an elastic medium. The unit of noise measurement is dB (decibel). The sources of noise are from objects with high amplitude fluctuations, in excess of the hearing threshold (70 dB), for example: heavy machinery in works, lightning, loud singing, etc. The noise affects the ears, then affects the central nervous system, then the cardiovascular system, the stomach and other organs, and then the hearing organs. To predict for areas that have not yet installed monitors, the author uses the CoKriging method.

Table 1. PM10 and dB data of air pollution stations in Binh Duong.

Stations	X	Y	PM10 (mg/m^3)	dB (A)
N	696.193	1.250.098	85	52.3
NT	655.890	1.241.092	92	58.1
DT1	693.004	1.204.617	105	63.5
DT2	686.008	1.206.206	93	66.1
DT3	681.042	1.214.323	114	59.6
DT4	690.640	1.214.132	162	71.4
DT5	687.438	1.205.692	160	66.3
DT6	692.090	1.205.134	259	65.0
GT1	688.151	1.213.933	500	76.5
GT2	706.634	1.220.991	154	75.9
GT3	678.398	1.231.367	175	71.4
CN1	684.214	1.222.794	219	67.6
CN2	697.081	1.223.852	162	65.0
CN3	696.411	1.224.187	513	64.4
CN4	678.238	1.243.845	34	66.0
CN5	688.598	1.236.343	47	65.7

The variogram $\gamma(h)$ can be defined as one-half the variance of the difference between the attribute values at all points separated by has followed [1] and [2]

$$\gamma(h) = \frac{1}{2N(h)} \sum_{i=1}^{N(h)} [Z(s_i) - Z(s_i + h)]^2, \tag{1}$$

where Z(s) indicates the value of the variable, and N(h) is the total number of pairs are separated by a distance h.

The second-order stationary conditions [3] and [4] one obtains

$$E[Z(s)] = \mu,$$

And the covariance

$$Cov[Z(s), Z(s+h)] = E[(Z(s) - \mu)(Z(s+h) - \mu)] = C(h). \tag{2}$$

The most common models are spherical, exponential, Gaussian, and pure nuclear effects [5] and [2]. Cross-validation technique is used to check the completeness and validity of the model.

The correlation coefficient r^2 shows the estimate and the true value. The most appropriate variogram was chosen based on the highest correlation coefficient.

Cokring: Recall that parameter $d = 2$ is the dimension of our geological domain D of interest, $n > 2$ is the number of sampling places/locations $s_i \in D$, and $k > 1$ is the number of pollutants under investigation.

Generally, suppose that at each spatial location s_i we observe $k > 1$ variables Z_j, described by a data matrix M of size $k \times n$ as follows:

$$\mathbf{M} = \begin{pmatrix} Z_1(s_1) \, Z_1(s_2) \cdots Z_1(s_i) \cdots Z_1(s_n) \\ \cdots \quad\quad \cdots \quad\quad \cdots \quad\quad \cdots \\ Z_j(s_1) \, Z_j(s_2) \cdots Z_j(s_i) \cdots Z_j(s_n) \\ \cdots \quad\quad \cdots \quad\quad \cdots \quad\quad \cdots \\ Z_k(s_1) \, Z_k(s_2) \cdots Z_k(s_i) \cdots Z_k(s_n) \end{pmatrix}, \tag{3}$$

for $j = 1, 2, \ldots, k$, and $i = 1, 2, \ldots, n$.

We predict $Z_1(s_0)$, the value of variable Z_1 at unobserved location s_0.

Given the fact that the *target variable* Z_1 occurs with other variables (call *co-located variables*), we explore the possibility of improving the prediction of variable Z_1 by taking into account the correlation of Z_1 with the other variables.

Definiton 1 [6, 7]. *The cokriging model of prediction takes the form*

$$\hat{Z}_1(s_0) = \sum_{j=1}^{k} \sum_{i=1}^{n} w_{ji} Z_j(s_i)$$
$$= w_{11} Z_1(s_1) + \cdots + w_{1n} Z_1(s_n) + \cdots + w_{k1} Z_k(s_1) + \cdots + w_{kn} Z_k(s_n). \tag{4}$$

Assuming that the sampling area is relatively homogeneous, i.e. distinct sampling points s_i have different values $Z_j(s_i)$ but their expectation are the same, we denote

$$\mu_j = \mathbf{E}[Z_j(s_i)] = \mathbf{E}[Z_j(s)],$$

for each pollutant $j = 1, ..., k$; for all $i = 1, ..., n$, and for any sampling point $s \in D$. We will examine *ordinary co-kriging* (the extension of ordinary kriging of a single variable to two or more variables). The expectation vector of k variables Z_j then is

$$\mathbf{E}[\mathbf{Z}(s)] = \begin{pmatrix} \mathbf{E}[Z_1(s)] \\ \mathbf{E}[Z_2(s)] \\ \vdots \\ \mathbf{E}[Z_k(s)] \end{pmatrix} = \begin{pmatrix} \mu_1 \\ \mu_2 \\ \vdots \\ \mu_k \end{pmatrix} = \mu.$$

We want the predictor $\hat{Z}_1(s_0)$ to be unbiased, that is $\mathbf{E}[\hat{Z}_1(s_0)] = \mu_1$, where

$$\mathbf{E}[\hat{Z}_1(s_0)] = \sum_{j=1}^{k} \sum_{i=1}^{n} w_{ji} \mathbf{E}[Z_j(s_i)] = \sum_{i=1}^{n} w_{1i} \mu_1 + \cdots + \sum_{i=1}^{n} w_{ki} \mu_k$$

$$= w_{11} \mathbf{E}[Z_1(s_1)] + \cdots + w_{1n} \mathbf{E}[Z_1(s_n)] + \cdots + w_{k1} \mathbf{E}[Z_k(s_1)] + \cdots + w_{kn} \mathbf{E}[Z_k(s_n)].$$

$$(5)$$

Definiton 2 [6, 7]. *The mean squared error (MSE) of prediction of Z_1 is given by.*

$$\mathbf{E}\left[\{Z_1(s_0) - \hat{Z}_1(s_0)\}^2\right] = \Sigma_1^2. \tag{6}$$

Therefore, to get $\mathbf{E}[\hat{Z}_1(s_0)] = \mu_1$ we must have the followings

$$\sum_{i=1}^{n} w_{1i} = 1, \ \sum_{i=1}^{n} w_{2i} = 0, \ \cdots, \ \sum_{i=1}^{n} w_{ki} = 0. \tag{7}$$

Co-kriging for Two Pollutants
Let's assume $k = 2$, in other words, we observe variables Z_1 and Z_2 (e.g. PM$_{10}$ and dB in our sample data) and we want to predict $Z = Z_1$.

Lemma 1 [6, 7]. The variance $\Sigma_1^2 = \mathbf{E}[\{Z_1(s_0) - \hat{Z}_1(s_0)\}^2]$ has expansion.

$$\Sigma_1^2 = \mathbf{E}[\{Z(s_0) - \mu_1\}^2] - 2\sum_{i=1}^{n} w_{1i} \mathbf{E}[(Z_1(s_0) - \mu_1)(Z_1(s_i) - \mu_1)]$$

$$- 2\sum_{i=1}^{n} w_{2i} \mathbf{E}[(Z_1(s_0) - \mu_1)(Z_2(s_i) - \mu_2)] + \sum_{i=1}^{n} \sum_{j=1}^{n} w_{1i} w_{1j} \mathbf{E}[(Z_1(s_i) - \mu_1)(Z_1(s_j) - \mu_1)]$$

$$+ \sum_{i=1}^{n} \sum_{j=1}^{n} w_{2i} w_{2j} \mathbf{E}[(Z_2(s_i) - \mu_2)(Z_2(s_j) - \mu_2)] + 2\sum_{i=1}^{n} \sum_{j=1}^{n} w_{1i} w_{2j} \mathbf{E}[(Z_1(s_i) - \mu_1)(Z_2(s_j) - \mu_2)].$$

$$(8)$$

Proof. See in Sect. 5.4 [8] or [3].

Theorem 1 [6, 7]. Consider the following optimization model min Σ_1^2 where.

$$\Sigma_1^2 = \mathbf{E}[\{Z(s_0) - \sum_{i=1}^{n} w_{1i}Z_1(s_i) - \sum_{i=1}^{n} w_{2i}Z_2(s_i)\}^2].$$

The above optimization model is converted into a kriging system of linear equations

$$\mathbf{G}w = c, \tag{9}$$

where vectors w,c have dimensions $(2n + 2) \times 1$ and $\mathbf{G}$ has dimension $(2n + 2) \times (2n + 2)$.

If the multivariate covariance model is strictly positive definite and if there is no data duplication, the optimal weights will be obtained via the vector

$$w = \mathbf{G}^{-1}c.$$

Proof. See (Paul, 2011) or (Webster, 2007, Sect. 10.4).

Algorithm for Coping with Unmeasured Data Points:
For this realistic data, we got $m = 16$ good data points. The main idea of the linear kriging in (4) is that the predicted value $\hat{Z}_1(s_0) = \sum_{j=1}^{2} \sum_{i=1}^{16} w_{ji}Z_j(s_i) = w_{11}Z_1(s_1) + \cdots + w_{116}Z_1(s_{16}) + w_{21}Z_2(s_1) + \cdots + w_{216}Z_2(s_{16})$, $w_{ji} \geq 0$ at certain unknown point s_0 in fact is just a convex combination of 16 observed value at $Z(s_i)$ at $m = 16$ monitoring points, where the weights w_i fulfill $\sum_{i=1}^{16} w_{1i} = 1$, $\sum_{i=1}^{16} w_{2i} = 0$.

Algorithm 1 Progressively Imputation

INPUT: a finite set V_0 of all n designed monitoring sites,
$V = \{s_1, s_2, \cdots, s_m\}$ of observable sites $(m \leq n)$, $V \subseteq V_0$,
a $k \times m$ data matrix M of k observable factors (monitored at m sites), modified from data matrix (3).
OUTPUT: the fully updated set V of n known sites with available data, from which observation $Z(s)$ at any location $s \in CH(V)$ (the convex hull of V) is estimated by Equation (4)
If $m = n$ stop, else proceed to next step.
while $m < n$ do
1. Select a site $s_0 \in V_0 \backslash V$ (an unmeasured site)
2. Set up the system (9) from data M and s_0
3. Compute the weight vector $w = \mathbf{G}^{-1} c$
4. Calculate the predicted value at s_0
5. Update $V := V \cup \{s_0\}$; update $m = |V|$; update data matrix M;
end while
return The full network V of all observable sites.

---

3   Results and Discussions

Anisotropy was tested by comparing variations in several directions 0°, 45°, 90°, and 135° with an angle tolerance of ±45° used to detect anisotropy.

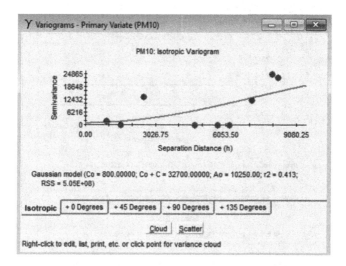

Fig. 3. Fitted variogram for the parameter PM10.

Figure 3 and 4 show fitted variogram for the parameters of PM_{10} and dB, respectively; and Fig. 5 shows fitted variogram for the parameters of both PM_{10} and dB, allfound by the isotropic-based Gaussian model, see Table 2.

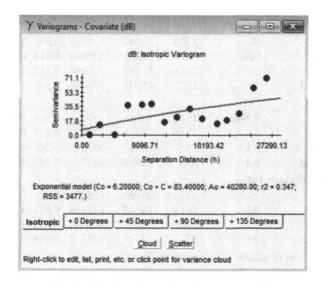

Fig. 4. Fitted variogram for the parameter dB.

Figure 3 shows fitted variogram for the parameter PM10. Gaussian model shows the best fitted omnidi-rectional variogram of air pollution obtained based on cross-validation. The variogram values are presented in Table 2.

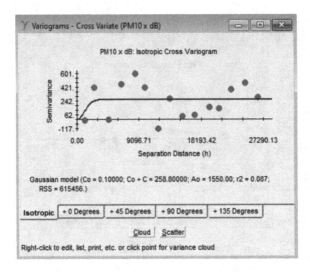

Fig. 5. Fitted variogram for two the parameter.

Table 2. Isotropic variograms values of PM_{10}, dB and two parameters

Data set and model	Estimates of parameters			RSS[a]	r^2	$\frac{C}{C_0+C}$
	Nugget (m)	Sill (m)	Range A			
	C_0	$C_0 + C$	(m)			
PM_{10} ($n = 16$)						
Linear	10	2.735	2.1482	5.66e08	0.351	11374.376
Gaussian	**800**	**32700**	**17754**	**5.05e08**	**0.413**	**0.976**
Spherical	10	26130	21100	5.79e08	0.335	1
Exponential	10	31120	43200	6.04e08	0.309	1
dB ($n = 16$)						
Linear	7.4884	45.936	26391	3390	0.364	0.837
Gaussian	0.1	32.96	9058.6	3789	0.289	0.997
Spherical	0.1	32.5	10590	3832	0.289	0.997
Exponential	**6.2**	**83.4**	**120840**	**3477**	**0.347**	**0.926**
PM_{10} and dB ($n = 16$)						
Linear	207.33	277.15	26390.5	658459	0.01	0.252
Gaussian	**0.1**	**258.8**	**2684.7**	**615456**	**0.087**	**1**
Spherical	0.1	256.4	3020	620895	0.092	1
Exponential	0.1	258.5	4500	631622	0.058	1

RSS[a] is the sum of squares of the residuals from the fitted function.

Thus, from the stations $s_1, s_2,..., s_{16}$ we find the best interpolation model based on RSS ($RSS = \sum_{i=1}^{n} e_i^2 = \sum_{i=1}^{n} (Z_i - \hat{Z}_i)^2$), r^2 and $C/(C_0 + C)$. Using the models found, we forecast for stations, where missing data occurred.

RSS represents the fit of the model to the data set, the lower the RSS indicates the better the model fits the data. r^2 is the fit of the model to the data; this value is not as strong as the Residual SS value.

Selecting the Best-Fit Model [7]: The model that uses interpolation is called optimal if it has the lowest error forecast. Few following statistics (integrated in GS+) can be used to explain the output of the model.

First, the residual sum of squares (RSS): a small RSS indicates a tight fit of the model to the data.

Second, the coefficient of determination, r^2: not strong for fitting the model as RSS, but used to look at the impact of change in the model parameters.

Third, the proportion $C/(C_0 + C)$ statistic provides a measure of the proportion of sample variance ($C_0 + C$) that is explained by spatially structured variance C.

This value will be 1.0 for a variogram with no nugget variance (where the curve passes through the origin).

Conversely, it will be 0 where there is no spatially dependent variation at the range specified, i.e. where there is a pure nugget effect.

Correlation coefficients are used to measure how strong a relationship is between two variables ($r = \dfrac{n(\sum xy) - (\sum x)(\sum y)}{\sqrt{n \sum x^2 - (\sum x)^2} \sqrt{n \sum y^2 - (\sum y)^2}}$).

Model checking: Selecting the right model for the data based on the results: regression coefficient, correlation coefficient and interpolation values, besides error values are standard error (SE) and standard error prediction (SE prediction) (Table 3).

Table 3. Result testing parameters of the model.

Coefficient regression	Coefficient correlation	SE	SE Prediction
1.044	0.994	0.021	5.440

Figure 6 shows the results of checking the error between the actual value and the estimated value using the cokriging method. The regression coefficient and the correlation coefficient are approximately equal to 1, the standard error is small (close to zero). Thus, the selected model is a suitable interpolation (Fig. 7).

From Fig. 8 and Fig. 9 show estimated errors of predicting PM10 concentrations 2D and 3D in Binh Duong by the discussed cokriging method. This shows that forecast areas close together have small forecast errors. Using the CoKriging interpolation method, we can predict air pollution levels for areas that have not yet installed monitoring points.

Based on the forecast map in Figs. 8 and 9, we can predict the air pollution concentration at locations around the air monitoring stations. Positions in the same color have a small prediction error. Through the use of CoKriging spatial interpolation

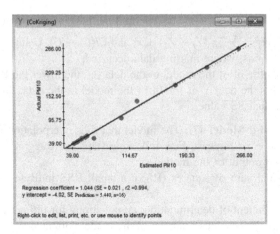

Fig. 6. Error testing result of prediction PM10.

Record	X-Coordinate	Y-Coordinate	Actual Z	Estimated Z	Error (E-A)
1	696193.00	1250098.00	39.00	40.67	1.67
2	655890.00	1241092.00	46.00	47.33	1.33
3	693004.00	1204617.00	52.00	51.99	-0.01
4	686008.00	1206206.00	43.00	44.53	1.53
5	681042.00	1214323.00	45.00	46.55	1.55
6	690640.00	1214132.00	101.00	104.37	3.37
7	687438.00	1205692.00	51.00	50.76	-0.24
8	692090.00	1205134.00	45.00	46.43	1.43
9	688151.00	1213933.00	266.00	258.97	-7.03
10	706634.00	1220991.00	178.00	175.43	-2.57
11	678398.00	1231367.00	55.00	55.85	0.85
12	684214.00	1222794.00	50.00	51.11	1.11
13	697081.00	1223852.00	52.00	67.63	15.63
14	696411.00	1224187.00	141.00	125.30	-15.70
15	678238.00	1243845.00	221.00	217.43	-3.57
16	688598.00	1236343.00	58.00	58.89	0.89

Fig. 7. Cross-Validation (CoKriging) of PM10.

model, we can predict air pollution levels for areas that have not yet installed air monitors. The higher the density of monitoring stations, the easier it is to choose the interpolation model and the more reliable the interpolation results and vice versa.

The prediction results of the model also have some limitations in terms of forecasting error. The reason is that in addition to the PM10 pollutant, there are other pollutants in the air such as TSP, CO, SO, NO2, PM25.

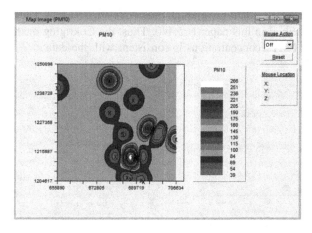

Fig. 8. The Cokriging interpolation method in 2D space.

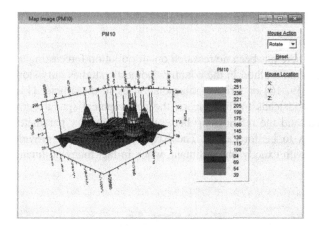

Fig. 9. The Cokriging interpolation method in 3D space.

4   Conclusion

CoKriging application to forecast PM10 concentration results in low error between estimated value and actual value. Therefore, the study shows that the efficiency and high reliability of geostatistics to build spatial prediction models. There is no way we can find the best model, only by experiment. The author must test all models, change the model parameters and finally choose the model that fits the data, the model with the lowest prediction error. When building the model, we should pay attention to the outliers, which will determine the error of the model, so we have to deal with them.

The following are the predicted results using other methods. Figure 10 shows the results of PM10 concentration prediction by the distance inverse method, which results in high predictive error 68,926. Figure 11 shows the results of PM10 concentration prediction by Kriging method giving high predictive error 71,912. The prediction error by CoKriging method in this paper is 5,440. Thus, the Cokriging method used in this paper to predict PM10 concentrations is consistent with the data.

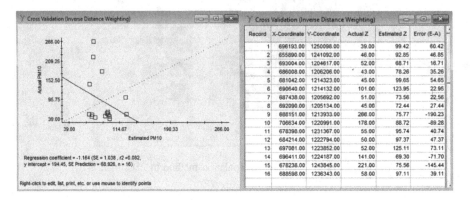

Fig. 10. Inverse distance weighting method.

Up to now, there has been no research on air pollution forecasting using CoKriging spatial interpolation method in the country. Domestic studies only stop at the level of data simulation [9, 10] or Kriging interpolation as in the article: [11, 12]. The data simulation method leads to high errors, the geographical spatial correlation has not been evaluated, and the relationship between the secondary parameters affecting the main parameters to be forecasted. The Kriging method only provides a predictive model for data with exactly one pollutant, when in fact many pollutants are related to each other.

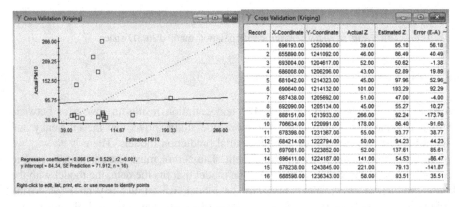

Fig. 11. Kriging method

Acknowledgment. The paper's author expresses his sincere thank to the scientists and the referees for their comments. The author thanks the anonymous reviewer whose helpful and valuable comments led to significant improvements to the final version of the paper. The author thanks the editor, the reviewer for facilitating the author's article to be published in the journal.

References

1. Ahmadi, S.H., Sedghamiz, A.: Geostatistical analysis of spatial and temporal variations of groundwater level. Environ. Monit. Assess. **129**, 277–294 (2007)
2. Kitadinis, P.K.: Introduction to Geostatistics: Applications to Hydrogeology. Cambridge University Press, Cambridge (2003)
3. Webster, R., Oliver, M.A.: Geostatistics for Enviromental Scientists, 2nd edn. Wiley, Chichester (2007). 6–8
4. Gentile, M., Courbin, F., Meylan, G.: Interpolating point spread function anisotropy. Astronomy and Astrophysics manuscript no. psf interpolation, 10 October 2012 (2012)
5. Isaaks, E., Srivastava, M.R.: An Introduction to Applied Geostatistics. Oxford University Press, New York (1989)
6. Nguyen, M.V.M., Nguyen, N.C.: Analyzing incomplete spatial data in air pollution prediction. Southeast-Asian J. Sci. **6**(2), 111–133 (2018)
7. Nguyen, C.N., Nguyen, M.V.M., Vo, L.P.: Co-kriging method for air pollution prediction: a case study in saigon. Thailand Stat. J. (2020). ISSN 2351–0676
8. Chiles, P., Delfiner, P.: Geostatistics - Modeling Spatial Uncertainty, 2nd edn. Wiley, Hoboken (2011)
9. Anh, P.T.V.: Application of airborne pollutant emission models in assessing the current state of the air environment in Hanoi area caused by industrial sources. In: 6th Women's Science Conference, pp. 8–17. Ha Noi National University (2001)
10. Yen, D.T.H.: Applying the Meti-lis model to calculate the emission of air pollutants from traffic and industrial activities in Thai Nguyen city, orienting to 2020. J. Sci. Technol. **106**(6) (2013)
11. Hà, P.T.S., Sơn, L.M.: Ứng dụng phương pháp nội suy Kiging khảo sát sự phân bố tầng đất yếu tuổi Holocen ở khu vực nội thành Thành phố Hồ Chí Minh. Tạp chí phát triển KH& CN Tập **10**(02), 43–53 (2007)
12. Trần, Q.Â.: Ứng dụng Variogram của địa thống kê để nghiên cứu một vài đặc điểm biến đổi hàm lượng đồng, Tạp chí địa chất số 190–191, Cục địa chất & khoáng sản Việt Nam (1989)

Author Index

Ali, Mumtaz   133
Anh, Duong Tuan   147, 255

Brodie, Joshua   1

Chan, Johnny   20, 192, 236
Chau, Vo Thi Ngoc   147
Coustaty, Mickael   77
Cu, Mina   20, 236

Dan, Tran Ngoc   71
Dung, Nguyen Viet   38

Guillaume, Jean-Loup   77

Han, Nguyen Van   71
Hien, Nguyen Van   255
Hoa, Nong Thi   91
Huong, Pham Thi Viet   38
Huy, Hoang Quang   38
Huynh, Hiep Xuan   56, 119, 179, 283

Kien, Nguyen Phan   38

Lai, Khai Dinh   105, 205
Le, Hanh My Thi   56
Le, Thai Hoang   105, 205, 300
Le, Tuan Hoang Viet   300

Ngo, Ha Quang Thinh   226, 267
Nguyen, Hai Thanh   56, 119, 179, 283
Nguyen, Phat Kieu   300
Nguyen, Sang Thanh   105
Nguyen, Thanh-Khoa   77
Nguyen, Thuy Thanh   205, 300

Nguyen, Xuan-Quang   164
Nhut, Nguyen Cong   323

Peko, Gabrielle   1, 20, 236
Pham-Quoc, Cuong   48, 164
Phan, Cang Anh   119, 179, 283
Phan, Cong Vinh   48
Phung, Bui Minh   71
Phuong, Nguyen Thu   38

Rakib, Abdur   133

Siricharoen, Waralak V.   314
Sundaram, David   1, 20, 236

Thinh, Tran Ngoc   164
Thuy, Huynh Thi Thu   147
Tran, De Cao   77
Tran, Hai Son   300
Tran, Phuc Quang   56
Tran, Tu Cam Thi   283
Truong, Khoa Tan   105
Truong, Loan Thanh Thi   119, 179
Tung, Nguyen Thanh   219

Uddin, Ijaz   133

Van Tao, Nguyen   91
Van, Hoang Thien   300
Vinh, Phan Cong   71, 133
Vo, Tuyet-Ngan   77
Vu, Tran Anh   38
Vu, Tuan Anh   48

Yang, Xin   192

Printed in the United States
by Baker & Taylor Publisher Services